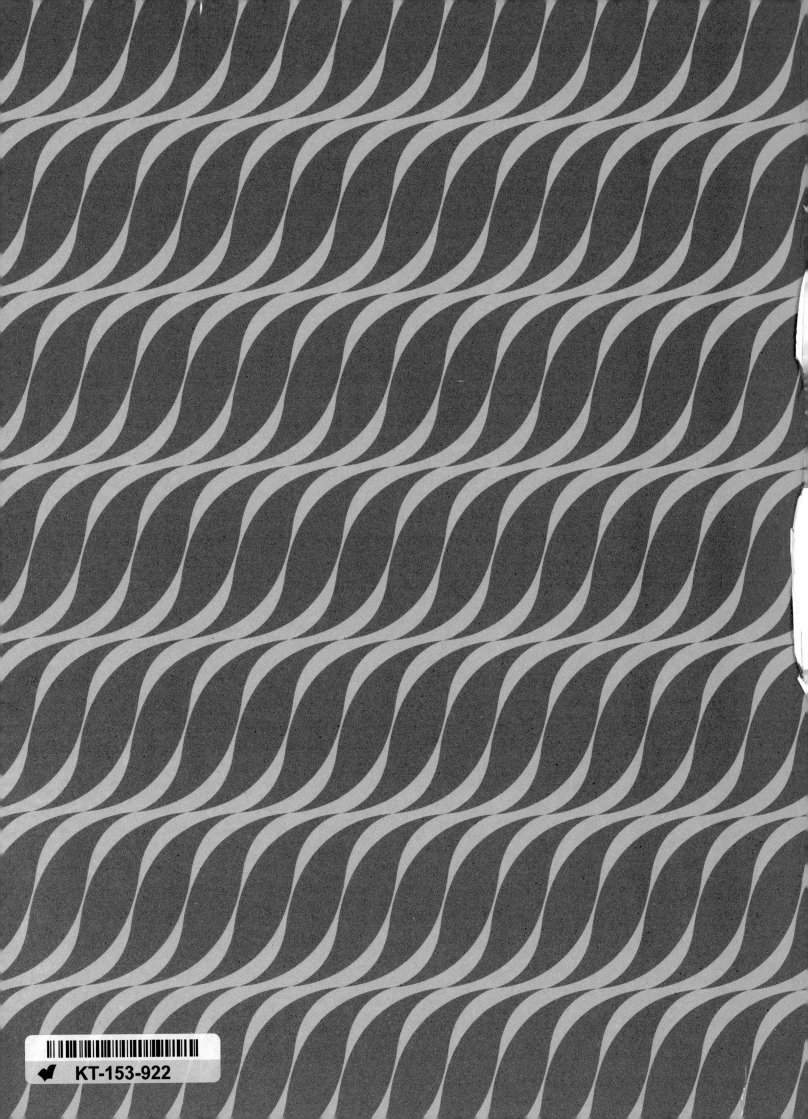

THE ILLUSTRATED HISTORY ENCYCLOPEDIA
RELIGION, SCIENCE, MEDICINE & WARFARE

THE ILLUSTRATED HISTORY ENCYCLOPEDIA
RELIGION, SCIENCE, MEDICINE & WARFARE

JOHN FARNDON • SIMON ADAMS

WILL FOWLER • BRIAN WARD

southwater

CONTENTS

Searching for Answers.....6

WORLD RELIGIONS.....10

SCIENCE AND TECHNOLOGY.....68

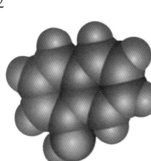

THE STORY OF MEDICINE.....126

MODERN WEAPONS AND WARFARE.....184

Searching for Answers

Human beings have rarely been prepared to accept life at face value. Throughout history, they have sought to investigate their world and to understand it. Then they have used their new knowledge to improve their own lives. This book looks at four of the most important aspects of this search for knowledge: religion, science, medicine and military technology.

NIKE
The Greek goddess Nike is shown on this coin. The ancient Greeks and Romans worshipped many different gods. They believed that religion affected every aspect of their daily life.

Faith and Understanding

Since the earliest times, humans have tried to make sense of their world. As they thought about the nature of the world and their position within it, they developed myths and religious beliefs to try to explain them. Aspects of life that could not readily be understood were explained as being controlled by superior beings, either spirits or gods. These beliefs were accompanied by religious rituals. People built temples where they could communicate with the gods by means of sacrifice and prayer.

All early religions were based on the idea that there were many gods, who had different characteristics and varying degrees of interest in humankind. However, between 1000BC and 1BC, religions emerged that were based on belief in a single god. The first monotheistic (mono meaning 'single' and theistic meaning 'related to god') belief system was Judaism. Christianity and Islam are the world's other main monotheistic religions. Belief in a single god has been the most successful type of religion in the Arab and Western worlds. However, Hinduism and other religions based on multiple gods are still very strong, especially in Asia. Buddhism also developed in India as people started to follow the teachings of a man called the Buddha

FINAL RESTING PLACE
The ancient Egyptians believed that everything in life was controlled by the gods. They built huge pyramids to house the bodies of their dead pharaohs (rulers). From here, the deceased could enter the next world, the realm of the gods.

CHIEF GOD
Although the Romans worshipped many gods, they believed that Jupiter held supreme power over all the other gods.

THE TEMPLE IN JERUSALEM
King Solomon built the first temple in Jerusalem, which became the centre of Jewish worship. The Jews worship one god, known as Yahweh. They also believe that they are God's chosen people.

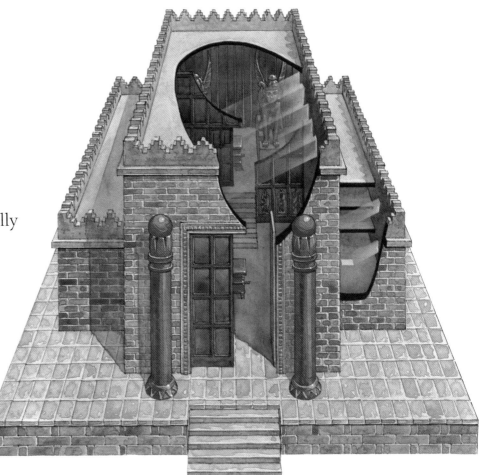

(the enlightened one). It is actually more a spiritual way of life than a true religion.

The Quest for Truth

Science is another way in which human beings seek to understand their world. People can also use an awareness of how things work to improve their way of life. From prehistoric times, humans began to invent devices and machines to help them carry out their daily tasks. However, the foundations of modern science and technology were laid by Greek thinkers, such as Archimedes, and by the skilful engineers of the Roman Empire.

During the Middle Ages, from AD1000–1500, the practice of alchemy emerged, which was the 'science' of trying to turn ordinary metals into gold. This paved the way for the development of modern chemistry during the 1600s. The 1700s are often known as the Age of Enlightenment because people began to question beliefs that had previously been accepted as 'fact'. Men, and later women, thinkers demanded increasingly rigorous proof before they would accept a piece of information as correct and true.

This mental approach was the real forerunner of modern scientific methods. It triggered the invention of instruments and thought processes that enabled scientists to look ever deeper into every aspect of life. The quest for knowledge prompted investigation into what lay

ORRERY
Once people accepted the idea that the Earth was just one of the planets, many became fascinated by how the planets circled the Sun. This orrery was built to show planetary movement.

CONQUERING SPACE
*The Mir space station spent
13 years as an orbiting laboratory. Space
exploration is now an everyday reality.*

beyond the Earth. Scientists and astronomers began to examine the workings of the universe to see how humans fit into the bigger picture.

A Healthy Body

Human beings have always been limited by their health and bodily wellbeing. The development of medicine has allowed people to extend their physical limits and to live longer, healthier lives. At its very earliest stages, medicine was a matter of herbal remedies found by trial and experiment. It was not regarded as something to do with the body alone, but as something that involved a spiritual or religious element. This point of view is still strong in parts of the world such as China, Africa and South America. Illness is seen as a reflection of the body being out of balance, or of a person having consciously or unconsciously fallen foul of the spirits or gods. Any cure therefore involves philosophical or religious aspects as much as physical ones.

From around 500BC, Greek thinkers and doctors realized that illness could result from natural causes, and that cures could be brought about by healthy eating, healthy living and the use of proven drugs. Further advances came around AD1000–1500, largely from physicians and thinkers living in the Islamic world. These far-sighted men relearned the thinking of the Greeks and then built on it to analyze disease and create medicines. Surgery developed more slowly, but the Islamic interest in alchemy led to the creation and accurate measurement of purer chemicals and better drugs.

PLANT CURES
The discovery of herbal medicine is attributed to Shen Nong. This legendary Chinese emperor is said to have lived around 2700BC. He described 365 different medicinal plants.

The thinking of Islamic doctors trickled slowly to the Western world. However, during the Middle Ages the powerful Christian Church promoted the old belief that disease was a punishment from God. Medicine in the West only began to develop from the 1500s as the power of the Church declined.

The Renaissance (c.1400–1600) marked a renewed interest in the learning of classical Greece and Rome, and stimulated the changes that marked the beginning of the modern times. During this period, medical pioneers began to study the anatomy of the human body and to understand more accurately how it worked. New scientific methods and instruments made it easier to establish facts. From this time, there was a slow but steady progress in medicine. Around 1850, medical

CLEAN AND SAFE
From the 1860s, operations were carried out in antiseptic conditions. Patients were also given chloroform to make them unconscious.

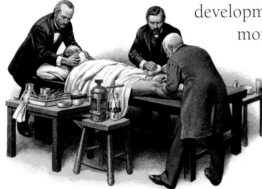

developments really started to accelerate. The reason for this was a more ready acceptance of scientific method after the Industrial Revolution. More and more scientific and technological breakthroughs were made. Doctors and researchers gained increased understanding of the human body and were able to make more sense of the biological and chemical principles that make it work.

Military Technology

One of the ways in which medical knowledge and skills increased was in the treatment of illness and injury in war. As a result of the technological advances during the Industrial Revolution, weapons and their killing power increased dramatically. The radical changes in materials and manufacturing capabilities meant that weapons could be mass-produced in their thousands. The rapid developments in physics and chemistry that accompanied industrial advancement also allowed designers to understand more clearly how weapons worked. They could improve the speed and power of ammunition, for example, by making elongated, explosive-filled shells rather than iron cannon balls. New explosives were also developed to replace gunpowder. These and other advances helped make weapons longer-ranged, more accurate and more devastating in their effect. By 1880, the machine gun had been invented and the submarine was almost a practical weapon, and powered, heavier-than-air craft were about to take to the skies. Advances in weaponry accelerated in World War I.

AUTOMATIC WEAPONS
The hand-cranked Gatling gun fired at a rate of 100–200 rpm. It had between six and ten barrels. Developed in 1862, it was used in the American Civil War.

Tanks were introduced and chemical weapons, in the form of poisonous gases, were used for the first time. In World War II there was another surge of development. Existing weapons were refined and the tank and the aircraft carrier came to the fore. New technologies allowed the introduction of radar, guided missiles and jet propulsion. Most decisively of all, the first atomic weapons were used to end World War II in 1945.

Military technology has continued to develop with great speed since that time. Today's weapons can be targeted more accurately and used over considerably longer ranges. Radar has become one of the many aspects of electronic warfare, and there have been enormous strides in the exploitation of computers for military purposes.

THE HELICOPTER
The rotary wing aircraft (or helicopter) was used at the close of World War II. A helicopter can be used in wartime to transport troops, casualties and stores. It can also rescue civilians and attack targets.

WORLD RELIGIONS

*Throughout history, human beings have sought to
make sense of their world through faith and
a system of moral and spiritual values.
This section explores all aspects of religion
from shamanism to the worship of a single god.*

BY SIMON ADAMS

Faith and Spirituality

▲ OHM SYMBOL
Every religion has its own symbol. This identifies the religion and its believers. Hindus use the Ohm symbol. Jews have the menorah (candlestick), Christians have the cross and Muslims use the hilal (crescent moon and star).

▼ KEY DATES
The panel below charts the history of religion, from the earliest religion of the ancient Egyptians to the new religions founded during the 1900s.

Tʜʀᴏᴜɢʜᴏᴜᴛ ʜᴜᴍᴀɴ ʜɪsᴛᴏʀʏ, people have asked questions about life and their place in the world. They have wondered why evil and suffering exist, how the world came into existence and how it might end. Above all, they have asked if there is a god who guides and directs the world, or whether events just roll on for ever without purpose or end.

There is no definite answer to these questions, but people have tried to make sense of their lives through religion. The first religions, such as Hinduism, were pantheistic, that is they involved the worship of many gods. With Judaism, a new type of religion known as monotheism (the worship of a single god) began. Christianity and Islam are also monotheistic religions.

At first sight the teachings of the various religions appear to be very different. In fact, they can be placed into two main groups. The first group includes Hinduism and Buddhism. These religions state that the world is a spiritual place, and that it is possible to escape the endless circle of birth, death and rebirth and reach a totally spiritual life. The second group includes Christianity and Islam. These religions say that the world is essentially good, but that humans make it bad. They urge people to behave well in order to change the world and make it a better place.

All the various religions use similar techniques to put across their messages. They tell stories and myths to explain complicated subjects in a way that is easy to understand. They use symbols that identify the faith and its believers and they use rituals, such as

▲ THE GOSPELS
All religions have their own holy book or books. These contain the words of God or the gods, as told to his earthly prophets (messengers). Jews have the Torah, Christians have the Bible, Sikhs have the Guru Granth Sahib and Muslims have the Qur'an. Many religions also have books of religious laws, such as the Jewish Talmud.

BC

c.3100 Kingdom of Egypt founded. The ancient Egyptians worship many gods.

c.3000 *I Ching* compiled.

c.2166 Birth of Abraham, founder of the Jewish nation.

c.2000 Celtic tribes practise a very local religion with their own group of gods.

Souvenir of a Hindu pilgrimage

c.1500 Hindu beliefs spread throughout northern India.

c.1200 Zoroaster lives in Persia.

c.900 Hindu beliefs are written down in the four *Vedas*.

600s Greek city-states link religion with government.

660 Legendary date of the unification of Japan and the start of the Shinto religion.

Tutankhamun's death mask

c.500s Mahavira founds Jainism.

c.500s Life of Lao-Tzu, legendary founder of Taoism.

551–479 Life of Confucius.

539–331 Zoroastrianism is the official religion of the Persian Empire.

Zoroastrian cup for Jashan ceremony

c.500 Jewish *Talmud* (laws) are written down.

c.500 The *Mahabharata*, a Hindu epic, is written.

The Buddha

485–405 Life of the Buddha.

c.250 Buddhism spreads to Sri Lanka and to Southeast Asia.

c.200 The *Ramayana*, the final Hindu epic, is written.

146 Greece comes under Roman rule. Many Greek gods are taken over and renamed by the Romans.

c.6BC–AD30 Life of Jesus Christ, founder of Christianity.

Christian baptism. Finally, religions develop societies that bind believers together. These techniques help worshippers to understand their faith and apply it in their daily lives.

Examining the development of the world's religions is one way to chart the history of humankind. Holy scriptures are the oldest written records we have. Not all the information contained in them need be read as historical fact. However, the latest archaeological discoveries are proving that many stories in the religious texts are based on true events.

At the start of the third millennium AD, the majority of the world's population follow a religion. There are also people, known as agnostics, who are not convinced that there is a god, but do not rule the possibility out. Atheists are people who do not believe in the existence of any god at all. Some people worship nature, while others, known as humanists, believe in the supremacy of human beings and their ability to make sensible decisions for themselves.

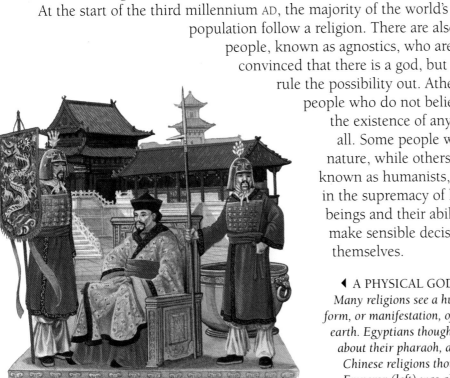

◀ A PHYSICAL GOD
Many religions see a human as a form, or manifestation, of their god on earth. Egyptians thought this way about their pharaoh, and some Chinese religions thought that the Emperor (left) was also a god.

▲ WORLD PICTURE
This is mandala, a Buddhist representation of the world through pictures and diagrams. Buddhists believe that it is possible to overcome suffering in the world if people follow guidelines to help them live a good life.

AD

c.30 The first Christian churches are founded.

100s Mahayana Buddhism emerges and gradually spreads to China.

313 Christianity is tolerated throughout Roman Empire. Many Romans convert to Christianity.

Jesus Christ

570–632 Life of Muhammad, the founder of Islam.

600s Islam spreads throughout Middle East and North Africa.

Muslim shahadah (statement of faith)

600s Buddhism spreads to Tibet and Japan.

680 Decisive split between the Sunni and Shi'ah Muslims.

800s Vikings spread their Norse religion throughout northern Europe.

1054 Christianity splits into Roman Catholic and Orthodox Churches.

1469–1539 Life of Guru Nanak, the first Sikh *guru.*

1517 Roman Catholic Church splits as the Reformation gives rise to Protestant churches.

1699 Guru Gobind Singh forms the *Khalsa* (Sikh community).

1830 Joseph Smith translates the *Book of Mormon.*

Modern Rastafarians

1863 The Baha'i religion is founded.

1870s The Jehovah's Witnesses are formed.

1930–74 Emperor Haile Selassie is Black Messiah to Rastafarians.

Israeli flag

1939–45 More than six million Jews are killed during World War II.

1954 L Ron Hubbard founds the Church of Scientology.

1954 Sun Myung Moon founds the Unification Church, or Moonies.

Ancient Egypt

T HE ANCIENT EGYPTIANS lived in the rich and fertile valley of the River Nile, which flowed from Central Africa in the south to the Mediterranean Sea in the north. From around 3100BC they built a great civilization along the river banks which lasted for almost 3,000 years. Ancient Egypt was governed by 31 dynasties (families) of kings, who were known as pharaohs. Pharaohs were believed to be gods on Earth.

Throughout their long history, the Egyptians worshipped many gods, each responsible for a different aspect of daily life. Their main god was Ra, the sun god. He was reborn every morning at dawn and travelled across the sky during the day. In the form of the Sun, Ra brought life to Egypt. He made the plants grow and the animals strong. The ancient Egyptians

▲ THE GREAT PYRAMIDS AT GIZA
Some pharaohs were buried in vast tombs called pyramids. About 100,000 people, many of them slaves, toiled for 20 years to build the Great Pyramid at Giza for Pharaoh Khufu. The shape might have been a symbol of the Sun's rays, or a stairway to heaven.

▶ FLOODS OF TEARS
Osiris was the god of farming. After he was killed by his jealous brother, Seth, Osiris became god of the underworld and the afterlife. Egyptians believed that the yearly flooding of the Nile marked the anniversary of Osiris's death when his queen, Isis, wept for him.

AFTER DEATH
The Egyptians believed that a dead person's spirit would always need a home to return to. That is why they took such trouble to embalm (preserve) dead bodies as mummies. The body was treated with special salt so that it would not rot. Then it was wrapped in linen bandages.

◀ MUMMY MASK
Tutankhamun was a pharaoh who died 3,500 years ago. In 1922 his tomb was discovered. The wrapped-up mummy was wearing a solid-gold death mask. The mummy had been placed in a nest of three ornate wooden coffins, inside a stone box called a sarcophagus.

▶ ANUBIS
The god Anubis led the dead person to the underworld. He was also the god responsible for embalming. Anubis was always shown with the head of a jackal, a type of wild dog. As real jackals often lived in cemeteries, the animal had come to be associated with death.

called their pharaohs the Sons of Ra. Pharaohs were said to be immortal, which meant they would never really die. They were buried in vast pyramids and, later, elaborate underground tombs. Special objects and treasures were buried with them, to ensure that they travelled safely to the afterlife.

The Egyptians believed that everything in life was controlled by the gods. They worshipped them in order to keep them happy and gain their protection. People tried to lead good lives so that, after death, they could enter the next world, which they called the Field of Reeds. They thought this was something like a perfect version of Egypt itself. To get there, first they had to pass through the dangerous *Duat* (underworld). Then they were judged by Osiris, god of the afterlife. If they had lived a good life and passed the test, they would

▲ IN THE BALANCE
In order to get into the heavenly kingdom after death, an Egyptian had to pass a test in a place known as the Hall of Two Truths. The person's heart was weighed to see if it was heavy with sin. If their heart was lighter than the Feather of Truth, the dead person had passed the test and was then presented to Osiris, god of the afterlife. If their heart was heavier, a monster called Ammit ate the heart and the person died forever.

live forever in the Field of Reeds.

The Egyptians placed detailed handbooks in their coffins to help them in this quest. These instruction manuals contained spells for the dead person to recite at each stage of the journey through the *Duat*. The most famous of these manuals is the *Book of the Dead*.

◄ CANOPIC JAR
The liver, lungs, intestines and stomach were removed from the body before it was mummified. The organs were dried out, wrapped in linen and stored in containers called canopic jars.

▶ CAT MUMMY
The Egyptians considered cats to be sacred. Some people even took their dead pet cat to the city of Bubastis, where the cat god Bastet was worshipped. There it would be embalmed and buried in a cat-shaped coffin in the cat cemetery.

▲ EYE OF HORUS
Lucky charms called amulets were wrapped in among a mummy's bandages. The eye amulet stood for the eye of the god Horus, son of Osiris and Isis. Horus lost his eye in a fight with his evil uncle Seth, but it was magically restored. The eye amulet symbolized the victory of good over evil, so everything behind it was protected from evil.

Key Dates

- c.3100BC The Egyptian kingdom is founded.

- c.2630BC First pyramid is built with stepped, not straight, sides.

- c.2528BC Great Pyramid built.

- c.2150BC Last pyramids built.

- 1504–1070BC Nearly all pharaohs, from Thutmose I to Ramses XI (and including the boy-king Tutankhamun), are buried in the Valley of the Kings.

- 332BC Egypt is conquered by the Greek ruler Alexander the Great.

- 30BC Egypt becomes part of the Roman Empire.

The Classical World

▲ EARTH AND SKY GOD
Zeus was the king of the gods. As ruler of the sky, he brought rain and storms. As ruler of the land, he took charge of morals and justice.

THE CIVILIZATION of the ancient Greeks began around 1575BC in Mycenae (southern Greece). The Greeks had no word for religion, yet religion affected every aspect of daily life. People believed that 12 major gods lived on Mount Olympus, the highest mountain in Greece. The god Zeus was their ruler. The gods rewarded good people and they intervened regularly in human affairs.

The Iliad, said to be written by the poet Homer around 800BC, tells the story of the historic siege of Troy by the Greeks. This event from real history is explained and presented as a

▶ THE DELPHIC ORACLE
Greeks used to visit the Temple of Apollo in Delphi to consult the oracle. This was the voice of the god Apollo, heard through a young priestess, the Pythia.

squabble between the gods. In *The Iliad*, the gods used the Greeks and Trojans to fight on their behalf.

In addition to the pantheon (collection) of 12 main gods, the Greeks believed in the existence of thousands of others. Some gods had more than one role. Athena was the goddess of wisdom and a war goddess, as well as the sacred spirit of the olive tree. She was also the patron (protector) of the city of Athens. Aphrodite was the goddess of love and beauty and also the sacred spirit of the myrtle tree.

The Greeks built temples where they could worship their gods. These were erected in the highest part of a city, which was known as the acropolis. People also built shrines in their homes where they could worship

ROMAN GODS AND BELIEFS

The city of Rome was founded in 753BC. The Roman Empire grew to one of the largest in the world. When they conquered Greece in 146BC, they added the Greek gods to their own. Often, they changed the gods' names into Latin. By the AD300s, however, many Romans had become Christians and the old gods were neglected.

◀ PAN'S PIPES
Pan was originally the Greek god of the countryside, later associated with the Roman god Faunus. He was usually shown as half-man, half-goat. Pan had many lovers, one of whom, Syrinx, escaped him by turning herself into a reed bed. From these reeds, Pan made a set of musical pipes.

◀ MITHRAIC TEMPLE
The Romans adopted the gods of many peoples they had conquered. Mithras was a Persian god of light and truth. There were Mithraic cults across the Roman Empire.

▶ NIKE
The Greek goddess Nike was known as Victoria to the ancient Romans. She was the goddess of victory. She had a devout following among soldiers in the Roman army.

their favourite gods. This might be a shrine to Hestia, goddess of the hearth (fireplace) and family life. Some gods were worshipped in secret by members of mystery cults. Believers went through a special initiation (joining) ceremony. Once they were in, they took part in elaborate rituals. The two most famous cults were those of Demeter, the goddess of farming and harvests, and Dionysus, the god of wine. Throughout the year, the Greeks celebrated their gods at numerous festivals and ceremonies. In Athens, 120 days of the year were dedicated to festivals.

Stories about the gods and their activities had explained the workings of the world. However, Greek philosophers worked out more everyday explanations. The most famous were Socrates (469–399BC), Plato (c.427–347BC) and Aristotle (384–322BC). As their philosophical ideas took hold, religion became less important to the Greeks and their gods became part of myth and legend.

▲ POSEIDON
Poseidon was god of earthquakes and the sea. He was associated with horses and was said to be the father of Pegasus, the winged horse. Greeks believed that Poseidon was the brother of Zeus and Hades. He was often shown carrying a three-pronged spear, called a trident.

▶ KINGDOMS OF THE GODS
Zeus ruled the land and sky, and Poseidon looked after the sea. Their brother, Hades, was god of the underworld. He ruled there with his wife, Persephone.

▼ JUPITER
The main god of the Romans was Jupiter. Like Zeus, he held supreme power over all the other gods, and showed his power through thunder storms and lightning.

▶ APOLLO
The Greek, and later Roman, god Apollo was associated with light, healing, music, poetry and education.

Greco-Roman gods

These Greek gods were adopted, or adapted, by the Romans. Their Roman names are in brackets.

- Aphrodite (Venus) goddess of love
- Apollo (Apollo) god of healing
- Ares (Mars) god of war
- Artemis (Diana) goddess of hunting
- Demeter (Ceres) goddess of grain
- Dionysus (Bacchus) god of wine
- Hades (Pluto) god of the underworld
- Hephaistos (Hephaestus) god of fire
- Hera (Juno) wife of Zeus (Jupiter)
- Hermes (Mercury) messenger god
- Persephone (Proserpina) goddess of death, queen to Hades (Pluto)
- Poseidon (Neptune) god of earthquakes and the sea
- Zeus (Jupiter) supreme god

Northern Europe

THE VIKINGS OF SCANDINAVIA lived in a cold and inhospitable world of long winters and short summers. They had to fight for their survival. Between the AD800s and 1000s they sailed overseas in search of new lands to conquer and settle. They soon earned a reputation as a warlike people.

Norse, or Scandinavian, religion reflected this harsh way of life. Its origins trace back to the earliest Northern European gods of the Bronze Age. The Vikings believed that the universe was made up of nine different worlds. These were connected by the world tree, Yggdrasil, which was often represented as a giant ash. This tree was thought to contain all the people yet to be born. The world inhabited by people was known as Midgard. The home of the gods was Asgard. The chief Norse god, Odin, lived here, along with all the other gods. He was god of both war and wisdom and had many supernatural powers.

◀ IN DEATH
Vikings were buried with the weapons and treasures that they would need for the next life. Viking chiefs were buried or put out to sea in their boats. Some were laid beneath burial mounds. Even the poorest person was buried with a sword or a brooch.

▶ VIKINGS AND CELTS
Vikings and Celts travelled far in search for new lands to settle. They took their religious beliefs with them. The Celts spread out from the Danube valley across Europe. Viking settlements ranged from North America in the far west to Russia in the east.

Map:
- Viking homelands
- Celtic homelands

NORTH SEA · GREAT BRITAIN · York · Dublin · London · ATLANTIC OCEAN · Paris · R. Rhine · R. Elbe · RUSSIA · Kiev · SPAIN · FRANCE · Seville · Rome · R. Danube · BLACK SEA · Constantinople · CASPIAN SEA · MEDITERRANEAN SEA

N

0 Kilometres 1000
0 Miles 600

THE CELTS
The Celts spread from their German homeland across the whole of western Europe from around 2000BC. As the Roman Empire expanded, however, the Celts were pushed to the edges of Europe, to Ireland, Scotland, Wales and Brittany. Different, local religions developed, each with its own group of gods. There were common themes, however. The Celts all believed in warrior-heroes with supernatural powers, and they all believed in the sacred Earth Mother. She was the goddess of fertility who brought them life.

▶ MISTLETOE
The druids were the high priests of Celtic religion. They performed the sacred rituals and often used mistletoe in their ceremonies. The plant is still important as part of Christmas festivities.

◀ HARVEST FESTIVAL
From around 2,000 years ago the Celts wove stalks of corn into human 'dollies' or other shapes. These objects were made to give thanks for a successful harvest.

▲ THE LINDISFARNE GOSPEL
The natural world was central to Celtic religion. Celtic influence can be seen in early Christian manuscripts, which were illuminated (illustrated) with pictures of animals and plants.

◀ FREYA
The goddess of love, Freya, was married to Odin, but he left her. Freya wept tears of gold and searched the skies for him in a cat-driven chariot.

▼ RIDE OF THE VALKYRIES
Odin was served by a band of female warriors called the Valkyries. After a battle, Odin and the Valkyries searched the battlefield for dead heroes, whom they carried to Valhalla (Viking heaven).

Vikings believed that the human world, Midgard, was constantly threatened by forces of darkness and evil, such as the frost giants, who covered the world with snow and ice. Thor, the god of thunder, tried to keep these giants away with his hammer. Many Vikings wore a hammer round their necks, or painted a hammer on their door, as protection against evil spirits.

The Vikings held many different beliefs about what happened after death. A sick person who died went to a serpent-filled kingdom ruled by Hel, a witchlike figure. Warriors who died in battle went to Valhalla. This was a huge communal hall, like a perfect version of a Viking longhouse. There were feasting and mock battles there.

By AD1000, many Vikings had become Christians. This is reflected in the late Viking belief that the world would end in one final battle, called the Ragnarok. The gods and forces of evil would destroy themselves in this battle. A new world would be born occupied by two people, Lif and Lifthrasir. Like Adam and Eve, they would worship one supreme god who lived in heaven.

◀ CELTIC CROSS
In around AD435, a Christian Briton, who later became St Patrick, went to Ireland to convert the Celts. He was successful, and Celtic art merged with Christian symbols, such as the cross.

▼ LINDISFARNE MONASTERY, NORTHUMBRIA
After the conversion of Ireland, Celtic-Christian missionaries took their religion back to England, and to Scotland. Celtic Christianity stressed the importance of missionary work, regular prayer and a modest lifestyle. In monasteries such as Lindisfarne, monks spent their time in prayer and study. They also educated the local people and converted them.

Key Dates

- c.2000BC Celtic peoples spread throughout western Europe.

- AD100 The Roman push the Celts to the edges of western Europe.

- c.AD435 St Patrick converts Celts in Ireland to Christianity.

- AD600s Celtic missionaries convert England and Scotland to Christianity.

- AD793 Vikings begin to raid Christian monasteries in Britain.

- AD800s Many Viking raids across northern and western Europe.

- 1000s Vikings begin to convert to Christianity.

Tribal Religions

THE ANCIENT RELIGIONS of Egypt, Greece and Rome disappeared with the fall of the civilizations that fostered them. The same is true of the religions practised by the great peoples of South America, the Mayans, Incas and Aztecs. Other religions, such as those followed by the Vikings and Celts, merged with other beliefs. However, some ancient religions survive to this day, even if they are restricted to one very small area. These are the religions practised by the tribal peoples of Africa, the Americas, Australasia and Asia.

Although these religions vary widely from place to place and people to people, they share much in common. For tribal peoples, the spiritual world plays a very important role in daily life.

The Maasai of East Africa worship a single god, who brings them life from the Sun and makes sure the crops grow. Most tribal peoples, however, believe that there are many gods and spirits. Some spirits are evil and good spirits must be summoned up to overcome them. The Kalabari of eastern Nigeria, for example, make ancestral screens on which they place pictures of their ancestors. Through these, they communicate with the spirit world and try to control the effect that spirits have on their lives. Elsewhere in Africa, local gods protect the oases and waterholes and help to heal the sick.

In all tribal religions, ritual plays an important part in a person's life. Birth, becoming an adult, marriage and death are all celebrated with elaborate ceremonies. Often the

▲ KUBA MASK
Many African peoples, such as the Kuba tribe of Zaire, make sacred masks. These represent the different spirits they call upon at ceremonies to celebrate birth, marriage, or death.

▶ TOTEM POLE
The Native Americans of the Pacific northwest coast carve elaborate totem poles out of tree trunks. Each pole provides a full history of a family. It records the family's earthly history and its relationship with the spirit world. A spirit might take the form of an animal, such as a bear, wolf or eagle.

ABORIGINAL RELIGION
The Aborigines of Australia trace their history back to a time called Dreamtime. This was the time of creation, when ancestral beings shaped the land and made all living things. These beings were half-human and half-animal. Aborigines consider these beings to be their ancestors and also believe that they live on forever as spirits.

◀ HOLY WATER
Aborigines believe that the land is sacred. Mountains, waterholes and other natural features are all places where the spirit world and the natural world combine.

▼ TELLING TALES
Stories of the Dreamtime have been passed down through the generations. One way has been through detailed bark paintings.

◀ ULURU
The ancestral beings created every aspect of the landscape, including Uluru (Ayers Rock). The rock has many sacred caves. It is a special place for all Aborigines.

◀ YANOMAMO SHAMAN
Shamans are healers who contact the spirit world in order to seek divine help. They are common in Siberia and Arctic North America, as well as among the many tribes of South America. These include the Yanomamo peoples who live in the Amazon rainforest, in Brazil.

people wear masks and beautiful costumes. In West Africa, the Mende people hold a masked dance, or masquerade, for young girls when they come of age. This unites all the young women and prepares them for marriage and motherhood. The Dogon of West Africa hold elaborate dances and chant in a secret language when someone dies.

Most common is the worship of ancestors and respect for elderly people in the tribe. This is common in tribes across the world, from the Native Americans to the people of Papua New Guinea. Stories of ancestors' exploits are passed down through the generations. Myths and legends explain how the world was formed and how good and evil came to exist side by side.

▼ BODY PAINT
Aborigines paint their bodies for special ceremonies. Each line of body paint may represent a different Dreamtime ancestor.

▲ GUM TREE
The Aborigines include the natural world in their ceremonies. Carved trees have been found, especially in New South Wales. These were a central part of Aboriginal coming-of-age and funeral rituals.

Key Dates

- c.40,000BC Aborigines from Southeast Asia settle in Australia.

- c.30,000BC First settlements by Amazon River, South America.

- c.1000BC Polynesians sail from Southeast Asia and settle in the Pacific Islands.

- c.500BC African societies expand south of the Sahara Desert.

- AD400 Polynesians reach Hawaii and Easter Island.

- 1000 Polynesian Maoris reach New Zealand.

- 1000–1600 Giant statues are erected on Easter Island.

Zoroastrianism

▲ THE PROPHET
Zoroaster lived in Persia about 1200BC, more than 600 years before the Buddha and 1,200 years before Christ. This makes him the earliest prophet of any world religion.

THE PROPHET ZOROASTER, OR ZARATHUSTRA as he is also called, was born in northeast Persia (modern-day Iran) around 1200BC. Not much is known about his life, except that he became a priest and was married with several children. His teachings soon became influential. When Cyrus the Great became king of Persia in 539BC, Zoroastrianism became the official religion of his vast empire. In later years, Persian armies spread the religion as far afield as Greece, Egypt and northern India.

For more than 1,000 years, until the arrival of Islam in the AD600s, Zoroastrianism remained a major religion throughout the Middle East. Today it is confined to small pockets in Iran, India – where followers are known as Parsis (Persians) – and East Africa. Zoroastrianism is also practised in a few cities in Europe and North America, but it has fewer than 130,000 believers worldwide.

▶ COMING OF AGE
Young Zoroastrians are welcomed into the faith when they are seven at a special ceremony called the Navjote. *The child is given two sacred objects, a white tunic and a length of cord. The cord, called the* kusti, *has 72 strands of thread. The way the strands join together to work as one has made the* kusti *a symbol of fellowship.*

THE THANKSGIVING CEREMONY
The Zoroastrian ceremony of Jashan (thanksgiving) is to ensure the harmony and well-being of both the spiritual and physical worlds. Zoroastrians offer thanks for their physical lives and ask for blessings from the spiritual world. The Amesha Spentas (spirit guardians of the seven good creations) and the spirits of good people who have died are all invited down to join the ceremony.

◀ AT THE CEREMONY
Jashan is presided over by a *zaotor*, the officiating priest, and a *raspi*, his assistant. Other priests may also be present.

▲ SEVEN GOOD CREATIONS
Everything at Jashan represents one of the seven good creations. A metal cup or tray represents the sky. Fruit represents plants and milk represents cattle. Wine represents humans. Burning sandalwood and frankincense represent the earth. Water and fire represent themselves. Seven flowerbuds represent the Amesha Spentas.

Zoroaster believed that the Supreme God, whom he called Ahura Mazda, had taught him through a series of visions. He learned that there are seven good creations – sky, water, earth, plants, cattle, humans and fire. Each of these is guarded by a spirit. The seven spirit guardians are known as the Amesha Spentas.

Zoroaster wrote his teachings down in 17 *gathas* (hymns) as part of the Zoroastrian sacred scripture, the *Avesta*. The *gathas* are very difficult to read and can be interpreted in many different ways.

According to Zoroaster, the world is a good place, although it contains evil. People can follow Ahura Mazda and live a good life, or they can choose to follow Angra Mainyu, the force of evil. These opposing forces are in constant conflict, but it is everyone's duty to follow good. If they do, they will be rewarded in the afterlife with happiness. If they follow evil, they will only find sorrow.

Zoroaster's teachings have been very influential, even if not many people practise his religion today. Its central ideas of the battle between good and evil and a final day of judgement had a large impact on Judaism, Christianity and Islam.

◀ GUARDIAN SPIRIT
Zoroastrians believe that everyone is looked over by a fravashi, *or guardian spirit. These spirits represent the good in people and help those that ask. The* fravashi *symbol can also represent a person's spiritual self or Ahura Mazda.*

▼ THE TOWER OF SILENCE
Zoroastrians believe that dead bodies provide a home for Angra Mainyu, the force of evil. Bodies cannot be buried in land or sea, nor can they be cremated, since earth, water and fire are all good creations. For this reason, they are left on top of a specially-built tower, the Dakhma (Tower of Silence), as a meal for the vultures.

▲ HOLY SMOKE
Fire is important to Zoroastrians. For them, it is the living symbol of Ahura Mazda. They worship in fire temples and offer prayers to the sacred fire.

▲ ASH SPOT
Before entering a fire temple, Zoroastrians remove their shoes. Once inside, they place a pinch of ash from the sacred fire on their forehead. Then they pray to the fire.

Key Dates

- c.1200BC Birth of Zoroaster.

- 539–331BC Zoroastrianism is the official religion of the Persian Empire.

- 331BC Alexander the Great destroys the Persian Empire and the manuscript of the *Avesta*.

- 129BC Zoroastrianism is again the official religion in Persia.

- c.AD400 The *Avesta* is rewritten.

- AD637 Islam becomes the main religion in Persia.

- AD716 Zoroastrians settle in Gujarat, India. These are the ancestors of modern-day Parsis.

Hinduism

▲ OHM
Every Hindu prayer that is said or sung includes the sound 'Ohm.' The part that looks like a '3' stands for the gods of creation, preservation and death. The part that looks like an 'O' is the silence of god.

THE WORD HINDU comes from the Persian word *sindhu*, which means 'river.' It refers to the religion of the people who lived by the River Indus around 2500BC. This ancient civilization was centred around the cities of Mohenjo-Daro and Harappa (in modern-day Pakistan). Over the centuries, the religion spread across northern India to the valley of the Ganges River.

In the 900s BC, the Hindu scriptures were written down. Two thousand years later Indian rulers took Hinduism to Sri Lanka and Southeast Asia. Today, it is practised around the world. There are more than 800 million Hindus, 700 million of whom live in India.

Hinduism does not have one central belief. It has evolved slowly over time, drawing in ideas from other religions. There are many different types of Hinduism and many different ways to be a Hindu.

Most Hindus believe that they have four aims in life. The first, *dharma*, is to live a good life by being kind to others and telling the truth. The second, *artha*, is to be wealthy and prosperous in life. *Kama* is to enjoy pleasure and *moksksha* is to be freed from the world and its desires.

Hindus also believe that they pass through four stages in life. These are being a student, then a householder, then a thinker and finally an ascetic (someone who is rid of all worldly pleasures). Not everyone achieves these four aims and stages, but if they do, they will be reincarnated (reborn) into a better life. For Hindus, this eternal cycle of life, death and then rebirth into a new life is very important.

◀ BRIDE AND GROOM
A Hindu marriage ceremony contains many religious rituals. At the end of the ceremony, the couple take seven steps, making a vow at each one. The steps represent food, strength, prosperity, well-being, children, happiness and harmony.

HINDU WORSHIP
Worship is an important part of Hindu religion. Hindus worship in temples, at shrines and in their own homes. Most people pray alone, rather than in large groups. Sunrise and sunset are the most popular times of day. Worship can involve singing, prayer and offering up gifts to the gods.

▶ HINDU TEMPLE
Temples have tall, ornate towers and four gateways that represent the four directions of the universe. Hindus visit the temple throughout the day to worship at its main icon (holy image).

◀ SITE OF LIGHT
Varanasi, on the banks of the Ganges, is the most important pilgrimage city in India. Varanasi is known as the City of Light, because it was here that the god Shiva's light reached up to the heavens.

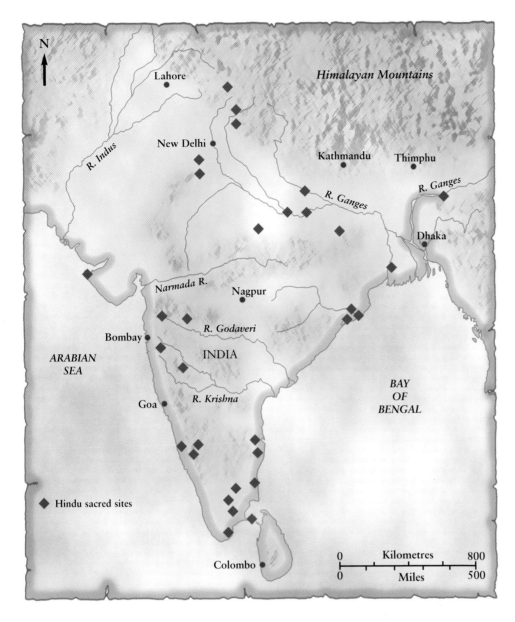

N

Lahore

Himalayan Mountains

New Delhi

R. *Indus*

Kathmandu   Thimphu

R. Ganges

R. *Ganges*

Dhaka

Narmada R.

Nagpur

R. Godaveri

Bombay

INDIA

ARABIAN
SEA

Goa   *R. Krishna*

BAY
OF
BENGAL

◆ Hindu sacred sites

	Kilometres	
0		800
0	Miles	500

Colombo

◄ THE BIRTH OF HINDUISM
Hinduism began in the Indus valley in present-day Pakistan. It spread throughout northern India, along the valley of the Ganges. In the early AD700s, Arab conquerors brought Islam to the valley of the Indus River. Over the next seven centuries, Islam spread slowly across northern India and sometimes there was conflict between Hindus and Muslims.

▼ HINDU PRIESTS
A brahmin (priest) looks after the temple and acts as a go-between between the worshipper and a god. Wandering priests or holy men are known as sadhus. These men lead an ascetic way of life. This means they give up worldly pleasures and wander from place to place begging for food.

▼ PILGRIMAGE
Going on a pilgrimage is an important part of Hindu worship. Places of pilgrimage include large cities, such as Varanasi and sacred rivers, such as the Ganges. Holy mountains, temples and small, local shrines are visited by pilgrims too.

▲ MEMENTO
To remind them of their pilgrimage, Hindu pilgrims often bring back small mementoes from the shrine they have visited.

Key Dates

- c.1500BC Hindu beliefs spread throughout northern India.

- c.900BC Hindu beliefs are written down in the four *Vedas*.

- c.500BC The *Mahabharata* written down by Vyasa, a wise man.

- c.300BC The *Ramayana* is written down by Valmiki, a poet.

- AD850–1200 Chola dynasty of northern India takes Hinduism to Sri Lanka and Southeast Asia.

- 1900s Hinduism spreads throughout world as Indians settle in Europe, Africa and the Americas.

Hindu Gods and Goddesses

HINDUS BELIEVE IN ONE SUPREME, ultimate god, Brahman, an unseen but all-powerful force who can appear in numerous forms. Some of these forms are worshipped by all Hindus, while others are worshipped only in one place or by a few people. The most important gods are those who created the world and its life and who are powerful enough to destroy it. There are gods of fire and war and many lesser gods that represent the forces of the natural world, such as the Sun and the wind.

Brahman brought the entire universe into existence. However, he is impersonal and takes no recognized appearance for his worshipers. Hindus therefore think of him in a variety of different appearances and worship him that way. The most important way in which Brahman makes himself known is through the Trimurti, a holy trio of three great gods. These are Brahma, Vishnu and Shiva. According to Hindu belief Brahma created the world, Vishnu preserves life and Shiva both destroys life and then recreates it.

Brahma is not worshipped like other gods, because after he created the world he had finished his work. However, when the world ends and needs to be recreated, he will return to create the world all over again. At that time he will be worshipped again.

Vishnu is known as the one who takes many different forms. He is very important because he preserves human life, the life of the world and the life of the universe itself. As a result, his different images are found in many temples and shrines.

▲ DANCE OF DESTRUCTION
Shiva is the destroyer and recreator of life. He is sometimes called the lord of the dance. He ends the dance of life so that a new dance can begin.

▼ BRAHMA
Brahma is the god of creation. After he created the first woman, he fell in love with her, but she hid herself from him. So Brahma grew three more heads so that he could see her from every angle.

GODS IN MANY FORMS

Hindus worship many minor gods. Some, such as Surya the sun god, Indra the god of war, and Vayu the wind god, are described in the Hindu scriptures. Others are specific to particular places. Hindus believe every part of Brahma's creation is divine and worship some animals, including Naga the snake god.

◀ THE ELEPHANT GOD
Ganesh is the remover of obstacles and also the lord of learning. His parents were Shiva and Parvati. One day Ganesh was protecting Parvati but his father did not recognise him and beheaded him. When he realised his mistake, Shiva replaced Ganesh's head with one from the first creature he saw, which was an elephant.

▲ LUCKY LAKSHMI
Lakshmi is one of the many friendly forms of the mother goddess. She is the goddess of fortune and brings wealth and good luck to her followers.

▼ MAHADEVI AS DURGA
Mahadevi is the Hindu mother goddess. She appears in many forms, both fiercesome and gentle. In one form she is the wife of Shiva. As Durga she is a fierce, demon-fighting warrior.

The third god of the trio is Shiva. Like Vishnu, he has many different forms and he has over a thousand names, such as Maheshvara, the lord of knowledge, and Mahakala, the lord of time. He is often shown with three faces. Two of the faces have opposite characteristics, such as male and female, or peace and war. The third face is always calm, to reconcile (bring together) the two opposites.

▶ RESTORING HARMONY
Vishnu is the god who preserves life, maintaining the balance between good and evil in the universe. If evil seems about to take control, Vishnu comes down to Earth to restore the balance. On Earth Vishnu takes the form of one of his ten incarnations, or avatars, the most important being Krishna. Nine of these avatars have visited the Earth already. The final one will arrive when the Earth is nearing the end of its current life. This tenth incarnation of Vishnu will destroy the world, then recreate it.

Kurma, the turtle

Matsya, the fish

Varaha, the boar

Narasimha, half-man, half-goat

Vamana, the dwarf

Rama

Krishna

Krishna with his mistress, Radha

Parasurama   *Buddha*   *Kalki*

▲ MONKEY GOD
The epic poem the *Ramayana* tells how the monkey god, Hanuman, helped Rama to defeat the demon king Ravana. Hanuman is worshipped as the god of strength and heroism.

▼ KARTTIKEYA
The boy god Karttikeya has many different names and there are many different stories about who his parents were. He was born to defeat evil and is often shown with a peacock, which is the national bird of India.

Ten Avatars of Vishnu

1. Matsya the fish, who saved the law-giver Manu during the Flood.
2. Kurma the turtle, who held the Earth on his back after the Flood.
3. Varaha the boar, who raised the land out of the water with his tusks.
4. Narasimha, who destroyed the demon king, Hiranyakasipu.
5. Vamana the dwarf, who tricked Hiranyakasipu's evil nephew, Bali.
6. Parasurama, who defeated an army of warriors with his axe.
7. Rama, who killed King Ravana.
8. Krishna, who told the *Bhagavad Gita* to Arjuna, his chariot driver.
9. Buddha, who founded Buddhism.
10. Kalki, who will appear at the end of the world on a white horse.

Hindu Scriptures

▲ A YOGI
Yogis are holy men who practise yoga, which means union of the individual soul with the universe. Yogis have played an important part in bringing Hindu teachings and scriptures to a wide audience in Europe and the Americas.

THE HINDU RELIGIOUS BOOKS were written down in Sanskrit (the ancient language of India) over the course of more than 1,000 years. Hindus have many different types of scripture, which fall into three groups.

The first group, the four *Vedas*, were originally passed down by word of mouth from generation to generation. *Veda* means 'knowledge.' The *Rig Veda* was the first to be written down in about 1200BC. It contains religious hymns. Next came the *Sama Veda*, which consists of chants for Hindus to sing as part of their worship, and the *Yajur Veda*, which contains words to be spoken by Hindu priests. The last one was written in about 900BC. This is the *Atharva Veda*, which is full of magic spells and incantations. Hindus believe the words of the *Vedas* are divine, so not a single word of them can be changed.

▲ THE VEDAS
The four Vedas *are the oldest Hindu scriptures of all. The oldest and best known, the* Rig Veda, *contains holy songs about the ancient gods of fire, earth, air and water. These were written to be accompanied by traditional Indian instruments, such as the sitar, shenai (a reed instrument) and the tabla (a type of drum).*

From around 700BC, Hindus began to wonder about the meaning of life and other philosophical questions. Over the next 400 years, this gave rise to the second major group of religious books. The *Upanishads* (sittings near a teacher) answer such questions as where we come from and why are we here. They explore the key concepts of Hinduism, such as reincarnation. They describe ordinary life as a cycle of birth, suffering, death and rebirth, and urge people to seek *moksha* (freedom from cycle of death and rebirth). The *Aranyakas* (forest books) deal with the meaning of rituals. The *Puranas* (ancient myths) contain stories of creation and the lives of the

FESTIVALS AND CELEBRATIONS

The Hindu year is filled with many festivals celebrating the gods and natural events, such as the end of winter or the rice harvest. Some are national festivals celebrated by Hindus all over the world. Others are celebrated only in particular parts of India.

▼ EFFIGIES FOR BURNING
Dusserah lasts nine days and is a celebration of good winning over evil. In southern India people burn effigies (models) of demons to symbolize Rama's victory over the evil king, Ravana.

◀ THE FESTIVAL OF LIGHTS
The five-day festival of Diwali celebrates the return of the god Rama from exile. Diwali is held in October or November. Candles are lit in every house so as to welcome Lakshmi, goddess of wealth.

▲ SPRING CELEBRATIONS
Holi, celebrated in March, marks the start of spring and the Hindu New Year. Holi is a fun festival. People of all castes (classes) join in by throwing coloured powders over each other.

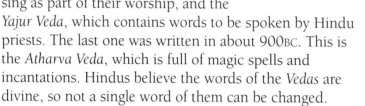

gods. As in the *Vedas*, the words in the *Upanishads* are holy and cannot be changed.

The final group of religious books are two epic poems. The first of these appeared in about 500BC. The *Mahabharata* is the longest poem in the world, with more than 200,000 lines. It includes myths and philosophical discussions. At the heart of the book is the *Bhagavad Gita* (Song of the Lord), which is a conversation between Krishna, one of the avatars of Vishnu, and his chariot driver, Arjuna. The second epic, the *Ramayana*, was written down in about 300BC. It tells the story of Rama, another avatar of Vishnu, and how he rescued his wife, Sita, who had been kidnapped by the demon king, Ravana, king of Lanka.

▲ AN ILLUSTRATION FROM THE MAHABHARATA
Much of the Mahabharata *concerns a long war between two families, the Kauravas and the Pandavas. Along the way there are many tales that explain aspects of history. One tells how the River Ganges came to be. Another describes the Great Flood.*

▲ SITA IN RAVANA'S PALACE
The Ramayana (Rama's Progress) *was a popular folk story long before it was written down. In it, the evil king Ravana captures Rama's wife, Sita. He carries her off to his palace in Lanka (modern-day Sri Lanka). It was years before Rama rescued her.*

▼ GANESH CHATURTHI
In September the birthday of Ganesh is celebrated all over India. Huge images of the elephant-headed god are paraded through the streets. Ganesh often holds sweets in his hand as he was very fond of them.

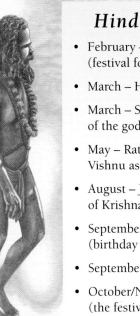

▶ HINDU HOLY MAN
Every 12 years, religious fairs or festivals are held in four different cities in India. Millions of people come to these events to bathe in the sacred rivers, listen to the teachings of the various *gurus* (teachers) and join in the many processions. Among those who make the pilgrimage to these events are *sadhus* (holy men).

Hindu Festivals

- February – Pongal-Sankranti (festival for the rice harvest)
- March – Holi (spring festival)
- March – Shivaratri (birthday of the god Shiva)
- May – Rathyatra (festival for Vishnu as lord of the universe)
- August – Janmashtami (birthday of Krishna, avatar of Vishnu)
- September – Ganesh Chaturthi (birthday of the god Ganesh)
- September/October – Dusserah
- October/November – Diwali (the festival of lights)

Jainism

THE JAIN RELIGION began in the valley of the Ganges River, India, in around 500BC. It slowly spread throughout northern India and today has 4.5 million followers in India, mainly in the business community. It also flourishes in Indian communities elsewhere in the world, such as in the USA.

Jainism was founded by a rich man, Mahavira. At the age of 29 he renounced (gave up) his wealth and became an ascetic, giving up worldy goods and begging for his food. He wanted to break the endless cycle of birth, life, death and rebirth, by finding enlightenment, or spiritual peace. After 12 years of fasting and meditation, he·achieved *kevala* (perfect knowledge). He then assembled a group of 12 followers and spent the next 30 years as a preacher until he starved to death at Pava, a village not far from his birthplace. Today Pava is one of the holiest sites of the Jain religion.

Jains take their name from *jina*. A *jina* is someone who has reached enlightenment. Jains believe that time is endless and is divided into a series of upward or downward movements that can last millions of years. In each of these movements, 24 *jinas* appear. Mahavira was the most recent. The *jinas* come to guide others towards enlightenment. They are also called *tirthankaras*.

Jains study the teachings of the *tirthankaras* and also take five vows to help them achieve spiritual peace. The vows are *ahimsa* (not to harm any living thing), *satya* (to speak the truth), *asteya* (not to steal), *brahmacharya* (to abstain from sexual activity) and *aparigraha* (not to become attached to people, places or possessions).

▲ PALM OF PEACE
The open palm is the official symbol of Jainism. It represents peace. Sometimes the word Ahimsa *(non-violence) is written on the palm.*

▼ RESPECT FOR LIFE
Monks and nuns often wear masks to stop them breathing in and killing insects. They also carry a brush to sweep insects out of the way so that they do not tread on them.

JAIN BELIEFS
Jains do not believe in a god and they do not pray to gods to help them in their lives. Instead, they study the works of the *tirthankaras* and practise meditation and self-discipline. They believe this is their only hope of release from the world and achieving spiritual liberation. Many Jains have jobs and live in the material world. Some Jains become monks or nuns to keep their mind uncluttered as they search for enlightenment.

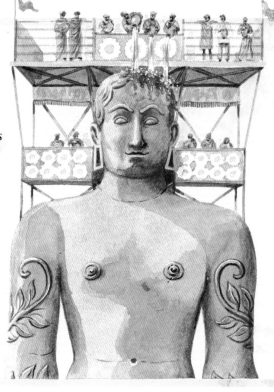

◀ LORD BAHUBALI
Bahubali defeated his half-brother in battle but did not kill him. Instead, he became a holy man. Jains consider him to be the first *tirthankara* of the present age. Every 12 years, pilgrims go to the Indian town of Sravanabegola to worship at his giant statue and anoint it with coloured water.

▲ PARSHVANATHA, 23RD TIRTHANKARA
The word tirthankara means 'builder of the ford.' Jains believe that they help people across samsara (the river of rebirth) to spiritual freedom. This page shows the 23rd Tirthankara.

Although there are not many Jains in the world today, their belief in non-violence has had a major effect on modern politics. The Indian leader Mahatma Gandhi, who led his country to independence from Britain in 1947, was profoundly influenced by the idea of non-violence, although he was not a Jain himself. Gandhi used it as a political weapon. Through his example, non-violent protest has become common in modern times, especially in the USA, where Martin Luther King and the Civil Rights movement achieved change peacefully in the 1960s.

▼ PLACE OF WORSHIP
A Jain temple is elaborately constructed, with many courtyards, balconies, domes and spires. At its centre is a shrine that contains a sacred image of one of the tirthankaras. Worshippers meditate quietly or chant a mantra (prayer).

▼ PICTURING THE UNIVERSE
The Jains see the universe, or *loka*, as divided into three main sections. At the bottom are eight hells and at the top are many heavens. In between is the *Madhya Loka* (middle world), which contains rings of continents and oceans. In the centre of these rings is the *Jambudvipa*, where Jains live.

▶ HEAVEN ON EARTH
Jain temples are meant to be earthly replicas of the *samasavarana* (the heavenly halls where the *tirthankaras* live). That is why Jain temples are so beautiful.

Key Dates

- c. 800BC Parsva, the last-but-one *tirthankara*, lives in India.

- c. 500BC Mahavira, the last *tirthankara*, founds Jainism, which spreads throughout northern India.

- c.AD300 Jainism splits into two groups, the Digambaras and Shvetambaras. They have different ideas about the status of women and how detached from daily life a Jain should be.

- AD981 Giant statue of Bahubali is built at Sravanabegola.

- 1900s The idea of non-violence influences political protests.

Buddhism

▲ THE EIGHTFOLD PATH
*An eight-spoked wheel is the
symbol for the Noble Eightfold
Path. These eight different
states of mind sum up the
Buddha's teaching on how
to find enlightenment.*

Buddhism was founded by Siddhartha Gautama, who became known as the Buddha (enlightened one). The Buddha was born in northern India in 485BC. By the time of his death in 405BC, his teachings had spread across India, eventually reaching Southeast Asia, Korea and Japan. Today, there are more than 330 million Buddhists around the world, mainly in eastern Asia but also in Europe and North America.

The Buddha taught that it was possible to overcome suffering in the world and become enlightened by following the Eightfold Path. The steps along this path are right knowledge, right attitude, right speech, right actions, right livelihood, right effort, right state of mind and right concentration. Buddhists must make sure that each of these aspects of their life is *samma* (right). The Eightfold Path involves a great deal of discipline, so Buddhists often find a teacher to help them. Once they have understood the path, they try to practise it. This takes them towards enlightenment and, ultimately, they aim for *nirvana* (a state of supreme happiness and bliss).

Nirvana is difficult to achieve, for Buddhists believe that we constantly travel through an endless cycle of life, death and rebirth, either as humans or in other forms. All these lives are subject to *karma* (the law of cause and effect). This means that every action has a result, either good or bad. If we do bad things, we increase our negative *karma* and keep being reborn into new lives. If we do good things, we gain positive *karma*.

Buddhists try to get rid of negative *karma* by

◀ BUDDHA'S FOOTPRINT
*The Buddha did not want his
followers to make him into a god,
so at first there were no statues of
him. He was shown only through
symbols, such as his footprint.*

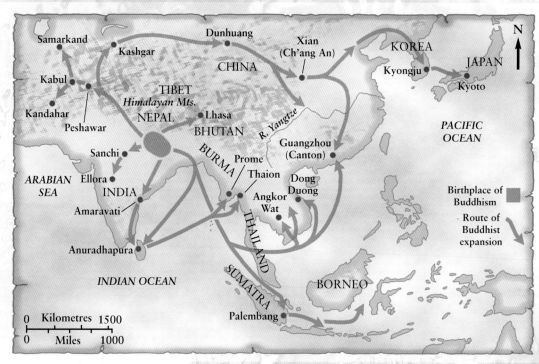

THE SPREAD OF BUDDHISM
Buddhism began in northern India in around 500BC and then spread to Sri Lanka, Southeast Asia and into Tibet, China and Japan. The early forms of Buddhism are known as Theravada (teaching of the elders). In the first century AD, a new branch of Buddhism developed called Mahayana (great vehicle).

▶ BUDDHISM DIVIDED
Theravada Buddhism is strongest in Sri Lanka and Southeast Asia. Mahayana Buddhism is practised in Tibet, Mongolia, China, Korea, Japan and Vietnam.

Samarkand · Kashgar · Dunhuang · Xian (Ch'ang An) · KOREA · JAPAN · Kyongju · Kyoto · CHINA · Kabul · TIBET · *Himalayan Mts.* · Kandahar · NEPAL · Lhasa · Peshawar · BHUTAN · R. Yangtze · Guangzhou (Canton) · PACIFIC OCEAN · Sanchi · BURMA · Prome · Thaion · Dong Duong · ARABIAN SEA · Ellora · INDIA · Angkor Wat · Amaravati · THAILAND · Anuradhapura · INDIAN OCEAN · SUMATRA · BORNEO · Palembang

N

Birthplace of Buddhism

Route of Buddhist expansion

0   Kilometres   1500
0   Miles   1000

▼ HUMAN FAILINGS
At the centre of the Wheel of Life are three animals. They symbolize the weaknesses that human beings must overcome. The pig represents greed. The cockerel stands for delusion (holding false beliefs). The last creature, the snake, symbolizes hatred.

following the Eightfold Path, doing good deeds and by meditating. They believe that if they succeed, they will be released from the law of *karma* and stop *samsara* (wandering from life to life). They will be free from suffering and achieve the peace of *nirvana*.

The Buddha preached that life is always changing and that people should not look for happiness in material things, such as wealth and possessions. Instead, they should get rid of fear, passion, greed, ignorance, selfishness, and all the other vices that keep them attached to the world. In this way, they become enlightened and can achieve *nirvana*.

▲ THE WHEEL OF LIFE
Buddhists believe that when a person dies, they are reborn into one of six realms (regions) of existence. The gods, the fighting gods, the hungry ghosts, hell, beasts and humans each have their own realm, shown on this thangka, *or religious drawing.*

◀ BUDDHIST MONK
The Buddha formed his own community of monks, the *Sangha*. Monks are an important part of Buddhism to this day. They teach people how to achieve *nirvana*, in return for food and clothes.

▶ BODHISATTVA
A person who has achieved enlightenment but decides to stay in the world to help others is known as a *bodhisattva* (one who is possessed of enlightenment).

Key Dates

- 485–405BC Life of the Buddha.

- 250BC Buddhism spreads to Sri Lanka and Southeast Asia.

- AD100s Mahayana Buddhism emerges.

- AD100s Buddhism spreads to China and Central Asia.

- AD300s Buddhism reaches Korea.

- AD600s Buddhism reaches Tibet and Japan.

- AD868 The sacred Buddhist text, the *Diamond Sutra*, is printed.

- 1000s Buddhism dies out in India as Muslim armies invade.

The Life of the Buddha

▲ LOTUS FLOWER
The waterlily or lotus flower often symbolizes Buddhism. The flower stands for enlightenment, because it grows out of slimy mud, which symbolizes suffering.

Prince Siddhartha Gautama was born into a royal family in northeastern India in 485BC. His father sheltered him from the suffering in the world, but while he was out of the palace one day Gautama came face to face with a sick man, then an old man and finally a dead man. He was only 29, but Gautama understood that sickness, old age and death would come to him eventually, too. He decided to follow a holy way of life in order to come to terms with the meaning of life. He left behind his wife and family and lived a poor life without any luxuries at all. He meditated every day and fasted (did not eat). Gautama suffered a great deal. His hair fell out and he grew thin and weak. After six years, Gautama decided that his extreme lifestyle was not the best way to find peace. He decided to find a middle way, somewhere between an ascetic, monk-like existence and a life in the everyday world.

One evening, Gautama was sitting in the shade of a bodhi tree (tree of enlightenment) in Bodh Gaya, a village in northeastern India. After meditating here for a long time, he achieved the state of perfect peace, or *nirvana*. From this moment on, he became known as the Buddha (enlightened one). Today the sacred Mahabodhi temple stands on the site of Buddha's enlightenment.

During his deep meditation the Buddha came to understand the Four Noble Truths. These are the central Buddhist teachings. By understanding these truths, and following the Eightfold Path of right living,

◀ GOLDEN BUDDHA
From around 200BC, people began to build statues of the Buddha. He is usually shown sitting cross-legged, with each foot resting on the opposite thigh. This is called the lotus position. It is used in yoga to help concentrate the mind.

BUDDHIST TEMPLES

When the Buddha died, his remains were divided and *stupas* (Buddhist burial mounds) were built over them. These soon became places of pilgrimage and were often decorated with elaborate carvings and encrusted with stone. Shrines and temples to the Buddha or *bodhisattvas* are found throughout the Buddhist world.

▶ KATHESIMBHU
Buddhists make pilgrimages to this stupa in Nepal to see relics of the Buddha.

◀ BOROBUDUR
The Buddhist temple at Borobudur on the Indonesian island of Java has a central stupa at the top. It is reached by climbing past eight terraces, shaped as squares and circles. These represent a Buddhist's journey from hell, through earthly life and up to heavenly worlds at the summit.

a person can rise above suffering and achieve the state of *nirvana*.

The Buddha gathered together a group of five disciples (followers) and took up a life as a holy teacher. For the next 45 years he travelled around northern India, teaching his message and begging for food. His first sermon was at Sarnath, near Varanasi in northeast India. He preached in a deer park, which is why some images of the Buddha show him with deer at his feet.

When the Buddha died, his last words to his followers were, "Do not cry. Have I not told you that it is in the nature of all things, however dear they may be to us, that we must part with them and leave them." He meant that Buddhists must not be too attached to anything, as this will only bring sorrow and suffering and will hinder them on their quest for *nirvana*.

◀ DEATH OF THE BUDDHA
When the Buddha died at the age of 80, he became known as the Tathagata (Thus-gone). Having achieved nirvana *when he died, the Buddha was not reborn into life again like other people. Buddhists believe he moved beyond life to a blissful state where he neither existed nor did not exist.*

▶ TEMPLE
At the centre of a Buddhist temple is a shrine that houses images of Buddha and other holy men. Leading off from it are rooms for meditation and teaching.

▼ MONASTERY
Buddhists as young as eight years old enter monasteries, where they study to become monks. Monasteries usually have classrooms, libraries, rooms for meditation and shrines.

▼ TRAVELLING TEMPLE
In Thailand, tiny temples containing a statue of the Buddha are carried to remote parts. This gives villagers a place to worship.

The Four Noble Truths

The Buddha revealed these Four Truths in his first sermon at Sarnath. They form the basis of all his other teachings. To understand them you must concentrate, and be peaceful.

1. Suffering exists in the world and so all existence is *dukka* (full of suffering and dissatisfaction).

2. Suffering exists because of *tamba* (the yearning for satisfaction).

3. The only way to overcome suffering is to achieve *nirvana*.

4. *Nirvana* can be reached by following the Eightfold Path.

Types of Buddhism

As BUDDHISM SPREAD from India throughout the rest of Eastern Asia, it changed. It adapted to local cultures and adopted elements from other religions. Early Buddhism emphasized the importance of meditation. It stressed that people are on their own in the world and can reach *nirvana* only through their own efforts. This strand of Buddhism is known as Theravada (the teaching of the elders). The other strand of Buddhism is known as Mahayana (great vehicle). Followers of Mahayana believe that people are not alone and that they must work together to achieve *nirvana*. Help also comes from the Buddha, other *buddhas* (enlightened ones) and

▲ PRAYER WHEEL
Tibetan Buddhists often carry a prayer wheel with a mantra *(chant) inside on a strip of paper. Each turn of the wheel counts as a single prayer.*

▶ WORLD PICTURE
A mandala *is a representation of the world through pictures and diagrams. It can be a vast temple, or a picture printed on paper or silk. Tantric Buddhists chant* mantras *over* mandalas *as they are made. They believe that they give off powerful energy.*

BUDDHISM ABROAD

Buddhism varies from country to country, but two aspects of the religion are common to Buddhists everywhere. Monks are important, especially to Tibetan Buddhists. Meditation is practised by all Buddhists, but especially by the Zen Buddhists of Japan. When they meditate, Buddhists rid their minds of all thoughts and find inner stillness. In this state, they can concentrate on gaining enlightenment.

◀ THE DALAI LAMA
The leader of Tibet is the Dalai Lama. The present Dalai Lama left Tibet in 1959, eight years after China first occupied his country. From his exile in India, he has campaigned peacefully for China to restore Tibet's independence.

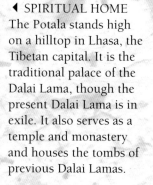

▲ HEADDRESS
Some Tibetan *lamas* wear headdresses for religious services. This one shows the five *buddhas* of meditation.

◀ SPIRITUAL HOME
The Potala stands high on a hilltop in Lhasa, the Tibetan capital. It is the traditional palace of the Dalai Lama, though the present Dalai Lama is in exile. It also serves as a temple and monastery and houses the tombs of previous Dalai Lamas.

bodhisattvas. *Bodhisattvas* are people who have already reached *nirvana*, but have chosen to stay in the world to help others achieve it too. Both Theravada and Mahayana Buddhists believe that the Buddha himself was only one in a long line of enlightened people, and that many other *buddhas* exist as well.

Mahayana Buddhism differs from country to country. In China, Buddhism was practised alongside the ancient Chinese religions of Confucianism and Taoism. Many *bodhisattvas* acquired Chinese names. In Tibet, the use of ritual, symbolism, meditation and magic became important. Tantric Buddhism, as it is known, uses mantras or sacred chants written in *tantras* (secret books) to help people attain *nirvana*. Spiritual teachers, known as *lamas*, educate people in Buddhism. *Lamas* are also said to guide a dying person's spirit between death and rebirth.

In Japan, Zen Buddhism adapted the Chinese practice of meditation. Zen meditation requires the person to sit cross-legged in the lotus position. As they meditate, they think about a *koan* (riddle), such as 'What is the sound of one hand clapping?'. The purpose behind such riddles is to make people focus on the meanings behind words. In this way, they escape their conventional ways of thinking and free their minds to reach *nirvana*. Zen meditation can take place in a garden, a teahouse or even through practising ancient arts, such as flower arranging or archery.

▶ THE BOOK OF BUDDHISM
This picture of the Buddha preaching is based on an illustration in the Diamond Sutra. This sacred Buddhist scroll is five metres long and contains one of the Buddha's sermons. It is the world's oldest printed book.

◀ JAPANESE TEAHOUSE
Teahouses are beautiful places to meditate. The *sado* (tea ceremony) was perfected in the 1500s by Sen Rikyu. He stressed the importance of *wabi* (simplicity) and *sabi* (peacefulness).

▼ ZEN GARDEN
Zen Buddhists create peaceful gardens as places for meditation. Instead of colourful flowers, there are rocks, sand and grass. Raking the sand into patterns can be a form of meditation in itself.

The Buddhist Year

- In India, Buddhist New Year is celebrated in March or April. In Tibet, it is celebrated in February.

- The birth of Buddha, known as Vesakha in Theravada Buddhism, is celebrated in May.

- In Tibet, Buddha's enlightenment is celebrated in May.

- Buddha's Asalha (first sermon) is celebrated by Theravada Buddhists in July.

- Kattika is a Theravada festival to celebrate missionaries who spread the Buddha's teachings. It is held in late November.

38 ❧ WORLD RELIGIONS ❧

Sikhism

THE SIKH RELIGION was founded by Guru Nanak. He was born in the Punjab province of what is now Pakistan and northwestern India in 1469. The Sikh holy book, the *Guru Granth Sahib*, was gathered together by the end of the 1500s. Despite persecution by Hindu and Muslim rulers of India, Sikhism slowly gained strength. Today there are more than 20 million Sikhs, mainly in the Punjab but also wherever Punjabis have settled in the world, notably Britain, East Africa, Malaysia, and North America. The word *sikh* is Punjabi for 'learner.' Sikhs see themselves as learning their faith from one true teacher, Sat Guru (the Sikh god). *Gurus* (teachers) reveal God's teachings. The Sikhs recognize 12 *gurus* in total. They are God, ten leaders of the faith, and the *Guru Granth Sahib*, the holy book.

The first *guru* was Nanak. He lived during a period of great conflict between Hindus and Muslims in India. Some Hindus were seeking a god above any religious conflict, and Nanak joined them in their search.

"There is no Hindu or Muslim, so whose path shall I follow?" he wondered. Nanak came to believe that there was one God, who created everything, and that everything depended on him. Nanak also believed that God does not appear on Earth but makes himself known through teachers, or *gurus*.

Sikh beliefs are summed up in the words of the *Mool Mantra*, the first hymn written by Guru Nanak.

◀ **THE KHANDA**
Every part of the Sikh emblem, the khanda, *has a meaning. The double-edged sword in the centre stands for truth and justice. The ring symbolizes the unity of God. The two curved swords at the bottom stand for spiritual and earthly power.*

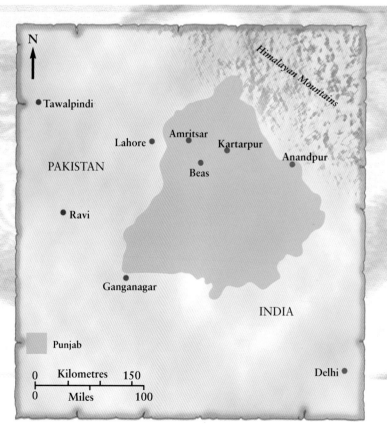

◀ GURU NANAK
The founder of the Sikh religion was born in the Punjab in 1469. Born a Hindu, Nanak did not agree with the religious wars at the time. He also felt that too much ritual made God distant to us.

THE SIKH HOMELAND
Sikhs were often under attack from Muslim, Hindu and Afghan armies so, in 1799, they established their own kingdom in the Punjab. This lasted until British forces occupied it in 1849. When the British left in 1947, the Punjab was split between India and Pakistan. Since the 1980s, some Sikhs have campaigned for the Punjab to become an independent Sikh state. This would be called Khalistan (the land of the *Khalsa*).

▲ GURU RAM DAS
Ram Das became the fourth *guru* in 1574. He founded the city of Amritsar. His followers dug out the Harimandir Sahib, the vast holy lake that surrounds the Golden Temple.

▶ THE GOLDEN TEMPLE
Guru Nanak saw that it was easy for worship to become a meaningless ritual. He said that God can always be found within oneself. However, as long as Sikhs understand that buildings are not holy in themselves, they can build temples at important holy sites. The Golden Temple at Amritsar, Punjab, is the holiest Sikh shrine. It was built in 1601 and contains the Guru Granth Sahib, the holy book of the Sikhs.

"There is only God. Truth is his name. He is the creator. He is without fear. He is without hate. He is timeless and without form. He is beyond death, the enlightened one. He can only be known by the Guru's grace." Sikhs meditate so that they can understand the *gurus'* teachings.

Nanak ensured that after his death another *guru* would take over and continue his work. Nanak died in 1539. Nine more *gurus* carried Sikhism forward until the death of Guru Gobind Singh in 1708. Guru Gobind Singh chose the Sikh holy scripture, not a person, to be his successor. That is why the scripture is called the *Guru Granth Sahib* and is considered to be the 11th guru. The holy book and its teachings guide the Sikh community to this day.

▼ GURU ARJAN
Arjan became the fifth *guru* in 1581. He collected all the hymns of previous *gurus* with his own contributions and combined them into the *Guru Granth Sahib*, the Sikh holy book. He died in 1606.

▲ GURU HAR KRISHAN
Har Krishan was only five when he became the eighth *guru* in 1661. He died of smallpox three years later. He·is the only *guru* to be shown without a beard, because he was too young to grow one.

▼ GURU GOBIND SINGH
Gobind Singh, the tenth *guru*, is the second-most important *guru* after Guru Nanak. He established the *Khalsa* (community of Sikhs) and resisted the Hindu and Muslim rulers of India.

Key Dates

- 1469–1539 Life of Guru Nanak, the first *guru*.

- 1577 Guru Ram Das founds the city of Amritsar.

- 1604 The *Guru Granth Sahib* is installed in the Golden Temple.

- 1699 Guru Gobind Singh forms the *Khalsa* (Sikh community).

- 1799 Maharajah Ranjit Singh founds an independent Sikh kingdom in the Punjab.

- 1849 The Punjab becomes part of British India.

- 1947 The Punjab is split between India and Pakistan.

Sikh Teachings

IN 1699 THE LAST of the ten *gurus*, Guru Gobind Singh, called the Sikhs together at the *mela* (fair) in Anandpur. He called for a volunteer who was willing to die for his faith. One man stepped forward and went into a tent with the *guru*, who came out soon afterwards with a bloody sword. Four more men then volunteered, and they also followed the guru into the tent. Then the *guru* opened the tent and revealed that all the five men were still alive.

This event marks the start of the *Khalsa* (Sikh community) whose members pledge to uphold the Sikh religion and defend all those in need, perhaps even to lose their lives for their faith. In order to make all Sikhs equal, Guru Gobind Singh gave all men the name Singh (lion) and all women the name Kaur (princess).

▲ THE CHAURI
The chauri, or whisk, is a symbol of authority. Just as a whisk was waved over a guru to keep the flies away in the Punjab, so the chauri is waved over the holy book to show respect for it.

▶ THE GURU GRANTH SAHIB
The Sikh holy book is a collection of teachings by Guru Nanak and other gurus. The book starts with verses written by Nanak, which are recited everyday by Sikhs in their morning prayers.

FESTIVALS
All Sikh festivals are times of meditation and thought. Sikhs hold two types of festival. *Gurpurbs* remember the birth or martyrdom of one of the ten gurus. Sikhs prepare for a *gurpurb* by reading the whole of the *Guru Granth Sahib*, which takes about 48 hours. *Melas* are fairs. They are times of strenuous activity, with sports events, mock battles, and firework displays.

▼ SIKH WEDDINGS
When Sikhs marry, the bride and groom's families are joined together as well. Verses from the *Guru Granth Sahib* are read out, and the couple walk around the holy book after each verse as part of their wedding vows.

▼ GOBIND SINGH'S BIRTHDAY
At the festival to celebrate Guru Gobind Singh's birthday, Sikhs read the *Guru Granth Sahib*, pray, meditate and sing together. People wear traditional costume.

kara

kirpan

kangha

◀ THE FIVE Ks ▶

When the Khalsa was founded in 1699, Guru Gobind Singh asked Sikhs to wear five symbols to show their allegiance to the Sikh community. These are known as the Five Ks, because their names all begin with the letter 'k.' They are kirpan *(a curved dagger),* kangha *(a comb),* kara *(a steel bangle),* kachh *(short pants worn as underwear) and* kesh *(uncut hair). Sikh boys and men wear a turban to keep their* kesh *tidy. However, the turban itself is not one of the Five Ks.*

Sikhs become members of the *Khalsa* in an initiation ceremony known as an *amrit sanskar*, which is often performed at the Vaisakhi festival held in April to commemorate the founding of the *Khalsa*. The ceremony is private, and takes place in the local *gurdwara* (Sikh temple). Many Sikhs wait until they are adults before joining the *Khalsa*, although boys as young as 14 do join. Women can join, but it is rare for them to do so. All candidates must be approved by existing members of the *Khalsa*.

At the ceremony, five members of the *Khalsa* each hand over one of the Five Ks to the new recruit. These are symbolic objects that all Sikhs must have. In return,

the young Sikh pledges to defend the faith, serve other people, pray every morning and evening, and not to smoke or drink alcohol. He is then given a sweet drink called *amrit* and says that "The *Khalsa* is of God and the victory is to God." After a few prayers, the new recruit is admitted to the *Khalsa*.

Sikh religious and community life revolves around the *gurdwara*. Its name means 'the door of the *guru*.' This is where the *Guru Granth Sahib* is kept, and where Sikhs gather to sing, meditate and study. There is no holy day of the week reserved for worship as in many of the other religions. Services can take place at any time.

▼ HOLY LITTER

The *Guru Granth Sahib* takes pride of place in any festival procession. It is carried on a litter by five Sikh elders, dressed in yellow and white. The litter is decorated with garlands.

▲ ANANDPUR FAIR

At the time of the Hindu festival of Holi, Sikhs gather for a *mela* (fair) to remember the life of Guru Gobind Singh. They hold athletic and horse-riding events and compete in the martial arts. The greatest of these *melas* is the Hola Mohalla in Anandpur, Punjab.

Sikh Festivals

- December/January – Guru Gobind Singh's birthday.

- February – Hola Mohalla, in memory of Guru Gobind Singh.

- April – Formation of the *Khalsa*.

- May – Martyrdom of Guru Arjan (1606).

- August – Celebration of the *Guru Granth Sahib* (1606).

- October – The Hindu festival of Diwali marks Guru Hargobind's release from prison in 1619.

- October – Guru Nanak's birthday.

- November – Martyrdom of Guru Tegh Bahadur (1675).

Religion in China

▲ THE I CHING
The I Ching *is based on the ancient art of divination, telling the future. Special disks might be thrown. The way they landed was then interpreted.*

CHINA DOES NOT have a single religion. Instead Chinese religion is made up of four separate religions and philosophies (ways of thinking). The main three are Confucianism, Buddhism and Taoism. Together, they are known as the *San-chiao* (the three ways). The fourth is the popular folk religion practised throughout the country. The Chinese practise all these religions in their daily lives, picking out those bits that seem most helpful or useful at the time. Few people follow just one.

The first way, Confucianism, is based on the practice of divination (foretelling the future). This is explained in five books, all compiled long before the birth of Confucius. The books are the *I Ching* (*Book of Changes*), the *Shih Ching* (*Book of Poetry*), the *Shu Ching* (*Book of History*), the *Li Chin* (*Book of Rites*) and the *Ch'un-ch'iu* (*Spring and Autumn Annals*). Confucius's own teachings are contained in the *Four Books of Confucianism*. Together these books produce a code of good behaviour for people to follow, rather than a formal religion for them to worship. Followers of Confucius can believe in any god or none.

▲ GOOD WORK
Confucius expected farmers to work hard and produce food for their family and country. Many Chinese festivals celebrate farmers' closeness to the land and their success in getting the harvest in.

Confucius tried to balance the opposing forces of *yin* (darkness) and *yang* (light) in the universe. He stressed the need for order and respect on Earth so that there will be a harmonious balance between heaven, Earth and human beings. To achieve this, people have to learn from the past to see how they should behave today. Confucius ignored existing religious beliefs and stressed instead the importance of serving other people. He said

CONFUCIANISM

Confucius was a philosopher and teacher who lived at a time of great disturbance in China. He wanted to bring order and peace to his country and taught that people should respect their ancestors and parents and work hard. *Li* (good conduct) was very important. Confucius taught that if everyone did their duty to the emperor and behaved well, then the country would be strong and at peace.

◀ RELIGIOUS RULER
Confucius's Chinese name, K'ung Fu-tzu, means 'master king.' His parents gave him this name because, when he was born, it was foretold that he would be a king without a crown.

▲ CHINESE TEMPLE
Confucius did not found a religion, but throughout China, shrines and temples were erected in his honour. Confucianism became the state religion.

▼ LOOKING
FORWARD
*Children are very
important in Chinese
life. They represent the
future of the family. In
the Chinese language,
the character for 'good'
(hao) shows a mother
and child, representing
harmony and fertility.*

▶ CONSULTING
THE I CHING
The I Ching *consists of 64
hexagrams (six lines) made up of
broken (yin) or unbroken (yang)
lines. Users draw stalks from a
container, and throw them to the
ground. Then, they consult the* I
Ching, *compare the way that their
sticks have fallen to what is in the
book and see what they foretell.*

that people should not do anything to other people that
they would not like others to do to them. Above all, he
taught that it was pointless to worship a god, or honour
your ancestors, if you did not serve other people first.
The second and fourth ways, Taoism and folk religions,
are described on the next page. The third way,
Buddhism, has already been described. Together, all
four ways showed people how to live their lives as
good citizens and therefore keep a balance between
yin and *yang* in their lives.

▲ EMPEROR TEAON-KWANG
The Chinese believed that the very first Chinese
emperors were gods and that their successors had a
mandate (approval) from heaven. Emperors were
worshipped and treated with great respect.

▼ BELL
Once, when Confucius
heard a bell ringing, he
decided to give up worldly
comforts and live on rice
and water for three months
as he meditated. To this
day, the Chinese believe
that bells calm the mind
and help clear thinking.

Key Dates

- c.3000BC The *I Ching* is written
  down by Wen Wang.

- 500sBC Life of Lao-Tzu.

- 551BC Confucius is born.

- c.495–485BC Confucius travels to
  neighbouring states in the hope
  of realizing his ideals.

- 479BC Confucius dies.

- 221BC China is united for the
  first time under Emperor Qin
  Shi Huangdi.

- 202BC–AD220 Under the Han
  dynasty, Confucianism becomes
  the official religion of China.

- AD100s Buddhism reaches China.

Taoism

▲ YIN AND YANG
Yin and yang *depend on each other and intertwine. The force of* yin *represents darkness, water and the female aspect of things. Its opposite,* yang, *represents light, activity, air and maleness.*

THE SECOND WAY of Chinese religion, alongside Confucianism and Buddhism, is Taoism. *Tao* means way, or path, and Taoists believe that there is a life force running through the natural world like a path. Taoists follow this path because it is the natural way and they do not struggle against it. The path is sometimes called the watercourse way, because like a river of water, the path flows in one direction. Like water, it is both powerful and life-giving. Taoists go with the flow of life. Taoist belief is summed up in the saying "Tao never acts, yet there is nothing that is not done."

The legendary founder of Taoism, Lao-tzu, lived at about the same time as Confucius, but little is known about him. He is supposed to be the author of the *Tao Te Ching,* one of the two major works of Taoism. The other is the *Chuang Tzu.*

From these books, two kinds of Taoism have developed – popular and philosophical. The popular form is concerned with religion and includes many gods, goddesses and spirits. Believers seek their help against the many demons that live in the world. They also use ritual and magic to capture the *Te* (power) that brings enlightenment and, they hope, immortality.

Philosophical Taoism is much more mystical and peaceful than religious Taoism. Followers gain an understanding of the Tao by meditation and control of their bodies. They attempt to live in harmony with the Tao. They believe that the body, mind and environment are closely linked and affect each other.

◀ LAO-TZU
The legendary founder of Taoism lived in China in about 500BC. He was probably a scholar. One day he travelled on his ox to a border post, where he was asked to write down his teachings. He did and the book he wrote is known as the Tao Te Ching. *After writing it, Lao-Tzu disappeared and was never heard of again.*

THE FOURTH WAY – CHINESE FOLK RELIGION

Popular religion in China is very festive, with everybody joining in parades and events. It is concerned with caring for dead ancestors and achieving a balance between the forces of *yin* and *yang*. The art of Feng Shui helps in this. Feng Shui is the practice of placing objects, buildings and even people in the best place to catch the currents of *ch'i* as they circulate.

▼ CHINESE DRAGON
People dressed as dragons, lions and other animals parade through the streets to celebrate Chinese New Year. The dragon brings happiness and good luck and represents the generous spirit of New Year.

▼ FORTUNE COOKIE
People give each other special biscuits called fortune cookies at New Year. Inside them are pieces of paper with a motto.

This belief is shown in the practice of a form of martial art called t'ai chi. Taoists believe that the body has invisible meridians (channels) that run through it carrying blood and *ch'i* (vital energy). The meridian lines feed the vital organs, such as the heart, and ensure a balance between *yin* and *yang*. If this balance is lost, or the flow of *ch'i* is disrupted, acupuncture needles can be used to rebalance the body and ease the flow of *ch'i*.

Taoism never became a major religion in China, although it gained ground during the 1st century AD. It remained popular until 1949 when the Chinese Communists took power. Communists believe that any religion stops people from working to help themselves, fooling them into just doing what they're told. It is for this reason that the new Chinese government destroyed many of the Taoist temples.

▲ RELIGIOUS TAOISM
Taoists believe in three star gods (shown here from the top left). These are the gods of long life, wealth and happiness. Taoists also recognize eight immortals (people who will never die), five of whom are shown here. The immortals show living people how to become immortal themselves.

▼ MARTIAL ART
T'ai chi is a form of exercise that focuses the mind and the body. People who practise it draw on the strength of the Earth and the ch'i *of the heavens.*

▼ BURNING MONEY
At a Chinese funeral, mourners burn fake money. The notes are meant as a bribe to the gods of the underworld so they will let the dead person through to heaven.

▼ A HOUSEHOLD SHRINE
Most houses have a shrine dedicated to a god. Popular gods include Fu Hsing, who brings happiness, and Tsai Shen, who brings wealth. Despite Communist disapproval of gods and religion, some homes place a picture of the first Communist leader, Chairman Mao, in pride of place at their shrine.

Chinese New Year

The major festival in China is New Year, which falls between 21 January and 19 February. Each New Year is associated with one of twelve animals.

- 2000 is the Year of the Dragon
- 2001 is the Year of the Snake
- 2002 is the Year of the Horse
- 2003 is the Year of the Goat
- 2004 is the Year of the Monkey
- 2005 is the Year of the Rooster
- 2006 is the Year of the Dog
- 2007 is the Year of the Pig
- 2008 is the Year of the Rat
- 2009 is the Year of the Ox
- 2010 is the Year of the Tiger
- 2011 is the Year of the Rabbit
- 2012 is the Year of the Dragon

Shinto

▲ TORII GATE
Every Shinto shrine is entered through a gate called a torii. *The torii separates the shrine from the ordinary world outside. It can be some distance from the shrine itself.*

THE ANCIENT RELIGION of Japan is called Shinto (way of the gods). The name was first given to the religion in the AD600s. It comes from the Chinese words *shen* (divine being) and *tao* (way). The religion itself, however, is much older, and dates back to Japanese prehistory, perhaps 1,000 years or more before. No one knows who founded Shinto, because it is so old.

The mysterious origins of Shinto are recorded in two books, the *Kojiki* and *Nihongi*, which were compiled at the beginning of the AD700s. Both books were influenced by Chinese thinking, brought to Japan by Buddhist and Confucian teachers.

Over the years, Shinto became the main religion of Japan, but the Japanese do not follow a single religion. Shinto is practised alongside Confucianism, Taoism, Buddhism and, more recently, Christianity. The Japanese take elements from each as they need them.

In many ways, Shinto is not really a religion. It is better described as a collection of attitudes and values about life and society that all Japanese people share. It emphasized the divinity of the emperor and the need to obey the government. There is no formal doctrine (set of beliefs) and no single book or collection that contains the main ideas of Shinto. However, all followers of Shinto believe in the forces of nature, which make themselves felt in *kami* (gods). *Kamis* live in every living thing. The Japanese

◀ TOSHO-GU SHRINE
Shrines are built to honour the kami *or past emperors. Tosho-gu Shrine in Ueno Park, Tokyo, was built in 1651 to commemorate the shogun (ruler) Tokugawa Ieyasu. The shrine's entrance is lined with lanterns. People go to shrines to escape the noise and pressure of everyday life. Sometimes they hang up little prayers that they have written.*

JAPANESE RELIGION

Shinto is the main religion in Japan, but it is quite common to see Buddhist priests at a Shinto shrine and sometimes temples to Buddha have been built within Shinto shrines. Elements of Confucianism and Taoism are also common in Japanese religion.

▶ HIROHITO
The Japanese believe their first emperor, Jimmu, was descended from Amaterasu, the sun goddess. In 1946 Emperor Hirohito said that he was human and renounced his divinity.

◀ MOUNT FUJI
Almost every mountain in Japan has its own god. Sengen-Sama is the goddess of Mount Fuji, the most famous and distinctive mountain in the country. Every year pilgrims climb the mountain at dawn to watch the sun rise.

worship about eight million different *kami* at national and local shrines. The Japanese consult the *kami* at the shrines, asking them for advice or support, and then they follow their instructions. Festivals and rituals play an important part in Shinto.

During the 1800s, Japan began to update its government and economy with ideas imported from Europe. Japanese citizens were given the freedom to worship as they pleased. However, Shinto remained important because it expressed beliefs that are still held by the Japanese people.

▶ THE SUN GODDESS
Amaterasu was the sun goddess who retired into a cave. The world was plunged into darkness and wicked gods created chaos. The good gods enticed Amaterasu out of the cave by making her curious about what was going on without her. Light and peace were then returned to the world.

▲ PORTABLE SHRINE
At a Shinto festival the kami (god) leaves the shrine and is carried through the streets in a mikoshi (portable shrine), to bless everyone in the community. As they process through the streets, the shrine-bearers shake the mikoshi to awaken the kami.

▲ A REQUEST
Japanese people often buy little plaques called *emas*, which they hang up at the temple or shrine. *Emas* are a request for help from the *kami*. This one asks for luck in love. Others request good health, or success in an exam or job interview.

▼ CHILDREN'S DAY
Carp kites are flown to mark Children's Day each May. The carp is a fish that has a long struggle upstream. This represents the difficult journey through life.

Key Dates

- 660BC According to legend, Japan was unified under the first emperor, Jimmu.
- AD600s Chinese Buddhism and Confucianism reach Japan.
- AD645 Reforms of the emperor decide that he is the Son of Heaven and a descendant of the sun goddess Amaterasu.
- AD700s The key Shinto texts, the *Kojiki* and *Nihongi* are compiled.
- 1945 Shinto loses its status as Japan's official state religion.
- 1946 Emperor Hirohito renounces his divinity.

Judaism

J UDAISM IS THE RELIGION of the Jewish people. Jews trace their origins back to Abraham (the Father of Many Nations), who lived in Mesopotamia (modern-day Iraq) more than 4,000 years ago. They believe that God revealed himself to Abraham and promised to make him the father of a great nation. Abraham and his family settled in Canaan (modern-day Israel), and this became the centre of Judaism. As Jews chose or were forced to settle elsewhere, the religion gradually spread. Today there are more than 13 million Jews worldwide, with large numbers in Israel, the USA, and in Russia, Ukraine and other countries of the former USSR.

▲ JEWISH LIGHTS
The menorah, a type of multi-branched candlestick, is a symbol of Judaism. A seven-branched menorah stood in King Solomon's temple in Jerusalem.

Judaism was the first great faith to believe that there is only one God. An important statement called the *Shema* (in the *Tenakh*, the Jewish holy book) says "Hear, O Israel: the Lord our God, the Lord is One."

Jews believe that God is the creator of the world, and that he chose their ancestors, the Israelites, to be his special people. He led the Israelites out of slavery in Egypt and brought them to Canaan, the Promised Land. God's holy name is the Hebrew (Jewish) word *Yhwh*, usually written as

▼ THE FERTILE CRESCENT
Most of the events in the Hebrew Bible took place in the region known as the Fertile Crescent. This is a huge arc of fertile land, stretching from the Tigris and Euphrates rivers in Mesopotamia (modern-day Iraq) and through the Jewish homeland of Israel to Egypt.

MODERN JEWISH GROUPS

Different customs have evolved in the various Jewish communities around the world. The two main groups are the Orthodox (traditional) Jews and the Reform Jews. Orthodox Jews stick to the traditional way of doing things. They hold their services in Hebrew, follow the ancient food laws, and separate men and women in the synagogue, the Jewish place of worship. Reform Jews reject traditional customs that seem old-fashioned to them. They hold their services in the local language, rather than Hebrew. They modify or discard the food laws, and they allow women to become rabbis.

▶ ETHIOPIAN JEWS
The Falasha are Jews who live in Ethiopia, east Africa. Their ancestors converted to Judaism more than 2,000 years ago. In the 1980s, about 45,000 Falasha emigrated to Israel to escape the war and drought in Ethiopia.

◀ THE TALMUD
Study of the scriptures is an important part of Jewish education. The main books are the Hebrew Bible, or *Tenakh* and the *Talmud*, a book of Jewish laws written in Babylon around 500BC.

Yahweh. Yahweh means 'I am' or 'I am who I am.'

Jews believe that God communicates with people through prophets. The greatest prophet was Moses, to whom God revealed the *Torah*, the first five books of the Bible. The *Torah* contains God's sacred laws, the best-known of which are the Ten Commandments. Keeping these laws is central to the Jewish way of life.

Jews believe that in the future, God will send a Messiah (anointed one), who will right all wrongs, reward good people and punish evil. His arrival will mark the end of history and the beginning of God's kingdom on Earth. Some Jews believe that when this happens the dead will be resurrected (brought back to eternal life). Other Jews believe that when they die their souls will go on living.

▲ THE GREAT FLOOD
According to the Bible, God sent a flood to destroy everything and rid the world of sin. Noah and his family were the only people to survive. Noah built an ark (huge boat), in which he saved his family and the animals.

▶ MODERN ISRAEL
Six million Jews were killed during the Holocaust in World War II. After the war, Jews stepped up their campaign to have their own country, where they could live and worship without threat of persecution. In 1948 the state of Israel was created as a Jewish homeland. Since then, thousands of Jews from all over the world have emigrated to Israel.

▲ RELIGIOUS TEACHER
Rabbis are the spiritual leaders for the Jewish community. They conduct services and teach children about Judaism.

▼ HASIDIC JEWS AT THE WESTERN WALL
Hasidism is a strict form of Judaism that originated in southeast Poland in the 1700s. It was founded by a Jewish scholar called Dov Baer. Hasidic Jews have many special customs. The men wear black suits and hats, and have side curls and beards. *Tzaddiqim* (Hasidic leaders) established new communities after World War II, when many Hasidic Jews were killed. These include the Lubavich sect in New York City.

Key Dates

- c.2166BC Birth of Abraham, the founder of the Jewish nation.

- c.586–537BC Judaism spreads beyond Canaan, when hundreds of Jews are forced into slavery in Babylon.

- c.500BC The *Talmud* is written.

- AD70 The Jewish population spreads throughout the Roman Empire. This is known as the Diaspora (dispersal).

- 1939–45 During World War II, six million Jews are killed by the Nazis during the Holocaust.

- 1948 The state of Israel is founded.

The Chosen People

▲ STAR OF DAVID
The Israeli flag features the six-pointed Star of David, which is a symbol of Judaism. In Hebrew, it is known as the Shield of David because King David had this star on his shield.

THE JEWS BELIEVE that they are God's chosen people. According to the Bible, the story of God's special relationship with the Jews started with Abraham. God asked him and his family to leave his home in Mesopotamia and travel to Canaan (modern-day Israel). In return for Abraham's faith and obedience, God promised that he would become the founder of a great nation, and that his descendants would inherit the land of Canaan. This agreement between God and Abraham is known as the covenant.

Many years later, God made another covenant with his people. Abraham's descendants, the Israelites, were living in slavery in Egypt. God chose Moses to be their leader and to take them out of Egypt to the Promised Land (Canaan). This is known as the Exodus. At Mount Sinai, God gave Moses Ten Commandments and promised to protect his chosen people if they kept these laws.

The journey to the Promised Land took a long time. The Bible says that the Israelites spent 40 years wandering in the wilderness, and that Moses died before they entered Canaan. Under his successor, Joshua, and later leaders, the Israelites gradually captured the land from its existing inhabitants.

The Israelites settled in Canaan, but over the years they stopped obeying God's laws. For this reason God allowed them to be threatened by the Philistines and other enemies. God renewed his covenant with the

▼ THE PROPHET EZEKIEL
Throughout Jewish history, God has spoken through prophets or wise men. Ezekiel was a priest who was deported to Babylon in 586BC. He told his fellow-exiles to keep their faith in God.

PLACES OF WORSHIP
Jews usually meet to worship at a synagogue. Prayers are held there in the morning, afternoon and evening each day, but many Jews only attend on Saturday, the Jewish Sabbath holy day. Worship is often led by the rabbi. It includes prayers and *Tenakh* readings.

▶ TEMPLE REMAINS
The Western Wall is all that is left of the temple in Jerusalem. It is a sacred place, where Jewish people go to pray. Some write prayers on pieces of paper, which they tuck between the blocks of stone in the wall.

◀ THE TEMPLE IN JERUSALEM
King Solomon built the first temple in Jerusalem, which became the centre of Jewish worship. His temple was destroyed by the Babylonians in 587BC, but later temples were built on the same site, the last by King Herod. This was destroyed by the Romans in AD70. The Western Wall is all that remains of it.

Israelites through David. He promised to make David a great king and to protect his people if they obeyed his laws. God told David to build a magnificent temple in Jerusalem as a sign of this covenant. The temple was eventually built by David's son, Solomon.

Hundreds of years later, in 586BC, Canaan was seized by the Babylonians, who took many Jews away to Babylon as slaves. In the Bible, the *Psalms* (songs) tell how the Jews missed their homeland during this period, but how they believed that God would return them to the Promised Land. Eventually Babylon was defeated by the Persians and the Jews returned home.

Jews today look back on their history. As they did in the past, they strongly believe that if they obey God, he will continue to look after them.

◀ KING SOLOMON
For much of their history, the Jews were ruled by a series of kings. King Solomon, the son of David, was famous for his wisdom. He built the first temple in Jerusalem.

▲ DAVID AND GOLIATH
As a shepherd boy, David killed the giant Goliath with just a stone and a sling. He later became the king of Israel. David established Jerusalem as the capital city of his kingdom.

▼ HOUSE OF WORSHIP
A synagogue is a place where Jews meet to pray and to study the *Tenakh*. All synagogues are built facing in the direction of Jerusalem. There is usually a cupboard in the end wall, known as the Ark of the Covenant, which contains the *Torah* scrolls. In Orthodox synagogues, men and women sit in separate areas.

▲ INCENSE BURNER
Incense is sometimes burned in Jewish synagogues. The smoke symbolizes people's prayers, rising up to God.

Key Dates

- c.2166BC Birth of Abraham.

- c.1700BC The Israelites move to Egypt to escape a famine.

- c.1446BC Moses leads the Israelites out of Egypt.

- c.1406BC The Israelites enter Canaan (the Promised Land).

- c.960BC Solomon completes the temple in Jerusalem.

- c.930BC The kingdom divides into Judah and Israel.

- c.586BC The Babylonians destroy the temple and enslave many Jews.

- c.537–445BC The Jews return to Judah and rebuild the temple.

Jewish Scriptures

THE HEBREW BIBLE IS the sacred book of the Jewish people. It also forms the first half of the Christian Bible, where it is known as the Old Testament. It tells the story of the Jewish people and their special relationship with God. The events it describes took place over a period of more than 2,000 years.

The Hebrew Bible is not one single book, but a collection of books written over many centuries by many different authors. It contains books of law, history, poetry and prophecy. The Jews group the books of their Bible into three main sections: the *Torah* (law), the *Nevi'im* (prophets) and the *Ketuvim* (writings).

The most important part of Hebrew Bible is the first five books, known as the *Torah*, or law. It contains the Ten Commandments and other laws given by God to Moses. The *Torah* also tells the story of the Jewish people from the time of their founder, Abraham, to the time of Moses. One of the most important themes of the *Torah*

▲ SPICE BOX
At the end of the Sabbath some Jews breathe in spices from a spice box to keep the sweet smell of the Sabbath with them all week.

◀ THE SHOFAR
The shofar is a trumpet made from a ram's horn. In ancient times, the Israelites used it to rally their warriors in battle and to summon people to worship. The shofar is still blown in synagogues at Yom Kippur (the Jewish fast) and Rosh Hashanah (Jewish New Year).

RITES AND RITUALS
Each week Jews keep their holy day, the Sabbath, the day of rest as ordered by God in the Ten Commandments. This starts with a family meal on Friday evening and lasts until sunset on Saturday. Throughout the year, Jews celebrate a number of festivals. Some of them commemorate specific events in Jewish history, such as the Exodus from Egypt. Other festivals are connected to the seasons and the events of the farming year.

▼ THE HAGADAH
At Pesach (Passover), Jewish families share a special meal, called the *seder*. During the meal they read from a part of the *Talmud* called the *Hagadah*. It tells how the Israelites escaped from Egypt.

▼ SUKKOT
At the autumn festival of Sukkot (the festival of booths) Jews remember the 40 years that they spent in the wilderness. They make booths (tents) out of leaves and branches to symbolize the ones that they used in the desert.

◄ TORAH COVERS

Each synagogue has a copy of the Torah, written on a long scroll. Jews believe that the Torah is too sacred to touch, so the reader uses a pointer to keep their place in the text. The Torah is often stored in a decorated, protective cover. Popular images on Torah covers include the lion, which represents the tribe of Judah, and the menorah.

▼ KOSHER FOOD

The Torah contains laws about food, which forbid Jews to eat certain types of meat, such as pork or rabbit, or to eat the blood of animals. Another law states that they cannot eat meat and milk in the same meal. Many Jews buy their food, especially meat, from special shops where it has been prepared according to the food laws. Food prepared in this way is called kosher.

is God's covenant (agreement), made first with Abraham and his descendants, and then again with Moses. This covenant showed the Jews that they were God's chosen people.

After the *Torah* is the section of the Bible known as the *Nebi'im*. This is made up of eight books, believed to have been written by Jewish prophets, including Samuel, Isaiah and Ezekiel. The *Nevi'im* continues the history of the Jews, from their conquest of the Promised Land up to the fall of the Jewish kings. In their books, the prophets explained the meaning of these events and warned the Jews about the dangers of disobeying God.

The remaining 11 books of the Hebrew Bible are called the *Ketuvim*. This section contains books of wisdom, poetry, prophecy and history. Among them is the *Book of Psalms*. This is a collection of hymns and prayers, many of which were written by King David.

▲ COMING OF AGE

Bar Mitzvah is the ceremony at which a boy becomes an adult member of the Jewish community. It happens when he is 13 years old and takes place in the synagogue. As part of the ceremony, the boy reads aloud from the *Torah*. Some Jews have a similar service to mark girls' entry into adulthood. This is called Bat Mitzvah.

▼ DECEMBER FESTIVAL

Hanukkah celebrates how the Jews reclaimed the temple from the Greek rulers in 164BC. The temple's lamp had only enough oil for one day, but burned for eight days. On each of the eight days of the festival, Jewish families light one more candle on a *menorah*. They do this using the ninth candle, or *shamash*, in the centre of the candlestick.

The Jewish Year

- February/March – Purim (celebrating how Esther saved the Jews from the Persians)

- March/April – Pesach or Passover (commemorating the Exodus, when the angel of death killed every first-born Egyptian, but passed over the Israelites)

- May/June – Shavuot (marking the giving of the law to Moses)

- September/October – Rosh Hashanah (Jewish New Year)

- September/October – Yom Kippur (the Day of Atonement)

- September/October – Sukkot

- December – Hanukkah

Christianity

THE FOUNDER OF CHRISTIANITY was Jesus Christ, a Jewish teacher and healer who lived in what is now Israel during the first century AD. His followers steadily grew in number. In the AD300s the Roman emperor, Constantine, decreed that Christianity should be tolerated throughout his empire. An important figure around that time was Augustine, who was bishop of Hippo (in modern-day Algeria, Africa) from AD396 until AD430. Augustine developed Christian thought in his *Confessions*, mixing them with Greek ideas. His interpretation of Christianity spread throughout Europe.

From the 1500s, as Europeans explored other continents, they took Christianity with them. Today Christians live on every continent of the globe. They total almost two billion, making Christianity the world's biggest religion.

Christians believe in one God. They believe that Jesus Christ was the Messiah promised in the Old Testament. The Christian God has three parts, known as the Holy Trinity. The Trinity consists of God the Father, God the Son (Jesus) and God the Holy Spirit.

Christians believe that God came to Earth in the form of a man, Jesus. He showed

▲ THE CROSS
Jesus was crucified (put to death on a cross), but Christians believe he rose from the dead. This has made the cross a symbol of Jesus's sacrifice. Christians see it as a symbol of victory and hope, too.

▲ THE VIRGIN MARY
The Bible says that Jesus's mother, Mary, was a virgin. The power of the Holy Spirit made her pregnant, so that Jesus could be born as a human being.

THE CHRISTIAN CHURCH

The first Christian Church was the Catholic (universal) Church, with the Pope at its head. In the AD1000s there was disagreement about the use of icons (holy pictures). This led to a split between the Catholic Church in Rome and the Orthodox Church, based in Constantinople. This is called the Great Schism (split). The Protestant churches were founded in the 1500s. This period is called the Reformation.

▲ MARTIN LUTHER
Luther was a German monk. He felt the Catholic Church abused its position of power. In protest, he founded the first Protestant church in the 1520s.

◀ ST PETER'S BASILICA
The Pope lives in the Vatican, a tiny country within the city of Rome. The Pope's church is St Peter's, begun in 1506 by Pope Julius II.

▶ JOHN CALVIN
Calvin set up a Protestant church in Switzerland. Like Luther, he tried to get rid of church traditions and simply follow the teachings of the Bible.

▼ ORTHODOX ICONS
Orthodox churches are usually full of beautiful icons. These are religious pictures or statues of Jesus, Mary, or the saints.

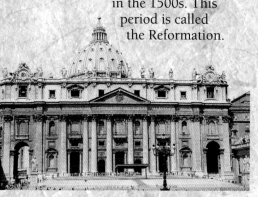

people how to confess the things they had done wrong in the past and have a fresh start with God. During his lifetime Jesus gathered a large body of followers. This alarmed the Romans, who occupied what is now Israel, and also the Jewish religious authorities, who feared Jesus was damaging their own power base. Jesus was put on trial and sentenced to death by crucifixion. When Jesus died, followers of Jesus believe that he paid the price for everyone's sins. According to the Bible, three days after his death, Jesus rose from the dead. Christians believe that when they die, they can look forward to eternal life in heaven.

Jesus said in the Bible that he is still with all Christians in spirit, and that he will come back at the end of the world to judge all people. Those who have faith in him will be saved and go to heaven. Those who have not will be banished to hell.

Jesus promised his disciples (followers) that after he was gone he would send a helper for them, the Holy Spirit. Christians believe this Spirit is still active in the world today.

▶ THE ASCENSION
Jesus appeared to his followers on many occasions in the 40 days following his resurrection, when he came back to life. Then one day he was taken up into heaven before his disciples' eyes. This event is known as the Ascension.

◀ EUROPE IN THE 1500S
During the Reformation, northern Europe became mostly Protestant, while southern Europe remained mostly Catholic. Most Orthodox Christians live in Russia and parts of eastern Europe, such as Greece and the Balkans.

Map legend:
- Roman Catholic regions
- Protestant regions
- Orthodox regions

NORWAY
SWEDEN
SCOTLAND
NORTH SEA
Dublin
Hamburg
IRELAND
WALES
ENGLAND
R. Rhine
HOLY ROMAN EMPIRE
BOHEMIA
Paris
Vienna
ATLANTIC OCEAN
R. Loire
FRANCE
SPAIN
PORTUGAL
Madrid
Rome
PAPAL STATES
R. Tagus
0 Kilometres 750
0 Miles 500
MEDITERRANEAN SEA

Key Dates

- c.AD30 Birth of the Christian Church. Jesus's disciples start to preach the Christian message.

- AD313 Emperor Constantine grants tolerance of Christianity. It eventually becomes the official religion of the Roman Empire.

- 1054 The Orthodox Church breaks away in the Great Schism.

- 1517 Martin Luther publicly criticizes the Catholic Church and starts the Reformation. Protestant churches are founded.

- 2000 Christians celebrate the millennium, 2,000 years after the traditional birth date of Jesus.

The Life of Jesus

JESUS CHRIST WAS BORN IN about 6 or 7BC in Judah (modern-day Israel), which was then a province of the Roman Empire. His mother was Mary, a young Jewish woman from Nazareth.

According to the Bible, the Angel Gabriel appeared to Mary and told her that she would have a child who would be God's son and the saviour of the world.

We know very little about Jesus' childhood, except that he lived in Nazareth and was brought up as a Jew. The Bible picks up the story when Jesus was in his early 30s. He was baptized in the River Jordan and spent

▲ JESUS
All that we know about Jesus's life comes from the accounts in the four gospels, the books of the Bible written specifically about Jesus.

▶ PARABLES
Jesus often told parables (stories about everyday life) to teach people about God in a way they could understand and remember. One of his most famous parables is the story of the good samaritan. It tells the story of a man who was helped by the one person he thought was his enemy.

WEEKLY WORSHIP

Christians gather together to worship God on Sunday and at other important festivals. They usually meet in a church, but some groups meet in people's homes. The most important form of Christian worship is the service known as communion, mass, or the Eucharist. At holy communion, Christians share bread and wine as Jesus did with his disciples at the Last Supper. Christian worship includes prayers, readings from the Bible, and singing religious songs called hymns.

◀ NOTRE-DAME CATHEDRAL
Huge cathedrals were built in Europe during the Middle Ages. One of the most beautiful is the Cathedral of Notre-Dame (Our Lady), in Paris, which was begun in 1163. It has three stained-glass windows.

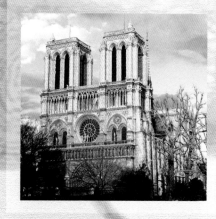

▲ MODERN CATHEDRAL
Not all cathedrals are old. The Cathedral of Christ the King, in Liverpool, England, dates from 1967.

◀ A PARISH CHURCH
Most Christians worship at a small local church, with members of their parish (community).

40 days fasting in the desert in preparation for his work. Then he travelled around the country, teaching people about God, healing the sick and performing miracles. He was accompanied by a group of 12 disciples (followers). Jesus told people that God's kingdom was coming and that they should ask God's forgiveness so they could be saved. Jesus became very popular and vast crowds of people came to hear him preach. However, he faced opposition from the Jewish religious authorities, who saw him as a threat.

After three years, Jesus travelled to Jerusalem for the Jewish festival of Pesach (Passover). According to the Bible he rode a donkey into the city, cheered on by crowds who threw palm branches in his path. Later in the week, Jesus and his disciples ate *seder* (the Pesach meal) together. This is now known as the Last Supper. Jesus shared bread and wine with his disciples. Later that night, Jesus was arrested, tried and found guilty by the religious authorities. The Roman governor of the province, Pontius Pilate, sentenced him to death. The following day, Jesus was forced to carry a wooden cross through the streets of Jerusalem to a place outside the city walls, where he was crucified. He died in the afternoon, and was buried by his friends and followers.

Three days later Jesus's followers discovered that his tomb was empty. An angel told them that Jesus was alive again. Jesus himself appeared to his astonished disciples on many occasions over the next few weeks. Forty days later, he was taken up into heaven. This marked the end of his life on Earth, but Christians believe that Jesus is still alive in heaven.

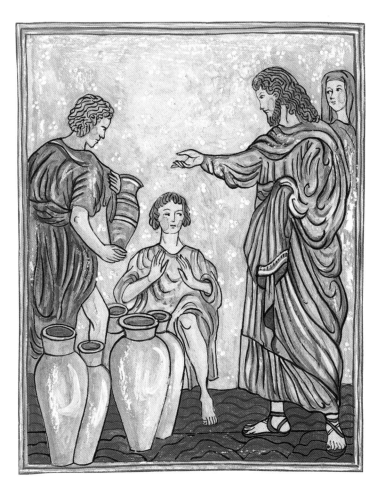

▲ THE WEDDING AT CANA
In the three years of his teaching, Jesus performed many miracles. His first was to turn jars of water into wine at a wedding. Jesus healed many people, and even brought a dead man, Lazarus, back to life. He also used miracles to demonstrate his power over nature, for example by calming a storm.

▲ HOLY COMMUNION
The bread and wine that Christians receive at communion represent the body and blood of Jesus. At the Last Supper, Jesus told his disciples to think of bread and wine in this way.

▼ FORMS OF WORSHIP
There are many styles of Christian worship. The Baptist Church, founded around 1611, is known for its lively services. Baptists celebrate Jesus with joyful singing and even dancing.

Key Dates

- c.6–7BC Jesus is born in Bethlehem. His family flees to Egypt to escape King Herod.

- c.4BC King Herod dies and Jesus's family returns to Nazareth.

- c.AD5–6 Jesus visits the temple at Jerusalem with his family where he is dedicated to God.

- c.AD28 Jesus is baptized in the River Jordan and starts his public teaching.

- c.AD30 Jesus is crucified in Jerusalem, but is resurrected after three days. About forty days later he ascends into heaven.

The Christian Scriptures

▲ GUTENBERG BIBLE
In the Middle Ages, when all books had to be copied out by hand, Christian monks produced some beautiful Bibles. The first printed edition was the Gutenberg Bible of 1455.

THE CHRISTIAN HOLY BOOK is the Bible. Christians believe that although the Bible was written by people, it was inspired by God. It is a collection of books written by different authors. These books are divided into two sections, the Old and New Testaments. The Old Testament consists of the Jewish scriptures. The New Testament deals with the life and teachings of Jesus Christ and the story of the early Christian church. All 27 books in the New Testament were written by early followers of Jesus, roughly between AD45 and AD97.

The first four books of the New Testament are the gospels of Matthew, Mark, Luke and John. The word gospel means 'good news' and refers to the good news that Jesus was the long-awaited Messiah. Together the gospels tell the story of Jesus's life. All four of the gospel writers were closely involved with Jesus or with his followers. Matthew and John were two of Jesus's disciples. Mark was probably a translator for Peter, another of the 12 disciples. Luke was a friend of Paul. Paul was not a disciple. He was a Jew who had persecuted the Christians but converted to Christianity after seeing a vision on the road to Damascus. After this, Paul travelled widely spreading the Christian message.

Each of the gospels tells the life of Jesus from a different viewpoint. All four concentrate on Jesus's ministry, his time teaching in Galilee, and on the events of the last week of his life.

The fifth book of the New Testament, *The Acts of the*

◀ ST ANDREW AND ST JAMES
The first four disciples that Jesus recruited were Peter, Andrew, James and John. After Jesus's death, they carried on preaching his message. Some died for their religion. King Herod Agrippa I of Judah had James beheaded around AD44 and Andrew was crucified in modern-day Turkey in the AD60s.

THE CHRISTIAN YEAR
Christians celebrate many festivals. Most commemorate events in Jesus's life. In some churches, saints are celebrated on the particular days dedicated to them. Festivals are marked with special church services and with other customs, such as giving Christmas presents or Easter eggs.

▲ EASTER EGGS
In some countries it is traditional to give and receive eggs at Easter, as a symbol of new life. Easter eggs may be real, or made of wood or chocolate.

◀ THE NATIVITY
At Christmas, Christian homes and churches often display models of the nativity, Jesus's birth in the stable in Bethlehem.

▲ PALM SUNDAY
Shortly before his death, Jesus rode into Jerusalem on a donkey. He was greeted by crowds of people, who laid palm branches in his path. Christians remember this event on Palm Sunday. At some churches, small crosses made of palm leaves are handed out to worshippers.

◀ RUINS AT EPHESUS
Paul was one of the first church leaders to see that the good news about Jesus was meant for all, not just Jews. He went on four journeys around the Mediterranean, telling people about Jesus and founding Christian churches in cities such as Ephesus in Turkey, and Corinth, in Greece.

Apostles, was written by Luke, the author of the third gospel. It tells what happened in the 30 years after Jesus's ascension into heaven. *Acts* describes the missionary work of the apostles, Jesus's specially appointed helpers, the life of the early Christian church, and Paul's travels.

The next 21 books are letters from the early Christian leaders to the newly founded churches, giving them advice and encouragement. Paul is believed to have written 13 of the letters. Other authors include the disciple Peter and Jesus's brother, James.

The final book of the Bible is the *Book of Revelation*. The writer, John, who may be the same John who wrote the fourth gospel, describes what will happen at the end of the world.

▲ A FRANCISCAN FRIAR
Monks or friars try to spread the Christian message by setting a good example. Francis, who later became a saint, founded his order of monks in 1209. The Franciscans live in poverty and in harmony with nature.

▶ PENTECOST
A few days after Jesus had ascended into heaven, his disciples gathered together on the Jewish festival of Shavuot. The Bible says that they suddenly heard a sound like rushing wind. They saw tongues of flame that came to rest on each of them. They were all filled with the power of the Holy Spirit and began to speak in tongues (other languages). Christians celebrate this event at the festival of Pentecost, or Whitsun.

Christian Festivals

- 25 December – Christmas (celebrates Jesus's birth)

- March/April – Lent (a 40-day fast that ends on Easter Sunday)

- March/April – Maundy Thursday (held the Thursday before Easter to celebrate the Last Supper)

- March/April – Good Friday (marks the crucifixion of Jesus)

- March/April – Easter Sunday (celebrates Jesus's resurrection)

- May/June – Pentecost or Whitsun (celebrates when the disciples received the Holy Spirit)

Islam

▲ SACRED SYMBOL
The hilal (crescent moon and star) is the symbol of Islam. It reminds Muslims that they follow a lunar calendar (a calendar based on the movements of the Moon), and that Allah created the stars. The hilal appears on the flags of some Muslim countries, including Pakistan, Singapore and Turkey.

ISLAM WAS FOUNDED by the prophet Muhammad. It began in the cities of al-Madinah (Medina) and Makkah (Mecca) in modern-day Saudi Arabia in about AD620. Muhammad received revelations from Allah (God) and began to preach his message.

Muhammad died in AD632, and within a few years the peoples of the Arabian peninsula had converted to Islam. The new religion soon had followers as far west as the Atlantic coast of Africa and as far east as India. Today, Islam is the world's second-largest religion, with more than a billion followers spread over almost every country.

The word Islam means 'surrender to the peace of Allah.' Muslims (followers of Islam) give themselves up to Allah's will. They believe that Allah is the one God, and that Muhammad was Allah's messenger.

Muslims believe that Allah sent many prophets (messengers) before sending Muhammad. These include holy men recognized by Jews and Christians, such as Adam, Ibrahim (Abraham), Musa (Moses), Dawud (David) and Isa (Jesus). Muhammad received revelations from Allah through the Angel Jibril (Gabriel) from the age of 40. He told his followers about these revelations. They were eventually written down in the Islamic holy book, the Qur'an.

Muslims believe that their faith is the final revelation of Allah. Every aspect of Muslim life is governed by the Five Pillars of Islam, duties that unite Muslims all over the world into a single community.

▶ THE SACRED KA'BAH
The Great Mosque at Makkah is set around the Ka'bah, a square building made of grey stone. In its eastern corner is the Black Stone. Muslims believe this fell to Earth as a sign of the covenant (agreement) between Allah and the prophet Ibrahim. Muslims believe that Ibrahim built the Ka'bah.

THE FIVE PILLARS OF ISLAM

Islam rests on five duties that all Muslims must obey and carry out. These are called the Five Pillars (supports) of Islam. They are based on the Qur'an and the actions of Muhammad. They give a sense of purpose to every Muslim's life.

◀ SHAHADAH
The first pillar is *shahadah*. This is the Muslim statement of faith – that Allah is the one true God, and that Muhammad was his prophet. This belief is stated each day in the call to prayer.

◀ SALAH
The second pillar is *salah*, the prayers that Muslims say five times a day. Wherever they are in the world, Muslims face towards the sacred Ka'bah in Makkah when they pray.

▼ CHARITY SCHOOL, OMAN
Every Muslim must give one-fortieth of his or her annual income to charities such as this religious school. This is called *zakat*, and is the third pillar.

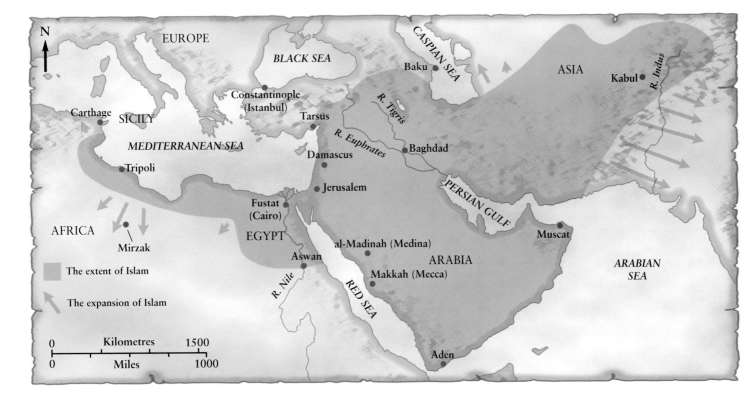

▶ HOLY SITE

Al-Aqsa (the Dome of the Rock) in Jerusalem is where Muhammad ascended into heaven in AD619 to meet Allah. It is sacred to Jews and Christians, too, as the ancient site of Solomon's temple. Other holy Muslim sites are the Great Mosque at Makkah and the tomb of Muhammad at al-Madinah.

▲ THE ISLAMIC WORLD

Islam began in the cities of Makkah and al-Madinah. It became the chief religion of the Arabian peninsula, spreading into Persia (modern-day Iran), Mesopotamia (modern-day Iraq) and North Africa. During the 1100s and 1200s, Christian knights known as Crusaders recaptured Jerusalem from Muslim control, but they failed to hold their gains for long.

▼ ID-UL-FITR

The fourth pillar is *sawm* (fasting). During the month of Ramadan, Muslims do not eat or drink during daylight hours. Muslims celebrate the end of Ramadan with a feast. They call this festival Id-ul-Fitr.

▶ TO BE A PILGRIM

During their lifetime all healthy Muslims must make at least one *hajj* (pilgrimage) to Makkah during the 12th month of the Islamic year. The *hajj* is the fifth pillar.

Key Dates

- AD570–632 Life of Muhammad.

- AD622 Muhammad's hijrah (flight) from Makkah to al-Madinah.

- AD630 Muhammad conquers Makkah.

- AD634 Muhammad's successor, Abu Bakr, conquers Arabia.

- AD638 Arab armies capture Jerusalem.

- AD651 Arab armies overrun Persia.

- AD711 Arab armies reach India.

- AD732 Arab armies conquer Spain.

- 1453 Muslim Ottoman Turks capture Constantinople.

- 1492 Last Muslim armies retreat from Spain.

The Life of Muhammad

▲ MIHRAB TO MAKKAH
Makkah is sacred to Muslims because it was there, in AD610, that Muhammad had his first vision of the Angel Jibril. Muslim mosques, such as this one at Aleppo, Syria, always feature a mihrab (an alcove in the wall that shows the direction of Makkah).

MUHAMMAD WAS BORN in the Arabian city of Makkah in AD570. He was orphaned as a child and brought up by his grandfather and then his uncle. He worked as a desert trader and in AD595 married Khadijah, a wealthy widow. Muhammad became wealthy and well-respected in the city. However, he was increasingly concerned about the worship of pagan gods at the Ka'bah, the sacred house said to have been built by Ibrahim. Muhammad used to go and pray and meditate in the mountains at Hira outside Makkah. In AD610 he was meditating when the

▶ HARUN AL-RASHID
In AD750 the Abbasid Dynasty took control of the Muslim world. They moved the capital from Damascus (in modern-day Syria) to Baghdad (in modern-day Iraq). Under Caliph (leader) Harun Al-Rashid (AD786–809), Baghdad became the centre of Islamic arts and learning.

ISLAMIC WORSHIP

The centre of the Islamic religion is the mosque. It is a space for prayer, worship, teaching and study. It also acts as a community centre for local Muslims. The main weekly service is usually held on Friday afternoon, but the mosque is open throughout the week for constant prayer and study.

◀ MOSQUE
Most mosques contain an outer courtyard with running water for *wudu* (washing before prayer). Inside is an area for prayer, with a pulpit and lectern.

▶ THE MINARET
Each mosque has a minaret (tower). A man called a *mu'adhin* or *muezzin* climbs it five times each day and calls Muslims to prayer.

▼ WOMEN AT WORSHIP
Muslim men and women pray separately. Most women worship at home, but some mosques have special areas reserved for women.

◀ PREACHING THE MESSAGE
This Turkish manuscript dates to the 1500s. It shows the Prophet Muhammad preaching to the people of Makkah after his first vision.

as the *hijrah* (emigration), marks the start of the Islamic Era. All Muslim calendars are dated AH (*Anno Hegirae* is Latin for 'year of the *hijrah*'). The year AD2000 is 1421AH in the Muslim calendar.

By AD630 Muhammad had a strong enough following to return in triumph to Makkah. He forgave his former enemies, and many became Muslims. After Muhammad's death in AD632, Islam became the major religion of the Middle East and North Africa. However it soon split into two groups, Sunnis and Shi'ahs. The two groups have many beliefs in common but the Sunnis believed that Muhammad's successors should be chosen by the Muslim community. The Shi'ahs believed that only the descendants of his cousin and son-in-law, Ali, could follow him. Most Muslims today are Sunnis. Ten per cent are Shi'ahs, and they live mainly in Iran.

Angel Jibril appeared to him and told him he would be Allah's messenger. Muhammad had further revelations for the rest his life. These include his famous night journey of AD619, when Jibril took him to Jersualem and then up to heaven to meet Allah. Muhammad tried to preach Allah's message to the people of Makkah, but they did not want to listen. In AD622 Muhammad fled the city and moved to al-Madinah. The people there did listen, and al-Madinah became the first Islamic city. For this reason, Muhammad's flight from Makkah, known

◀ IMAM
The main official at the mosque is called the *imam* (chief). He leads the prayers. Sermons are read by the *khatib* (preacher).

▶ SAJJADA
Muslims use a *sajjada* (prayer mat) to make sure that they pray on a clean space. Many mats have a picture of a mosque. Some feature an inbuilt compass so that the user always knows the direction of Makkah and which way to face as he prays.

Key Dates

- AD595 Muhammad marries Khadijah, a wealthy widow.
- AD610 Muhammad's vision of Jibril in a cave on Mt Hira.
- AD619 Muhammad's Night Journey with Jibril to Jerusalem.
- AD622 Muhammad's *hijrah*.
- AD630 Muhammad captures Makkah.
- AD632 Muhammad dies in Makkah and is buried in al-Madinah.
- AD632 Abu Bakr becomes the first caliph (Muslim ruler).
- AD680 Sunni/Shi'ah split.

The Qur'an

▲ CALLIGRAPHY

Muslims are forbidden to depict Allah or Muhammad in paintings. They decorate the Qur'an with geometric or floral designs and with intricate calligraphy (writing). This lettering is the Arabic script for 'Allah.'

MUHAMMAD TOLD his followers all the teachings that Allah had passed on to him through the Angel Jibril. They learned his revelations by heart and dictated them to scribes, who wrote them down in what became the Qur'an, which means 'revelation.' Muslims believe that earlier messages from Allah to his prophets had been corrupted or ignored. They believe that the Qur'an is the true word of Allah. As it was spoken by Muhammad in Arabic, the Qur'an can only be written and recited in Arabic, regardless of the language of the believer. Muslims believe that the Qur'an is perfect and therefore it cannot be translated into any other language, only interpreted.

Copies of the Qur'an are always beautifully illustrated. Muslims believe that making the word of Allah beautiful is in itself an act of worship.

The Qur'an is divided into 114 *surahs* (chapters). It starts by saying that Allah is the one true god. Then it discusses Allah's role in history and Muhammad's role as Allah's prophet. The Qur'an describes Allah's last judgement on his people and the need to help other people. It tells Muslims how to behave, as well as how to treat other people and animals. However, not everything is covered by the Qur'an, so Muslims also study the *Sunnah*, too. This book contains accounts of the words and deeds of Muhammad and his close followers. The *Sunnah* helps Muslims to gain a clear understanding of the Qur'an. Muslim laws are taken from both the Qur'an and the *Sunnah*. These laws, known as the *Shari'ah*,

◀ PATHWAY TO ALLAH

Islamic law is known as the Shari'ah. *This is an Arabic word meaning a track that leads camels to a waterhole. In the same way, Muslims who obey the* Shari'ah *will be led to Allah. The* Shari'ah *guides Muslims on their faith and behaviour. It is taught in law schools, such as this one, throughout the Islamic world.*

THE SUFIS

Sufis are Muslims, who can be either Sunnis or Shi'ahs. They place complete obedience and trust in Allah. They try to get closer to Allah through dance and music. Sufi beliefs are passed down through the generations by saints and teachers. Many Sufis are involved in education and community work.

▲ A SUFI

No one really knows how Sufis got their name. The word might come from *suf*, a basic woollen garment that early Sufis wore. Sufis turn their back on the world. They do not own many possessions and they often take vows of poverty.

▶ SOULFUL SINGER

Sufis believe that music is both a path to Allah and a means of spiritual healing. They sing *qawwalis*, trance-like hypnotic songs that build up to an ecstatic climax. *Qawwali* singers such as Nusrat Fateh Ali Khan have achieved international fame.

▲ DERVISHES

Some Sufis dance and spin to forget the things around them and get closer to Allah. They are known as Whirling Dervishes.

provide detailed instructions to Muslims as to how to lead a good life. Sunni Muslims follow one of four different schools or interpretations of the *Shari'ah*. The Shi'ahs also follow the teachings of the first *imams*, the spiritual leaders descended from Ali, Muhammad's cousin. They follow the teachings of individual thinkers, too. The greatest thinkers are known as *ayatollahs* (signs of Allah).

◄ THE QUR'AN
The Qur'an was prepared in about AD650 by Uthman, the third successor to Muhammad. Muslims consider it to be the perfect word of Allah. Only Muslims who have been ceremonially washed can touch it.

▶ SHI'AH LEADER
Muslims interpret the Qur'an in different ways. Ayatollah Khomeini was leader of Iran between 1979 and 1989. He interpreted the Qur'an very strictly. During his decade of power, he applied its teachings to every aspect of political and social life in his country.

▼ QAWWALI SHRINE, DELHI
One of the main Sufi shrines, dedicated to the Sufi saint Nizamuddin Awliya, is in Delhi, India. Its community of *qawwali* singers trace their ancestors back to Amir Khusrau (1253–1325). He was the founder of *qawwali* music.

▲ THE SIMURG
Sufis use a mythical bird, the *simurg*, to symbolize their search for unity with Allah. Its name is Persian for '30 birds.' The *simurg's* multi-coloured feathers represent every other bird that there is.

The Islamic Year

The Islamic calendar has 12 lunar months, each with 29 or 30 days.

- Muharram is the first month.

- Muslims celebrate the birthday of Muhammad on the 12th day of Rabi'I, the third month.

- Ramadan is the ninth month, when Muslims fast during daylight hours.

- Id-ul-Fitr (the breaking of the fast) is celebrated at the start of Shawal, the tenth month.

- Dhul-Hijjah, the 12th month, is when Muslims make their *hajj* (pilgrimage) to Makkah.

Modern Religions

THE MAJOR RELIGIONS of the world were all formed more than 1,350 years ago. New religions are still being founded today, as people seek fresh answers to the age-old questions about the meaning of life and our place in the world. Some new religions, such as the Baha'i faith, are born out of existing ones. Others, such as the Moonies, are created by a visionary leader, who starts a completely new faith. All new religions borrow elements from existing ones and add new ideas of their own.

Both Islam and Christianity have inspired new religions. The Baha'i faith began in Iran in 1844, when a Shi'ah Muslim, Siyyid Ali-Muhammad, announced he was a *Bab* (gate) through which Allah communicates with his people. He predicted that a new prophet would arrive to lead Allah's people. Baha'is believe that Baha'u'llah (1817–92) was that prophet. Baha'u'llah was persecuted throughout the Middle East. Eventually he was exiled to Acre, in what is now Israel. From there, the Baha'i faith has spread throughout the world.

Christianity produced the Mormons and the Jehovah's Witnesses. Both of these believe that the second coming of Jesus Christ is close, a belief shared

▲ MARY BAKER EDDY
Christian Scientists believe that illness can be cured by prayer and so believers do not take medicines or even accept blood transfusions. The religion was founded by the American Mary Baker Eddy (1821-1910).

▶ MORMONS
The Church of Jesus Christ of Latter-Day Saints are better known as the Mormons. Their name comes from the Book of Mormon, *which their founder Joseph Smith (1805–44) claimed to have translated under God's guidance. Mormons believe the book is equal to the Old and New Testaments of the Bible. Here you can see the first Mormon church leaders.*

RASTAFARIANISM
Rastafarians believe that they are the descendants of the 12 tribes of Israel. They worship the Hebrew God, whom they call Jah. They believe that the white world is godless, and that black people will eventually return to Africa to achieve their freedom. Their messiah, after whom they take their name, is Haile Selassie, the only black leader in Africa to keep his country independent of white, European rule.

◀ THE ETHIOPIAN FLAG
The green, yellow and red colours on the flag of Ethiopia have been adopted by Rastafarians as their own personal colours. They have also added black, which appears on the flag designed by Marcus Garvey.

◀ DREADLOCKS
Rastas wear their hair in dreadlocks. The style is inspired by the description in the Bible of the mane of the Lion of Judah. It is also an outward sign that Rastas refuse to conform to the expectations of white people.

▶ BLACK ACTIVIST
In 1914 Jamaican-born Marcus Garvey set up the Universal Negro Improvement Association. He urged black people to assert themselves and return to Africa. He said a Black Messiah would appear there to redeem (save) black people.

◀ THE MOONIES
The Unification Church was founded in Korea by Sun Myung Moon in 1954. The Moonies hold mass weddings, at which the couples are purified so that their children will be born without sin.

▲ THE RAELIANS
The UFO writer Claude Vorilhon formed the Raëlian cult in 1973. He also renamed himself Raël. Raëlians believe that one day extraterrestrials will land on Earth. According to Raël, these aliens are what we have mistaken for gods or God in all the world's religions. The Raëlian symbol represents star systems inside bigger star systems.

by the Seventh Day Adventists and other new Christian churches. Rastafarians believe in the Old Testament but worship a visionary leader, the Ethiopian emperor Haile Selassie.

Although all the new religions are very different, they often share two central beliefs. The first is the idea that a new messiah or prophet has arrived to lead the people. The second is that the end of the world is coming soon. New Christian religions also believe that Jesus Christ will return to lead the world for 1,000 years, a belief known as millennarianism. Members of cults such as Heaven's Gate try to speed up the process of the end of the world with mass suicides.

Whatever their beliefs and differences, the new religions show us that as long as there is suffering and cruelty in the world, people will continue to look for new ideas and beliefs that make sense of the world.

▼ THE BLACK MESSIAH
Haile Selassie (Might of the Trinity) was the emperor of Ethiopia from 1930 until 1974. He was also known as Prince Ras Tafari. Rastafarians believe that he was the Black Messiah prophesied in 1916 by the black Jamaican activist Marcus Garvey.

▲ BOB MARLEY
Reggae is a music style that grew up in Jamaica in the 1950s and 1960s. It gained worldwide fame through the singing of Bob Marley. Many reggae stars are rastas. They sing about their faith in their songs.

Key Dates

- 1830 Joseph Smith translates the *Book of Mormon*.

- 1863 Baha'u'llah declares that he is the new prophet.

- 1870s Charles Taze Russell forms the Jehovah's Witnesses.

- 1930–74 Haile Selassie (Ras Tafari) rules Ethiopia.

- 1954 L Ron Hubbard founds the Church of Scientology.

- 1954 Sun Myung Moon founds the Unification Church in Korea.

- 1977 Marshall Applewhite founds the Heaven's Gate cult.

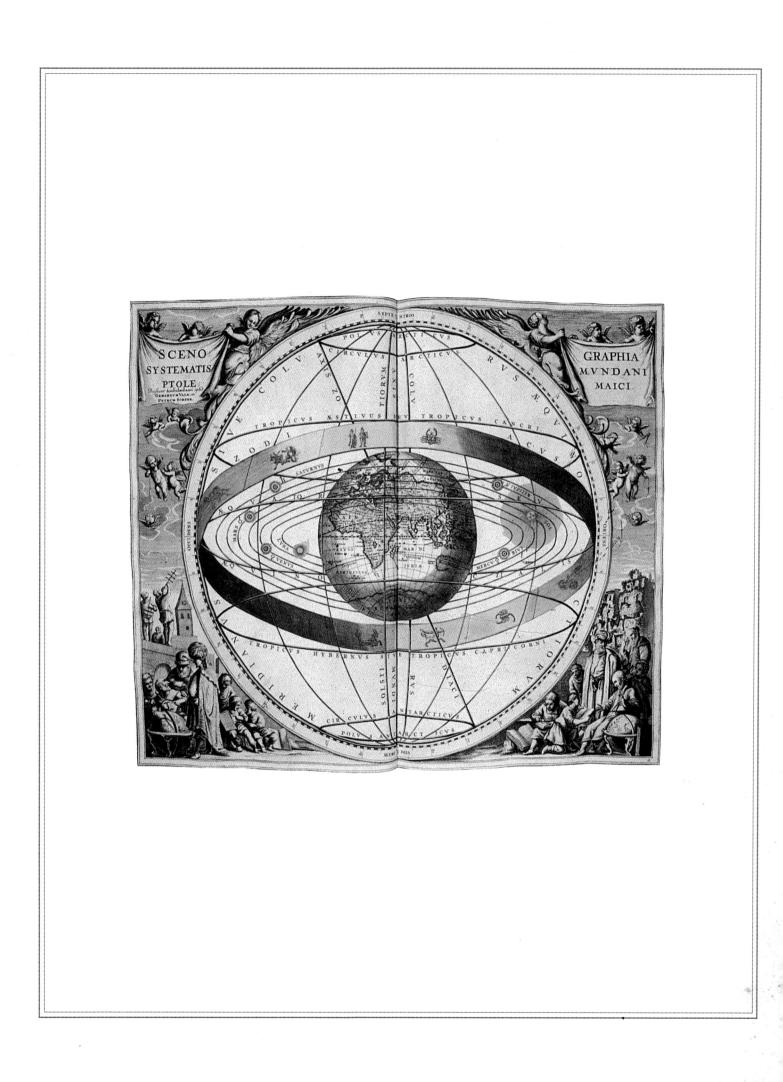

SCIENCE AND TECHNOLOGY

Science and technology have changed the face of our planet, from astronomical discoveries made in ancient Greece to recent advances such as genetic engineering. This section explores how human beings have attempted to master an understanding of their world.

BY JOHN FARNDON

Understanding the World

▲ PYTHAGORAS
Great thinkers such as Pythagoras of Samos (560–480BC) are essential to scientific progress. Without the input of people like Pythagoras, Albert Einstein and Louis Pasteur there would be no scientific advances at all.

▼ KEY DATES
This panel charts the progress of science through the ages, from the invention of the wheel to the creation of the World Wide Web.

SCIENCE AND TECHNOLOGY SEEM VERY modern ideas, but humans have been striving to understand the world and inventing machines to help them ever since they first walked on the Earth 30,000 years ago.

The earliest people lived simply by hunting animals and gathering fruit and there was no need for science to be anything but basic. But as people settled down to farm around 10,000 years ago, the first towns and cities were built in the Middle East and life became much more complicated. At once science and technology began to develop apace to meet their varied needs. The Babylonians, for instance, created numbers and mathematics to keep track of goods and taxes. The Egyptians studied astronomy to help them make a calendar. And the astonishing achievements of Greek thinkers like Archimedes and the engineers of the Roman empire laid the foundations of modern science and technology.

Their achievements were almost lost with the collapse of the Roman empire, which plunged Europe

▼ OVERCOMING PROBLEMS
Most of the great explorers had used square-sailed ships, which were limited in their manoeuvrability. The development of new technology, such as this caravel with its triangular sails which could sail almost directly into the wind, opened up new possibilities.

EUROPE

c.3200BC The wheel is invented in Sumeria.

c.2500BC The Ancient Egyptians devise a 365-day calendar.

c.1500BC The Babylonians develop numbers.

c.300BC Euclid writes *Elements of Geometry.*

c.250BC Archimedes establishes the mathematical rules for levers.

221-206BC The Great Wall of China is built.

AD130 Galen writes his medical books.

140 Ptolemy writes *Almagest.*

c.850 Al-Kharwarizmi introduces algebra.

1492 Christopher Columbus sails across the Atlantic.

1543 Copernicus shows that the Earth circles the Sun.

1610 Galileo spies Jupiter's moons through a telescope.

1628 Harvey shows how the heart circulates blood.

1661 Boyle introduces the idea of chemical elements and compounds.

1686 Newton establishes his three laws of motion and his theory of gravity.

1698 Savery invents the first practical steam engine.

1735 Linnaeus groups plants into species and genera.

1752 Franklin shows lightning is electricity.

1783 The Montgolfier brothers' balloon carries two men aloft.

1789 Lavoisier writes the first list of elements.

1804 Trevithick builds the first steam locomotive.

1808 Dalton proposes his atomic theory of chemical elements.

1830 Faraday and Henry find that electricity can be generated by magnetism.

1825 The first passenger railway, from Stockton to Darlington.

▲ FIRST CARS
The invention of the motor car has had a huge impact on transport throughout the world. The slow and noisy early cars have been replaced by quieter, safer and more economical models. Prices have come down, and the range of makes is now greater than ever. The car has, in fact, been so successful that many countries are now trying to limit car ownership because of the impact on the environment.

into the Dark Ages. But scientific thought continued to flourish in the Islamic east, and further east in China. And as eastern ideas gradually filtered into Europe in the 15th century, European scholars began to rediscover Greek and Roman science, and make new discoveries of their own.

The next 100 years brought great shocks to established ideas. First, in 1492, Columbus sailed across the Atlantic to discover a whole new, undreamed of continent. Then, in 1543, Copernicus showed that the Earth, far from being the centre of the Universe, was just one of the planets circling around the Sun.

Deep thinkers realized that ancient ideas could not necessarily be trusted: the only way to learn the truth was to look and learn for themselves. Observation and experiment became the basis of a new approach to science which has led to a huge range of discoveries such as Newton's laws of motion, Dalton's atoms, Darwin's theory of the evolution of life and many more – right up to recent breakthroughs in the science of genetics. Trade and industry, meanwhile, have fuelled a revolution in technology which began with the steam-powered factory machines of the late 18th century and continues to gather pace with the latest computer technology of today.

▼ MIR
Despite a number of mishaps, the Soviet Mir spacecraft stayed up in space for over 13 years, between 1986 and 1999, and made more than 76,000 orbits of the Earth. It was a temporary home to many astronauts – and Russian Valery Polyakov spent a record 437 continuous days aboard.

1830s Babbage designs his 'Analytic Engine'.

1856 Mendel discovers the basic laws of heredity.

1858 Darwin and Wallace suggest the theory of evolution by natural selection.

1861 Pasteur shows many diseases are caused by germs.

1862 Lenoir builds the first internal combustion engine car.

1862 Maxwell proposes that light is electromagnetic radiation.

1888 Hertz discovers radio waves.

1895 Röntgen discovers X-rays.

1897 Thomson discovers electrons and Becquerel discovers radioactivity.

1900 Planck suggests quantum.

1903 The Wright brothers make the first controlled, powered flight.

1905 & 1915 Einstein's Special and General Theories of Relativity.

1908 Ford's Model T, the first mass-produced car.

1911 Rutherford shows atom has a nucleus circled by electrons.

1923 Wegener suggests continental drift.

1927-9 Hubble realizes there are other galaxies and the universe is expanding.

1928 Fleming discovers penicillin.

1935 Carrothers develops nylon.

1939 Hahn and Strassman split a uranium atom.

1945 The USAF drop atomic bombs on Nagasaki and Hiroshima.

1948 Shockley, Bardeen and Brattain invent the transistor.

1953 Crick and Watson show DNA, the gene molecule in living cells, has a double-spiral shape.

1957 Sputnik is the first spacecraft to orbit the Earth.

1961 Gagarin is the first man in space.

1967 Nirenberg and Khorana show how the genetic code works. Gurdon creates the first animal clone.

1969 Armstrong and Aldrin are the first men on the Moon.

1989 Berners-Lee creates the World Wide Web.

Inventing Mathematics

▲ CUNEIFORM
The first writing came hand in hand with the development of numbers. This is Sumerian cuneiform (wedge-form) writing.

PEOPLE PROBABLY LEARNED TO count using numbers many, many thousands of years ago. In fact, even small animals have a basic number sense. Birds usually know how many babies they have, for instance. However, it was only when primitive hunters began to settle down and farm around 10,000 years ago that people started to think in terms of larger numbers. Then, for the first time, people needed to count things properly. They needed to count how many sheep they were selling at the market, how many bags of wheat they were buying, and so on. So the first farms and the first towns appeared in the Middle East, together with the first numbers, in the ancient civilizations of people such as the Sumerians.

People probably started by counting on fingers. This idea worked well, as it still does today, but fingers do not help you to remember how many. So people began to make the first number records by dropping stones, shells or clay discs one by one into a bag. In Sumeria, about 6,000 years ago, someone had the bright idea of making scratch marks on a clay tablet – one mark for each thing they were counting. Soon the Babylonians learned to use different shaped marks for larger numbers. This system is still the basis of our modern number system – except that instead of using different marks for larger numbers, we simply use a different symbol for each number up to nine, and then put the symbols in different positions for the larger numbers.

The early civilizations also developed mathematical skills. First, there was arithmetic. This is the art of working things out by numbers – by addition, subtraction, multiplication and division. Arithmetic is the oldest of all the mathematical skills. We know that the Babylonians and Sumerians were skilled in arithmetic at

◄ SUMERIAN ACCOUNTANTS
The accountants of the ancient civilization of Sumeria may have written down the first numbers over 6,000 years ago. To keep track of tax accounts and payments, they scratched marks on soft clay tablets. The tablets hardened to make a permanent record.

THE GREAT GEOMETERS
The first great masters of geometry were the ancient Greeks, such as Pythagoras, Eudoxus and in particular Euclid, who lived between about 330 and 275BC. Geometry is actually a Greek word meaning "earth measurement". Euclid's book *Elements* was such a brilliantly thorough study of geometry that it became the framework for geometry for thousands of years. Even today, mathematicians still refer to all the geometry of flat surfaces – lines, points, shapes and solids – as Euclidean geometry.

▶ EARLY GEOMETRY
Most basic geometry is about lines and the angles between them – and how they make up two kinds of shape, or figure: circles and polygons. The Greek geometers used to analyse these shapes in particular ways. They might try to calculate the area of a triangle, for instance, or work out the relationship between particular angles.

A
B

Right-angle triangle

C

◄ PYTHAGORAS
Pythagoras of Samos (560–480BC) was one of the first great mathematicians. He is a rather mysterious figure, who believed that numbers were the perfect basis of life. He is most famous for his theory about right-angled triangles. His theory showed that if you square the two sides next to the right angle, the two add up to the third side squared. (Squaring simply means multiplying a number by itself.) This was expressed by Pythagoras in the following, famous, formula:

$$A{\times}A + B{\times}B = C{\times}C$$
$$\text{or}$$
$$A^2 + B^2 = C^2$$

least 5,000 years ago. Babylonian schoolchildren learned how to multiply and divide, and they used arithmetical tables to help with complex sums.

Arithmetic was developed to keep the accounts that were the key to power in the ancient civilizations. Accounts and arithmetic were vital. For example, they helped to work out how much tax people owed. Many of those skilled in arithmetic were highly honoured. In fact, they were often feared, for when mathematicians first learned to make quick mathematic calculations it seemed like magic. The arithmetic processes developed in ancient China seemed so tricky and clever that they were still being used by Chinese "mind-readers" in the music halls of Europe in the early 20th century.

Another skill was geometry, which is the mathematics of shapes. It was probably first invented to help people work out the area of their land. Geometry was developed by the ancient Egyptians over 4,000 years ago to help them build perfect pyramids.

▼ THE PERFECT PYRAMID
The Great Pyramids of ancient Egypt still astonish us with their geometric precision, and an amazing discovery showed us just how the Egyptians did it. In 1858, while holidaying in Egypt, the Scottish historian Alexander Rhind bought an ancient papyrus written by an Egyptian scribe called Ahmes around 1650BC. The Rhind Papyrus showed that the ancient Egyptians knew a great deal about the geometry of triangles, which is vital in building the pyramids. For example, they knew how to work out the height of a pyramid from the length of its shadow on the ground.

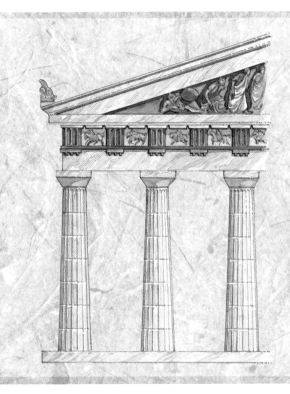

◄ TRIANGULAR FRIEZE
The ancient Greeks were fascinated by perfect geometric shapes, which is reflected in their elegant temples. These graceful buildings were among the first to be built using geometric rules, with beautifully proportioned rectangles crowned by triangular friezes. At this time, geometry was not only used in the building of temples, it was the basis for practical engineering too. In fact, much of our knowledge of geometry is based on the theories of ancient Greeks.

Key Dates

- 1500BC Babylonians develop a number system.

- 530BC Pythagoras devises his theory about right-angled triangles.

- 300BC Euclid writes his *Elements of Geometry*, the most influential mathematics book ever written.

- 300BC The Hindus develop their own number system.

- 220BC Archimedes finds a way of measuring the volume of spheres.

- 200BC Appolonius analyses slices across cones – parabolas and ellipses.

- AD662 Hindu number system develops into decimal system we now use.

Star Gazing

ASTRONOMY DATES BACK TO the earliest days of humankind, when prehistoric hunters gazed up at the sky to work out which night might give them a full moon for hunting. When people began to settle down to farm 10,000 years ago, astronomy helped farmers to know when seasons would come and go. Indeed, astronomy played such a vital role in early civilizations that astronomers were often high priests. Many ancient monuments have strong links with astronomy. The standing stones in Stonehenge in England, for instance, are aligned with the rising sun on the solstices, the longest and shortest days of the year. Shafts in Egypt's Great Pyramids point at the star group called Orion.

By the time the ancient Greek astronomer Hipparchus of Rhodes (170–127BC) began to study the sky, astronomy was already an ancient art. Hipparchus was a skilled observer, but much of his work was based on old Babylonian records rescued from the ruins of the Persian Empire by Alexander the Great. Even so, his achievement was stupendous. He was the first great astronomer, and he laid the foundations for astronomy for almost 2,000 years.

Excited by spotting a new star in 134BC, Hipparchus began to make a catalogue of the 850 stars whose positions were then known. This catalogue, adapted by Ptolemy, was still being used in the 16th century. Hipparchus also compared stars by giving each one a "Magnitude" from one to six, depending on how bright it

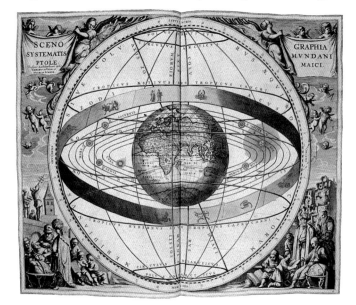

▲ PTOLEMY'S MAP
Early European maps were based on a work called Geography, *by the astronomer Ptolemy. It was because Ptolemy underestimated the size of the world that Columbus set out for Asia, sailing west across the Atlantic Ocean. This then inspired his discovery of the Americas.*

THE CONSTELLATIONS

To help find their way around the night sky, astronomers in ancient Babylon and Egypt looked for patterns of stars, or constellations. They named each star pattern after a mythical figure. On star maps, you often see these figures drawn over the stars, as if the stars were a giant "painting by numbers" book.

There is no real link between the stars in a constellation; they simply look close together. But the system is so effective that astronomers still use it, though they have added a few extra constellations. Each ancient civilization had its own names for constellations, and the names we use today come from Greek myths. The names are written, not in Greek, but in their Roman (Latin) equivalent, such as Cygnus (the Swan) and Ursa Major (the Great Bear).

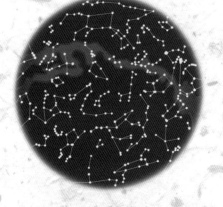

▲ NORTHERN HEMISPHERE
These are some of the 88 constellations, or star groups, that are recognized by astronomers today. There are many other stars in the sky; the constellations simply make groups of the brightest stars.

▲ SOUTHERN HEMISPHERE
A different set of constellations is visible from the Southern Hemisphere (half of the world). Indeed many, such as Crux (the Southern Cross), would have been completely unknown to ancient Greeks.

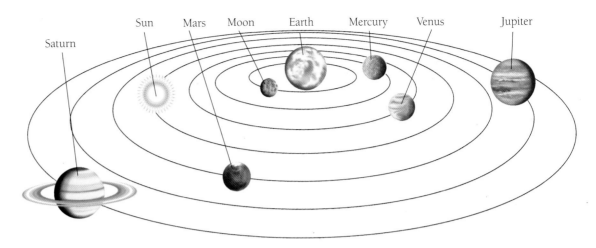

Saturn Sun Mars Moon Earth Mercury Venus Jupiter

▼ CLAY TABLETS

Many of the earliest astronomical records were kept by the Babylonians who kept records on clay tablets like this one.

looked. The brightest star is Sirius (the Dog Star), which he called a First-Magnitude star; the faintest star was called a Sixth-Magnitude star. The idea of star magnitude is very important to astronomers even today, although the scale has been refined.

Hipparchus measured things in the sky very exactly, considering he only had his own eyes to guide him. He made some amazingly precise measurements of the movements of the heavens. He calculated the length of a year, for instance, to within less than seven minutes. He also discovered that the relative positions of the stars on the equinoxes (March 21 and December 21) slowly shift round, and worked out that they take 26,000 years to return to the same place.

Sadly, hardly any of Hipparchus' work survives as he

▲ THE WANDERERS

Early astronomers such as Ptolemy knew that the world was round, but they believed that the Earth was the centre of the Universe and everything revolved around it. They knew of only five planets – Mercury, Venus, Mars, Jupiter and Saturn.

The early astronomers had no telescopes, so the planets looked just like stars, only they were brighter. What makes planets different is that the position of the stars in the night sky is fixed and they only move as the Earth turns. The planets, however, wander through the sky like the Sun and the Moon. This is why they are called planets, which is the Greek word for "wanderers".

wrote it. We know of it because it was developed by the astronomer Ptolemy (AD90–170), who wrote four books summarizing Greek astronomical ideas in the 2nd century AD, including *Almagest* (Arabic for "The Greatest"). These books became the cornerstone of western and Arab astronomy until the 16th century.

◄ EGYPTIAN ASTRONOMY

Here you can see an Egyptian drawing of the goddess Nut holding up the sky. The ancient Egyptians relied on astronomy to give them times and dates. They performed some religious ceremonies, for instance, at certain times during the night when the constellations reached a particular place in the sky.

The most important date was the time when Sirius, the brightest star in the sky, appeared after being hidden behind the Sun for many months. This date was important as it coincided with the annual floods of the River Nile, which made the Egyptian soils fertile.

Key Dates

- 2800BC The ancient Egyptian astronomer Imhotep aligns the first great pyramid perfectly with the Sun.

- 2500BC The ancient Egyptians devise a 365-day calendar.

- 550BC Greek astronomer Anaximander suggests the Earth is a globe hanging in space.

- c.200BC Eratosthenes calculates the size of the Earth.

- 134BC Hipparchus catalogues 850 stars and devises a magnitude scale for stars.

- AD140 In *Almagest* Ptolemy describes the motions of the planets and catalogues stars and planets.

The First Scientist

▲ ARCHIMEDES
The great scientist Archimedes was killed when the Romans invaded Syracuse. Some say he was working on a theory when he died.

ARCHIMEDES WAS THE WORLD'S first great scientist. Of course, others had studied scientific subjects before, but Archimedes was the first to think about problems in the scientific way that we now take for granted. He came up with abstract theories that could be proved or disproved by practical experiments and by mathematical calculations.

Archimedes lived in Syracuse in Sicily, which was a Greek colony at the time. He was born there around 285BC, and spent most of his life in the city studying geometry and inventing all kinds of fantastic machines. These included the famous Archimedes' screw, a device for pumping water, and many war machines which he built for the defence of Syracuse. Archimedes was regarded with awe in his lifetime, and there are many stories about him.

The most famous is about a task that the king of Syracuse once set him. The king wanted to know if his crown was pure gold – or if the crafty goldsmith had mixed in some cheaper metal as he suspected. Archimedes was thinking about this tricky problem in the bath one day when suddenly he noticed how the water level rose the deeper he sank into the bath. The story goes that he leaped out of his bath and ran naked through the streets to the king, shouting at the top of his voice "Eureka! Eureka!", which means "I've got it! I've got it!". Later, he showed the king his idea. First, he immersed in water a piece of gold that weighed the same as the crown. Then he immersed the crown itself and discovered that the water level was different. Archimedes then concluded that the

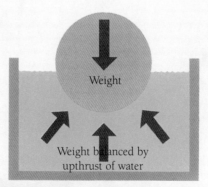

◀ ARCHIMEDES' SCREW
Archimedes' screw is a very simple but effective pump. Inside a tube is a spiral, which scoops up the water as someone turns the handle at the top. Such pumps are still in use 2,000 years later in some places in the Middle East. They lift water from irrigation canals and rivers onto dry fields.

FLOATING AND SINKING

One of Archimedes' great breakthroughs was the discovery that an object weighs less in water than in air – which is why you can lift quite a heavy person when in a swimming pool. The reason for this "buoyancy" is the natural upward push, or upthrust, of the water.

When an object is immersed in water, its weight pushes down. But the water, as Archimedes realized, pushes back up with a force equal to the weight of water the object pushes out of the way. So the object sinks until its weight is exactly equal to the upthrust of the water, at which point it floats. So objects that weigh less than the water displaced will float and those that weigh more will sink.

Weight

Weight balanced by upthrust of water

▲ BUOYANCY
If you drop a barrel weighing 100g into water, it will sink until it displaces (pushes out of the way) a volume of water weighing 100g. It floats at this point because the upthrust created by pushing 100g of water out of the way exactly balances with the weight of the barrel.

▲ WHY SHIPS FLOAT
When the first iron ships were made in the 18th century, many people were convinced they would sink because iron is too heavy to float. They were right; iron is too heavy to float. But iron and steel ships float because their hulls are full of air, and so they can safely sink until enough water is displaced to match the weight of the iron in the hull.

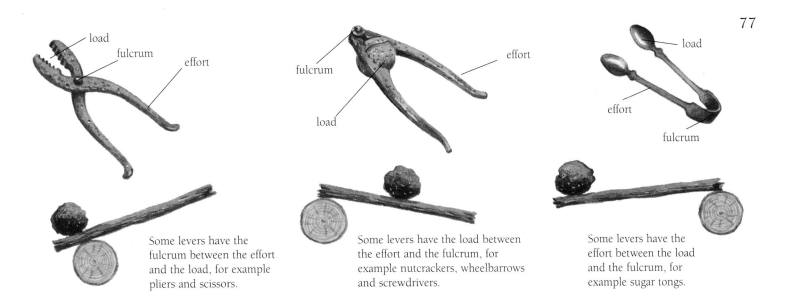

Some levers have the fulcrum between the effort and the load, for example pliers and scissors.

Some levers have the load between the effort and the fulcrum, for example nutcrackers, wheelbarrows and screwdrivers.

Some levers have the effort between the load and the fulcrum, for example sugar tongs.

crown was not pure gold because the difference in water levels showed that the crown had a different volume to the gold, although they were the same weight. This proved that it must have been made of a different metal. The goldsmith was executed.

Whether this story is true or not, it is typical of Archimedes' amazingly neat and elegant scientific solutions to awkward questions. He also tried to approach problems mathematically. He was probably not the first to realize that if you put a weight on each end of a seesaw, the lighter weight must be farther away if the two weights are to balance. Archimedes, though, showed that the ratio of the weights goes down in exact mathematical proportion to the distance they must be from the pivot of the seesaw – and he proved this also mathematically. In the same way, he had the brilliant insight that every object has a centre of gravity – a

▲ LEVERS AND FORCES

Archimedes' brilliant insight was to analyse mathematically an everyday tool such as a lever. If a lever, such as a plank of wood, pivots around one point, called the fulcrum, the effort you apply on one side of the fulcrum can move a load on the other side. What Archimedes found was that the load you could move with a certain amount of effort depended exactly on the relative distance of the effort and load from the fulcrum. Working out load, force, distance and so on mathematically is now one of the cornerstones of science.

single point from which all its weight seems to hang – and he proved it mathematically.

Sadly much of Archimedes' work has been lost. Yet his approach to science – using mathematics to understand the physical world – is the basis of the most advanced science today. Almost 1,900 years after Archimedes' death, the great Italian scientist Galileo said, "Without Archimedes I could have achieved nothing."

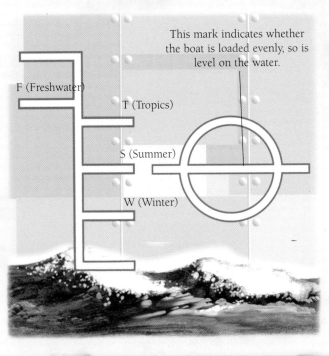

This mark indicates whether the boat is loaded evenly, so is level on the water.

F (Freshwater)

T (Tropics)

S (Summer)

W (Winter)

◀ PLIMSOLL MARK

The density of water (how tightly together its particles are packed) changes depending on its temperature and on whether it is fresh (non-salty) or sea water. Ships float higher in cold or salty water because it is more dense and creates more upthrust.

Some ships are marked with a set of lines, called a Plimsoll mark, to show the safe levels to which cargo can be loaded on board – in the tropics, in freshwater, in summer and in winter.

Key Dates

- c.450BC Empedocles suggests all substances are made from four elements: earth, air, fire and water.

- c.335BC Theophrastus writes the first scientific book on plants.

- c.350BC Aristotle lays down rules for science.

- 250BC Archimedes discovers principles of buoyancy and forms mathematical rules for levers.

- c.AD70 Hero of Alexander invents a pump, a fountain and a steam turbine.

- c.AD100 Chinese thinker Zhang Heng makes a seismoscope to record earthquakes.

Roman Engineers

▲ ROMAN BUILDINGS
This temple is an excellent example of Roman architecture. To create buildings such as this, the Roman's would use bricks to form a strong and long lasting structure.

ANCIENT ROME HAD few of the great thinkers that made ancient Greece so remarkable. However, it had many clever, practical men, and the Romans were the greatest engineers and builders of the ancient world. Their bridges, roads and aqueducts are marvels of ingenious, efficient large-scale construction, and many of them are still standing today, over 2,000 years on. Some, such as the eight aqueducts that supply Rome with water, are still in use, working as well as they ever did. It is hard to imagine many modern structures lasting quite so long.

Much of the Romans' engineering was connected with their military conquests, and engineers travelled with the armies to build roads and bridges. A sound knowledge of engineering was an essential skill for an officer, and soldiers provided much of the labour for the major construction works. Whenever the Romans conquered a new territory, one of the army's first tasks was to lay out cities to a standard plan, build roads to supply the army and lay on a clean water supply.

The Romans inherited some of their construction techniques from the Greeks and the Etruscans. They added to the Greek knowledge, and pushed Greek techniques to new levels, and added a number of features of their own. One of the keys to Roman engineering was the arch. The arch is a simple but clever way of making strong bridges. A flat piece of stone across two posts can only take so much weight before snapping. But in an arch the stones are pushed harder together when weight is placed on them, so the arch actually becomes stronger.

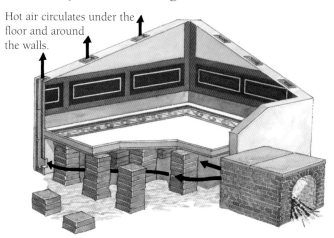

Hot air circulates under the floor and around the walls.

▲ UNDERFLOOR HEATING
We tend to think of central heating as a modern invention, but many Roman villas (houses) had a space under the floor called a hypocaust. Warm air from the hot bricks of a furnace circulated through this space, keeping the floor warm and the house very cosy.

ROMAN ROADS

None of the Romans' engineering achievements has had more impact than their road system. The Romans began building roads in 334BC, and by the time their empire was at its peak they had laid down more than 85,000km of roads, including the famous Appian Way running 660km through Italy.

During this time most roads were simple, rough dirt tracks, which were impassable with mud in winter. In contrast the Romans laid smooth, hard-surfaced roads that cut as straight as an arrow across marshes, lakes, gorges and hills. Using these roads, their soldiers could move around the empire with astonishing speed.

▲ ROMAN ROUTES
Even today, roads in many parts of the world quickly become impassable in bad weather. The Romans, however, built their roads to be used in all seasons. They built strong stone bridges high above rivers, and raised roads above ground that was liable to flooding on embankments called aggers. They even made grooves in the road to guide trucks.

Another feature of Roman engineering was cement. The Romans made bricks on an unprecedented scale, and Roman bridges and buildings are the first great brick structures. At first, the structures were mortared together with a mixture of sand, lime and water. In the 2nd century BC a new ingredient was added: volcanic sand found near the modern town of Pozzuoli in Italy. This ingredient, now called pozzolana, turned mortar into an incredibly tough cement that hardens even underwater. Pozzolanic mortars were so strong and cheap that the Romans began to build with cement only and dispense with the bricks. Eventually, they added stones to make concrete.

With the arch and pozzolanic cement, the Romans could build bridges and aqueducts on a massive scale, such as the famous Pont du Gard near Nîmes in France and the 780m-long Segovia aqueduct in Spain. The fact that these bridges have survived almost 2,000 years testifies to both their strength and durability.

▶ BUILDING AN AQUEDUCT
Building a Roman aqueduct was a massive job involving hundreds and sometimes thousands of men. To build each arch, the engineers constructed a framework of wood on which they laid the stones. Towering scaffolds of wood enabled them to build rows of arches which were 100m or more high.

▶ A ROMAN ROAD
To build their roads, the Romans laid a deep solid foundation of large stone. They covered this with a smooth surface of flat stones, with a raised centre, or "crown", so that water would drain off either side. They also dug ditches along the sides of the road to carry the water away.

Key Dates

- c.3200BC The wheel is invented in Sumeria.

- 2800BC The ancient Egyptians build the first pyramid.

- 1470BC Pharaoh Sesostris builds first Suez Canal, linking the river Nile to the Red Sea.

- 480BC Xerxes of Persia builds a bridge of boats across the Hellespont.

- 312BC The Appian Way, the first great Roman road, is built.

- 221–206BC The Great Wall of China is built.

- c.AD200 By this time the Romans have built over 80,000km of roads.

Where and When

▲ SHIP'S COMPASS
The compasses that ships use utilize a suspended, magnetized needle that aligns itself in a north-south direction with the Earth's magnetic field.

I N THE MIDDLE AGES THE Europeans knew little of the world. Maps were inaccurate and showed Asia to the east only vaguely. To the south, Africa faded off into a mystery land filled with monsters and dangerous peoples. To the west there was nothing at all. It was still not absolutely certain that the world was round. Perhaps it ended in empty space? Even in Europe itself, charts were so inaccurate and navigation methods so unreliable that ships stayed in sight of land to be sure of finding their way.

Then, in the 14th century, the great Mongol Empire in Asia collapsed. The roads to China and the East, along which silks and spices were brought, were cut off. So bold European mariners set out westwards to find their way to the East by sea. From 1400, ship after ship sailed from Europe. At first they ventured south around the unknown west of Africa in small ships called caravels. The mariners were often Portuguese, sent out by Prince Henry "the Navigator" (1394–1460) from his base at Sagres. They pushed on, cape by cape, until Bartolomeu Dias rounded Africa's southern tip in 1488. Nine years later, Vasco da Gama sailed right round to India. In the

▼ THE CARAVEL
Up until the 15th century, most European ships were square-rigged, which meant they could only sail in much the same direction as the wind. Most of the great explorers, including Columbus, used a small revolutionary ship called a caravel, which had triangular "lateen" sails adopted from Arab dhows. With these sails, a caravel could sail almost directly into the wind.

THE SEARCH FOR LONGITUDE

Finding longitude was for a long time a problem in navigation. In theory you can work it out from the Sun's position in the sky, comparing this to its position at the same time at a longitude you know. However, you must know the exact time. Huygens had made an accurate pendulum clock in the 1670s, but it was too sensitive to keep good time aboard a tossing ship. The solution was the chronometer, a very accurate, stormproof clock made in the 1720s by John Harrison (1693–1776). It used balance springs, rather than a pendulum, to keep time.

◀ HUYGENS' CLOCK
The pendulum clock, invented by Christiaan Huygens in the 1670s, was the world's first accurate timepiece.

◀ HARRISON'S CHRONOMETER
It took John Harrison decades to persuade the authorities that his chronometer was indeed the solution to the longitude problem. This is his second version.

▲ LATITUDE
Latitude says how far north or south you are in degrees. Lines of latitude are called parallels because they form rings around the Earth parallel to the Equator. You can work out latitude from the Sun's height in the sky at noon. The higher it is, the nearer the Equator you are.

▲ LONGITUDE
Longitude says how far east or west you are in degrees. Lines of longitude, or meridians, run from pole to pole, dividing the world like orange segments. You can work out your longitude from the time it is when the Sun is at its highest.

meantime, in 1492 Christopher Columbus took a great gamble and set out west across the open Atlantic, hoping to reach China. Instead, he found the New World of the Americas waiting to be explored. Finally in 1522, fewer than 90 years after the voyages of discovery began, Ferdinand Magellan's ship *Victoria* sailed all the way around the world. Now there could be no doubt; the world is round.

Maps improved vastly as each voyage brought new knowledge, and map "projections" were devised to show the round world on flat paper and parchment. Yet these early projections helped sailors little, since a straight course at sea was an elaborate line on the map. In 1552 Dutch mapmaker Gerhardus Mercator invented a new projection. It treated the map of the world as if it were projected onto a cylinder, which could then be rolled out and lay flat. Although Mercator's projection made countries near the Poles look far too big, it meant that sailors could plot a straight course by compass simply by drawing a straight line on the map.

At the same time, navigation at sea made startling progress. Early sailors had steered entirely by the stars – they had only a vague idea where they were during the day, and no idea at all if the sky clouded over. From the 12th century on, European sailors used a magnetic needle to find north at all times. This however, only gave them a direction to steer; it did not tell them where they were. From the 14th century, sailors used an astrolabe to get an idea of their latitude – how far north or south of the Equator – by measuring the height of a star or the Sun at noon. The great breakthrough, came with the invention of the cross-staff in the 16th century. Sailors used it to measure the angle between the horizon and the Pole Star and so work out their latitude precisely. Now the problem was longitude – how far east or west they were. For centuries, the only way to work out a ship's longitude was to guess how far it had come by "dead reckoning". This involved trailing a knotted rope in the water to keep a constant track of the ship's speed. However, this was not very accurate, so the problem of longitude was to tax some of the greatest minds over the next few centuries.

▶ GREENWICH
The great observatory at Greenwich, London, was set up in 1675. Its brief from King Charles II was to map the movements of the heavens so accurately that the longitude problem could be solved. The problem was not solved here, but the observatory sits on the Prime Meridian, the first line of longitude.

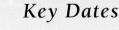

▲ HOW FAR NORTH?
The mirror sextant was developed in the mid-1700s from the cross-staff to measure latitude accurately. It became the main navigation aid for sailors until the days of electronic technology after World War II. It has one mirror that you point at the horizon, and another mirror that you adjust until the Sun (or a star) is reflected in it at exactly the same height as the horizon. The degree of adjustment you need to make to the second mirror gives the latitude. The sextant gets its name from its shape, which is one-sixth of a circle.

Key Dates

- 1488 Bartolomeu Dias sails round the southern tip of Africa.

- 1492 Christopher Columbus sails across the Atlantic.

- 1497 Vasco da Gama sails round Africa to India.

- 1497 John Cabot discovers Canada while trying to find a way to Asia.

- 1501 Amerigo Vespucci realizes South America is a whole new continent.

- 1513 Vasco de Bilboa of Spain sails into the Pacific Ocean.

- 1519 Ferdinand Magellan leads the first voyage around the world.

The Great Anatomists

NOTHING IS CLOSER TO us than the human body, yet it has taken as long to explore it as it has to explore the Earth. For thousands of years medicine was based as much on superstition as on research. The first doctor that we know about was Imhotep, who lived in ancient Egypt 4,600 years ago. People travelled from far and wide to be treated by him, and after his death he was made a god. The greatest physician of the ancient world was the Roman Galen, born around AD130. Like

▲ LEONARDO DA VINCI
Da Vinci (1452–1519) is best known for his few master paintings, such as the Mona Lisa *and the* Last Supper. *His curiosity led him to study everything from human anatomy to astronomy with the same remarkable insight.*

▼ DA VINCI'S ANATOMICAL DRAWINGS
To draw human figures exactly, many artists in the Renaissance began to study human anatomy for themselves. Some, such as da Vinci, made their own dissections, and their knowledge of the human body often outstripped that of physicians.

THE POWER OF THE MICROSCOPE

People never suspected that many things were far too small for the eye to see until the microscope was invented in around 1590. Soon, using a simple microscope made with a drop of water, the Dutch scientist Anton van Leeuwenhoek found that the world is full of tiny micro-organisms such as bacteria.

In the 1660s Italian physician Marcello Malphigi (1628–1694) began to use a microscope to study the human body. He made many discoveries of tiny structures such as the tastebuds on the tongue. He did not, however, restrict himself to the study of humans, but he studied plants and animals in great detail as well.

▼ MICROSCOPES
Early microscopes magnified things many times by combining two lenses. One lens, called the objective lens, bends light rays apart to create an enlarged image, but this image is still very small. A second lens, called the eyepiece lens, acts like a magnifying glass to make this tiny image visible.

his contemporaries, Galen learned about the body by studying ancient manuscripts, but he also took a scientific approach and cut up animals to see how their bodies worked. He recorded his findings in many books describing the skeleton, the muscles and the nerves. Respect for Galen was so great that for more than 1,000 years, doctors would consult Galen's books rather than look at a body.

During the Renaissance in Italy in the 15th and 16th centuries, physicians began to consider that it might be better to look at real bodies, rather than at Galen's texts. They retrieved dead bodies from graveyards and cut them up to see exactly how they were put together. This is called dissection. The focus of this revolution was the University of Padua, where a brilliant German, Andreas Vesalius (1514–1564), was professor of surgery and anatomy. (Anatomy is the study of the way the human body is put together.) When dissection had been done in the past, it was usually done for the physicians by a butcher. Vesalius, though, began dissecting corpses himself, and asked the Flemish artist Jan van Calcar to draw very accurately what he found. In 1543, Vesalius published his findings in a textbook of anatomy called *De humani corposi fabrica* (On the Structure of the Human Body), which became the most influential medical book ever written.

Inspired by Vesalius's work, other physicians began to make their own dissections. Piece by piece, a very detailed picture of human anatomy began to build up. In the 1550s, for instance, Vesalius's colleague Gabriel Fallopio (1523–1562) discovered the tubes that link a

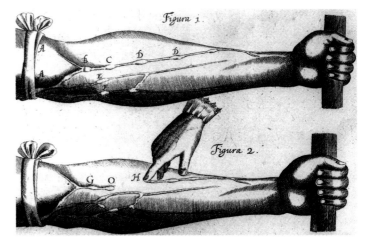

▲ BLOOD CIRCULATION

The English physician William Harvey (1578–1657) was one of the many great scientists who studied at the University of Padua in the 1500s and 1600s. Harvey's great insight was to realize that blood flows out from the heart through arteries and back through veins, making a complete one-way circulation of the blood.

female's ovaries to the uterus. These are now known as the Fallopian tubes. He also identified various other parts of the female reproductive system. Another colleague, Matteo Corti, discovered minute structures in the inner ear.

Gradually, physicians began to learn about physiology too (the science of the workings of the body). In 1590, for instance, Santorio Sanctorius showed how to measure pulse and body temperature. In 1628 William Harvey showed that the heart is a pump, and that blood circulates round and round the body. In this way the foundations for our current knowledge of the human body were built bit by bit.

▶ MALPHIGI
Marcello Malphigi was the first person to apply the power of the newly invented microscope to the human body. He made the first microscopic studies of human tissues, discovering the tiny structures present in the body. In 1661 Malphigi discovered capillaries, the minute blood vessels that were the missing link in Harvey's blood circulation.

Key Dates

- 480BC Hippocrates is one of the first great doctors.

- c.AD130 Galen writes his medical treatises.

- 1543 Vesalius publishes his book *De Humani Corporis Fabrica*.

- 1550 Gabriel Fallopio studies the human body in minute detail.

- 1590 Santorio Sanctorius creates science of physiology, and shows how to measure pulse and temperature.

- 1628 William Harvey shows how the heart circulates blood.

- 1661 Marcello Malphigi sees tiny blood vessels called capillaries under a microscope.

The Moving Earth

▲ COPERNICUS
The astronomer Copernicus spent most of his life studying old astronomical texts at Frauenberg Cathedral in Germany. His theories literally shook the world.

UNTIL THE 16TH century, nearly everyone was certain that the Earth was at the centre of the Universe, and that the Moon, the Sun, the planets and the stars revolved around it. Then a Polish astronomer, Nicolaus Copernicus, began to think there was something strange about the path of the planets through the sky.

Most of the time, the planets follow a smooth curved path, but every now and then some of them perform a small backward loop through the sky. Ancient astronomers, including the brilliant Ptolemy, had explained this by suggesting that everything in the Universe worked by an ingenious system of epicycles, or wheels within wheels. This elaborate system did not quite ring true with Copernicus. He noted, for example, that the stars seem sometimes nearer and sometimes farther away. "Why should this be?" he asked.

Then Copernicus had a simple but brilliant idea. What if the Earth was not the fixed centre of the Universe, but was one of the planets revolving around

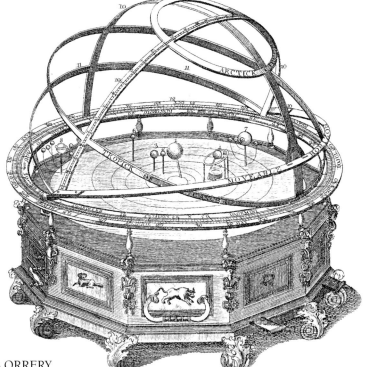

▲ ORRERY
Once people accepted the idea that the Earth was just one of the planets circling the Sun, they became fascinated by how this system worked. In 1710 a Scottish clockmaker called George Graham built a clockwork model to show how the planets moved. He built the model for his patron, the 4th Earl of Orrery. Orreries, as they came to be known, were soon very popular.

the Sun? Then the strange movement of the planets and the varying distance of the stars would be explained very simply. He wrote his ideas in a book called *De revolutionibus orbium coelestium* (On the Revolutions of the Heavenly Spheres), which was published just after he died in 1543.

GALILEO'S TELESCOPE

Galileo did not invent the telescope, but he was the first person to make one for looking at the night sky. He encountered an extraordinary amount of prejudice and scepticism. One professor said that he refused to waste his time looking through this silly device "to see what no-one but Galileo has seen. Besides, it gives me a headache." "It's all a trick!" said others.

When an excited Galileo tried to show the professors at Bologna the four moons of Jupiter he had seen through his telescope, all the "most excellent men and noble doctors" insisted that "the instrument lies!". Father Clavius, the professor of mathematics, laughed and said he would show them the moons of Jupiter too if he had time to paint them onto the lens.

▲ GALILEO
Galileo Galilei (1564–1642) was one of the greatest scientists of all times. He made many important scientific discoveries, but none that caused as much controversy as his support for Copernicus's ideas.

▶ POWERFUL TELESCOPES
In 1609 Galileo heard of the invention of the telescope in the Netherlands. He quickly learned how to make his own telescope. His telescopes were increasingly powerful, magnifying up to 20 times.

No single idea in history has changed our view of the Universe, and our place in it, quite so much. At first, only a few astronomers took much notice of Copernicus's new theory. After all, people had been publishing mad ideas for centuries. Then early in the 17th century, the famous Italian scientist Galileo began to look at the night sky with a new device called the telescope. What Galileo saw through his telescope proved that Copernicus's ideas were not just an interesting theory – they were really true.

Galileo saw two things that confirmed this view for him. The first was the fact that he could see four moons circling Jupiter – the first proof that the Earth is not at the centre of things. The second was the fact that he could see Venus has phases like our Moon. (Phases are the way the Moon seems to change shape as we see its bright sunlit side from a different angle.) The nature of Venus's phases showed it must be moving around the Sun, not the Earth.

Catholic teaching at that time was based on the idea that the Earth was the fixed centre of the Universe. When Galileo published his findings in a book called *The Starry Messenger* in 1513, he was declared a heretic by the cardinals in Rome. When threatened with torture, Galileo was forced to deny that the Earth moves. Legend says that he muttered *"eppur si muove"* ("yet it does move") after. The Catholic Church did not retract its sentence on Galileo until 13 October 1992.

▼ COPERNICUS'S MAP OF THE HEAVENS
Copernicus's map showed that the Earth was not at the centre of the Universe and gave us the "heliocentric", or Sun-centred, Universe. Now we know, of course, that not even the Sun is the centre of the Universe. It is just one of many billions of stars.

◀ JUPITER'S MOONS
In January 1610, Galileo was looking at the planet Jupiter through his telescope when he saw what could only be four tiny moons circling it. Up until then, most people thought everything in the Universe was circling the Earth. Yet here were four moons circling just one of the planets in the solar system. Jupiter is now known to have 16 moons. The four that Galileo saw are called Galilean moons.

Key Dates

- 300BC Greek astronomer Aristarchus suggests that the Earth revolves around the Sun.

- 1543 Copernicus suggests that the Earth circles the Sun.

- 1550 Johann Kepler recognizes that the planets follow elliptical, not circular, paths.

- 1610 With his telescope Galileo sees mountains on the Moon and four moons orbiting the planet Jupiter.

- 1665 Isaac Newton uses the theory of gravity to explain how the planets move.

- 1781 William Herschel discovers the planet Uranus.

Force and Motion

▲ ISAAC NEWTON
Isaac Newton (1642–1727) showed the link between force and motion in his three laws of motion. He realized that a force he called gravity makes things fall and keeps the planets orbiting the Sun.

THE 17TH CENTURY WAS THE first real age of science, when brilliant men such as Galileo, Huygens, Boyle, Newton, Liebnitz and Leeuwenhoek made many important discoveries. Of all their achievements, however, perhaps none was as important as the understanding of forces and motion.

The philosophers of ancient Greece had known a great deal about "statics" – things that are not moving. Though when it came to movement, or "dynamics", they were often baffled. They could see, for instance, that a plough moves because the oxen pulls it, and that an arrow flies because of the force of the bow. But how, they wondered, did an arrow keep on flying through the air after it left the bow – if there was nothing to pull it along? The Greek philosopher Aristotle made his common-sense assertion that you must have a force to keep something moving – just as your bike will slow to a halt if you stop pedalling.

Yet common sense can be wrong, and it took the genius of Galileo and Newton to realize it. After a series

▼ THE TOWER OF PISA
Galileo was the first to appreciate that gravity accelerates downwards anything falling by exactly the same amount. In other words, things will fall at the same speed no matter how heavy they are. Legend has it that he demonstrated this by dropping two objects of different weights from the Leaning Tower of Pisa in Italy. The two objects will have hit the ground at the same time.

NEWTON AND GRAVITY
No one knew why planets circle round the Sun or why things fall to the ground until one day around 1665, when Newton was thinking in an orchard. As an apple fell to the ground, Newton wondered if the apple was not just falling, but actually being pulled to the Earth by an invisible force. From this simple but brilliant idea, Newton developed his theory of gravity, a universal force that tries to pull all matter to together. Without gravity, the whole Universe would disintegrate.

Newton showed that the force of gravity is the same everywhere, and that the pull between two things depends on their mass (the amount of matter in them) and the square of the distance between them.

▲ NEWTON'S PRINCIPIA
Newton's *Philosophiae naturalis principia mathematica* (The Mathematical Principles of Natural Philosophy), in which he set out the laws of motion, is the most influential science book ever written.

▶ BAROMETER
By the mid-1600s scientists knew about force and motion, and about gravity. The picture of what made things move was completed when they learned about pressure. In 1644 one of Galileo's students, Evangelista Torricelli, showed that air is not empty space but a substance.

In a famous experiment, Torricelli showed that air has so much substance it can press hard enough to hold up a column of liquid mercury in a tube. In this experiment, Torricelli made the first barometer, the first device for measuring air pressure. Before long, he realized the value of the barometer for forecasting weather.

of experiments – notably rolling balls down slopes – Galileo realized that you do not need force to keep something moving. Exactly the opposite is true. An object will keep moving at the same speed unless a force slows it down. This is why an arrow flies on through the air. It only falls to the ground because the resistance of the air (a force) slows it down enough for gravity (another force) to pull it down. This is the idea of inertia. Galileo realized that there is no real difference between something that is moving at a steady speed and something that is not moving at all – both are unaffected by forces. But to make the object go faster or slower, or begin to move, a force is needed.

Further experiments, this time with swinging weights, led Galileo to a second crucial insight. If something moves faster, then the rate it accelerates depends on the strength of the force moving it faster

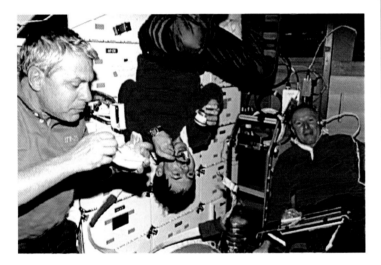

and how heavy the object is. A large force accelerates a light object rapidly, while a small force accelerates a heavy object slowly.

Galileo's ideas made huge leaps in the understanding of force and motion. In 1642, the year he died, another scientific genius, Isaac Newton, was born. It was Newton who drew these ideas together and laid the basis of the science of dynamics. In his remarkable book *Philosophiae naturalis principia mathematica* (The Mathematical Principles of Natural Philosophy), published in 1684, Newton established three fundamental laws, which together account for all types of motion.

The first two laws were Galileo's two insights about inertia and acceleration. Newton's third law showed that whenever a force pushes or pulls on one thing, it must push or pull on another thing equally in the opposite direction (see below). Newton's three laws gave scientists a clear understanding of how force and motion are related, and a way of analyzing them mathematically. Morever, together with Newton's insight into the force of gravity (the pull between two things), these laws seemed to account for every single movement in the Universe, large or small – from the jumping of a flea to the movements of the planets.

◀ WEIGHTLESSNESS
In a spaceship orbiting the Earth, the crew floats weightless. You might think that gravity is not working, just as Newton had predicted. The reality is that gravity is in fact still acting as a force, but the spaceship is hurtling round the Earth so fast that its effects are cancelled out.

▼ THE THREE LAWS
Newton's laws of motion are involved in every single movement in the Universe. They can be seen in action in a frog jumping from a lily pad.

Newton's first law says an object accelerates (or decelerates) only when a force is applied. In other words, you need force to make a still object move (inertia) or to make a moving object slow down or speed up (momentum). To jump from the lily pad, the frog needs to use the force of its leg muscles.

The second law says that the acceleration depends on the size of the force and the object's mass. So the frog will take off faster if it gives a stronger kick (or is less heavy).

The third law says that when a force pushes or acts one way, an equal force pushes in the opposite direction. So as the frog takes off, its kick pushes the lily pad back.

Key Dates

- 1638 Galileo publishes his theories on speed and forces.

- 1644 Evangelista Torricelli demonstrates the reality of air pressure and invents the barometer.

- 1646 Blaise Pascal shows how air pressure drops the higher you go.

- 1650 Otto von Guericke invents the air pump.

- 1660 Robert Boyle shows how the volume and pressure of a gas vary.

- 1686 Newton publishes his work *The Mathematical Principles of Natural Philosophy*. It contains his theory of gravity and three laws of motion.

Atoms and Matter

▲ JOSEPH PRIESTLEY
Joseph Priestley (1733–1804) is the English scientist who discovered the gas in air that Lavoisier later called oxygen. This is the gas we need to breathe, and fire needs to burn.

THANKS TO NEWTON AND Galileo, scientists in the 17th century knew a lot about how and why things moved, but they knew little about what things are made of. In ancient Greece 2,000 years earlier, philosophers thought all substances were made of just four basic things, or elements – earth, water, air and fire. In the Middle Ages men called alchemists had tried heating and mixing substances to see how to change one into another. They discovered new substances such as nitric acid and sulphuric acid, but still agreed with the idea of four elements.

The first chemist to really doubt this idea was Irishman Robert Boyle (1627–1691), who carried out experiments with all kinds of substances. In his book *The Sceptical Chemist*, Boyle suggested that everything is made from a handful of basic substances, or "elements", each made up from a tiny lump called an "elementary corpuscle". Boyle believed that all the substances in the world are compounds made from these corpuscles joined together in different ways.

▼ LAVOISIER IN HIS LABORATORY
Lavoisier's carefully weighed experiments showed that air, one of the four basic elements of the ancient Greeks, is actually a mixture of different gases, mainly oxygen and nitrogen. He also showed that another of the basic elements, water, is a compound of hydrogen and oxygen.

DALTON AND ATOMIC THEORY

The idea that all matter is really made of tiny particles called atoms was first suggested by the Greek philosopher Democritus in the 5th century BC. Later, in the 17th century, it was championed by Boyle with his elementary corpuscles.

The English chemist John Dalton (1766–1844) put forward the first real atomic theory and gave the first proof of it. By comparing the relative weights of the elements in different samples of different compounds (chemical combinations of elements), Dalton was able to deduce how much an atom of each element actually weighs.

DALTON'S MODEL OF WATER MOLECULES

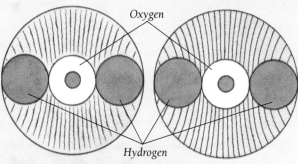

Oxygen

Hydrogen

▲ DALTON'S ATOMIC MODEL
Dalton's theory showed that compounds are formed when the atoms of one element join with the atoms of another. Dalton believed that water was made when a hydrogen atom links with an oxygen atom. Italian physicist Amedio Avogadro later showed that each atom of oxygen joined with two hydrogen atoms, not one, to make water.

▼ DALTON'S ELEMENTS.
In 1808 Dalton published the first list of chemicals, complete with his estimated weights for individual atoms, or "atomic weights".

▶ MINER'S FRIEND
With the idea of chemical elements established, chemists raced to discover new ones. Dalton's 1803 notebooks show just 20 elements. By 1830 chemists knew of 55. Flamboyant English scientist Sir Humphry Davy (1778–1829) discovered sodium and potassium, and showed that chlorine and aluminium were elements. Davy is best remembered for inventing the miner's safety lamp, which greatly reduced the risk of explosions underground.

The alchemists believed that one substance could be changed into another – that was why they had searched for the "philosopher's stone", a substance that would transform ordinary "base" metal into gold. If Boyle's theory of elements was true, the alchemists were wrong; substances could only be mixed together differently, but not actually changed. The scene was set for a controversy that raged throughout the 18th century.

The debate focused on burning. If you look at wood turning to ash as it burns, or at metal turning rusty, the alchemists argued, it seems quite clear that substances can change. An alchemist called Georg Stahl suggested in the early 18th century that anything burnable contains a special "active" substance called phlogiston, which dissolves into the air when it burns. If this is so, anything that burns must surely become lighter as it loses phlogiston. Does this happen?

A French chemist Antoine Lavoisier (1743–1794) realized that the way to settle the argument was to weigh substances carefully before and after burning. In a brilliant experiment, Lavoisier burned a piece of tin inside a sealed container. The tin was actually heavier after burning – contrary to the phlogiston theory – but the air became lighter. So there was really no change in weight at all – substances were simply changing places! It was also clear that rather than losing something (phlogiston) to the air, the tin was taking something from it. Lavoisier later realized this was the gas oxygen, that had recently been discovered in England by scientist Joseph Priestley.

Lavoisier's experiment was a turning point in our understanding of matter for three reasons. First, it put accurate scientific measurement firmly at the heart of chemistry. Second, it demolished the phlogiston theory and showed that burning is a process involving oxygen. Third, it showed that substances do not change even in a process as dramatic as burning; they simply change places. So Lavoisier put Boyle's idea of elements firmly on the map. Indeed, he made the first real list of chemical elements. Quite rightly, he has been called the father of modern chemistry.

◀ MENDELEYEV
Dmitri Mendeleyev was a Russian chemist who lived from 1834 to 1907. In the 1860s he realized that if the 60 elements known then were arranged in order of increasing atomic weight, then elements with similar chemical characteristics could be arranged in eight neat vertical groups. This arrangement, later known as the periodic table, has become central to our understanding of the elements. Scientists today continue to use Mendeleyev's table to assist them in their work and experiments.

Key Dates

- 1661 Robert Boyle introduces the idea of elements and compounds.

- 1756 Joseph Black deduces the presence of carbon dioxide in the air.

- 1774 Joseph Priestley discovers many new gases, including ammonia.

- 1784 Henry Cavendish shows water is a compound of hydrogen and oxygen.

- 1789 Lavoisier writes the first list of elements and disproves the phlogiston theory.

- 1808 John Dalton proposes his atomic theory of chemical elements.

- 1818 Jöns Bezelius publishes the first table of atomic weights for the elements.

Factory and Furnace

▲ IRON BRIDGE
Iron was the new material of the Industrial Age. In 1779 the first all-iron bridge was built in Coalbrookdale in Shropshire.

UNTIL 1750, MOST people lived in country villages, raising animals and growing crops. Then two great revolutions started in Britain and changed things forever. A revolution in farming drove poor labourers off the land. A revolution in industry saw cottage crafts give way to great factories. People who were driven off the land came to work in the factories, and the first great industrial cities grew up.

These revolutions were fuelled by the growth of European colonies and trade around the world. Colonies were vast new markets for goods such as clothes and cutlery. In the past people had made things slowly by hand. Now enterprising men realized they could make a fortune by producing huge quantities of goods quickly and cheaply for the new markets. They began to invent machines to speed things up, increase production and reduce the number of people to be paid.

At first, the clothing industry was the main focus. Traditionally, yarn was made by spinning together fibres, such as cotton, with a foot-driven spinning wheel. Cloth was made from yarn by weaving it on a loom by hand.

THE COMING OF WATERWAYS
The traditional horse and cart could not transport all the goods produced by the new factories, and within a few decades thousands of kilometres of massive canals were built across Europe. Using thousands of construction workers these canals were then the biggest, most complex things ever built by humans.

▶ NEWCOMEN'S ENGINE
Newcomen's 1712 beam engine was the first practical steam engine. Steam drove a piston up and down to rock the beam that pumped water from the mines. It was heavy on coal but worked.

◀ SEVERN CANAL
The great canal-building era began in 1761 with James Brindley's Bridgewater Canal from Manchester. Soon the Grand Trunk Canal linked the rivers Mersey and Trent, and the Severn Canal linked the Thames and Bristol Channel. The area around Birmingham became the hub of a national canal network.

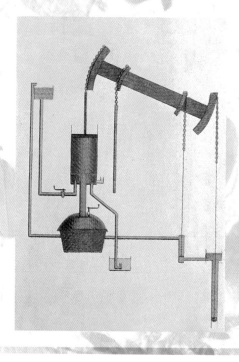

Then in 1733, John Kay built a machine called a flying shuttle. Kay's shuttle wove cloth so fast that the spinners could not make enough yarn. In 1764 Lancashire weaver James Hargreaves created the spinning jenny to spin yarn on eight spindles at once. This was a machine for home use, but a bigger breakthrough was Richard Arkwright's water frame of 1766. The water frame was a spinning machine driven by a water wheel. In 1771 Arkwright installed a series of water frames in a mill in Cromford in Derbyshire, England, to create the world's first large factory.

The early factories were water powered, but could they be powered by steam? Steam would be more powerful and there would be no need to locate factories by rivers. Thomas Savery had created a steam engine for pumping water out of mines in 1698, and a version developed by Newcomen in the 1720s was installed in many mines. Newcomen's engine was expensive to run, but in the 1780s James Watt created a cheaper engine. It gave power anywhere, and steam engines soon took over in factories.

The success of steam power depended on machine tools to shape metal, such as John Wilkinson's 1775 metal borer, and on iron and coal. Coal produced heat to make, or "smelt", iron. In the past iron had been smelted with charcoal. Then, in 1713, Abraham Darby found out how to smelt with coke, a kind of processed coal. Soon huge amounts of iron were churned out by coke-smelters. The combination of big steam-powered machines, cheap iron and coal proved unstoppable, and the quiet rural ways gave way to the big cities and noisy factories.

▼ THE INDUSTRIAL TOWN

The vast new towns of the Industrial Revolution, such as Birmingham and Leeds, were different from any town before. Noisy, smoky factories loomed over neatly packed rows of tiny brick houses – home to tens of thousands of factory workers. The coming of the railways in the 1840s completed the picture.

▶ ARKWRIGHT'S WATER FRAME

The Industrial Revolution got under way with the invention of numerous ingenious machines for making cloth. The crucial breakthrough was the move from machines powered by humans or horses alone, to machines powered first by massive waterwheels and later by steam. The invention of a cotton-spinning machine called a frame by Sir Richard Arkwright (1732–1792) in 1766 was a turning point. Arkwright had originally designed the spinners to be turned by horsepower. Then in 1771 he adapted it to run on water power, which is why it came to be called the water frame.

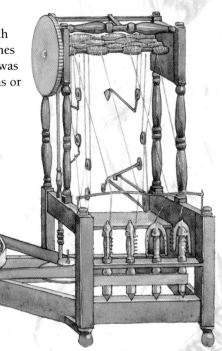

Key Dates

- 1698 Thomas Savery invents the first practical steam engine.

- 1722 Thomas Newcomen improves the steam engine.

- 1713 Abraham Darby smelts iron with coke.

- 1733 John Kay invents the flying shuttle weaving machine.

- 1764 James Hargreaves invents the spinning jenny to spin yarn.

- 1766 Richard Arkwright invents the water frame for spinning by water power.

- 1782 James Watt creates a cheap-to-run steam engine for powering machines.

The Charged World

▲ MICHAEL FARADAY
(1791–1867)
The son of a blacksmith, Michael Faraday grew up to become one of the greatest experimental scientists of all time. He laid the foundation of our knowledge of electricity and magnetism.

IT WOULD BE HARD TO IMAGINE a world without electricity. Not only is it the energy that powers everything from toasters to televisions, but it is one of the fundamental forces in the Universe that holds all matter together. Yet until the late 18th century scientists knew almost nothing about electricity. The ancient Greeks knew that when you rubbed a kind of resin called amber with cloth it attracts fluff. The word "electricity" comes from *elektron*, the Greek word for amber. For thousands of years amber attraction was considered a minor curiosity.

In the 18th century scientists such as the French chemist Charles Dufay (1698–1739) and English physicist Stephen Gray (1666–1736) began to investigate electricity. They soon discovered, not only that various substances could conduct (transmit) the same attraction to fluff as amber, but also that rubbing two similar substances together made them repel each other, not attract. This attraction and repulsion came to be called positive and negative electrical "charge".

▶ THE DYNAMO
The discovery of the link between electricity and magnetism led to the development of the dynamo. It could generate electricity by turning magnets between electrical coils. In 1873 Belgian Zénobe Gramme built the first practical generator. By 1882 power stations were supplying electric power to both London and New York.

By the mid-1700s some machines could generate quite large charges when a handle was turned to rub glass on sulphur. The charge could even be stored in a special glass jar called a Leyden jar – then suddenly let out via a metal chain to create a spark. Seeing these sparks, American statesman and inventor Benjamin Franklin (1706–1790) wondered if they were the same as lightning. He attached a metal chain like that of a Leyden jar to a kite sent up in a thunderstorm. The lightning sent a spark from the chain – only much bigger than expected – and Franklin was lucky to survive.

ELECTRICAL PROGRESS

Faraday's and Henry's discovery of a way to generate electricity may have transformed our lives more than any other single scientific discovery. For thousands of years, people had seen at night by candle light, kept in touch with messages carried on foot or horseback and heard music only when someone played an instrument near them. The discovery of electricity changed all this.

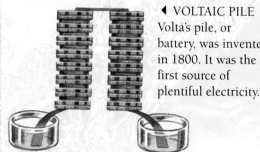

◀ VOLTAIC PILE
Volta's pile, or battery, was invented in 1800. It was the first source of plentiful electricity.

▲ EDISON'S PHONOGRAPH
The first record player, Edison's phonograph of 1877, was mechanical. The arrival of electrical sound recording in the 1920s, including sound on TV and film, made sound and music more accessible.

▲ EDISON'S ELECTRIC LIGHT BULB
The electric light bulb was invented independently by Sir Joseph Swan in the UK in 1878, and by Thomas Edison in the USA in 1879.

▶ FARADAY AT WORK
*Michael Faraday spent his life working at the
Royal Institution in London, where his exciting
and brilliantly clear public demonstrations of
the latest electrical discoveries were famous.
For one show he built a big metal cage. He
stepped inside it with his instruments while his
assistant charged up the cage to 100,000 volts
– a terrifying crackle of sparks ran around it.
Faraday knew that he would be safe inside the
cage because the charge courses around the
outside. Such electrically safe cocoons are now
called Faraday cages.*

People were so excited by Franklin's
discovery that demonstrations of
electrical effects became very
fashionable. When Italian anatomist
Luigi Galvani (1737–1798) found that
a dead frog's legs hung on a railing
twitched in a thunderstorm, people
wondered if they had found the very
force of life itself – animal electricity. Alessandro Volta
(1745–1827) realized that it was not the life force that
made the electricity to twitch the frog's legs, but simply
a chemical in the metal railing. Soon scientists realized
that an electrical charge could be made to flow in a
circular path from one side, or "terminal", of a battery
to the other.

The real breakthrough, however, was the discovery
of the link between electricity and magnetism. In 1819,
Danish physicist Hans Øersted suggested that an
electrical current has a magnetic effect, turning the
needle of a compass. Little more than a decade later
Joseph Henry (1797–1878) in America and Michael
Faraday (1791–1867) in Britain proved that the
opposite is in fact true – that it is actually a magnet that
has an electrical effect. When a magnet is moved near
an electric circuit, it generates a surge of electricity in
the circuit. Using this principle – called electromagnetic
induction – huge machines could be built to generate
large quantities of electricity. The way was now open for
the development of every modern appliance from
electric lighting to the Internet.

▲ ALEXANDER BELL
Bell (1847–1922) was the Scottish-born
American inventor of the telephone and
a pioneer of sound recording.

▼ THE FIRST TELEPHONE
When Alexander Bell invented
the telephone in 1876, electric
telegraphs were already widely
used to send messages along an
electric cable, simply by
switching the current on and off.
Bell found a way of carrying the
vibrations of the voice in a
similar electric signal.

Key Dates

- 250BC Parthians invent the battery.
- 1710s Stephen Gray transmits electricity 100m along a silk thread.
- 1752 Benjamin Franklin shows that lightning is electricity.
- 1800 Alessandro Volta makes the first modern battery.
- 1819 Hans Øersted discovers an electric current creates a magnetic field.
- 1820 Georg Ohm shows that the flow of an electric current depends on the resistance of a wire.
- 1830 Joseph Henry and Michael Faraday discover how an electrical current can be generated by magnetism.

Steam Power

▲ TREVITHICK'S STEAM
LOCOMOTIVE
*The age of modern powered land
transport began in 1804 with
Trevithick's locomotive, the world's
first steam railway locomotive. It
ran on a mine track in Wales.*

FOR TENS OF thousands of years, human beings had managed with the power provided by wind, water or sheer muscle. Then with the Industrial Revolution of the 18th century came the first steam engines, bringing huge amounts of controllable, and reliable power.

The idea of using steam for power dates back to the 1st century AD, to an ancient Greek mathematician called Hero from Alexandria in Egypt. He came up with the idea of using jets of steam to rotate a kettle-like vessel. However, it was not until the 18th century that steam engines became a practical reality.

Most of the early steam engines, including those built by James Watt, were fixed engines, which provided power for working machines and pumps in factories and mines. Then in 1769 a French army engineer called Nicolas-Joseph Cugnot (1725–1804) built a massive three-wheeled cart that was driven along by a steam engine at walking pace.

The problem with using steam to drive vehicles such as this was that steam engines were incredibly heavy. Weight though, would not be a problem in boats. In 1783 the Marquis Claude de Jouffroy d'Abbans, a French nobleman, built a massive steamboat that churned up the Saone River near Lyon, in France, for 15 minutes before the pounding of the engines shook it to bits. The boat sailed only once, but in 1787 John Fitch, an American inventor, made the first successful steamboat with an engine driving a

▲ THE ROCKET
In Stephenson's famous *Rocket* the cylinder that drove the wheels was almost horizontal. This made it so powerful that it easily won the first locomotive speed trials in 1829.

THE FIRST PASSENGER RAILWAYS
The first steam locomotives were built to haul coal trucks around mines. On 27 September 1825 a father and son, George and Robert Stephenson, ran the first passenger train from Darlington to Stockton in the north of England. Over 450 people rode in the train's open wagons that day, pulled by the Stephensons' locomotive *Active* (later renamed *Locomotion*), and the 13km journey was completed in just 30 minutes. The railway age had begun.

▲ THE LIVERPOOL AND MANCHESTER
The 64km-long Liverpool and Manchester railway, which opened on 15 September 1830, was the first real passenger railway. On the opening day, it also claimed the first railway casualty: Home Secretary William Huskisson was killed under the wheels of a locomotive.

series of paddles on each side of the boat. In 1790 Fitch started the world's first steam service on the Delaware River. In 1802, in Scotland, another steam pioneer William Symington (1763–1831) built a steam tug, the *Charlotte Dundas*. It was so powerful that it could pull two 70-ton barges.

The steamboat really arrived when American engineer Robert Fulton (1765–1815) made the first successful passenger steamboats in 1807. They carried people 240km up the Hudson River between New York and Albany. This journey, which took four days by sailing ship, took Fulton's steamboats less than a day.

Three years earlier, Cornish engineer Richard Trevithick had shown that heavy steam vehicles – or "locomotives" as they came to be called – could move more easily on rails. In 1804 he fired up the world's first steam railway

locomotive at Pendarren ironworks in Wales. Even rails did not solve the problem at once, because Trevithick's locomotive cracked the cast-iron tracks. But the success of the concept was clear. Cast-iron rails were soon replaced with wrought-iron and, later, steel rails that could take much more weight. Within 15 years steam locomotives were running on short railways all over Britain. The age of steam travel had begun.

▲ HMS *THESEUS*
Steamships gained in power and reliability and, in the 1880s many navies began to build steam-power warships like HMS Theseus.

◀ *THE GREAT EASTERN*
In 1819 the New York-built Savannah, *a sailing ship equipped with a steam engine, made the first Atlantic crossing using steam power. The age of regular transatlantic steam passenger services began in 1837 with the launch of the* Great Western, *one of three giant steam ships designed by British engineer Isambard Kingdom Brunel. Brunel's* Great Eastern, *launched in 1858, was the biggest ship launched in the 1800s – 211m long and weighing almost 19,000 tons.*

▶ STEAM SPEED
Steam locomotives were the cutting edge of technology in Victorian Britain. Brilliant men such as James Nasmyth (1808–1890) went into locomotive design in the same way that talented designers are now drawn into electronic and space technology. As a result, steam locomotives rapidly became more and more efficient.

By the 1880s trains were running the 640km from London to Edinburgh in little more than 7 hours, often hitting speeds of over 110kmh. Just 40 years earlier the journey had taken 12 gruelling days in a coach.

Key Dates

- 1783 Claude d'Abbans sails the first steamboat on the Saone near Lyon in France.

- 1804 Richard Trevithick builds first steam-powered railway locomotive.

- 1807 Robert Fulton opens the first passenger steamboat service.

- 1819 The *Savannah* makes the first steam-powered crossing of the Atlantic.

- 1823 George and Robert Stephenson begin to build railway locomotives.

- 1825 Stockton and Darlington railway opens.

- 1830 Liverpool and Manchester railway opens.

The Story of Life

▲ CHARLES DARWIN
Charles Darwin (1809–1882) was one of the most influential scientists of his day. His theory of evolution is one of the most important ever scientific breakthroughs.

IN THE 18TH CENTURY travellers returning to Europe brought news of thousands of previously unknown plants and animals which they had found on their travels around the world. To try and make sense of these finds, the great Swedish botanist Carl Linnaeus (1707–1778) devised a system of classifying plants and animals into the many species and genera (groups of species) that we still use today.

People began to wonder how all this variety of life had come to be. Perhaps the variety had developed, little by little, over time, but how did this gradual development, or evolution, work? How did new species appear? In 1808 a French naturalist called Jean Lamarck suggested that it happened because animals can change during their lives. For example, organs and muscles which are used a lot become stronger. In this way useful developments are then passed on to an animal's offspring. This was the first proper theory of evolution, but few people were convinced as they could see that strong parents could produce weak offspring.

▼ DINOSAUR SKELETON
Darwin's theory of evolution arose partly from the first discovery in the 1820s and 1830s of the fossilized bones of huge extinct reptiles that came to be called dinosaurs. In 1824, William Buckland found the jaw of Megalosaurus. The following year, Gideon Mantell found a giant tooth of a creature he called Iguanodon. Soon many more dinosaur fossils were found.

DARWIN'S THEORY
Darwin's theory depends on the fact that no two living things are alike. Some may start life with features that make them better able to survive. For example, an animal might have long legs to help it escape predators. Individuals with such valuable features have a better chance of surviving and having offspring that inherit these features. Slowly, over many generations, better adapted animals and plants survive and flourish, while others die out or find a new home. In this way, all the millions of species that we know about today gradually evolved.

▼ THE EVOLUTION OF THE HORSE
Species may die out, but they leave behind similar but better adapted offspring species. The earliest horse, called Eohippus or "dawn horse", was tiny – only 25–50cm high at the shoulder – and had four toes on each of its front feet. Fossils have shown that a chain of about 30 species, spread over 60 million years, led step by step from Eohippus to the modern horse. Each species is slightly bigger and has fewer toes than its ancestors.

Hyracotherium Mesohippus Merychippus Equus

In the 1820s and 1830s geologists and naturalists made a series of discoveries that were to pave the way for a new theory of evolution, proposed by Erasmus Darwin's grandson Charles. Geologists discovered that the Earth was much older than had previously been thought, and that the landscape of today has evolved over millions of years. At the same time, naturalists discovered more fossils of long dead creatures, including dinosaurs, showing that many more species had once lived on Earth than are alive today.

Charles Darwin made a long trip around the world on a ship called the *Beagle*, on which he was employed as a botanist. He began to develop a theory of evolution which depended on species developing as gradually as the landscape. He found an explanation for how this happened in the ideas of the economist Thomas Malthus, who suggested that when populations grow too big for the available resources the weak slowly die out. In the same way, Darwin suggested, species slowly

▲ THE VOYAGE OF THE *BEAGLE*
Between 1831 and 1836, Darwin travelled aboard HMS Beagle *as it voyaged around the world on a scientific expedition. He studied plants and animals everywhere the ship landed, including on the Galapagos Islands in the Pacific. While Darwin was sorting through the material that he brought back he developed the idea of evolution.*

◀ UNIQUE WILDLIFE
This is a giant tortoise that lives on the Galapagos Islands (Galapagos means "giant tortoise"). Here Darwin found wildlife unique to the islands.

evolve by natural selection as they compete for limited resources – with only the fittest surviving.

English naturalist Alfred Wallace (1823–1913) independently proposed a theory of evolution similar to Darwin's, and they published their ideas jointly in 1858. It was Darwin's research that gave the theory substance, which is why it is called Darwin's theory. Many people were shocked by Darwin's ideas, but his evidence was hard to ignore and his theory gradually gained acceptance. Most scientists today see it as one of the greatest-ever scientific breakthroughs.

These finches have longer, thinner beaks for catching insects.

These finches have short, stout beaks for cracking seeds. The bird on the right, has evolved a slightly longer beak as it eats both insects and seeds.

▲ THE GALAPAGOS FINCHES
When Darwin landed in the Galapagos Islands in the Pacific he found slightly different species of finch on each island. These small but significant variations made it clear to Darwin that species must gradually change through time. He thought species changed in different ways in different places, even if they start the same.

Key Dates

- 1735 Carl Linnaeus groups plants into different species, and sub-groups.

- 1788 James Hutton realizes the Earth is many millions of years old.

- 1801 Jean Lamarck proposes that animal species evolve in response to their habitat.

- 1820s William Buckland and Gideon Mantell discover the first fossils of dinosaurs.

- 1830 Charles Lyell's *Principles of Natural Geology* shows that landscapes evolved gradually.

- 1858 Charles Darwin and Alfred Wallace suggest the theory of evolution by natural selection.

On the Road

▲ THE MODEL T
Cars were toys for the rich in the early days. Then the age of mass motoring dawned in 1908, when Henry Ford launched the Model T Ford, the world's first mass-produced car. By assembling the car on a moving production line from standardized parts, the Model T could be made so cheaply that people barely able to afford a horse and buggy could easily buy a car. Within five years, 250,000 Americans owned a Model T.

THE STORY OF THE motor car really began in the summer of 1862, when Frenchman Étienne Lenoir drove his small self-propelled cart out through the forests of Vincennes, near Paris, with its small engine slowly thumping. Lenoir's was not the first powered car however. At the Chinese court a Jesuit priest called Padre Verbiest built one as long ago as 1672. Nicolas Cugnot built one in 1769, and over the next 100 years there were many others, including Goldsworthy Gurney's famous steam carriages. The problem was that all of these vehicles were powered by steam engines, which tended to be either cumbersome or very expensive to make.

Lenoir's breakthrough was to make a neat little engine that worked by internal combustion – that is, by

▲ FIRST CARS
The idea of steam cars seems quaint nowadays, but many of the first successful motor cars were driven by steam. The steam engine was, after all, a tried and tested form of engine.

burning gas inside a cylinder. Lenoir's gas internal combustion engine was much lighter because it needed neither a tank of water nor a bunker of coal. He set up his engine on an old horse cart so that it drove the

HISTORY OF CARS

Cars have come a long way Since the Benz Motorwagen rolled out of the works in 1888. The earliest cars were coach built, one by one, for the rich, but the Ford Model T showed that mass production was the way forwards. By the 1930s mass production meant many ordinary people could afford cars, but the rich still had coach-built beauties. Cars then were designed mostly by experience and trial-and-error. Car design today relies more on the computer.

▲ 1886 DAIMLER
Gottlieb Daimler was one of the pioneers of motoring. Unlike Benz, who set out to build a motor vehicle from scratch, Daimler fitted an engine to a horse carriage. Like many of the first cars, this had wooden-spoked wheels like a horse cart.

▼ 1901 OLDSMOBILE
This was one of the most popular cars of its time. The Oldsmobile was made by the American Ransom Eli Olds (1864-1950). His 1901 Oldsmobile was steered with a tiller like a boat, rather than with a steering wheel. Many early cars used this means of steering.

▲ MORRIS OXFORD
Millions of Americans had their own cars by the 1920s, thanks to Ford. In the rest of the world cars were still costly. Prices did come down, and soon middle-class families were buying modest saloons such as the Austin Ten, the Opel Kadett and the Morris.

◄ MAN WITH FLAG
After a few accidents early on, cars were seen as highly dangerous machines. For 30 years from 1865, the "Red Flag" Act meant that motor vehicles in Britain had to be preceded by a man on foot waving a red flag. It was not until 1896 that this restriction was lifted and the speed limit raised to 19kmh. New York had a Red Flag Act until 1901.

wheels via a chain around the axles. Another Frenchman, Alphonse Beau de Rochas, soon improved the efficiency of Lenoir's engine by using an extra movement, or "stroke", of the piston to squeeze the gas before burning it, making a four-stroke engine. Four-stroke engines are the engines still used in most cars today.

A few years later an Austrian called Siegfried Marcus managed to make an internal combustion engine that ran on petrol instead of gas. His secret was to create a simple but ingenious device called a carburettor, which turned the petrol into vapour. In 1873, Marcus built what is now thought to be the world's oldest petrol-engined car.

It had wheels like a cart, but a small steering wheel. It looked more like a car than a horse cart with an engine.

Despite these successes, petrol-engined cars were still at the experimental stage. Many people believed the future of the car lay with tried and tested steam engines. Indeed the land speed record was broken in 1906 not by a petrol-engined car but by a steam car, the Stanley steamer, travelling at an astonishing 206kmh! The breakthrough for the petrol engine came with the three-wheel car developed by German engineer Karl Benz and his wife Berta in the 1880s. In 1888, the Benz Patent-Motorwagen became the first motor car ever made for sale to the public. It was such a success that within a decade the Benz factory in Mannheim was turning out 600 cars a year. The age of the motor car had begun.

▲ FUTURISTIC CAR
Motor manufacturers are always trying to improve their cars. Top speed, fuel economy, safety, and looking good are all important factors to consider. Manufacturers want to find a car that balances these elements.

▲ VOLKSWAGEN BEETLE
The biggest selling car ever, the Volkswagen "Beetle", was developed in Germany in the 1940s as a compact and affordable "people's car".

▲ MORRIS MINI
The 1959 Mini was the first tiny family car. To save space, its designer Alex Issigonis placed the engine across the car, to drive the front wheels.

► MCLAREN F1
Designed to be the ultimate road-going car, plans for Gordon Murray's McLaren F1 were released to the public in March 1989. It has a top speed of 231mph.

Key Dates

- 1672 Padre Verbiest builds the world's first steam carriage in China.

- 1769 Nicolas Cugnot builds three-wheeled steam carriage.

- 1862 Étienne Lenoir builds the first vehicle powered by an internal combustion engine.

- 1865 Alphonse Beau de Rochas builds first four-stroke internal combustion engine.

- 1873 Siegfried Marcus builds the first petrol-powered car.

- 1888 Karl Benz builds the world's first petrol-engined car for sale.

- 1908 Henry Ford launches the first mass-produced car, the Ford Model T.

Off the Ground

▲ ORVILLE WRIGHT
Orville Wright was at the controls of his plane, the Flyer, *for the world's first controlled flight. He was the younger of the two Wright brothers. He was born in 1871, in Dayton, Ohio, and died in 1948.*

THERE WAS PROBABLY NEVER a time when people did not look up and long to fly like the birds. In ancient Greece there was a myth about an inventor called Daedalus, who made himself wings of feathers and flew high in the sky. Long after, there were those who believed they could mimic the birds and their flapping wings. In the Middle Ages, many a reckless pioneer strapped on wings and launched themselves over cliffs and from high towers – only to plummet to the ground.

In the 15th century the brilliant Italian artist and thinker Leonardo da Vinci designed a flying machine with pedal-power wings, which he called an "ornithopter". It was never built and would never have flown, because it was far too heavy. Men did get off the ground every now and then. In ancient China the military lifted lookouts aloft on giant kites over 3,000 years ago.

In 1783 two men were carried high in the air over Paris in a giant paper balloon made by the Montgolfier brothers. It was filled with hot air, which rises because it is less dense than cold air. Both kites and balloons were at the mercy of the wind, however, and many inventors believed the future of flight lay with wings.

The great pioneer of winged flight was the British engineer Sir George Cayley (1773–1857). After a series of experiments with kites, Cayley worked out that a wing lifts because when it curves this boosts air pressure underneath, and reduces it above. All modern aircraft are based on the kite-like model glider Cayley built in 1804, with its up-angled front wing and stabilizing tail. In 1853, at the age of 80, he built a full-size glider which is said to have carried his terrified coachman through the air for several hundred metres.

After Cayley, various experimenters tried their luck with gliders. No one

▶ THE WRIGHT BROTHER'S FIRST FLIGHT
One of the secrets of the Wright brothers' success at Kitty Hawk was their development of a way to stop the plane from rolling from side to side – something that had proved the downfall of many earlier planes. Their Flyer *had wires to "warp", or twist, the wings to lift one side or the other. This meant that it could not only fly level but also make balanced, banked turns.*

FLYING AHEAD

When Wilbur Wright took their plane, the *Flyer*, to France in 1908, it was clear that the Wrights were far head of pioneers in Europe, such as Louis Blériot. Before long, aircraft were making rapid progress everywhere. On 25 July 1909, Blériot flew across the English Channel. The military demands of World War 1, which began in 1914, gave a tremendous boost to aircraft development. By the time the war was over in 1918, aircraft were reliable enough for the first regular passenger flights to begin.

▶ FIRST HANG-GLIDER
The Wright brothers' ideas on control in flight were preceded in the 1890s by Otto Lilienthal's pioneering flights with craft such as hang-gliders. Sadly, Lilienthal was killed flying in 1896.

▲ 1917 BIPLANE
The fighter aircraft of World War 1 were incredibly flimsy machines, made of fabric stretched over a wooden frame. They were usually biplanes – they had two sets of wings – because single wings were far too fragile.

▲ JUMBO JET
The age of mass air travel began with the first jet airliner, the Comet 4, in 1952. Now millions of people fly each year in giant jets such as the Boeing 747 jumbo jet. These aircraft fly high above the clouds and winds so the journey is smooth and comfortable.

had any idea how to control their craft in the air until, in the 1890s, a brave young German called Otto Lilienthal built a series of fragile gliders rather like modern hang-gliders. He succeeded in making the world's first controlled flights in them.

With a glider, a person could fly on wings at last, but not for long. What was needed for sustained flight was an engine. As long ago as 1845 two Englishmen, William Henson and John Stringfellow, built a working model of a plane powered by a lightweight steam engine, which may well have made a successful trial flight. Steam engines were too weak or too heavy, and it was the development of the petrol engine that proved to be the breakthrough. Even with a petrol engine a single wing did not provide enough lift, so experimenters tried adding more and more wings.

Then, one cold Thursday in December 1903 at Kitty Hawk in the USA, a petrol-engined, biplane (double-winged) flying machine built by the brothers Orville and Wilbur Wright rose shakily into the air. It flew 40m and then landed safely. It was the world's first controlled, powered, sustained flight.

▼ CONCORDE
By the time the Anglo-French Concorde was built in the 1960s, millions of people were being zoomed around the world each year in high-speed jet airliners. Concorde remains the only successful airliner to carry passengers at supersonic speeds, that is well above the speed of sound.

▶ STEALTH BOMBER
In 1988, after years of secret development, the US Air Force unveiled its B-2 "stealth" bomber – the most advanced military plane in the world at the time. This sinister-looking aircraft is designed to fly at incredibly high speeds at low altitudes – and be almost invisible to enemy radar. A few years later, it was joined by the F-117 "stealth" fighter. Stealth bombers were used heavily in 1999 in the US bombing raids on Serbia and Kosovo.

Key Dates

- 1783 Two men fly in the Montgolfier brothers' hot-air balloon.

- 1804 Sir George Cayley builds a model kite with wings and a tail.

- 1853 Cayley builds a full-size glider.

- 1890 Clement Ader makes the first powered flight in a steam-powered plane, the *Eole*.

- 1896 Samuel Langley flies 1km in his steam-powered *Aerodrome*.

- 1903 Orville and Wilbur Wright make the first controlled, powered flight in the *Flyer*.

- 1909 Louis Blériot flies across the English Channel.

Rays and Radiation

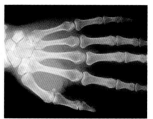

▲ SEE-THROUGH HAND
X-rays reveal the bones inside a living hand because they shine straight through skin and muscle, and are only blocked by bone.

IN 1864 SCOTTISH SCIENTIST James Clark Maxwell made the brilliant deduction that light is a kind of wave created by the combined effects of electricity and magnetism. He also predicted that light might just be one of many kinds of "electromagnetic" radiation. Scientists were keen to find out, and in 1888 German physicist Heinrich Hertz built a circuit to send big sparks across a gap between two metal balls. If Maxwell was right, the sparks would send out waves of electromagnetic radiation. But they might not be visible like light. So Hertz set up another electric circuit to detect them. The waves created pulses of current in this circuit, which Hertz saw as tiny sparks across another gap. By moving the receiving circuit, he worked out just how long the waves were. They proved to be much longer than light waves, and are now known as radio waves.

About the same time, others were experimenting with discharge tubes. Scientists had known for 100 years or more that a bottle from which air is sucked glows eerily if you put electrodes (electric terminals) into it and fire a spark between them. Discharge tubes gave a near-perfect vacuum (space without air), and the spark between the electrodes made the tube glow brightly. Sometimes even the

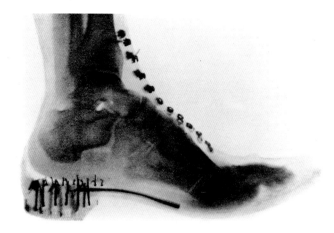

▲ FIRST X-RAY
In 1895, Röntgen shone X-rays through his wife's shoe to make a photo of the bones of her foot inside the shoe.

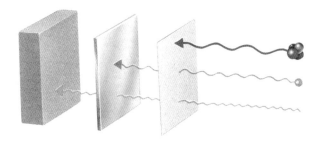

▲ RADIOACTIVITY
We now know that radioactivity is three kinds of particle shot out by atoms as they disintegrate naturally: alpha, beta and gamma particles. Each kind of particle has the power to penetrate different materials.

THE TV TUBE
The cathode-ray tube was not just behind the discovery of electrons and radioactivity. Most TV and computer screens are also cathode-ray tubes. The stream of electrons discovered by Thomson is what makes your TV or computer screen glow.

▼ PRISM AND SPECTRUM
In the 1600s Newton showed that light is made of a spectrum, or range, of different colours. We now know that light itself is part of a much wider spectrum of electromagnetic radiation. The radio waves that beam out TV signals are just part of this spectrum.

▲ BAIRD'S TELEVISION ATTEMPTS
John Logie Baird (1888–1946) was the Scottish inventor who made television a reality. Television had no single inventor, but it was Baird who made the the first true TV pictures in 1926. Baird transmitted TV pictures by telephone line from London to Glasgow in 1928.

▶ THE CURIES IN THEIR LABORATORY
The Curies were among the greatest of all scientific experimenters. Their combination of brilliant insight and exact, patient work led them not only to discover the true nature of radioactivity – radiation from atoms – but to prove it too.

glass glowed. The glowing was named "cathode rays" because it seems to come from the negative terminal, or cathode. If the tube was empty, how was the spark crossing from one electrode to another? In 1897, J. J. Thomson guessed the spark was a stream of tiny bits of atoms, which he called electrons. For the first time, scientists saw that the atom is not just a solid ball, but contains smaller, subatomic particles.

Meanwhile, in 1895 the discharge tube helped Wilhelm Röntgen to discover another kind of radiation. Röntgen found that, even when passed through thick card, some rays from the tube made a sheet of fluorescent material glow. Although card could block out light it could not stop these new mystery rays, which he called X-rays. Within a few weeks he had taken a picture of the bones in his wife's foot by shining X-rays through it and onto a photographic plate.

In the same year French scientist Henri Poincaré was wondering why the glass in discharge tubes often glowed as well as the sparks. Perhaps radiation might be emitted not only by electricity but by certain substances too. Soon, Antoine Becquerel discovered this when he left uranium salts in a dark drawer on photographic paper. A few weeks later there was a perfect image of a copper cross that had been lying on the paper. There was no light or electricity to form the image, so where was the radiation coming from?

Marie and Pierre Curie soon found the intensity of radiation was in exact proportion to the amount of uranium. They realized it must be coming from the uranium atoms themselves, and called this atomic radiation "radioactivity". In fact, not only uranium, but also many other elements are radioactive, including two new elements discovered by the Curies – radium and polonium. Since this crucial discovery many uses for radioactivity have been found, but so too have its dangers. Marie Curie herself died of cancer brought on by overexposure to radioactivity.

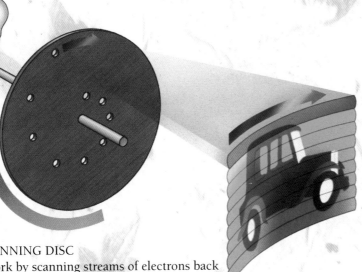

▲ BAIRD'S SPINNING DISC
Modern TVs work by scanning streams of electrons back and forth inside a cathode-ray tube. Baird's system was entirely mechanical, using a rapidly spinning disc drilled with holes. The holes let different parts of the picture shine through onto different light-sensitive electric cells.

Key Dates

- 1864 James Clerk Maxwell says that light is electromagnetic radiation.

- 1888 Heinrich Hertz discovers radio waves.

- 1895 Wilhelm Röntgen discovers X-rays.

- 1897 J. J. Thomson discovers electrons.

- 1897 Antoine Becquerel discovers radioactivity.

- 1898 Marie and Pierre Curie discover the radioactive elements radium and polonium.

- 1898–1900 Ernest Rutherford finds that radioactivity is emissions of alpha, beta and gamma particles.

Space and Time

▲ MICHELSON
Albert Michelson (1852-1931) became the first American scientist to win the Nobel Prize in 1907.

IN 1905, A TALENTED YOUNG scientist called Albert Einstein came up with his special theory of relativity. The theory is not easy to understand, but it has revolutionized the way in which scientists think about space and time. Its origins date back to 1610, when Galileo was thinking about how things moved and described a ship at sea. Shut yourself in a cabin, Galileo suggested, and you see fish in a fish tank swimming in all directions just as easily when the ship is moving as when it is at anchor. For the fish, the ship's motion is irrelevant. In the same way, when you walk around you are never aware that the ground beneath your feet is a planet whizzing through space at 100,000kmh. So we can only detect movement through space in relation to something else.

Half a century later, a Dutch astronomer called Owe Roemer added another dimension to the picture – time. Roemer realized that because the light took ten minutes to travel across space to the Earth, he was seeing the eclipse of Jupiter's moons in 1676 ten minutes after it actually

▲ EINSTEIN AND E=MC²
Einstein's theory of relativity is not just about space and time; it involves energy too. Energy is how vigorously something can move. Something moving fast clearly has a lot of energy, called kinetic energy. The energy of a heavy ball perched on a hilltop is called potential energy. Scientists knew that kinetic and potential energy are interchangeable – the ball might roll downhill, for instance.

Einstein went further and showed that mass, energy and movement are interchangeable. They are swapping over all the time – energy into mass, mass into movement and so on. Since light is the fastest moving thing, it clearly plays an important role in the relationship between energy, mass and movement. Einstein linked them in a famous equation: energy equals mass times the speed of light squared, or $E=mc^2$. This equation shows how a very little mass can give an enormous amount of energy.

TIME MACHINES

Ever since people realized earlier this century that time is just a dimension, many have fantasized about the possibility of travelling backwards or forwards in time. Stories such as H. G. Wells's *The Time Machine* and the films such as the *Back to the Future* series centre on amazing time machines that can whisk you millions of years into the past or the future, or in some cases just a few minutes or days. Scientists are now beginning to think these may not be just pure fantasies. If time is just another dimension, like length and breadth, what is to stop us from travelling in time to visit the past or the future, just as we travel through space? Einstein himself said it was impossible, and though some scientists think we could do it by bending space–time in some way, no one has yet come up with any convincing ideas of just how it might be possible.

◄ DOCTOR WHO'S TARDIS
The popular television series Doctor Who had the time-travelling Doctor moving around time and space in his TARDIS, which was disguised as a police box. TARDIS stands for "Time And Relative Dimensions In Space". The TARDIS is famous because it warps space and time, and is best known for being many times larger inside than it appears to be on the outside.

▶ THE FOURTH DIMENSION

*Einstein's proof that everything is relative upsets
our commonsense idea of time. We see time
passing as one thing happens after another – as
the hands tick round on a clock. It seems time can
move in only one direction, from past to future.
But many laws in science, such as Newton's laws
of motion, work just as well whether time goes
forward or backward. In theory, time could run
backwards just like a video replay. Einstein's
theory showed that this is not just theory, but
reality. Many scientists now prefer to think of
time, not as a one-way train, but as a dimension,
like length, depth and breadth. The three space
dimensions – length, breadth and depth – combine
with the time dimension to make the fourth
dimension of space–time.*

occurred. In the same way, when we see a star four million light-years away, we see it as it was four million years ago. Someone elsewhere in the Universe would see the eclipse at a different time. So the timing of events depends on where you are. If this is true, how do you know which is the right time? Is it the time you set on your watch, or the time your friend on a distant planet sets? The fact is you do not know. You can only tell the time in relation to something else, such as the position of the Sun in the sky or the position of a distant star.

Despite this, 120 years ago most people were sure that behind all this relative time and space there was real, or "absolute", time and real movement. In 1887, two American scientists, Michelson and Morley, set out to prove it with an ingenious experiment. They reasoned that a beam of light moving the same way as the Earth should

whizz along slightly slower than one shooting past the opposite way – just as an overtaking bike passes you more slowly than one coming towards you at the same speed. So they tried to measure the speed of light in different directions. Any difference would show that the Earth was moving absolutely. Yet they detected no difference in the speed of light, in whichever direction they measured it.

Einstein then came to a startling conclusion, which he published as his theory of special relativity. It demolished the idea of absolute time and space for ever. Einstein showed not only that light is the fastest thing in the Universe – but that it always passes you at the same speed, no matter where you are or how fast you are going. You can never catch up with a beam of light. Einstein realized that every measurement must be relative, because not even light can help to give an absolute measurement.

◀ KILLING YOUR GRANDPARENTS

A famous argument against the possibility of time travel is about killing your grandparents. The argument asks, what if you travelled back in time to before your parents were born and killed your grandparents? Then neither your parents nor you could have been born. But if you were never born, who killed your grandparents? This kind of problem is called a paradox. Some scientists get round it with the idea of parallel universes, different versions of history that all exist at the same time, running in parallel.

Key Dates

- 1610 Galileo suggests the idea of relative motion.
- 1676 Owe Roemer realizes that light takes time to reach us across space.
- 1887 Michelson and Morley show that the speed of light is the same in all directions.
- 1900 Max Planck invents quantum theory to explain why radiation varies in steps rather than continuously.
- 1905 Albert Einstein publishes his theory of special relativity.
- 1915 Einstein publishes his theory of general relativity.

The Big Universe

▲ EDWIN HUBBLE
Hubble (1889–1953) was an exceptional man. He had trained at Chicago and Oxford in law, and taken up professional boxing, before turning to astronomy.

Up until the 20th century, astronomers thought the Universe was little bigger than our own Milky Way Galaxy, with the Sun at its centre. All the Universe consisted of, they thought, were the few hundred thousand stars they could see with the most powerful telescopes of the day. The largest estimates put the Universe at no more than a few thousand light-years across (one light-year is 9,460 billion km, the distance light travels in a year). There were fuzzy spiral patches of light they could see through telescopes, but these were thought to be clouds of some kind. They were called spiral nebulae, from the Greek word for "cloud".

In 1918 an American astronomer called Harlow Shapley made an astonishing discovery. Shapley was working at the Mount Wilson Observatory near Los Angeles. He was studying ball-shaped clusters of stars called globular clusters through the observatory's powerful telescope. He wondered why they seemed to be concentrated in one half of the sky, and guessed that this is because the Earth is not at the centre of the

Galaxy as had been thought – but right out at the edge, looking inwards. He also realized that if this is so, then the Galaxy must be much, much bigger than anyone thought – perhaps as big as 100,000 light-years across.

The discoveries that we are not at the centre of the Galaxy but at the edge, and that the Galaxy is gigantic, were in some ways as dramatic as Copernicus's discovery that the Earth is not at the centre of the Solar System. Even as Shapley was publishing his ideas, a new and even more powerful telescope was being installed at Mount Wilson. It enabled a young

▲ THE ANDROMEDA GALAXY
The Andromeda Galaxy is the nearest galaxy beyond our own, and the only one visible with the naked eye. But as Hubble's study of Cepheid variable stars within it showed, even this nearby galaxy is over two million light-years away. Thousands of other galaxies, which are visible only through powerful telescopes, are many billions of light-years away.

BIG BANG

Hubble's discovery that the Universe is getting bigger led to an amazing theory about the history of the Universe. If the Universe is expanding as Hubble showed, it must have been smaller at one time. Indeed, all the signs are that it was once very, very small indeed – perhaps smaller than an atom. The Universe began with an unimaginably gigantic explosion called the Big Bang. It was so big that the galaxies are still being flung out from it today.

◀ THE AFTERGLOW OF THE BIG BANG
The Big Bang theory seemed a very good explanation of the way the Universe is expanding. But there was little real proof until 1992, when the Cosmic Background Explorer (COBE) took a picture of the whole sky showing the microwave radiation coming towards us from all over space. This radiation is the afterglow of the Big Bang, and the slightly uneven pattern shown by the COBE picture confirmed astronomer's theories. Without this unevenness the galaxies could never have formed, so the Big Bang theory could not be correct.

▶ THE STORY OF THE UNIVERSE

By calculating back from the speed of the galaxies, we can estimate the universe began about 14 billion years ago. Gradually, astronomers have been piecing together the history of the Universe, from the time the first stars and galaxies formed, perhaps 13 billion years ago, through the beginnings of the Earth 4,567 million years ago, the beginning of life some 3,500 million years ago, the age of the dinosaurs 210–65 million years ago, down to the modern age.

astronomer called Edwin Hubble to make even more astonishing discoveries.

Using the new telescope, Hubble began to look at the spiral nebulae – in particular the nebulae we now know as the Andromeda Galaxy. He could see that it was much more than a fuzzy patch of light, and actually contained stars. Among these stars he could see special stars called Cepheid variables, which are so predictable in their brightness that we can use them as distance markers in the sky. The Cepheid variables showed Hubble that Andromeda is several hundred thousand light-years away – far beyond the edge of the Galaxy.

Soon it became clear that many of the fuzzy patches of light in the night sky were other galaxies of stars, even farther away. Suddenly the Universe seemed much, much bigger than anyone had dreamed of. In 1927 Hubble made an even more amazing discovery. While studying the light from 18 galaxies,

he noticed that the light from each one had a slightly different red tinge. He realized that this was because the galaxies are zooming away from us so fast that light waves are actually stretched out and become redder. Remarkably, the farther away the galaxies are, the faster they seem to be moving away from us. Hubble realized that this is because the Universe is expanding.

So within ten years the Universe which was thought to be just a few thousand light-years across was found to be many millions, and it was known to be growing bigger at an absolutely astonishing rate. Astronomers can now see galaxies 13 billion light-years away – zooming away from us at nearly the speed of sound.

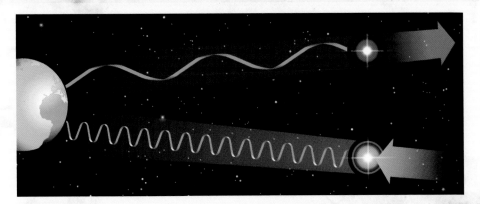

▲ RED SHIFT

We know galaxies are speeding away from us because their light is "red shifted". If a light source is rushing away, each light wave is sent from a little farther on – and so gets stretched out. As the light waves are stretched out, the light appears redder. The most distant galaxies have such huge red shifts that they must be moving very, very fast. Red shift is based on the observation by Austrian physicist Christian Doppler (1803–1853) that sound waves moving away are stretched out in the same way. The roar of a train coming towards you is high-pitched. As it zooms on past and away, the pitch drops as the sound waves become longer.

Key Dates

- 1918 Harlow Shapley shows that Earth is on the edge of the Galaxy.

- 1929 Hubble shows Andromeda is a galaxy beyond our own.

- 1927 Hubble realizes that other galaxies are flying away from us – and the Universe is expanding.

- 1927 Abbé George Lemaitre pioneers the idea that the Universe began in a Big Bang.

- 1948 Alpher and Herman suggest the Big Bang left behind weak radiation.

- 1964 Penzias and Wilson detect weak cosmic background radiation, providing evidence for the Big Bang.

Miracle Cures

▲ ALEXANDER
FLEMING
The discovery of penicillin, the first antibiotic, by Scottish bacteriologist Alexander Fleming (1881–1955) was one of the great medical breakthroughs of the 20th century. For the first time doctors had a powerful weapon against a wide range of diseases.

IN 1900 DISEASE WAS A frighteningly normal part of life – and death. Few large families of children ever grew up without at least one of them dying. The introduction of vaccination began to save many people from catching diseases such as smallpox. Doctors could do very little once anyone actually became ill, except tend them and pray. To catch a disease such as tuberculosis or syphilis was very likely to be a death sentence.

The main reason for doctors' helplessness in the face of infectious (catching) diseases was the fact they had no idea what caused them. Then, in the late 19th century, thanks to the work of scientists such as Louis Pasteur, it finally became clear that it was tiny, microscopically small germs such as bacteria and viruses that were to blame.

Gradually medical scientists, especially those in Germany, began to realize that it might be possible to fight infectious disease with chemicals that targeted the germs but left the body unharmed. A very dedicated scientist called Paul Ehrlich believed that the key was to find chemical "magic bullets" that could be aimed at

▲ ERNST CHAIN
Along with Howard Florey, Chain continued the research into penicillin that had been started by Alexander Fleming. The value of the three men's work was recognized in 1945 when they were awarded the Nobel Prize in Medicine.

ANTIBIOTICS
Antibiotics work by attacking germ cells, but not body cells, and they have proved remarkably effective at treating a variety of bacterial diseases, including pneumonia, meningitis, scarlet fever, syphilis, tuberculosis and other infections. There are at least 70 useful antibiotics. Most are used against bacterial infections, but some attack fungal diseases and a few are designed to work against cancer. Diseases caused by viruses, however, cannot be treated by antibiotics in any way.

▼ HOW ANTIBIOTICS WORK
Antibiotics fight germs in a number of ways. Some antibiotics make the germ cell's skin leak vital nutrients or let in poisonous substances, but they have no affect on human cell skins. Others, such as penicillin, work by stopping the germ cell's tough skin from forming. Human cells do not have the same tough skins, so they are left unharmed. A third kind of antibiotic, including streptomycin and rifampicin, interferes with chemical processes inside the germ cell.

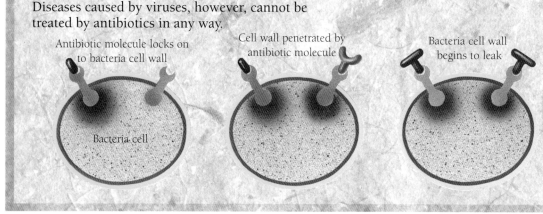

Antibiotic molecule locks on to bacteria cell wall

Bacteria cell

Cell wall penetrated by antibiotic molecule

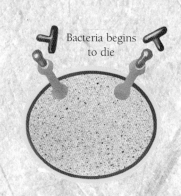

Bacteria cell wall begins to leak

Bacteria begins to die

germs. With his colleague, Sahachiro Hata, Ehrlich worked to find such a cure for syphilis – a terrible disease that had killed millions of people over the centuries. In 1910 he discovered the chemical arsphenamine, which was sold under the name Salvarsan. It wiped out the germ that causes syphilis while leaving body cells virtually unharmed.

For the first time, doctors had a powerful weapon against a disease, and the search was now on for similar chemical treatments for other diseases. The early hopes were dashed, and it was not until the 1930s that scientists discovered a group of chemicals called sulfonamides that were deadly to a wide range of bacteria. In the meantime, a British scientist called Alexander Fleming had made a remarkable discovery.

In 1928 Fleming was working in his laboratory in St Mary's Hospital, London, when he noticed a strange thing. He had been culturing (growing) the staphylococcus bacteria in a dish and it had grown mouldy. What was remarkable was that the bacteria seemed to have died wherever the mould was. Fleming had a hunch that this mould, called *Penicillium notatum,* could be useful against disease.

Fleming himself was unable to find out if his hunch was true, but ten years later Howard Florey, Ernst Chain and others took up the idea and developed the first antibiotic drug, penicillin. "Antibiotic" means germ-attacking. Penicillin, one of the miracle drugs of the 20th century, has saved many, many millions of people from dying from a wide range of infectious diseases, including tuberculosis. Since then, thousands of other

▲ CLEAN BILL OF HEALTH
In the 1850s Austrian Ignaz Semmelweiss found that he could save women from dying in childbirth in hospital by getting his medical students to wash their hands to stop the spread of infection. Later, Joseph Lister introduced carbolic to kill germs in surgery. These antiseptic (germ-killing) techniques were not miracle cures, but they made hospitals, such as this smallpox hospital, much, much safer.

antibiotic drugs have been discovered. In the early 1940s, for instance, the American scientist Selman Waksman found the antibiotic streptomycin in soil fungi. Some antibiotics come from nature, mainly moulds and fungi, and some have been made artificially from chemicals. None has proved as effective and safe against such a broad range of diseases as penicillin.

◀ NEW DRUGS
In the past, drugs either occurred naturally or they were created in the laboratory. In future, some may be created in cyberspace, as chemists put computer models of molecules together with models of body cells to see how they react, which is what this chemist is doing. Computers may be able to trawl through millions of different ways of putting atoms together very quickly to find the perfect "magic bullet" that targets the disease precisely.

Key Dates

- 1867 Joseph Lister shows the value of antiseptic surgery.

- 1860s Louis Pasteur insists that many diseases are caused by germs.

- 1876 Robert Koch proves germs can cause disease.

- 1910 Ehrlich and Hata find Salvarsan is a cure for syphilis.

- 1928 Florey, Chain and others turn penicillin into the first antibiotic.

- 1942 Waksman discovers streptomycin.

- 1951 Frank Burnet discovers how the immune system attacks germs but not body cells.

Nuclear Power

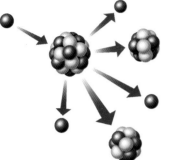

▲ NUCLEAR FISSION
In nuclear fission, an atom is split by the impact of a tiny neutron. As it splits into two smaller atoms, it releases a lot of energy and two more neutrons, which may split further atoms.

No SCIENTIFIC DISCOVERY has been so awesome as that of nuclear energy, the energy in the nucleus of every atom in the Universe. Nuclear energy is not only the energy that makes nuclear weapons, it is the energy that keeps every star in the Universe burning. Until the 20th century, this vast power was undreamed of. Scientists knew that matter was made of atoms, but they thought atoms were no more lively than billiard balls. No one knew what energy really was.

Albert Einstein had a brilliant insight in his theory of special relativity of 1905. He showed that energy and matter are flip sides of the same basic thing, swapping back and forth all the time. His famous equation $E=mc^2$ gave this swap a real quantity. E is energy, and m the mass, or quantity, of matter; c is the speed of light, which is huge. If the mass of a tiny atom could be changed to energy, some scientists believed it would yield a huge amount of power.

At the same time, scientists such as Neils Bohr were probing the atom and finding that it is not just a ball. First, they found it holds tiny electrons whizzing around a nucleus, or core, of larger protons.

▼ NUCLEAR MUSHROOM
When a nuclear bomb explodes on the ground, a huge fireball vaporizes everything on the ground and turns it into a blast of hot gases and dust that shoots far up into the sky. When this blast reaches the stratosphere, one of the layers of the atmosphere that finishes 50km from the earth's surface, it begins to cool and some of the gases condense into dust. As the dust begins to fall it billows out in a distinctive mushroom-shaped cloud. Often radioactive particles drop back to the ground.

THE MANHATTAN PROJECT

The bombs dropped on Hiroshima and Nagasaki were developed in a secret programme called the Manhattan Project by a team at Los Alamos in New Mexico. On 16 July 1945, the Los Alamos team exploded the first atomic bomb in the desert, to the amazement of spectators in bunkers 9km away.

The team achieved the critical mass of fission material (plutonium-239 and uranium-235) in two ways. One was to smash two lumps together from opposite ends of a tube, a system called "Thin Man". The other was to wrap explosive around a ball of fission material and smash it together ("Fat Man"). The Hiroshima bomb was a uranium-235 "Thin Man". The Nagasaki bomb was a plutonium -239 "Fat Man".

▲ J. ROBERT OPPENHEIMER
Oppenheimer (1904–1967) led the Los Alamos team but he later opposed hydrogen bombs. These are powerful nuclear bombs based not on the fission (splitting) of atoms, but on the fusion (joining together) of tiny hydrogen atoms.

▼ NAGASAKI
The effect of the nuclear bombs on Hiroshima and Nagasaki was so terrible that no one has used them in warfare again. The bombs obliterated huge areas of both cities and killed over 100,000 people instantly. Many of those who survived the initial blast died slow and painful deaths from the after-effects of radiation.

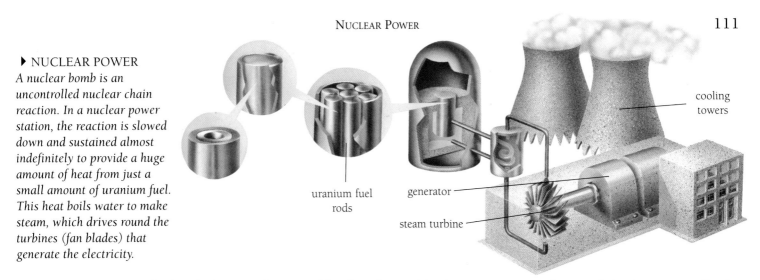

▶ NUCLEAR POWER
A nuclear bomb is an uncontrolled nuclear chain reaction. In a nuclear power station, the reaction is slowed down and sustained almost indefinitely to provide a huge amount of heat from just a small amount of uranium fuel. This heat boils water to make steam, which drives round the turbines (fan blades) that generate the electricity.

uranium fuel rods

generator

steam turbine

cooling towers

Then, in 1932, James Chadwick discovered a second kind of particle in the nucleus – the neutron.

At once, Italian atom scientist Enrico Fermi tried firing neutrons at the nuclei of uranium atoms. He found different atoms forming, and guessed that the neutrons had joined onto the uranium atoms to make bigger atoms of an unknown element, which he called element 93. But Fermi was wrong. In 1939, German scientists Otto Hahn and Fritz Strassman repeated Fermi's experiment. What they found was not a new element, but something even more astonishing – so astonishing that Hahn hardly dared believe it. It was another physicist, Lise Meitner who announced to the world what Fermi, Hahn and Strassman had done. They had split the uranium atom in two, making smaller atoms including barium. This splitting of the atom is called fission.

When the uranium atom split, it not only released a lot of energy, but also split off two neutrons. What if these two neutrons zoomed off to split two new atoms? These atoms would then, in turn, release two more neutrons, which

would split more atoms, and so on. Scientists soon realized this could become a rapidly escalating chain reaction of atom splitting. A chain reaction such as this would unleash a huge amount of energy as more and more atoms split.

Normally, chain reactions will not start in uranium because only a few uranium atoms are of the kind that splits easily, namely uranium-235. Most are tougher uranium-238 atoms. To make a bomb or a nuclear power plant, you need to pack enough uranium-235 into a small space to sustain a chain reaction. This is known as the critical mass.

During World War II, scientists in both Germany and the USA worked furiously to achieve the critical mass, since neither wanted to be last to make the atomic bomb. The Americans realized that another atom – plutonium-239 – might be used instead of uranium-235. At 3.45 p.m. on 2 December 1942, a team in Chicago led by Fermi used plutonium-239 to achieve a fission chain reaction for the first time. In August 1945, American fission bombs devastated the Japanese cities of Hiroshima and Nagasaki.

▲ NUCLEAR POWER PLANT
Nuclear reactions release huge amounts of energy, but they create dangerous radioactivity too. Radioactivity can make people very ill or even kill them. Many people suffered radiation sickness after the Hiroshima and Nagasaki bombs. Even nuclear power plants can have dangerous leaks. A serious nuclear accident occurred when the Chernobyl reactor, in the Ukraine, went wrong in April 1986, spreading radioactive material over a vast area. The radioactive material produced by nuclear power stations must be stored safely for hundreds of years until it loses its radioactivity.

Key Dates

- 1905 Einstein reveals the theoretical power of the atom in special relativity.

- 1911 Rutherford proposes that atoms have a nucleus, circled by electrons.

- 1919 Rutherford discovers the proton.

- 1932 Chadwick discovers the neutron.

- 1939 Hahn and Strassman split a uranium atom.

- 1942 Fermi's team achieve the first fission chain reaction.

- 1945 July 16: Oppenheimer's team explode the first atomic bomb.

- 1945 August: US Air Force drop atomic bombs on Nagasaki and Hiroshima.

Lifeplan

EVERY LIVING THING — EVERY human, animal and plant – is made up from millions of tiny packages called cells. Inside each cell is a remarkable chemical molecule called DNA. It is the basis of all life. The DNA in human body cells not only tells each cell how to play its part in keeping the body alive, but it also carries all the instructions for making a new human being. The discovery of DNA's shape by James Watson and Francis Crick in 1953 was one of the major scientific breakthroughs of the 20th century, and the impact of their discovery on our lives has already been huge.

DNA (deoxyribonucleic acid) was discovered in1869 by a Swiss student called Friedrich Miescher. Miescher was looking at pus on old bandages under a microscope when he saw tiny knots in the nucleus, or core, of

▲ DNA
DNA is one of the largest molecules known, weighing 500 million times more than a molecule of sugar. It is very thin, but very long – if stretched out it would be over 40cm long. The molecule is usually coiled up, but it is made from two thin strands wrapped around each other in a twin spiral, or "double helix". It is rather like a long twisted rope ladder, with rungs made of chemicals called bases.

▲ FAMILY
Everyone has their own unique DNA, and it is so distinctive that it can be used to prove who you are, like a fingerprint. You get half your DNA from your mother and half from your father. There are sequences of bases in your DNA that are so similar to both your mother's and your father's that an analysis of your DNA proves who your parents are. DNA is also the reason why we all bear some resemblance to our parents.

the pus cells. His tutor Ernst Hoppe-Sayler analyzed these nuclear knots chemically and found they were acidic, so they called the substance nucleic acid. No one at the time had much inkling of its real significance.

Seventy-six years later, in 1945, American bacteriologist Oswald Avery was studying influenza bacteria when he noticed that DNA could turn a harmless bacteria into a dangerous one – as if it was giving instructions. In 1952 Alfred Hershey and Martha Chase showed that this is

THE CHEMICALS OF LIFE
The study of the chemicals of life, such as DNA, is called organic chemistry, or biochemistry. It is also known as carbon chemistry because, remarkably, all life depends on chemicals that include atoms of carbon. There are literally millions of these carbon compounds, because carbon atoms are uniquely able to form links with other atoms. Some, such as proteins and amino acids, are more important than others.

▶ NICOTINE MOLECULE
Many organic compounds are based on a ring, or hexagon, of six carbon atoms. This is a model of the compound nicotine, found in the dried leaves of the tobacco plant. It is a poison used as an insecticide. It is also the chemical in cigarettes that makes people addicted to smoking.

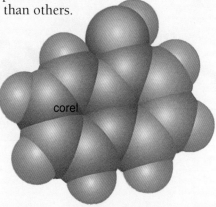

corel

▼ PROTEINS
Proteins are the basic material of all living cells. They are built up from different combinations of chemicals called amino acids. All these amino acids are present in each cell, like these cells from around human teeth. To make a protein, DNA must instruct the cell to make the right combination of amino acids.

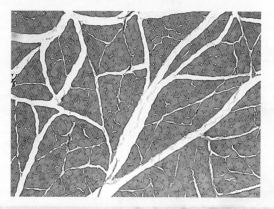

just what DNA does. Once DNA's importance became clear, the race was on to find out how it worked. It was crucial to discover the shape of this long and complex molecule. In 1952 Rosalind Franklin, a young woman working at Imperial College in London, photographed DNA using X-rays, but could not figure out its structure. The young American Watson and Englishman Crick were then working on DNA at the Cavendish Laboratory in Cambridge. When they saw Rosalind Franklin's photographs, they suddenly realized that the DNA molecule is shaped like a double helix – that is, like a rope ladder twisted in a spiral.

After this great discovery, biochemists began to take DNA apart piece by piece under microscopes, then put it together again to find out how it gave instructions. The search focused on the four different chemicals making up the "rungs" of the ladder: guanine, cytosine, adenine and thymine. Erwin Chagraff found that these four "bases" only pair up in certain ways – guanine links only with cytosine; adenine only with thymine.

It soon became clear that the key to DNA lies in the order, or sequence, of the bases along each of the molecule's two long strands. Like the bits of a computer, the sequence of bases works as a code. The bases are like letters of the alphabet, and the sequence is broken up into "sentences" called genes. The code in each gene is the cell's instructions to make a particular protein, one of the basic materials of life. The complete gene code, or genetic code, was finally worked out in 1967 by American biochemists Marshall Nirenberg and Indian-American Har Khorana, earning them the Nobel Prize.

▲ STAYING ALIVE
Not only humans, but every living thing in the world has a DNA molecule in each of its body cells. This remarkable molecule tells the cell exactly what to do in keeping the living thing's body together, whether it is a bear or a salmon. It is also a complete copy of instructions for making an entirely new bear or salmon.

▲ THE GENETIC CODE
The key to the DNA code lies in the sequence of chemical bases along each strand, shown here in the form of a DNA fingerprint. These bases are a bit like letters of the alphabet, and the sequence is broken up into "sentences" called genes. Each gene provides the instructions to make a particular set of proteins.

Key Dates

- 1869 Miescher discovers DNA.

- 1945 Avery discovers that DNA issues life instructions to living things.

- 1952 Hershey and Chase show that DNA carries genetic instructions.

- 1953 Watson and Crick show that DNA has a double-helix (spiral) structure.

- 1954 Chagraff shows that DNA's four "bases" only join together in certain ways.

- 1961 Brenner and Crick show how so-called "letters" in the DNA code are formed by triplets of bases.

- 1967 Nirenberg and Har Khorana show how the genetic code works.

The Power of the Processor

▲ MICROCHIP
Microprocessors are made from thousands of tiny transistors joined in circuits and printed onto a tiny slice of silicon, or silicon chip. The biggest parts of a chip are not its circuits and switches – the tiny patch in the centre – but the connecting teeth along its sides.

THE COMPUTER'S ORIGINS date back 5,000 years when people in Asia used abacuses to do sums. An abacus is a simple frame with rows of sliding beads, but a skilled user can do complex computations very quickly. In the 1600s, men such as French mathematician Blaise Pascal, built adding machines with gears and dials.

The first real computer was an "analytic engine" designed in the 1830s by Englishman Charles Babbage with the poet Byron's daughter Ada Lovelace. This machine would have used cards punched with holes to control the movement of rods and gears, and so make complex calculations. Crude mechanical systems though, were not up to the task and Babbage never built it.

During the next 100 years, people built increasingly clever calculators using punch cards to control rods and dials. These were just adding machines and could not do the complex sums we expect of a computer. Mechanical devices were too big and noisy. In 1944, Howard Aiken and IBM did build a basic computer using punch cards, but it was over 15m long and had less computing power than a modern pocket calculator!

The way forwards for computers was to replace mechanics with electronics. Electronics are at the heart of most modern technologies, from CD players to rocket control systems. They work by using electricity to send signals. Inside every electronic device there are lots of small electric circuits, which continually switch on and off telling the device what to do. Unlike electric light switches on the wall, electronic switches work automatically.

The first electronic device, called a valve, was invented in 1904. It looked like an electric lightbulb and was used in radios and TVs. In 1939 American physicist John Atasanoff built a valve computer at Iowa University. A few years later, during World War II, an English mathematician called Alan Turing developed a giant valve

◀ VIRTUAL REALITY
Virtual reality (VR) systems build a picture electronically to create the impression of a real 3D space. They were developed in the 1960s in simulators that taught jet pilots how to fly. With VR, people can operate a computer-guided device in dangerous or difficult places, for example in an underwater wreck or inside the body.

THE TRANSISTOR

In the 1940s, TVs and other electronic devices relied on huge, hot-running glass tubes (rather like lightbulbs) for fine control over electric currents. Then John Bardeen and his colleagues showed the same control could be achieved with tiny, solid lumps of semiconductor materials – special materials such as germanium and silicon that conduct electricity only when warmed up by another electric current. The development of integrated circuits and microchips, on which all modern electronic technology relies, stems from this discovery.

◀ BARDEEN AND COLLEAGUES
The transistor was created by three scientists working together at the Bell Laboratories in 1948 – John Bardeen, William Shockley and Walter Brattain.

Random Access Memory (RAM)

screen

keyboard

Read Only Memory (ROM)

computer called Colossus to break the secret German 'Enigma' codes. Turing also created many of the basic rules of computing. Valves were used in the first electronic computers built for sale in the early 1950s, called first-generation computers. However, the valves were big, got very, very hot and kept failing.

The big breakthrough came when valves were replaced with transistors. Transistors are switches, like valves, but they are made from special "semiconductor" materials such as silicon and germanium, which can change their ability to conduct electricity. Transistors are lumps of these material inserted with electrodes (conductors). These can be very small and robust.

With transistors, computers moved on to the second and third generations in the 1950s and 1960s, but they were still small and expensive. Then, in 1958, American Jack Kilby put the connections for two transistors inside one 10mm-long crystal of silicon – he had made the world's first integrated circuit, or microchip.

Soon microchips were getting smaller and smaller, and electronic circuits became increasingly complicated as scientists discovered new ways of squeezing more and more components into a single chip. Nowadays, microchips, or silicon chips, range from simple circuits for electric kettles to complex high-speed

microprocessors with millions of transistors capable of running computer programs at very high speeds.

With integrated circuits, computers could start to be miniaturized. Heat ceased to be a real problem, and a great deal of computing power could be packed into a tiny space. The first computer based on a microprocessor was the Intel of 1974, moving computers into the fourth and fifth generations. Since then, they have progressed in leaps and bounds in terms of reliability, speed and power. Today's computers are packed into such compact and inexpensive packages that the average household in most developed countries can now have their own high-powered computer.

◀ COMPUTER GRAPHICS
The sophisticated graphics (pictures) now seen on ordinary home computers require levels of computing power that would have been envied by the scientists guiding spacecraft through the Solar System just 15 years ago. Every computer we use is still built around the microprocessor.

◀ SCREEN AND KEYBOARD
The keyboard and TV-like screen of the computer are so familiar that we take them for granted. Flat screens which are thin enough to hang on the wall have already been developed. So too have voice-operating systems that may make the keyboard redundant.

◀ ELEMENTS OF A COMPUTER
Inside a computer are a number of microchips. Some of a computer's memory, called the ROM (read-only memory), is built into these microchips. A computer also has chips for RAM (random-access memory), which takes new data and instructions whenever needed. Data can also be stored on magnetic patterns on removable discs, or on the laser-guided bumps on a CD.

At the heart of every computer is a powerful microchip called the central processing unit (CPU). The CPU is the part that works things out, within guidelines set by the ROM, and processes and controls all the programs by sending data to the right place in the RAM.

▲ TRANSISTOR
The modern computer was born when the transistor was invented in 1948. Modern microprocessors contain millions of transistors packed onto tiny silicon chips, but they still work in the same way as this single transistor.

Key Dates

- 1642 Pascal invents an adding machine.
- 1835 Babbage begins to build his programmable analytic engine.
- 1847 George Boole devises the basis of computer logic.
- 1930 Vannevar Bush builds a mechanical computer.
- 1937 Atsanoff builds a digital electronic computer.
- 1939 Aiken builds a valve computer.
- 1948 Shockley, Bardeen and Brattain invent the transistor.
- 1958 Jack Kilby invents silicon chip.

Space Age

▲ THE EARTH
FROM SPACE
Viewing the Earth from space has been one of the most extraordinarily powerful experiences of the space age. It makes clear what we had never been able to see before – that the Earth is an almost perfect sphere. It has also made us much more aware of the frailty of our planet.

THE CONQUERING OF SPACE has been one of the great human achievements of the 20th century. What was barely a fantasy 100 years ago is now an everyday reality. Over 100 artificial satellites are launched into space every year, manned space flights are commonplace and space probes have visited all but one of the planets in the Solar System. The *Mir* space station was recently abandoned after 13 years as an orbiting laboratory in space.

The space age began on 4 October 1957 when the Soviet Union launched *Sputnik* (later called *Sputnik 1*). It was blasted straight up by powerful rockets, and as the rockets fell away *Sputnik* soared on upwards, levelled out and hurtled into the first-ever orbit of the Earth. A month later, the first living creature went into space in *Sputnik 2* – a dog called Laika. Sadly, Laika never came back.

On 12 April 1961, brave Russian cosmonaut Yuri Gagarin went up in *Vostok 1* to become the first man in space. *Vostok 1* took Gagarin once around the Earth before re-entering the atmosphere and parachuting into the ocean. A few months later US astronaut Alan Shephard went up, and in June 1963 Valentina Tereshkova became the first woman in space in *Vostok 6*. In 1965, Russian Alexei Leonov stepped outside a spacecraft in space, floating on the end of a cable.

During the early years of the space age, the United States and Soviet Union were engaged in a bitter rivalry called the Cold War. Each was determined to beat the other in the "space race". Throughout the 1960s and 1970s, each nation was spurred on to ever more spectacular and showy

◀ GAGARIN
Born of a poor Russian farming family, Yuri Gagarin became the most famous person in the world in 1961 when Vostok 1 made him the first man in space. His flight around the Earth lasted just 1 hour 48 minutes, but it was a spectacular moment in human history. Sadly, Gagarin died only seven years later at the age of 34 while testing a new plane.

EXPLORING SPACE

On 17 July 1969 the giant *Saturn V* rocket launched three astronauts towards the Moon on the *Apollo 11* mission. Three days later, the Apollo command module was circling the Moon. While Michael Collins stayed in the command module, Neil Armstrong and Buzz Aldrin went down to the Moon's surface in the lunar module. On 20 July, Neil Armstrong opened the hatch and climbed out onto the Moon.

▶ THE LUNAR MODULE
Armstrong and Aldrin went down to the Moon's surface in the tiny lunar module, which was little bigger than a caravan. When it landed, four legs supported it on big pads on the soft, dusty surface.

▲ FIRST STEPS
Neil Armstrong was the first man on the Moon. As he climbed down the ladder of the lunar module and stepped onto the Moon's surface, he said these now famous words: "That's one small step for a man, one giant leap for mankind."

▶ MIR
Despite a number of mishaps, the Soviet Mir *spacecraft stayed up in space for over 13 years, between 1986 and 1999, and made more than 76,000 orbits of the Earth. It was a temporary home to many astronauts – and Russian Valery Polyakov spent a record 437 continuous days aboard.*

achievements. Both the USA and USSR sent probes to the same planets, including Venus (the American *Mariners* and the Soviet *Veneras*) and Mars. Both sent probes to the Moon. Then, in July 1969, the Americans went ahead by putting men on the Moon (see below). The Soviets could go no better, but within two years they launched *Salyut 1*, the first space station.

Although these achievements were spectacular, the space race cost the two superpowers a fortune, and by the end of the 1970s it began to slow down. Today the Cold War is over, co-operation in space is the spirit of the day, and the Americans and Russians are working with Canada, Europe and Japan to build a huge international space station (ISO), which is being assembled in space piece by piece.

One cause of controversy among those involved in space exploration has been whether to focus on manned or unmanned exploration. Unmanned probes are cheaper, safer and faster than manned vehicles, and can make trips far too risky for human beings to attempt. No manned probe is ever likely to descend into Saturn's atmosphere or venture out beyond the edge of the Solar System – partly because manned spacecraft must return.

Unmanned probes have already visited most of the Solar System's planets. They have landed on Mars and Venus and they have told us a huge amount about all the planets. Unmanned probes can never give as full a picture as human observers, and cannot react so well to unexpected events. Manned spacecraft have been sent to the Moon, but sending people to the planet Mars is far trickier. Even the journey itself would take many months and would be a tremendous ordeal for astronauts. Most experts think astronauts may land on Mars by 2020.

▲ MARS LANDING
No manned spacecraft has landed on another planet, but many unmanned probes have landed on Mars. In July 1997, the US *Mars Pathfinder* touched down on Mars and beamed back "live" TV pictures from the planet. Two days later, it sent out a wheeled robot vehicle called *Sojourner* to survey the surrounding area.

▼ THE SPACE SHUTTLE
Early spacecraft were usable only for one flight, but the US space shuttle of 1981 was the first reusable craft, landing again with the aid of plane-like wings. It made short flights in space much easier.

Key Dates

- 1957 *Sputnik* is the first spacecraft to orbit the Earth.

- 1957 Laika the dog is the first living creature in space.

- 1961 Yuri Gagarin is the first man in space.

- 1961 Alan Shephard is the first American in space.

- 1963 Valentina Tereshkova is the first womna in space.

- 1965 Alexei Leonov does the first space walk.

- 1969 Neil Armstrong and Buzz Aldrin are the first men to land on the Moon.

Instant Contact

▲ TELEPHONES
Since it was invented by Alexander Graham Bell in 1876, the telephone has become a vital part of our lives, giving us the instant contact we now take for granted.

THE AGE OF INSTANT communication began when American painter and inventor Samuel Morse invented the electric telegraph in the 1830s. The telegraph linked two places by electric wire. By simply switching the current rapidly on and off, a message could be sent in a code of pulses, called Morse code. For the first time, people could send messages almost instantly over long distances. On 24 May 1844, Morse sent this message from Washington, D.C., to Baltimore over the world's first commercial telegraph line: "What hath God wrought".

Newspapers quickly began to use the Morse telegraph to send news stories, and by the 1860s the telegraph was the main means of long-distance communication in the United States, linking all major cities. Thanks to the backing of American banker Cyrus W. Field and British physicist Lord Kelvin, a telegraph cable was laid all the way under the Atlantic in 1866. The benefit was instant. Once, even

urgent messages between London and New York had taken weeks to get through. Suddenly, via the transatlantic cable, contact between people had become almost instant.

However, messages still had to be transmitted in an elaborate code. A few years later, in Boston, USA, Scotsman Alexander Graham Bell found a way to transmit not just single pulses down the telegraph wire, but multiple pulses. In 1875 he found a way to transmit all the vibrations made by sounds as multiple pulses. On 10 March 1876, he transmitted human speech for

▼ THE INVENTION OF RADIO
The telegraph and the telephone rely on a physical connection by wire. In 1895 Guglielmo Marconi transmitted a Morse message across empty space using pulses of radio waves.

INTERNET
The Internet is a vast network linking millions of computers around the world. It transmits huge amounts of information, including words, images and sounds. It began in the 1960s when the American army developed a network called ARPAnet to link military and government computers in case of nuclear war. Soon places like universities developed their own networks.

In 1983, the university networks merged with ARPAnet to form the Internet. Now anyone with a computer, a modem and a phone line can join. Originally the Internet was just used for electronic mail (e-mail) and transferring files. But there was a huge explosion of interest in the Internet after Tim Berners-Lee of the CERN laboratories in Switzerland developed the World Wide Web in 1989 for finding your way round Internet sites.

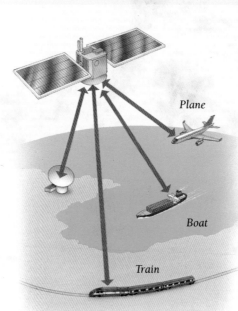

Plane

Boat

Train

Satellites links will soon connect be able to link you to the internet wherever you are

◀ THE NET
Just as you can talk on the phone, so computers can talk to each other on the Internet. Every computer has its own "address" where it can receive messages, like a telephone number. Computers that have a "site" – a window of information open to all – have a website address too.

When you access the Net, your computer connects via a local phone line to a big computer called a net provider. This, in turn, is linked to a bigger computer called a main hub. Each main hub is connected to about 100 other main hubs around the world. Some messages travel between main hubs by phone lines and others are linked by satellite. Either way, they are incredibly fast and are called "fast-truck connections".

the first time, saying to his colleague in another room: "Watson, come here. I want you!" By the end of the 19th century every major city in the world was linked by telephone.

Over the next 90 years, nearly every household in North America and Europe acquired a phone. People took it for granted that they could pick up the phone and chat to friends at opposite ends of the country. When it came to international calls, there were often long delays – either because the line was crowded or because the signal took time to get through. Also, some countries did not have a cable link.

When the space age dawned in the 1960s, communications companies were quick to take advantage of the satellites being fired up into space. Telephone signals were translated into microwaves (like the rays in a microwave oven) and bounced around the world off satellites. Suddenly even the most out of the way places could join the telephone network cheaply, and people could speak almost instantly to people across the far side of the world. Communications satellites transmit not only telephone messages instantly, but they also handle TV and radio signals as well.

The telephone network was speeded up even further when fibre-optic cables began to be used in the 1970s. A laser or a light-emitting diode (LED) translates the electric signals of a telephone call into light impulses.

These are shone along a thin, transparent glass or plastic strand called an optical fibre. The light impulses are reflected off the internal surfaces of the fibre, and so they travel much faster and more cleanly than a conventional electric signal.

In the early 1980s several companies had begun to market cellular telephones, which used no wires at all. They sent and received messages via microwaves sent to special receiving stations. By the mid-1990s, a huge number of people used the compact mobile phones developed from these first chunky cell phones. The great revolution of the 1990s has been the Internet, which links computers all around the world using the telephone network.

▲ COMMUNICATIONS SATELLITE
Since the first communications satellite, called Telstar, was launched in 1962, satellites have dramatically accelerated the speed and ease with which all kinds of messages – from telephone conversations to TV broadcasts – can be beamed around the world.

▶ THE WORLD WIDE WEB
The World Wide Web is an amazingly clever way of finding your way around information on all the computers in the Internet. The information you can reach is set up as "sites" on all the millions of individual computers in the Net. The Web makes "hyperlinks" (fast links) to all the sites that contain the word you select. To find the right sites, you need a browser, which is a computer program that searches the entire Net.

Key Dates

- 1844 Morse sends the first telegraph message.

- 1866 The first telegraph is sent through the transatlantic cable.

- 1876 Bell sends the first telephone message.

- 1963 The first communications satellite is launched.

- 1960s The US military develops ARPAnet to link computers.

- 1983 ARPAnet merges with university links to form the Internet.

- 1989 Tim Berners Lee develops the World Wide Web.

The Moving Earth

▲ LYSTROSAURUS
Finding fossils of Lystrosaurus in Antarctica was crucial evidence for the theory that the continents were once joined. Lystrosaurus is a reptile known to have lived in China, Africa and India 200 million years ago – and the best explanation for finding fossils in all four places is that all four places were once joined together.

IN RECENT YEARS geologists have made the startling discovery that the Earth's surface is broken into 20 or so giant slabs called "tectonic plates". Even more startling is the fact that these plates are moving slowly around the Earth. As they move the plates carry the oceans and the continents with them, so that they drift around the world. This discovery revolutionized our understanding of the Earth's surface, showing us why and where earthquakes and volcanoes occur and a great deal more.

The idea that the continents have moved is so astonishing that when a young German meteorologist called Alfred Wegener (1880–1930) first suggested it in 1923, he was ridiculed. "Utter damn rot!" sneered the President of the American Philosophical Society.

Yet it was not an altogether new idea. In the 17th century the English thinker Francis Bacon had noticed how strangely alike the coasts of South America and

◀ KOBE QUAKE
The idea of tectonic plates that move has transformed scientists' understanding of how earthquakes happen. One day they may be able to predict earthquakes such as the one that hit Kobe, in Japan, in 1996.

Africa are, and in the early 19th century a German explorer had noticed remarkable similarities between the rocks of Brazil and those of the African Congo. No one thought much of this until naturalists found not only identical turtles, snakes and lizards in both South America and Africa, but fossils of the ancient reptile Mesosaurus in both Brazil and South Africa.

The accepted explanation was that the continents had once been joined by necks of land that had since vanished. The evidence was weak, but by the time Wegener came up with his theory, the idea of land bridges was firmly entrenched. Wegener's theory was that all the continents had once been joined in a single huge landmass which he called Pangaea, which had split up hundreds of millions of years ago.

Only in the 1950s, when geologists began to explore the ocean floor, did evidence in favour of Wegener start to emerge. First, oceanographers found a great ridge

EARTHQUAKE AND VOLCANO ZONES
Soon after the idea of tectonic plates was developed, geologists realized that the world's major earthquake and volcano zones coincide with the boundaries between the plates. It has now become clear that most major earthquakes are triggered by the immense forces generated as plates grind together. When one plate drags past another, the rock on either side of the boundary bends and stretches a little way, then may snap suddenly. This sudden rupture sends shock waves, called seismic waves, shuddering through the ground causing earthquakes.

▶ MONITORING VOLCANOES
Most of the world's most explosive volcanoes occur in an arc along the edge of what are called "convergent" plate margins (places where two tectonic plates are coming together). Volcanologists learn about volcanoes from studying less violent volcanoes away from plate margins and above hot spots in the Earth's interior, such as this one.

◀ ERUPTING VOLCANO
Here you can actually see the molten lava exploding from the Earth's crust, where the pressure has become too great.

winding along the middle of the ocean floor through all the world's oceans, like a seam on a baseball. At the crest of this ridge was a deep central rift, or canyon.

In 1960 an American geologist, Harry Hess, stunned geologists by suggesting that the ocean floors might not be fixed, but were spreading rapidly from the mid-ocean ridge. As hot material wells up from the Earth's interior through the ridge's central rift, Hess suggested, it pushes the two halves of the ocean apart. Geologists were sceptical until, in the late 1960s, Frederick Vine and Drummond Matthews found stripes of strong and weak magnetism in the rocks on either side of the ridge. These stripes, they realized, must indicate ancient

switches in the Earth's magnetic field, and so the stripes recorded the spreading of the ocean floor like the growth rings in a tree. A few years later, scientists on the research ship *Glomar Challenger* found that rocks got older the farther away from the ridge they were.

If Hess's theory that the ocean floor is spreading was right, then it seemed likely that Wegener's theory of continental drift was right too. In the 1980s geologists began to measure the distance between continents with astonishing accuracy, using laser beams bounced off satellites. They found that the continents really are moving, but the speed of this movement varies from place to place. North America and Europe are moving over 2cm farther apart every year, which is faster than the rate at which a fingernail grows.

▼ KINDS OF VOLCANO
The movement of the plates creates different kinds of volcano. Where the plates are pulling apart – along the mid-ocean ridge, for instance – volcanoes ooze lava gently all the time, often bubbling up through the gap. The lava often flows out to form shallow shield volcanoes. Where the plates are pushing together, volcanoes are much more unpredictable and explosive – thick magma piles up steep, cone-shaped volcanoes.

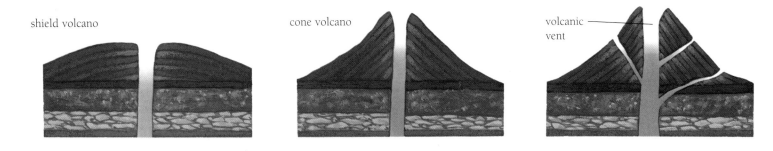

shield volcano   cone volcano   volcanic vent

▶ QUAKE WATCH
All around the world seismographic stations, such as the one shown here, are continually monitoring the earthquake vibrations generated as the Earth's tectonic plates grind together. The most violent earthquakes tend to occur in places where plates are sliding past each other – for example along the San Andreas fault in California, USA – or where one plate slides under another.

Key Dates

- 1923 Alfred Wegener suggests the idea of continental drift.

- 1956 Maurice Ewing, Bruce Heezen and Marie Tharp discover the mid-ocean ridge.

- 1960 Harry Hess suggests that the ocean floors are spreading away from the mid-ocean ridge.

- 1963 Frederick Vine and Drummond Matthews find proof of ocean floor spreading in magnetic reversals in sea-bed rocks.

- 1967 Discovery of Lystrosaurus fossils in Antarctica.

- 1983 Satellites measure how fast tectonic plates are moving.

Artificial Materials

▲ ETHENE MOLECULE
Ethene is a gas extracted from oil and natural gas. Ethene molecules are made from four hydrogen atoms and two carbon atoms. Long chains of these molecules are put together to make polythene and PVC.

In the past, people made things largely with natural materials such as wood and wool. During the 20th century, scientists developed an increasing range of synthetic, or manufactured, materials with properties that natural materials could not possibly match.

One of the biggest groups of synthetic materials are plastics, which are used in everything from spacecraft and car parts to bottles and artificial body parts. Plastics are incredibly light and can be moulded into any shape. What gives plastic its special quality is the shape of its molecules (the smallest particles). With only a few exceptions, plastics are made from long organic (natural) molecules called polymers, which are made from lots of smaller molecules called monomers. Polythene, for instance, is a chain of 50,000 tiny molecules of an oil-extract called ethene.

A few polymers occur naturally, such as the tough fibre in plants known as cellulose. In the mid-1800s, scientists already knew that cellulose could be made into a brittle substance called cellulose nitrate. Then, in 1862, British chemist Alexander Parkes discovered that by adding camphor he could make cellulose nitrate tough but bendy and easy to mould. The new material "Parkesine" never took off, but in 1869 American John Hyatt created a similar substance called celluloid. At first it was used simply to make billiard balls, but when Kodak started to make photographic film with it in 1889, its success was assured.

▼ RACING YACHT
To achieve lightness and strength, racing yachts are made from an increasing range of synthetic materials instead of the traditional wood and cotton. Typically the hull is a composite such as fibreglass or carbon-reinforced plastic, while the sails are made of a tough, light, completely waterproof nylon material.

POLYMER QUALITIES
Some polymers occur naturally, such as the cellulose in wood and cotton, but most are now manufactured. They are all long chains of smaller molecules, altered slightly and repeated many times. In many polymers, the long molecules get tangled up like spaghetti, and it is the way they are tangled that gives a polymer its strength. If the strands are held tightly together, the result is a stiff plastic such as perspex. If the strands slip over one another easily, it makes a bendy plastic such as polythene. Forcing the molecules through tiny holes lines them up to form a fibre such as nylon.

▶ LAVA LAMP
Plastics are easy to mould into almost any shape while warm, and once set they hold their shape well. The clear cover for this lamp is moulded plastic – typical of the fashion for moulded plastic in the 1960s and 1970s.

◀ PVC
Polyvinyl chloride (PVC) is a synthetic polymer introduced in the 1920s. It can be either rigid or flexible. Rigid PVC is used for making objects such as bottles. Flexible PVC is used for making raincoats, garden hoses and electrical insulation.

Since then hundreds of plastics and other synthetic polymers have been developed, including Plexiglass, polythene PVC, cellophane and a huge range of artificial fibres. The first of the synthetic fibres was nylon, which was created in the 1930s by Wallace Carothers, a chemist with the Du Pont company. In the 1920s, Carothers had found a way of making fibres out of very long polymer molecules stretched out in a machine called a molecular still. The stretching made the fibres strong and elastic, but they melted at very low temperatures. In 1935 he tried using a combination of chemicals called polyhexamethylene adipamide, which came to be called nylon. Within a few years, Du Pont researchers had found a way of making the basic ingredients from petroleum, natural gas and agricultural byproducts, and the first nylon products went on sale in 1939. People were so excited by this amazing new material that nylon mania swept the USA, and by the end of World War II everyone was wearing nylon-based clothes, and nylon stockings were a

◀ RACING CYCLIST
Lightness really counts for a racing cyclist. This world-beating bike, instead of being made of metal like most bikes, is moulded from carbon-reinforced plastic which is far lighter than metal. Even the weight of the cyclist's clothes, shoes and helmet is important. The synthetic fibre Lycra meets these requirements perfectly, in a way that no natural material can match.

must for every woman. Nylon's toughness, elasticity and mouldability soon made it valued for home furnishings, cars and machinery as well as for clothes.

Since the introduction of nylon a whole new range of artificial fibres has been developed, including polyesters and Lycra, with a huge variety of uses. The big new area of polymer-based synthetic materials is "composites", which are made by combining two substances to obtain a material that has the qualities of both. Typically, one of the materials is a polymer. In carbon-reinforced plastic, tough carbon fibres are set within a polymer to make an amazingly strong but light material that is used to make anything from tennis rackets to racing car bodies. Kevlar, developed by Du Pont in 1971, is a composite based on nylon fibres set inside another polymer.

▲ BAKELITE
Bakelite was the first entirely synthetic plastic, invented by Leo Baekeland in 1909. It was made by treating phenol resin made from coal tar with formaldehyde. Like earlier plastics, it could be moulded, but once moulded it set hard and was heatproof. Bakelite was also a good electrical insulator, so it was used for switches and plugs. It was also used to make radios, telephones, kitchenware, cameras and much more.

▼ PLASTIC DUCK
Plastics are so easily moulded and so easy to make in bright colours that they have become very popular materials for making toys.

Key Dates

- 1862 Alexander Parkes invents Parkesine, the first artificial polymer.

- 1869 John Hyatt invents celluloid.

- 1889 Kodak uses celluloid to make photographic film.

- 1909 Leo Baekeland invents Bakelite, the first entirely synthetic plastic.

- 1920 PVC is developed.

- 1935 Carothers develops nylon.

- 1939 Du Pont launches nylon.

- 1950s Carbon-fibre materials introduced.

- 1971 Kevlar created by Du Pont.

Life Changing

▲ GM TOMATOES
Many foods in our shops are already made with crops that have been genetically modified in some way. The genetically modified (GM) foods look no different from other foods.

D URING THE 1950s, scientists discovered that all the instructions for life were carried in genetic code on the remarkable DNA molecule coiled inside every living cell. It took a while to crack the genetic code, but as they finally did, so scientists began to realize that they might be able to manipulate it as a means of changing life's instructions.

In 1971, American microbiologists Daniel Nathans and Hamilton Smith discovered some chemicals called restriction enzymes. Restriction enzymes are like biological scissors, and they can be used to snip DNA in particular places. Other scientists soon found a biological glue – another enzyme, called DNA ligase, that can stick DNA back together. A few years later, American biochemist Paul Berg realized that by using restriction enzymes to cut DNA, and DNA ligase to glue it back together again, it would be possible to create entirely new and different DNA molecules. He called these new molecules "recombinant DNA". The remarkable thing about recombinant DNA was that it could be made to order, making it completely different from anything that had ever existed before. This discovery was the beginning of what is now called genetic engineering. Scientists soon found, for instance, that they could turn bacteria into protein factories by altering their genes. They simply

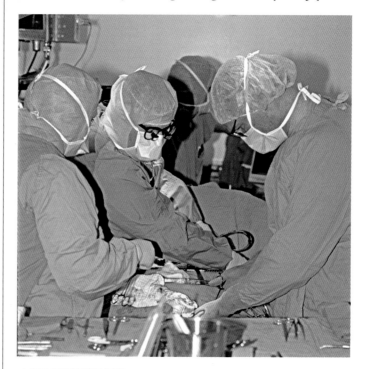

▲ HEART DISEASE
Many illnesses are inherited in the genes from parents, such as a risk of heart disease. One key area of genetic research focuses on ways of manipulating genes to cure genetic disorders such as these.

PERFECT REPLICAS

Usually each plant and animal has its own unique genes, which are different from those of every other plant and animal. You have a mix of genes from your mother, father and grandparents, plus some that are your own and no one else's. "Cloning" means creating an organism (living thing) with exactly the same genes as another. The first clone was made when John Gurdon put the nucleus from a tadpole's gut cell, complete with DNA, into a frog's egg. The egg grew into a new tadpole, identical to the first.

Normally, new organisms grow from sex cells (from both parents) in which genes are mixed up. The DNA in each cell is a complete set of genes. Cloning uses the DNA from any body cell to grow a new creature. Since the new creature has the same genes, it is a perfect replica.

◀ DOLLY THE SHEEP
In 1997 Ian Wilmut and colleagues at Edinburgh's Roslin Institute made the first clone of an adult mammal. The clone was a sheep called Dolly. Scientists had thought adult mammals could not be cloned, but Dolly proved otherwise. Dolly grew from the nucleus of a cell taken from the teats of a Finn Dorset ewe and inserted in an egg in the womb of a Scottish Blackface ewe. The egg grew there to be born as a lamb with identical genes to the Finn Dorset ewe.

extracted the DNA from the bacteria, cut the right gene out of their DNA, inserted the one for the protein and put it back in the bacteria. As the bacteria multiplied they would become a growing factory for the protein.

One valuable protein soon made like this was interferon. Interferons are proteins made by the human body which protect us against some viruses. However, the body makes only a tiny amount. By inserting doctored DNA into bacteria, lots of interferon can be made reasonably cheaply. In the 1980s, scientists found how to use bacteria to make enzymes for detergents and melanin for suntan lotion, and also how to heighten the resistance of crops to pests and disease. Later, they discovered how to use sheep to produce insulin in their milk for diabetics. Using recombinant gene techniques, scientists began to realize there is no reason why, in future, we should not be able to transfer any gene from one living thing to another. Soon they were investigating not only how to get bacteria and other living things to make certain substances, but many other things. Some scientists, for instance, began to work on how genetic disorders – illnesses inherited from your parents via your genes – might be cured. Others looked at how the genes of crops and farm animals might be modified to give them particular qualities. By adding to crops the genes from plants known to be distasteful or poisonous to crop pests, for instance, crops might be made pest resistant. By adding the antifreeze genes from Antarctic fish, other crops could be made frost-resistant. However, as such experiments in the genetic modification of crops continued, they began to cause some public concern.

▶ GM CROPS
The idea of genetic modification of crops has become a topic of heated debate. Many scientists believe that genetic modification could dramatically boost crop production and reduce the need for pesticides. Others believe the introduction of unnatural genes might have a devastating effect on natural ecosystems.

▼ IDENTICAL TWINS
Identical twins are the nearest nature provides to human clones. In theory, they both have identical genes because they grow from the same egg which splits in two. In practice, however, many small differences appear as the twins develop inside their mother's womb.

Key Dates

- 1967 Gurdon creates the first clone from a tadpole.

- 1970 Khorana creates the first truly artificial gene.

- 1971 Nathans and Smith discover restriction enzymes to snip DNA.

- 1973 Paul Berg discovers recombinant DNA techniques.

- 1973 Boyer uses recombinant DNA to create a chimera (combination of two species).

- 1975 Milstein produces the first monoclonal (single cell clone) antibodies.

- 1997 Wilmut and colleagues clone Dolly the sheep, the first adult mammal clone.

THE STORY
OF MEDICINE

*The story of medicine begins with the prehistoric
process of skull-drilling. Laboratory-grown spare body
parts are some of the latest, but by no means the last,
medical achievements. This section explores how advances
in medicine have enabled human beings to live longer,
more comfortable lives.*

BY BRIAN WARD

Medicine through the Ages

What is medicine? And what is health? In different cultures and at different times you would have received widely varying answers to these questions. In the modern Western medical tradition, the main objective is to get rid of disease, and then to keep people healthy. In earlier times, Western medicine depended on a muddled mixture of prayer, folk remedies and theories going back to the Arab civilizations and beyond that to the ancient Greeks. True advances in medical care did not take place until the 1800s, and it was not until the 1900s that medicine was able to reduce the high death rates caused by infections. Eastern medicine took a different line, which was that the whole body had to be treated in order to keep it healthy and to prevent disease from appearing. Now, in the 2000s, Western medicine has begun to accept the idea of keeping the whole body healthy, it has come full circle.

Disease is when the normal body does not function properly, but it is more difficult to define health. A person aged 70 or more may feel that they are in perfect health, but a younger person would not be happy to experience the aches, pains and breathlessness that often accompany ageing. So health needs to be considered in terms of our

▲ TRADITIONAL MEDICINES
Chinese medicine developed from a totally different background to science-based Western medicine. It treats the whole body by restoring the balance of forces flowing within it. There is growing interest in this and other forms of traditional medicine.

▼ KEY DATES
The panel charts the history of medicine, from the earliest uses of herbs and magic as cures, to the invention of state-of-the-art technologies.

▼ CAUTERIZING IRON
Medical techniques become out-dated as better knowledge and technology lead to an improved way of doing things. For centuries, a red-hot iron was used to seal or cauterize the blood vessels and prevent bleeding after surgery. This agonizing process usually led to infection. Today, high-tech laser beams seal a wound safely and painlessly.

Paracelsus

ANCIENT TIMES

15,000BC Cave paintings in France show shamanic rituals.

2700sBC Legendary Shen Nong discovers herbalism.

2600sBC Imhotep describes ancient Egyptian medicine.

c.2000BC Legendary date for the writing of the *Nei Ching*.

1700sBC Code of Hammurabi lays down laws for doctors.

Hammurabi, king of Babylon

1550BC Ebers papyrus records Egyptian medical practices.

1200BC Asclepius sets up healing centres in ancient Greece.

460BC Birth of Hippocrates, who founds Greek medicine.

Hippocrates

c.300 BC The medical school and library at Alexandria is founded.

AD40–c.90 Dioscorides writes manual of herbal medicine.

AD129-216 Galen enlarges on earlier Greek writings and begins experimental medical studies.

THE MIDDLE AGES

AD832 Non-Islamic medical texts are translated in Baghdad.

AD800s Rhazes prepares his medical compendium.

AD1000s Avicenna produces the *Canon of Medicine*.

1100–1300 Medical schools are founded throughout Europe.

1215 The Pope decrees that all doctors need Church approval.

1200s–1300s Professional medical organizations are set up.

1258 Medical texts preserved by the Arabs flow back to the West.

THE RENAISSANCE

1527 Paracelsus lays the ground for studies into chemical treatment of diseases.

1543 Vesalius publishes accurate illustrations of human anatomy.

1628 William Harvey publishes his theory of blood circulation.

1665 King Charles II and the royal court flee London during the Great Plague.

expectations for normal life. Even ageing itself is thought of almost as a disease in some Western cultures, where people are living longer. Thanks to modern medicine, today people can live an active life into extreme old age, while in earlier times they might have been crippled by heart disease or arthritis. However, in some developing countries where malnutrition and infection are common, 40 years is still considered to be a good life expectancy.

Killer diseases, that used to wipe out as many as half of the children in a family, have been brought under control by drugs and vaccination in Western countries. However, nature still has a few surprises for modern medicine. New diseases such as AIDs have appeared and these are not yet under control. Some of the old, familiar microbes have found ways to beat modern antibiotics and are threatening health once more. The only real conquest of disease has been the eradication of smallpox. There are a few more diseases, such as polio, measles and leprosy, that might be conquered soon.

Medicine has made other huge advances. Doctors have the technology with which to examine almost every part of the body. Scientists are beginning to understand the complex chemical reactions that power the body. Surgery, which has been performed for thousands of years, has made great leaps with the techniques for transplantation of body organs and artificial organs. One thing is certain – no one *can* be certain what advances medicine will make in the future.

▲ HIV VIRUS
Recent understanding of the structure of viruses such as HIV has revealed how they overcome the body's natural immune defences. Research into viruses can reveal their weak points, so that effective drugs can be designed to attack them.

MODERN TIMES

1673 Van Leeuwenhoek makes the first microscope and discovers microbes.

1714 Gabriel Fahrenheit invents the mercury thermometer.

1796 Edward Jenner vaccinates against smallpox using cowpox.

1819 René Laënnec introduces the first stethoscope.

Laënnec's stethoscope

1847 Ignaz Semmelweiss demonstrates that infection is spread by unwashed hands.

1853 Queen Victoria uses chloroform as an anaesthetic during childbirth.

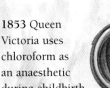

1854 John Snow demonstrates that cholera is spread through contaminated drinking water.

Chloroform mask

1865 Joseph Lister carries out the first operation using carbolic acid as an antiseptic.

1878 Louis Pasteur presents his case for the germ theory of infection.

1882 Robert Koch discovers the tubercle bacillus that causes TB.

1885 Louis Pasteur successfully tests his rabies vaccine.

1895 X-rays are discovered by Wilhelm Röntgen.

1898 Marie Curie discovers the radioactive element radium.

1901–2 Blood groups are described by Karl Landsteiner, making transfusion practical.

1902 Frederick Treves makes removal of the appendix a popular treatment for appendicitis.

Marie Curie

1928 Alexander Fleming discovers penicillin.

1953 James Watson and Francis Crick discover the structure of DNA.

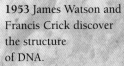

DNA

1954 The first successful kidney transplant is performed.

1955 Jonas Salk introduces the first polio vaccine.

1961 Thalidomide (a sedative) is withdrawn after causing birth defects.

1964 Christiaan Barnard carries out the first heart transplant.

1974 The last natural case of smallpox occurs.

1983 HIV is identified in France and the USA.

Earliest Medicine

▲ TREPANNING TOOLS
Stone Age people used a drill to cut a hole in the skull. This was a wooden stick with a sharpened piece of flint at the tip. Flints were later used with a bow drill. Sometimes the drill was tipped with volcanic glass or even a shark's tooth.

EARLY PEOPLE'S REMAINS contain evidence of attempts at medical care. The most striking of these are skulls with neatly drilled or cut holes. The process of making these holes is called trepanning. The holes may have been made to allow a disease to escape from the body. Trepanned skulls have been found in Europe and in South America. Remarkably, some of them show signs that the cut edges of bone had healed, so the patient had survived for some time after the operation. Some even show evidence of being trepanned on several different occasions.

Herbal medicine was probably also practised from the earliest times. It can still be seen in the great apes, such as chimpanzees. Chimps sometimes chew herbs that are not part of their normal diet, probably for their medicinal effects. The remains of herbs are not uncommon in ancient burials, and have also been found in association with the burials of Neanderthals,

who were ancient relatives of modern people.

Although prehistoric people must have suffered from many diseases, they probably did not experience the rapidly spreading infections that later caused epidemics. They lived in small groups, so there were not enough people for diseases to spread quickly.

By 3000BC people were beginning to live in huge cities, such as Babylon. Epidemic diseases appeared, many of which are recorded in ancient documents and carvings. By the 1700sBC Babylonian doctors had to follow a number of laws. These were written down in the Code of Hammurabi. One practice was to sacrifice animals and look at their organs to work out if the patient would die.

The ancient Egyptians left careful records that describe a whole range of medical

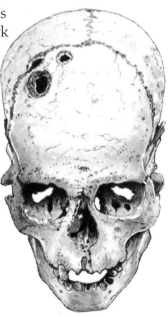

▶ HOLES IN THE HEAD
This skull was found in Jericho and dates to 2000BC. It has three carefully cut trepanning holes, together with a healed hole. The holes are round, which tells us that they must have been drilled into the skull. In other skull finds, there are square holes, that were cut out with a knife.

MESOPOTAMIA AND EGYPT
The oldest surviving medical text is the Ebers papyrus from Egypt. It dates back to about 1550BC. This papyrus scroll is more than 20 metres long and describes many diseases and remedies. It includes over 700 drugs and 800 medicine recipes. There is even a cure for crocodile bites! The Ebers papyrus has instructions for mixing up these medicines into ointments, poultices (compresses), pills and inhalations. There are also descriptions of protective amulets (charms) and spells. Many of the medicines would have had little effect, but some were drugs still familiar today, including opium and cannabis.

▼ THE FIRST DOCTOR
Imhotep was an ancient Egyptian scribe and priest who lived 4,500 years ago. He left many detailed descriptions of diseases and treatments. After his death, he was made into a god.

◀ SURGICAL TOOLS
These bronze and copper knives are from ancient Mesopotamia. They may have been used to remove organs from dead bodies.

▶ CODE OF CONDUCT
Hammurabi, king of Babylon, laid down 17 rules for doctors in the Code of Hammurabi, his collection of all Babylonian laws. The rules included guidelines on punishments for doctors if their treatment did not work.

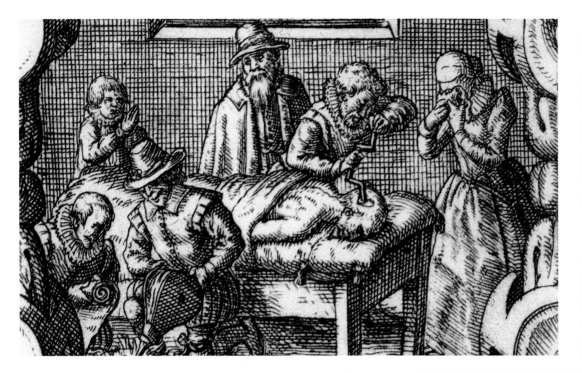

▼ MEDICINE IN THE WILD
Animals such as this baby gorilla search out medicinal herbs in order to treat their ailments. Even carnivores, such as cats, sometimes chew leaves and stems. This may be a way to obtain extra nutrients.

procedures and drugs. Egyptian doctors began to specialize in treating particular organs or diseases. The most famous was Imhotep, who was also a high priest, an architect and an astrologer. The Egyptians believed that spirits crept into the body and caused disease. They used surgery to set broken bones and sew up wounds. However, they took little interest in internal anatomy (the inside workings of the human body). This is surprising, as they must have learnt about it through their interest in mummifying (preserving) the bodies of the dead. Most Egyptian medicine consisted of herbal treatments.

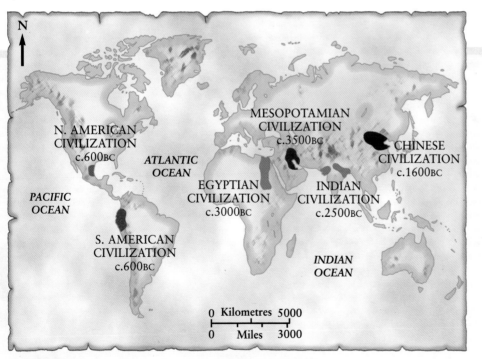

▲ EARLIEST MEDICINE
Finds or written records provide evidence of medicine practised by the civilizations shown here, but it is almost certain that medicine was known in all ancient cultures.

Key Dates

- 10,000–2000BC Evidence of ancient Egyptian medical practice.

- 5000BC Trepanned skull at Ensisheim, France, is the oldest evidence we have of trepanning.

- c.2686–2613BC Life of the Egyptian doctor, Imhotep.

- 1792–1750BC Hammurabi rules in Babylon.

- 1550BC The Ebers papyrus is written in Egypt.

- 650BC Mesopotamian clay tablets describe herbal cures and accurately describe a *migtu* (epileptic seizure).

Shamans and the Supernatural

A S ISOLATED COMMUNITIES developed, so did the idea of an individual who could combine the function of healer with the ability to speak to the gods and spirits. In some early French cave paintings, made about 17,000 years ago, there are pictures of men in animal masks performing ritual dances. These are what we call shamans, and they still exist in many cultures around the world. Shamans are found in Arctic regions and especially in Siberia, among some Native North Americans and South Americans, in Southeast Asia and in the Pacific Islands. In West Africa, shamans are often known as medicine men or witch doctors. Their activities include medical treatment with drugs and prayer, and sometimes the laying of curses on an enemy. People believe that shamans also have the power to cause illness, to ensure fertility or the birth of male children, and to prevent disease by the use of ointments, talismans (charms) and fetishes (magical objects). Shamans are thought to talk with gods, spirits

▲ ASHANTI DOLL
Shamans heal by magic. They often use dolls to represent their patients, or to represent the spirits that will aid in the healing ceremony.

▶ SHAMAN HEALING CEREMONY
During the healing ritual, such as this ceremony in Cameroon, West Africa, the shaman dances around the patient and chants prayers to the spirits.

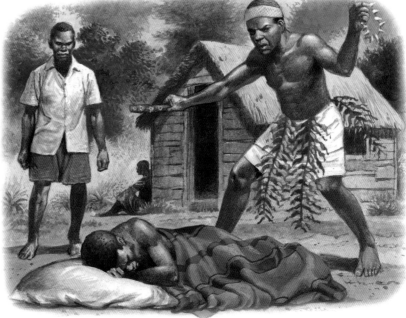

NATIVE AMERICAN MEDICINE

All the Native American tribes had shamans. Those of the Ojibwa tribe formed secret societies and even specialized in particular types of medicine, such as herbalism. Disease was often seen as punishment for bad behaviour or for not worshipping the spirits properly. The Navajo cure was to appeal to the spirits by means of songs, dance, prayer, sweat baths, massage and making sand paintings. Bull-roarers were used to invoke (call up) wind or rain and drive out evil spirits. Healing ceremonies were lengthy. They were used to treat both physical disorders, such as blindness, and mental illness.

▶ MEDICINE MAN
There were over 300 different tribes of Native Americans and they all had different ways of life and traditions. This medicine man is from the Blackfoot tribe, who lived on the plains of the northwestern USA in what is now the state of Montana.

◀ MAGIC NECKLACE
This magical amulet was worn by an Apache medicine man. It is made from glass beads and human teeth, some of which are still embedded in part of the jawbone.

and the dead. They often ask the spirits for special favours, such as a good harvest, or victory in battle over other villages or tribes.

The shaman usually acts as a local religious leader. Shamanism is not organized like the major world religions. It is a collection of a whole range of folk beliefs and myths. The shaman is able to leave his body and enter a trance, where they do not appear to be aware of what is going on around them. He does this through the use of drugs, dancing, music or, sometimes, an epileptic fit.

In most cultures where shamans exist, illness is blamed on the soul leaving the body. In a trance, the shaman finds the soul, which may have been stolen by witchcraft or magic, and persuades it to return to the body. This is a long process, often made dangerous by the use of drugs. If the patient dies, the shaman has to make a treacherous voyage to take the soul of the dead person safely to its new home.

Sometimes an illness is blamed on an object that has been put inside the sick person by magic. In these cases the shaman sucks hard at the affected area, then spits out pieces of wood or stone. These are said to be the cause of the problem. Shamans use various types of instruments and charms for their cures, such as hollow bones to suck out poison, sharp flints for cutting the skin and causing bleeding and, often, masks and other ritual clothing.

◀ BAHUNGANA FETISH
This fetish carries a medicine bag, just like the one a shaman uses to carry his potions. It is festooned with small magical figures that help to give it power.

▶ YOMBE FETISH
This fetish comes from the Yombe tribe of the Republic of Congo. It can be used to cure or curse, by driving nails into the image during a magical ritual. The nail is pushed into the part of the body that needs to be made better or harmed.

▼ SQUAWROOT
North American medicine men used the roots of the black cohosh, or squawroot, as a painkiller. It has now been adopted by Western herbalists.

▶ SAND PAINTING
The Native Americans used grains of coloured sand to create magical pictures called sand paintings. Some were big enough for the sick person to sit in the middle of them during the healing ceremony.

Key Dates

- 15,000BC French cave paintings show evidence of ritual dances.

- c.3000BC An amber horse from this date shows the use of amulets to ward off evil spirits and sickness.

- AD1492 Christopher Columbus 'discovers' the Americas.

- 1520s Cabeza de Vaca witnesses medicine men curing the sick by blowing on the patient.

- 1800s Tradition of medicine men disappears as European settlers destroy and fragment Native American tribes.

Chinese Medicine

▲ YIN AND YANG
This symbol for yin *and* yang *represents the rule of opposites that is so important in Chinese medicine. Yin is the force that represents qualities such as darkness. Its opposite, yang, stands for qualities such as light. Chinese medicine attempts to restore the balance between these opposites.*

CHINESE MEDICINE developed over thousands of years, almost without any outside influences from other medical systems. The *Nei Ching* (Book of Medicine) is an ancient medical work. According to legend, it was written over 4,000 years ago by the Yellow Emperor, Huang Ti. The book was more likely to have been written some time about 200BC, but it has formed the basis for most Chinese medical literature since.

Chinese medicine is largely based on the concept of *yin* and *yang*, which stand for opposing states and conditions. *Yin* represents states such as feminine, dark and wet. *Yang* represents the opposing states of masculine, light and dry. In the *Nei ching, yin* and *yang* are said to control the body, which is thought of as a tiny country with rulers and administrators. The 'country' also has a communication system of 12 rivers, based on the great rivers of China. These rivers divide into much smaller channels which carry blood and a liquid called *ch'i* (vital energy). These channels connect organs to one another. For example, the kidney connects to the ear, the lungs to the nose and the heart to the tongue. When these channels are in good working order, the body is healthy. Points along the channels can be used to influence the flow of *ch'i*.

As with Hinduism, Chinese religions discouraged dissection. For this reason, medicine was based largely

▶ HUANG TI
The Yellow Emperor, Huang Ti, lived from 2698BC to 2598BC. He was said to be the author of the great Chinese medical work called the Nei Ching. *This forms the basis of all Chinese medicine.*

RESTORING THE BALANCE
The Chinese doctor was only paid as long as his patient remained healthy. So if a patient became ill, it was very important to restore the balance of *ch'i* and other elements within the body. This was done with a mixture of exercise, contemplation (thought or meditation), diet and other means. Many Chinese drugs were made from ingredients that were believed to have special effects. For example, organs from a tiger were thought to pass on some of that animal's power.

▶ DOCTOR AND PATIENT
Traditional Chinese medicine involves long discussion between the doctor and patient. The doctor treats the whole body, not just a small diseased part.

◀ MAMMOTH TEETH
So-called dragon teeth are still ground up and widely used in Chinese medicine. Of course, there are no such creatures as dragons. Huge teeth taken from the dug-up remains of ancient mammoths are often used by pharmacists, but so are the teeth of many other extinct animals, including those of the huge ape, *Gigantopithecus*.

▼ GINSENG
This root contains many substances which have powerful effects on the body. Extracts are widely used as a stimulant or tonic. The ginseng root may have appealed to early Chinese pharmacists because it looked a bit like a human body.

◀ PAGE FROM THE NEI CHING
The Nei Ching *explains how the forces* yin *and* yang *interact and affect the flow of* ch'i. *According to the* Nei Ching, *the human body, like all other matter, is made of five basic elements – fire, earth, water, metal and wood.*

▶ SHEN NONG
This legendary emperor lived in the 2700sBC and is said to have discovered Chinese herbal medicine. He described 365 different medical plants. His teachings were written down about 2,000 years ago in a book called the Bencao Jing.

on these channels and their influences on the body. Treatments often involved the use of acupuncture, where needles were inserted into one of the hundreds of points where *ch'i* channels were thought to run. This stimulated (perked up) the flow of *ch'i* and restored good health. Sometimes cones of dried herbs were burned on the skin at these points, for the same purpose. Acupuncture has been practised for more than 4,500 years. It remains central to Chinese medicine and is also used in the West, especially as a treatment for pain and a cure for addiction (dependency on a drug).

Chinese medicine depends mostly on herbal remedies. Many of these herbs have been incorporated into Western medicine, such as castor oil, camphor, chaulmoogra oil to treat leprosy and iron to treat anaemia. Ginseng is a widely-known Chinese remedy, used to keep a person alert, called a stimulant. The ancient Chinese invented vaccination as a way to treat smallpox. They injected a small amount of pus from a smallpox sore into healthy people. This gave them a mild form of the disease and made them immune (resistant) to full-blown infection. Europeans did not discover vaccination until the AD1700s.

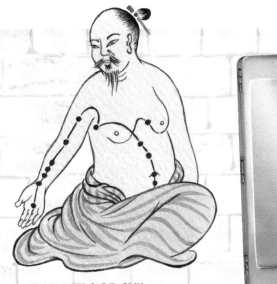

▲ CHANNELS OF CH'I
Acupuncture needles are inserted through the skin at points along lines called meridians (channels). The point where the acupuncturist inserts the needle may be a long way from the part of the body that needs treatment.

◀ ACUPUNCTURE NEEDLES
Acupuncturists (people who practise acupuncture) use very long needles. They may be inserted as deeply as 25 cm into the body. Then the needles are wiggled or twirled to restore the flow of *ch'i*. Modern acupuncturists often pass a small electrical current through the needle.

Key Dates

- 2700sBC Life of legendary emperor Shen Nong, who discovered herbal medicine.

- 2698–2598BC The reign of Huang Ti, legendary founder of Chinese medicine.

- 200sBC The *Nei Ching* is written.

- AD280 Wang Shu-ho writes his 12-volume *Mei Ching* (Book of the Pulse).

- 1601 Yang Chi-chou writes his ten-volume *Ch'en-Chiu Ta-Ch'eng*, describing acupuncture.

- 1600s The first descriptions of Chinese medical practice reach the West.

Hippocrates and the Greeks

THE ANCIENT GREEK DOCTOR Asclepius lived in about 1200BC. According to legend, he was so successful in curing disease that he became a god. The sick went and slept in his temples, known as *asklepia*. They believed that Asclepius would cure them in the night. Diet and mineral baths were part of the cure but treatment of disease was almost entirely a matter for prayer and magical rituals. However, from about 400BC Greek philosophers began to look for a more practical approach to disease.

The ancient Greeks had contact with the Middle East and Asia, due to the conquests of Alexander the Great. In India they may have come across Vedic beliefs. This could explain how Greek philosophers came to believe that the universe was made up of four elements – air, earth, fire and water. This led to the idea that the body was made

▲ SERPENT AND STAFF
A snake coiled around a wooden staff was the symbol of the physician Asclepius, who lived around 1200BC. Even today, it is still used as a sign for the medical profession in many countries around the world.

▲ THE FOUR HUMOURS
This medieval illustration shows the four humours. Greek philosophers held that the body was made up of these four elements – blood, phlegm, yellow bile or choler, and black bile or melancholy. These had to be kept in balance.

TREATING DISEASE

Hippocrates and his fellow doctors believed their job was to help the body to heal itself. Drugs were seldom used, although opium was used to relieve pain. Surgery was understood but was not very common. The Greeks have left behind detailed descriptions of trepanning, even advising surgeons to dip the knife or drill into cold water every now and then so it did not become too hot from rubbing against the bone. The writings of Hippocrates include a method for treating a dislocated (out of joint) shoulder that is still in use today. It is called the Hippocratic method.

▶ MANDRAKE
The root of the mandrake plant was believed to be a powerful magical charm because it looked rather like a human body. Mandrake is actually very poisonous.

▼ GREEK DOCTOR
Greek doctors travelled about to meet their patients, on trips called *epidemics*. They were skilled in examining patients and accurate in diagnosing diseases, but they had only limited treatments available.

▲ BLOODLETTING
This Greek vase, made in about 470BC, shows a doctor preparing to bleed a patient by opening a vein. The blood would have been collected in the jar hanging on the wall behind them.

◀ FATHER OF MEDICINE
Hippocrates was the greatest of the ancient Greek doctors, and his influence persists to this day. He is said to have written more than 70 books on medicine and surgery. The Hippocratic Oath (promise) outlined the responsibilites that Hippocrates believed doctors had to their patients and to society. Doctors still try to live up to these today.

▶ VOTIVE TABLET
It was common to dedicate a tablet to the gods in thanks for a cure. This votive tablet is dedicated to Asclepius, probably in thanks for treatment of varicose veins, which can be seen on the leg that Asclepius is holding.

up of four humours (elements), too.

This belief was held by Hippocrates, the father of Western medicine. He was born in Kos around 460BC. Little is known about him. Even his surviving medical works were actually written by other people. Hippocrates said that diseases had natural causes. He stressed the importance of diagnosis and encouraged doctors to write down all they could about how a disease developed. He thought the body would heal itself and that this process could be sped up through diet, exercise and rest. These helped to restore the balance of the humours. If the disease did not respond, humours were removed by bloodletting (removing blood), or by making the patient sweat. These treatments often worked, even though the reasoning behind them was wrong. This is probably why the theory of humours survived into the 1800s in Western medicine, and so did Hippocratic treatments.

▶ SPREAD OF GREEK MEDICINE
Ancient Greek ideas spread around the Mediterranean, and through the Middle East and Egypt. In turn, herbal remedies and treatments from these areas were incorporated into Greek medicine.

Key Dates

- 1200BC Asclepius sets up healing centres. He is later worshipped as a god.

- 490–430BC Life of Empedocles, who described the four humours.

- 460–377BC Life of Hippocrates.

- 429BC An important medical school is founded at Cyrene.

- 356–323BC Life of Alexander the Great, whose empire stretched as far as India.

- c.300BC The famous medical school is founded at Alexandria.

- c.100BC Greek doctors take their knowledge to Rome.

Roman Medicine

▲ CELSUS
In around 25BC, the Roman nobleman Celsus wrote his huge encyclopedia. One of its volumes, De medicina, recorded all that was known about Greek and Roman medicine.

THE FAMOUS GREEK school at Alexandria remained the centre for medical teaching, even after the Romans conquered the Greeks. Asclepiades of Bithynia (in modern-day Turkey) lived from 124BC until 40BC. He took Greek ideas about medicine to Rome. He did not believe in the healing power of nature, nor that humours caused disease. He recommended treatments such as poultices, massage, good diet and plenty of fresh air. Asclepiades was also the first to study mental illness. He prescribed music, occupational therapy (work) and exercise, together with plenty of wine to sedate them (make them calm or sleepy).

The Romans mostly employed Greek doctors. Even then, many people preferred to treat ailments themselves with herbs and charms. Cornelius Celsus, a Roman nobleman, wrote a detailed history of medicine in about 25BC. Doctors used this work up until the 1400s. It described diseases of the eyes, nose and ears, hernias, bladder stones and other common conditions.

▼ CUPPING
The Romans and Greeks drew foul humours out of the body in a process called cupping. A piece of lint was set alight and placed inside a cup, which was pressed against the skin, an open wound, or a surgical cut. As the oxygen was used up the cup became a vacuum (airless space). This created suction (like in a vacuum cleaner) that sucked out the 'vicious humours.'

LEARNING FROM COMBAT
According to Galen, much disease resulted from an excess of blood, one of the four humours. This surplus blood might putrefy (rot) in some part of the body, and should be removed by bloodletting. Sometimes patients were even bled until they became unconscious. Like Galen's other teachings, bloodletting persisted until the 1800s, resulting in many unnecessary deaths.

◀ ROMAN GLADIATOR
Before moving to Rome, Galen was physician to the gladiators in Alexandria. He must have gained useful experience of anatomy and surgery by treating these professional fighters.

▲ BATTLEFIELD MEDICINE
The Roman army was the first to use doctors on the battlefield. They set up field hospitals to provide instant medical care.

▶ SURGICAL HOOK
Roman surgeons used a bronze hook to tease apart the tissue during an operation. This kept the blood vessels and muscles out of the way and gave the doctor a clear view.

◄ PUBLIC BATHS
The Romans took great care of their bodies. They spent many hours in the public baths, soaking in hot water or enjoying a massage. This helped them to avoid infections caused by poor hygiene.

▼ ROMAN AQUEDUCT
Clean water supplies were an important public health measure introduced by the Romans. Aqueducts were bridges that carried supplies of fresh water from sources many kilometres away.

During the 1st and 2nd centuries AD, many Greek doctors travelled to Rome. Claudius Galen moved to Rome in AD162 and went on to become the physician to five different Roman emperors. He was so influential that his writings were accepted for the next 1,500 years. Galen developed Hippocrates' theories about humours but, unlike the Greeks, he believed in experimenting.

Human dissection was not permitted, so Galen learnt about anatomy by dissecting monkeys and other animals. As a result, many of his assumptions were later proved wrong. Galen showed that blood ebbs and flows as the heart beats, but he never realized that it flows around the body. He wrote at least 350 books about medicine, some describing very complex operations. Galen's works were so respected that they went unchallenged for centuries. Even his mistakes were widely accepted up until the 1500s, when doctors

began to experiment once more.

While Greek influence accounted for most medical advances in Rome, the Romans made important advances in maintaining public health, which reduced infectious disease. Fresh water was piped into the cities and public baths were built. There was proper sanitation and rubbish clearance. Clinics and hospitals were built and there were also army doctors who treated soldiers' battle wounds.

▲ FOLDING SCALPEL
The Romans used scalpels like this to cut open a body for surgery. It folded when not in use to prevent any accidental cuts.

▼ ARMY HOSPITAL
This model shows an army hospital, or *valetudinarium*. The Romans developed a sophisticated system of care for their soldiers. Hospitals on this scale did not appear again for nearly a thousand years.

Key Dates

- c.100–44BC Life of Julius Caesar, who employs doctors in the army.

- 53BC–AD7 Life of Cornelius Celsus, author of *De medicina*.

- AD40–c.90 Life of Nero's army surgeon, Dioscorides, who describes around 600 plants and over 1,000 drugs in his book, *De materia medica*.

- AD77 Pliny the Elder's *Historia Naturalis* describes surgery and herbal remedies.

- c.AD100 Soranus writes about birth control and pregnancy.

- AD129–216 Life of Galen, who expands on Greek writings.

The Arab World

DURING THE PERIOD of the Byzantine Empire (AD300–1453), the works of Greek and Roman doctors were collected together. Some appeared in the languages used at the fringes of the empire, such as Persian and Syrian.

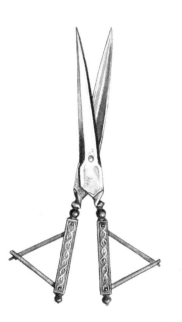

▲ SURGICAL SCISSORS
Scissors were developed as a more precise way to cut through tissue than knives or scalpels.

▶ AVICENNA
Avicenna was a Persian doctor working within the Arab Empire. His book, the Canon of Medicine, *was used across the Middle East and Europe for centuries.*

Meanwhile the Arab Empire was growing in power and influence. It conquered Persia and Syria. At first, the Arabs favoured their own traditional remedies, but as the power of the Islamic religion increased in the Arab Empire, many traditional treatments were lost. Doctors began to turn to ancient Greek ideas and translated Greek texts into Arabic. This meant that ancient Greek learning spread throughout the Arab Empire, into Europe and around the Mediterranean.

Important centres of learning sprang up in Baghdad, Cairo and Damascus in the Middle East, and in Toledo, Cordoba and Seville in what is now Spain. Arab scientists and doctors published copies of the early medical works. Some of these were later translated into Latin and used in European medical schools from the 1200s.

Arab medicine did not contribute much new knowledge, but Arab writers made detailed descriptions of diseases and their diagnoses. Surgery suffered in early years, because dissection was banned, so little was known about anatomy. However, an Arab surgeon in Cordoba wrote a text on surgical techniques and others developed techniques for surgery on the eye and the internal organs. The Arabs were interested in alchemy (trying to transform cheap metals into gold, and searching for a source of eternal life). Their alchemical experiments led them to find many

MEDICAL PIONEERS

Not all of the medical scholars were Arabs. Many were Persians, Jews or Christians living within the Arab Empire. Rhazes was a Persian who put together a huge medical compendium. Maimonides was a Jewish doctor born in the 1100s. He became physician to the Saracen ruler Saladin. His extensive writings on medicine were based on Greek ideas.

◀ RHAZES
The Persian physician Rhazes was born in the AD800s. He wrote more than 200 books on a huge range of subjects. He was admired for his medical care of the poor.

▲ EYE SURGERY
Cataracts is an eye condition that clouds the lens of the eye and eventually leads to blindness. Arab physicians developed a technique for dislodging the clouded lens and pushing it clear of the field of vision. This allowed some degree of sight to be restored.

drugs by accident. Alchemists also developed techniques for purifying chemicals that are still used today. Arab pharmacists complied long lists of these herbal remedies, gathered from the places they conquered. Some describe more than 3,000 different

drugs. Some of these drugs were very unusual. The real value of Arab writings, however, was how carefully they recorded information. These great works were painstakingly copied and circulated throughout the Arab Empire.

◀ MIXING MEDICINES
Persian and Arab apothecaries (chemists) developed many methods for preparing medicines. These Persians are boiling the ingredients of a medicine over a brazier (a container of burning coals).

▼ PESTLE AND MORTAR
The simplest way to make up a herbal medicine was to grind its ingredients together using a pestle and mortar. This made a powder that could be mixed with water and drunk, or made into a paste or ointment. They are still in common use today.

▼ MEDICINE IN THE ARAB EMPIRE
The Arab Empire spread widely around the Mediterranean and the Middle East and adopted the traditional remedies of the regions it conquered. Arab scholars preserved ancient Greek and Roman traditions and wrote down the newest medical discoveries.

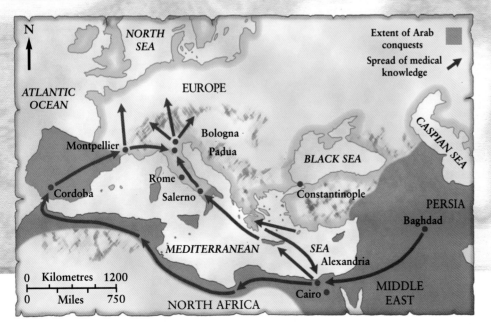

Key Dates

- AD620s Muhammad founds Islam.

- AD832 Baghdad is established as a centre of learning.

- AD850 Muslim scholar at-Tabari compiles medical writings of Greece, Rome, Persia and India.

- c.AD865–928 Life of Rhazes.

- AD980–1037 Life of Avicenna.

- 1174 Maimonides is appointed as court physician to Saladin.

- 1236 Christians gain Cordoba.

- 1258 Mongol warriors sack Baghdad. Medical information preserved by the Arabs begins to flow back to the West.

Galen's Legacy

▲ URINE GAZING
During the 1200s and 1300s, there were few ways to diagnose a disease. One method was to examine the patient's urine. Its colour, cloudiness and even its taste were carefully noted.

▶ MEDICAL GIANTS
In this edition of Galen's works published in 1528, Galen is shown with two other medical geniuses. Hippocrates is on the left and Avicenna on the right.

AFTER THE EMPEROR Constantine made Christianity the official religion of the Roman Empire, the power of Greek medicine and Galenic teaching began to fade. Once more, religion became more influential than practical medicine. Sickness was often seen as punishment from God for past sins. Prayer and pilgrimages to holy relics were the recommended cures for most diseases and cults of healing saints sprang up.

The Church's opinion of medicine was summed up by St Bernard who lived from AD1090 until 1153. He said that going to the doctor was not proper behaviour. Trying to cure a disease was seen as interfering with God's punishment. A dying person was more likely to call a priest than a doctor.

Christian saints became associated with different diseases. St Christopher dealt with epilepsy, St Roch was the patron saint of plague victims, St Apollonia looked after those with toothache and St Margaret kept women safe during childbirth.

However, the sick did receive some practical care. Many monasteries offered care of the sick. Hospitals were built across Europe, often alongside healing shrines (holy places). Special hospitals were built for lepers, who were treated with especial horror and considered 'unclean.'

Medical knowledge began to improve in the AD1000s, when a

FALSE BELIEFS
Throughout the Middle Ages, superstition formed part of medical practice. Herbals were books that listed the medicinal properties of plants. A few of these did have the promised effect, but most were useless. Bleeding, the use of leeches, enemas and deliberate vomiting were all recommended. Following the ideas of Hippocrates, these methods were thought to restore the balance of the humours.

◀ LUNGWORT
Many plants were used in medicine on the basis of their appearance. This practice was known as the doctrine of signatures. The leaves of lungwort were thought to look like the lung, so this plant was used to treat lung disease.

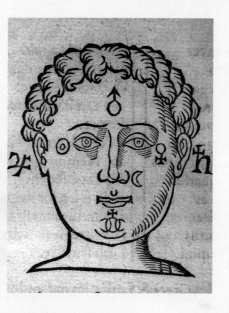

◀ ASTROLOGY
Many strange theories developed to explain how disease progressed. Astrology was thought to show an association with diseased body parts.

▶ PURGING
Powerful drugs were given to cause vomiting. Being sick was believed to rid the body of poisons.

small group of doctors began work at Salerno, in Italy. They formed an influential medical school and revived ancient ideas, especially those of Galen. People assumed Galen's teachings were accurate, even though some were changed or missed out in translation and others had been wrong in the first place. Doctors treated their patients with diets and drugs, many of which were imported from the East.

Surgery became a separate branch of medicine and was carried out by barber-surgeons. Barber-surgeons provided a range of services. They cut hair, pulled out teeth, gave enemas (injected fluids into the rectum) and let blood.

At least one Greek technique was challenged. Hippocrates had recommended leaving open wounds to become septic. Henri de Mondeville, a French surgeon who lived from 1260 until 1320, had different ideas. He advised closing the wound as soon as possible and keeping it dry and covered to prevent infection. Thanks to de Modeville, many limbs and lives were saved.

▼ CAUTERIZING IRON
To stop bleeding, medieval doctors used to apply a red-hot iron to coagulate (thicken) the blood. This caused agonizing pain. Cauterization was not very hygienic and many wounds became infected.

▲ LEECHES
Bloodletting was a treatment for most illnesses. People often used freshwater leeches to suck out the blood. Recently, the use of leeches has been reintroduced as a way to reduce serious bruising.

▼ POMANDER
In medieval times, people thought that foul smells spread disease. Many carried scented pomanders about with them to drive these smells away. The simplest pomanders were oranges stuck with aromatic spices called cloves.

▲ HOLY EYES
St Lucy of Syracuse became the patron saint of eye disease. According to legend, she plucked out her own eyes but they grew back. Many sick people still pray to saints.

Key Dates

- 1100–1300 Medical schools and hospitals are founded throughout Europe.
- 1100s Trotula joins the Salerno medical school. She writes the first complete work on women's health and another on skin disease.
- 1200s–1300s Physicians and surgeons begin to form into professional organizations.
- 1215 Pope Innocent III decrees that all doctors must be approved by the Church and bans lepers from the Church.
- 1260–1320 Henri de Mondeville recommends closing wounds.

Renaissance Discoveries

THE RENAISSANCE was the period in European history that lasted from the 1400s until the 1600s. Before then, European medicine was based on theory rather than practice. Then Renaissance scientists and physicians began to question the old Greek writings on medicine. Some brave individuals even challenged the Church's teachings on the effect of the soul on the body. This change of approach was not the result of renewed interest in Greek and Roman medicine. It was led by people who rejected tradition and wished to discover and investigate. Scientists began to dissect human

▲ THERMOMETER
Unlike a modern one, this mercury thermometer from the 1400s had to be kept in the patient's mouth for up to 25 minutes.

▶ VESALIUS
This picture by Eduoard Hamman was made during the 1800s. It shows how Vesalius dissected human bodies so that he could make extremely detailed anatomical drawings.

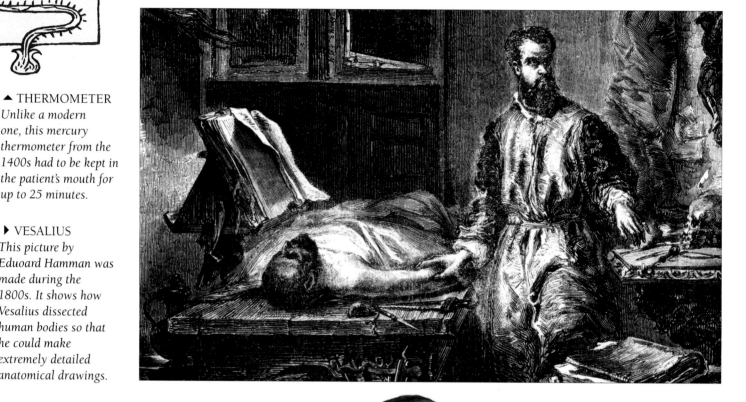

MEDICAL REVOLUTIONARIES

The ideas of Hippocrates and Galen had been followed for so long without question, that it was difficult to abandon them. New ideas did not always offer a comforting solution to medical problems and many traditional doctors did not welcome them. Despite opposition, revolutionary scientists and doctors persevered and made some ground-breaking discoveries.

▼ MARCELLO MALPIGHI
The Italian biologist and doctor Malpighi was able to complete part of the story of blood circulation. He discovered the capillary vessels that link arteries and veins, which Harvey had been unable to see.

▶ PARACELSUS
Paracelsus was a Swiss doctor. His belief in alchemy, which flew in the face of fashion, nevertheless led him to discover important new drugs. In this way, Paracelsus pioneered chemical treatment of disease.

▲ WILLIAM HARVEY
Harvey was the first person to prove that the heart pumped blood through the body, which he did by identifying the direction of blood flow. He even demonstrated his discovery to King Charles I.

bodies. The first anatomists were puzzled to see that their findings did not match Galen's descriptions. Their new knowledge led to great advances in surgery.

The greatest revolution in the understanding of anatomy and physiology came from the work of the Flemish physician Andreas Vesalius. In 1543 he published his detailed drawings of dissections of the human body. Vesalius was Professor of Anatomy at the University of Padua, Italy. One of his successors, Hieronymus Fabricius, studied the function of the valves in the veins and established that they made the blood flow in one direction. He tried to blend his findings with those of Galen, so he did not realize that the blood circulated through the body. One of his students, an Englishman called William Harvey, was able to contribute to the story by demonstrating the circulation of the blood. However, even Harvey missed the final link because he did not realize how blood passes from the arteries to the veins.

As people realized that many ancient manuscripts and descriptions were inaccurate, they collected new descriptions of medicinal plants in books called herbals. This led to the discovery of many plants and drugs previously unknown in Western Europe. These included the rhubarb root (first described in a Chinese herbal over 4,000 years earlier), which was used to cleanse the bowels. Explorers to the New World, especially the Spanish and Portuguese, brought back amazing new plants, while travellers to the Far East brought back new drugs and remedies, too.

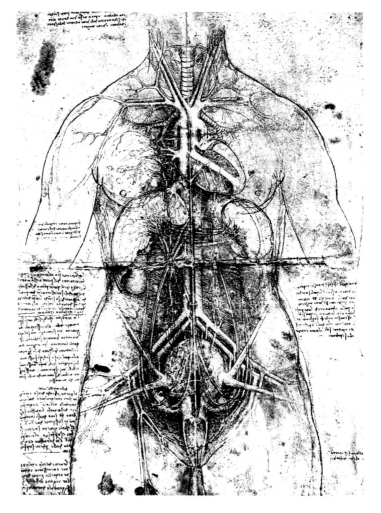

▲ THE MAJOR ORGANS OF THE BODY
Leonardo Da Vinci's anatomical drawings were undoubted works of art. Often, however, they were highly inaccurate. Da Vinci made guesses rather than performing detailed dissections himself.

▲ AMBROISE PARÉ
Paré was a French army surgeon who came to realize that cauterizing wounds often resulted in the patient dying. He developed a gentler form of dressing and tying off of severed blood vessels, making a huge advance in surgical care.

▼ GIROLAMO FRACASTORO
This Italian formulated the idea that infection could spread from one person to another by physical contact, or through the air. He guessed that this might be caused by tiny living organisms, which he called 'seeds.' However, he could not prove his theory, so it was largely dismissed.

Key Dates

- 1482 Pope Sixtus IV allows the dissection of executed criminals.

- 1527 Paracelsus burns the books of Avicenna and Galen.

- 1537 Ambroise Paré develops his concept of wound care.

- 1540 Barber-Surgeons' Company is founded in England.

- 1546 Fracastoro publishes his theories on germs and disease.

- 1628 William Harvey publishes his theory of blood circulation.

- 1661 Marcello Malpighi publishes his theory on the circulation of the blood through the lungs.

Plague and Pestilence

▲ FLEA
Bubonic plague is spread by the bite of a flea that has fed on the blood of an infected rat. European towns and cities were infested with rats during the 1300s and 1400s.

IN AD540 A TERRIBLE DISEASE broke out in Europe. This epidemic is known as Justinian's Plague, after the Byzantine emperor at the time. So many people died that the his empire was almost destroyed. Over 800 years later, during the 1300s, the plague reappeared in Europe. This outbreak is known as the Black Death. Between 1348 and 1351 it killed around 20 million people.

The plague had reached Constantinople in 1347, carried by traders fleeing from the advance of Mongol warriors from Asia. They brought the disease with them from the steppes (grasslands) where they originally lived. Although humans can catch it, plague is a disease of rodents, and especially of the black rat. Infected rats were bitten by fleas that fed on their blood. When the host rat died, the fleas looked for a new source of food. They bit people, who then became infected with the plague.

Infected people developed swellings around the neck, armpits and groin, and bled beneath the skin, producing sores called buboes. They died at such a rate that bodies were just dumped in huge pits. Doctors were helpless to treat the plague. Isolating infected people did not help, because rats were everywhere. Once most of the rats died, the plague slowly vanished. However, it came back again at intervals. There was another serious outbreak during the 1800s. The plague is still around today, for example in the USA.

Bubonic plague was not the only pestilence to strike Europe in the Middle Ages. Leprosy was common.

▲ SPREAD OF THE PLAGUE
In 1347 the bubonic plague arrived at the trading post of Kaffa (modern-day Feodosiya, in Ukraine). Merchants unwittingly carried the disease to Constantinople. From there, it soon spread rapidly throughout Europe.

THE BLACK DEATH
The mortality (death rate) from the Black Death was so huge that it changed the whole structure of European society. The ancient feudal system of serfs who worked their masters' land broke down. There were not enough people to work the land. Often, whole villages were abandoned. Wealthy people fled the cities as outbreaks of plague approached, but the rats travelled with them, so the disease continued unchecked.

▶ THE TOWN CRIER
'Bring out your dead' was the message called out at the height of the plague by the town criers, who were the only way of spreading news quickly, as most people could not read. Strangers were often barred from entering plague-free areas.

▲ FAST FUNERALS
People died from the plague in huge numbers. Only the rich were buried in individual graves like this one. Most bodies were dumped into huge communal graves, known as plague pits.

▶ THE TRIUMPH
OF DEATH
Pieter Bruegel painted his
Triumph of Death in
about 1562. It features
nightmarish skeletons
and gives some idea of the
hysterical fear caused by
the plague. The title of
the painting refers to the
commonly-held belief that
the Black Death was a
victory for the forces of evil.

▼ PLAGUE VICTIM
This illustration appeared in
the Toggenberg Bible in the
1400s. It clearly shows the
huge buboes, or swellings,
that covered a plague
victim's body.

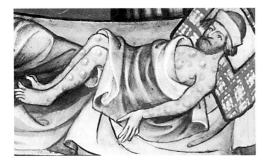

Although the disease is not very infectious, lepers were feared and treated as social outcasts. There were also epidemics of cholera and typhoid. Cholera was especially feared because it killed most people who caught it and no one understood what caused it. It was caused by sewage and rubbish in rivers. People picked up the bacteria causing these diseases from contaminated drinking water and food.

Medicine was powerless against these epidemics, so prayer was the only option for the terrified people when disease broke out.

▶ PLAGUE HOUSE
The doors of houses where plague victims lived were marked with a red cross. Some houses were sealed up, even if there were healthy people still living inside.

◀ DR DEATH
Plague doctors offered to cure or prevent the disease. To keep themselves clear of infection they wore strange costumes. They stuffed their headdresses with sweet-smelling herbs and carried amulets and pomanders.

Key Dates

- AD540 Justinian's Plague attacks Constantinople.

- 1347 Plague reaches the Black Sea coast. It spreads all over Europe from Constantinople within two years.

- 1349 Jews are blamed for the plague and massacred in Strasbourg, Mainz and Frankfurt.

- 1377 The Italian port of Dubrovnik quarantines itself, followed by the ports of Venice and Pisa, also in Italy, and Marseilles, in France.

- 1665 The Great Plague attacks London. King Charles II and his court flee to the countryside.

Making a Diagnosis

D IAGNOSIS IS THE skill of identifying a disease. It is carried out by observing signs and symptoms of the illness. Until recently there were few medical tests to help a doctor identify a disease. Instead, doctors talked to their patients, examined them and looked at their behaviour.

In Greece, at the time of Hippocrates, doctors tried to identify their patient's disease so they could reach their prognosis (say how the disease would develop). A doctor's reputation rested on how accurately he predicted whether the patient would recover or die. Hippocrates taught that every single observation could be significant. Greek doctors used all of their senses in making their diagnosis. Touch, taste, sight, hearing and smell could all provide valuable clues. These principles still apply for modern doctors.

By Galen's time, taking the pulse had become a part of diagnosis. Galen gave instructions on how to take the

◀ CLINICAL THERMOMETER
The modern digital thermometer is quick and easy to use, and is also extremely accurate. It does not contain the poisonous mercury used in traditional thermometers, which were fragile and easily broken.

▶ USING THE STETHOSCOPE
The stethoscope introduced by Laënnec's in 1819 was awkward to use, because it was rigid. Unlike the modern stethoscope, which has a bendy rubber tube, it was not easy to move around in order to detect sounds in different areas.

TOOLS OF THE TRADE
Diagnosis improved with the invention of instruments that allowed the doctor to find out what was going on inside the body. A whole range of new observations could be made, and these were added to the findings from old methods, such as interviewing the patient. Better measurements of pulse rate, blood pressure and temperature all helped towards accurate diagnosis.

◀ LAËNNEC'S STETHOSCOPE
In 1819 the French physician René Laënnec introduced the first stethoscope. It was a wooden device, almost 23 cm long, that amplified the sounds of the chest.

▼ THE STETHOSCOPE TODAY
The modern stethoscope is a simple lightweight device. It allows doctors and nursing staff to listen to the sounds of the lungs and the heart. It often gives an early warning of illness.

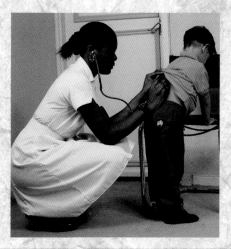

Early opthalmoscope   *Modern opthalmoscope*

▲ EYE SPY
Doctors use instruments called ophthalmoscopes to examine a patient's eye. The earliest were little more than powerful magnifying glasses. The modern instrument has powerful lenses and lights that allow the doctor to see right to the back of the eyeball.

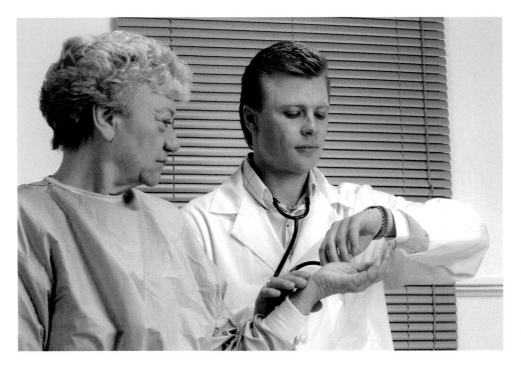

pulse. The findings could be described as 'fast' or 'normal.'

In the Arab world, diagnosis involved careful examination of the affected parts, checking the pulse and examining the urine. Arab doctors did not disclose their findings to anyone else in case they frightened the patient. In most of Europe, diagnosis was rather haphazard, because disease was seen as a punishment from God. This meant its cause could not be questioned and the disease could not be treated, except with prayer. Sometimes the diagnosis was obvious to all, such as in cases of leprosy or plague, but even then the doctor was not able to cure the patient.

It was not until the 1700s that real advances were made in the art of diagnosis. In 1761, a Viennese doctor called Leopold Auenbrugger discovered that thumping on a patient's chest produced sounds which could indicate lung disease. The technique was reluctantly accepted and is still in use today. However, most doctors did not perform physical examinations, and still formed their diagnosis by interviewing the patient. Auscultation (sounding the chest) improved with the invention of the stethoscope in 1816. This also allowed doctors to hear the heart properly, and diagnose different heart diseases.

Examination of the urine was a popular method of diagnosis for all sorts of disease. Its colour, odour and even its taste were thought to reveal the state of the patient's health. Urine tests are still used in some forms of diagnosis today, for example to identify diabetes or pregnancy.

▲ COUNTING THE BEATS
Taking a person's pulse tells the doctor how fast the heart is beating. With each heartbeat, the arteries bulge slightly. The arteries at the wrist are very close to the skin surface, so the doctor can feel them bulge with his or her fingertip.

▼ BLOOD CHEMISTRY
Blood tests are used to measure changes in the chemical make up of the blood. These changes can indicate that a person is suffering from an infection, diabetes or some other hormonal disorder, or that a woman is pregnant.

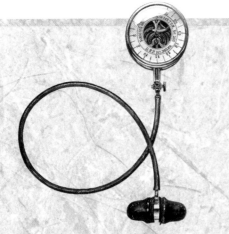

▲ UNDER PRESSURE
The sphygmomanometer is used to measure blood pressure. First the doctor puts an inflatable sleeve on the patient's arm. This is pumped up to close off the blood flow through the arteries. As the sleeve is slowly deflated, the device measures the blood pressure.

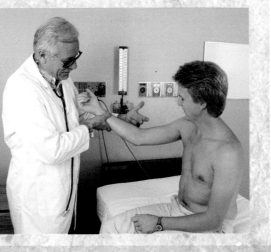

Key Dates

- 1714 Gabriel Fahrenheit invents the mercury thermometer.

- 1761 Leopold Auenbrugger publishes his findings on sounding the chest.

- 1819 René Laënnec introduces the first stethoscope.

- 1851 Hermann von Helmhotz invents the ophthalmoscope.

- 1868 Carl Wunderlich promotes widespread use of the thermometer.

- 1895 Wilhelm Röntgen discovers x-rays.

- 1896 Scipione Riva-Rocci invents the sphygmomanometer.

The Rise of Surgery

▲ JOHN HUNTER
Born in Scotland in 1728, John Hunter was very important to modern surgery. He changed people's views so that they saw it as a proper medical discipline. He put together a huge collection of medical specimens, which today is in the Hunterian Museum, in Glasgow.

SURGERY IS PROBABLY the oldest medical skill. Even pressing a hand over a cut to stop it bleeding is a form of surgery. Prehistoric skeletons show signs of bone-setting to repair broken limbs, and holes drilled into skulls in the process of trepanning. Some ancient civilizations practised very sophisticated surgery, with operations on the eyes, and even on the intestines. However, during the Middle Ages, the skill was almost lost. Surgery was not taught in most European medical schools. It was left to barbers and other unskilled people to carry out surgery, usually as a last resort. During the Renaissance, there were attempts to improve matters. The United Company of Barber-Surgeons was set up in London in 1540 to give guidelines to people carrying out operations. However, most patients still died through infections due to lack of hygiene.

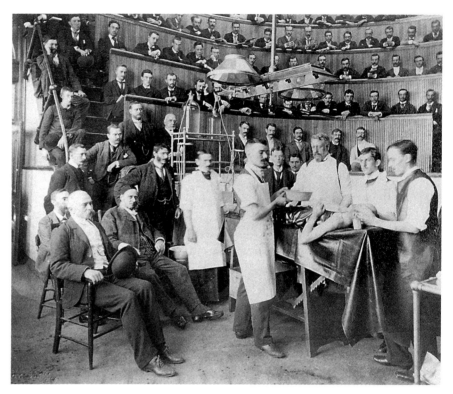

▶ SURGERY IN THE ROUND
This photograph, taken in 1898, shows surgery being performed at the Bellevue Hospital, New York. Fellow surgeons and medical students look on, so that they can learn the latest surgical techniques.

EARLY SURGERY
Surgery was carried out in ancient Mesopotamia as long ago as 2000BC, and in India in 100BC. The Indian surgeons were especially skilful and left behind detailed descriptions of delicate operations to remove cataracts from the eye. In ancient China, however, any invasion of the body was discouraged and surgery was seldom practised. Advanced surgery was practised by the ancient Greeks and the Romans, and spread into the Arab Empire, eventually returning to Europe much later.

▼ HUA TUO
Surgical treatment was discouraged in ancient China. Its only record is of Hua Tuo operating on the arm of General Kuan Yun. Hua Tuo was executed for treason when he offered to perform a trepanning operation on Prince Tsao Tsao. The prince suspected a plot to murder him.

◀ BLEEDING A PATIENT
Bloodletting was one of the earliest and most common forms of surgery. In later times it was carried out by barber-surgeons. Bloodletting was used to treat almost all diseases. Patients were usually already very ill. The loss of blood often weakened them so much that they died.

In 1547, the French surgeon Ambroise Paré abandoned the traditional, agonizing cauterization of wounds with a red-hot iron. He found that he could tie off the blood vessels to prevent blood loss, with far less shock and mortality in his patients. It was another two centuries before any further advances were made.

By the 1700s, improved knowledge of anatomy meant that the removal of tumours and bladder stones were common operations. Amputations were carried out in less than five minutes to minimize pain and shock. Patients were sedated (quietened) with opium or alcohol and held down by attendants. However, many still died due to infection caused during surgery.

From the 1760s the British surgeon John Hunter turned surgery from amateur butchery into a scientific profession. He lectured, wrote widely, and collected huge numbers of medical specimens. Hunter was an expert dissector. As the number of hospitals had increased, so had the number of unclaimed dead bodies, which could be sent to the anatomy schools and used for training student surgeons.

Once pain and infection could be controlled, surgery became less risky. Operations became common for minor problems. Appendicitis had been recognized back in the 1500s, but surgery to remove the appendix was regarded as very dangerous. Then, in 1902, Frederic Treves drained an abcess on the appendix of the Prince of Wales, just before he was crowned Edward VIII. This won Treves a knighthood and, from then on, surgery to remove the appendix became highly fashionable.

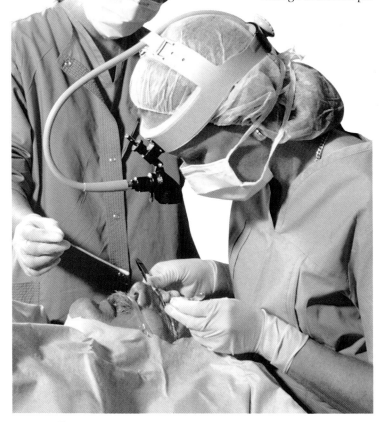

▼ EYE OPERATION
Modern surgery demands very precise instruments. This eye surgeon is using a scalpel that has a tiny blade made from diamond, which is extremely sharp. The doctor sees into the eye by means of a powerful magnifier. Some operations are so delicate that they are carried out looking through a microscope.

▲ LOSING A LEG
Amputations were a brutal business. They had to be carried out very swiftly so the patients would not die from bleeding and shock. In this picture, printed in 1618, the barber-surgeon already has cauterizing irons heating in the fire, ready to seal the wound.

▼ BLOOD STOPPER
The tourniquet was developed to stop blood loss after an amputation. The strap was fastened tightly around the limb above the place where the cut was to be made. Then the screw was tightened down to squeeze the arteries and cut off the blood flow.

▲ SURGICAL SAW
At first, ordinary carpenters' saws were used for amputations. Later, specialized surgical saws were produced.

Key Dates

- AD600s The Ayurvedic *Sushrita-Samhita* describes over 120 types of steel surgical instrument.

- 1728–1793 Life of John Hunter, who revolutionizes the teaching and practice of surgery.

- 1793 French army surgeon Dominique-Jean Larrey introduces the first ambulance service, *ambulances volantes*.

- 1809 American Ephraim McDowell pioneers gynaecological surgery when he removes a tumour from a woman's ovary.

- 1902 Frederic Treves treats the Prince of Wales' appendicitis.

Germ-free and pain-free

▲ KEEPING CLEAN
Washing the hands is still one of the most important ways to limit the spread of infection, both in hospitals and in the home. Modern surgical staff use antibacterial soap to prevent infection.

▶ IGNAZ SEMMELWEISS
Semmelweiss realized that lack of hygiene was causing many deaths among his patients so he insisted on rigorous washing. His views were considered outrageous and he was forced out of his hospital in Vienna.

SURGERY IN THE 1600s was a very dangerous business. There was no concept of hygiene. Surgeons worked in their normal clothes, which became splashed with blood. They used instruments in consecutive operations without any attempt at cleaning. Childbirth fever was a particular hazard, killing many women within a few days of giving birth. A Hungarian doctor, Ignaz Semmelweiss, realized that patients were more likely to suffer infection after being examined by medical students who had been carrying out dissections. He saw that when students had not visited the dissection rooms, infection did not occur. As a result, Semmelweiss insisted on high standards of hygiene in his hospital, and this cut the death rate dramatically. He

was violently opposed by many medical colleagues, however, and eventually had to leave his practice in Vienna.

At this time no one realized that microbes spread disease. It was not until the 1860s that the concept of bacterial infection was established as a result of the work of Louis Pasteur. The British surgeon Joseph Lister made the next major advance. He was alarmed at how many people died of severe bone fractures. Lister observed that if a bone was broken without penetrating the skin, infection seldom occurred. If a bone fragment punctured the skin, exposing it to the air, there was usually an infection, and this led to amputation or death.

When Lister found out about Pasteur's work, he realized that it was not air that caused the problem, but bacteria contaminating the wound. Lister had heard that carbolic acid could be used to kill bacteria in sewage, so he tried spraying a mist of diluted carbolic acid on wounds. His experiment had dramatic results. Out of his first 11 patients, only one died. This discovery was resisted at first, but as it became

KILLING THE PAIN

Anaesthesia has a long history. The ancient Greeks used drugs to provide pain relief. By the 1800s, opium was widely used as a soporific (to make the patient sleepy). Alcohol was also used in surgery to help the patient relax. Ether and nitrous oxide were the first modern anaesthetics. They were introduced at about the same time and were both inhaled. Shortly afterwards, chloroform was introduced. After initial resistance, all three of these anaesthetics were enthusiastically accepted and became very widely used.

▼ WILLIAM MORTON
Morton was an American dentist who experimented with the effects of ether as an anaesthetic. In 1846 he anaesthetized a patient for the surgeon John Collins Warren.

▲ FIRST FAILURE
In 1848, Hannah Greener became the first person to die from the poisonous effects of chloroform. Greener had only had a minor operation to remove a toenail.

▼ CHLOROFORM MASK
Chloroform and ether were both applied by soaking a cloth mask. The mask's wire frame closely covered the nose and mouth so that the chloroform or ether fumes were breathed in by the patient.

accepted it was possible to carry out routine operations with hardly any risk to the patient. Asepsis (keeping free from infection) was safer than allowing a bacterial infection to take hold and then trying to treat it with antiseptics. To achieve this surgeons tried to keep bacteria away from wounds by sterilizing their instruments and wearing masks and gowns.

At about the same time that asepsis was discovered, several doctors discovered how pain could be relieved by the use of anaesthetics. In 1846 the American dentist Thomas Morton showed how ether could be used to eliminate pain during surgery, while John Warren also experimented with the use of nitrous oxide (laughing gas). Nitrous oxide had been used for a while as a party novelty. Breathing in the gas made people collapse in fits of giggles. Chloroform was another form of anaesthetic. After John Snow gave it to Queen Victoria during the birth of Prince Leopold, its use became more widespread.

▲ STEAM SPRAY
Joseph Lister invented the carbolic steam spray. It produced a fine mist of mild carbolic acid in the operating room and killed bacteria. The death rate among Lister's patients fell from 50 per cent to 5 per cent.

◄ UNDER THE KNIFE
From the 1860s, operations were carried out in antiseptic conditions. A carbolic steam spray pumped an antibacterial mist into the room. Surgery was not only safer, it was more comfortable for the patient. A chloroform mask kept them unconscious during the operation.

▶ THE MODERN ANAESTHETIST
Anaesthesia is now usually carried out using a mixture of gases. Anaesthesia depresses (slows down) all of the body's functions, so the patient's condition must be carefully monitored during surgery.

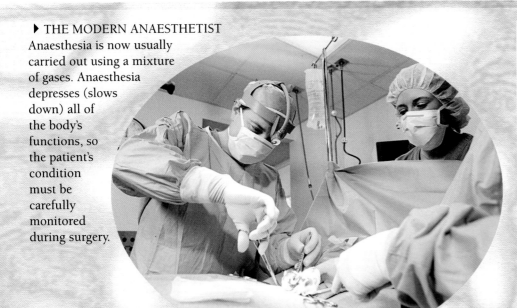

Key Dates

- 1800 Humphrey Davy reports that nitrous oxide can produce unconsciousness.

- 1831 Chloroform is discovered.

- 1844 Horace Wells uses nitrous oxide to anaesthetize a patient.

- 1846 William Morton uses ether to anaesthetize a patient.

- 1847 Ignaz Semmelweiss makes his staff wash their hands.

- 1865 Joseph Lister uses his carbolic steam spray in surgery.

- 1884 Cocaine is used as a local anaesthetic, pain-killing drug.

- 1886 Aseptic surgery begins.

Quacks and Charlatans

▲ KOLA MARQUE
This French poster is advertizing a stimulant containing the drug cocaine. Some quack cures were completely useless. Others, such as Kola Marque, contained dangerous and addictive ingredients.

IT IS EASY FOR US to dismiss doctors in the past as being quacks or charlatans (people who swindled their patients by selling them useless cures). This was certainly true of some of them, but their strange activities need to be put into the context of the level of scientific learning of the time. For instance, it would not have been possible to convince Hippocrates or Galen about the existence of bacteria, or that bacteria cause disease, because it was only possible to see them through a microscope.

▶ QUACK MEDICINES
Salespeople drew attention to their wares by any means at their disposal. Many wore outrageous and eye-catching outfits, and they all perfected their own style of patter (sales talk).

Although surgery could sometimes be effective, most medicine was not able to cure disease. Doctors were forced to desperate measures in order to find cures. Sometimes a patient recovered by natural means, but then the experimental method used by the doctor would be accepted as a miracle cure.

Prayer and the use of holy relics might be dismissed as quack medicine, but they are still widely used today, along with the laying on of hands (blessing the patient) and other forms of therapy based upon spiritual cure.

In Britain, quackery flourished in the 1700s. Outlandish cures were sold on street corners and at fairs and markets. During the 1800s people realized that quacks were exploiting the sick with cures and treatments that had no value at all.

Medical associations, such as the Royal Colleges in Britain, were set up. These professional organizations kept out charlatans and regulated the activities of doctors who were members. They also checked that the doctors were skilled enough to

FALSE HOPES
As medicine becomes more advanced, cures that were once promoted by respectable doctors are rejected as quackery. For example, spa baths were a popular cure in Western Europe around 1900. They have now dropped out of favour, and many doctors would consider their use as quack medicine. However, they are still mainstream practice in parts of Eastern Europe.

◀ ELECTRICAL CORSETS
Electricity was considered a magical cure-all in the 1700s and 1800s. Electrical currents were applied to parts of the body to cure a whole range of conditions.

▼ MUDBATHS
Baths in hot mud are widely used to treat diseases such as arthritis, especially in Eastern Europe. Elsewhere, mud treatments are considered harmless, but ineffective.

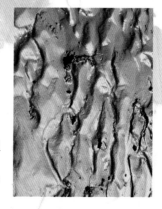

▲ FRANZ MESMER
The German physician Franz Mesmer developed techniques for what we now call hypnosis (putting someone into a trance). He called his discovery animal magnetism, and used it to treat patients who suffered from hysteria. His cures sometimes worked, even though they were scientific nonsense. Eventually, Mesmer was exposed as a fraud.

◀ MORISON'S PILLS
During the 1800s, Morison's Pills achieved huge commercial success throughout Europe and the USA. They were said to cure all sorts of disease, but were found to be merely a mixture of powerful laxatives. This cartoon from the period pokes fun at people who believed in such unreliable cures. It suggests that the man has taken so many Morison's Pills that they have taken root in his stomach and made his skin sprout with grass!

perform their job. Gradually, laws were passed to stop products being sold with outrageous promises.

Lydia Pinkham's Vegetable Compound, introduced in 1873, was one of the most popular quack remedies – probably beccause it contained huge quantities of alcohol. This was sold first as a treatment for 'female weaknesses' and later as a cure for just about anything.

In the USA, quacks advertized cancer cures at high prices. These were aimed at desperate cancer sufferers, willing to pay almost any price for life. Quacks had to pay heavy fines if they were caught, but the practice still exists. Since the 1970s many people dying from cancer have visited Mexico to buy a so-called cure called laetrile, which is in fact poisonous. The same happens with AIDS, where unscrupulous dealers sell dubious pills and potions to those infected with HIV.

◀ FRANZ GALL
The German doctor Franz Gall developed the concept of phrenology. Phrenology is a form of diagnosis based on examining the skull. Gall claimed that skull shape revealed the functions of parts of the brain. He 'read' the skull by feeling for bumps. Phrenology survived for many years, but it is no longer considered to have any use to medicine.

▼ PHRENOLOGY
This porcelain head is marked with the regions identified by Franz Gall. Each area was identified with an aspect of a person's personality or behaviour, such as secretativeness or wit.

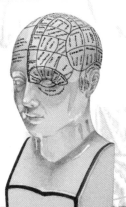

Key Dates

- 1700s Benjamin Franklin praises air bathing (sitting naked in front of an open window).

- 1775 Franz Mesmer develops his theory of animal magnetism.

- 1780 James Graham opens his Temple of Health in London.

- 1810s Franz Gall develops the concept of phrenology.

- 1970s Laetrile is promoted as a cure for cancer.

- 1991 The American Cancer Society declares laetrile is poisonous, but it remains on sale, especially on the Internet.

Public Health

▲ CHOLERA
This image from the 1800s shows cholera in the form of a spectre that descends on the Earth to claim its victims. More than 7,000 Londoners died in the 1832 outbreak.

PUBLIC HEALTH is not a new idea. The Romans understood the need for clean water supplies and built huge aqueducts to bring in water to the centre of their cities, along with water pipes and public baths. They also constructed elaborate sewage systems to remove waste from their cities. The Romans were not even the first to build aqueducts. The Etruscans had started to build them in 312BC.

Ancient Chinese and Indian religious writings had recommended good diet and hygiene to protect health, but in medieval Europe, all of this was forgotten. The Church frowned on washing, as it seemed too much like a bodily pleasure. There was no concept of hygiene, and sewage and rubbish were just thrown out into the street. It is no coincidence that during this period Europe was ravaged by plague, leprosy, tuberculosis (TB, also known as consumption),

typhoid and cholera. People thought that these diseases were spread by miasma (unpleasant smells). This idea probably did encourage some disposal of waste. The miasmic theory of infection persisted into the 1800s, until the effects of bacteria were finally demonstrated.

The cholera epidemics had already brought matters to a head. For centuries the River Thames had been London's sewer and source of drinking water. It was black and stinking, and finally everyone had had enough. The government commissioned a report from a civil servant called John Chadwick, which turned out to be the most influential document ever prepared on the subject of public health. It was published in 1842. The report described the probable causes of disease in the poorer parts of London, and also suggested practical ways to solve the problem. These public health measures included supplying houses with clean running water and proper sewage drainage.

Not long after this came the first proof of the risks from contaminated water, during a terrible cholera outbreak in 1854. John Snow, a London doctor, realized that many cholera cases were clustered in a small area near Broad Street. Investigation showed that they all drew their water from a public pump. Snow removed the pump handle, and within a few days the epidemic stopped. Even so, it took several years for the medical profession to accept that cholera was not spread by foul air, but by drinking water contaminated by sewage.

CLEAN SOLUTIONS

Flushing toilets and clean running water in the home remained novelties into the 1800s. Before then, people had to visit public pumps and taps for their water. In the late 1800s local authorities began to demolish the worst slums and replace them with better housing. By the 1900s children's health was improving. Schools provided meals for the poorest, and medical inspections allowed disease to be detected early on.

▶ FOUL WATERS
Dr John Snow started as a surgeon in Newcastle-upon-Tyne, England, and moved to London in 1836. After halting the cholera epidemic he recommended improvements sewerage.

▶ WATER CLOSET
Flushing toilets, such as this one from the 1880s, were a great improvement in public health. The first toilets were often elaborately decorated and were almost works of art.

▲ AMERICAN SINK (1888)
The 19th-century kitchen was not always very hygienic. Hot water on tap was a rare luxury. Cleanliness depended on having enough servants to scrub all the work surfaces and floors, which often harboured germs.

▶ LONDON LIVING CONDITIONS
During the 1800s, living conditions for the poor were atrocious. They lived in cramped housing without proper sanitation. These people are going through the rubbish on the river. Such conditions provided an ideal breeding ground for disease.

▼ BUILDING A SEWER
Repeated outbreaks of disease finally led to the building of sewers, such as this one being dug in London in 1862. These enormous mains sewers were connected to outfalls far down the Thames, where the tides could sweep the sewage away.

▲ ROYAL VICTORIA HOSPITAL, MONTREAL
Many hospitals were built in the 1800s, such as this one in Canada. These were often magnificent buildings, but as there were still few effective medical treatments, many patients came to hospital to die.

Key Dates

- c.1700 BC King Minos of Crete has a flushing toilet in his palace.

- 312 BC The Etruscans build the first aqueduct.

- AD300s Two-seater toilet, shaped like a temple, in use in Greece.

- c.1590 John Harrington invents the flushing toilet.

- 1770–1915 Development of the modern water closet, or toilet.

- 1854 John Snow shows dirty water is the cause of cholera.

- 1880s Most British cities have sewage treatment plants, after the Public Health Act of 1875.

Microbe Hunters

▲ BACTERIA
Researchers grow bacteria on agar jelly in petri dishes. They draw a contaminated glass rod across the surface of the jelly and the colonies grow in a streak along this line.

BACK IN THE RENAISSANCE, people had speculated that contact with an infected person might spread disease, but no one knew why. Then, in the early 1700s, the Dutch scientist Antonie van Leeuwenhoek described tiny animals that he saw when looking at body fluids under a microscope. These might, it was thought, be associated with disease.

Two hundred years later, the French scientist Louis Pasteur finally proved that microbes (germs) cause disease. First, he proved that microbes made milk sour and wine ferment. He also found that heat treatment killed off these microbes. This process, known as pasteurization, is still used to help preserve milk today. Pasteur went on to show how bacteria caused disease in chickens, and also caused anthrax, a severe infection that affects cattle and humans.

Robert Koch was a German doctor who was also studying anthrax. Using some of Koch's bacteria, Pasteur made a vaccine to prevent the disease in livestock. He went on to an even greater triumph, which was a vaccine for the killer disease rabies. Pasteur was unable to find the organism that caused rabies, because it is a virus, invisible except under a high-powered electron microscope.

Koch was a very painstaking scientist who was aware of the

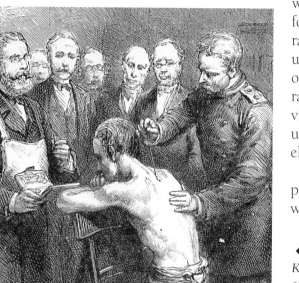

◀ ROBERT KOCH
Koch became famous as the conqueror of diphtheria. Here, he is examining a patient with TB. Koch managed to reveal the bacterium responsible for causing TB, but he failed to produce an effective vaccine against it.

ON THE TRAIL

Colonization (settlement) of the warmer parts of the world introduced Europeans to a whole range of tropical diseases, to which they had no natural immunity. West Africa, in particular, was nicknamed 'the white man's grave.' Malaria, yellow fever and many other tropical diseases spread by insect bites caused prolonged disease and death. It was not until 1897 that it was realized that a mosquito bite could spread malaria. Within a few years people discovered that bites from infected insects also caused sleeping sickness, plague and yellow fever.

▶ THE FIRST MICROSCOPE
Van Leeuwenhoek was an expert at making lenses. He developed the first practical microscope in 1671. He jealously hid his technique for making lenses, but he did share his discoveries by describing what he saw.

▲ MAGGOTS
In 1699 Francesco Redi showed that maggots did not appear on meat that had been kept free of flies. Before then, people had thought that life just appeared on decaying materials. We now know that the flies laid their eggs in the meat.

▼ RUDOLF VIRCHOW
Virchow demonstrated that disease did not arise spontaneously from humours, but that 'all cells come from cells.' In other words, bacteria give rise to more bacteria, rather than appearing on their own.

need to identify disease organisms accurately. He laid down rules for proving that a particular microbe is the cause of a disease that are still followed today. Koch said that a microbe must be present in every case of the disease. It must be grown experimentally and in laboratory animals, and it must also be found when the disease is transmitted to another animal. Following these rules, Koch was able to prove that tuberculosis

(TB) was caused by a bacterium. Next he travelled to Egypt and India to study cholera. He proved that it, too, was caused by a bacterium. Koch discovered that it lived in the human gut and was spread by polluted water. By 1883 he had provided scientific evidence for John Snow's earlier findings on the causes of cholera. Koch went on to discover the organisms responsible for diphtheria, typhoid, leprosy and many other infections.

◀ **LOUIS PASTEUR**
Pasteur's experiments proved that life did not arise from nowhere. He explained how microbes are responsible for making things go off and also for diseases.

▼ **GERM EXPERIMENT**
Pasteur proved that microbes exist with this experiment. He heated a nutrient broth (a substance in which bacteria will grow) in a flask. This killed any microbes already there. He sealed the flask to stop any new microbes getting in. The broth did not spoil until he opened the flask and germs were allowed to enter it from the air.

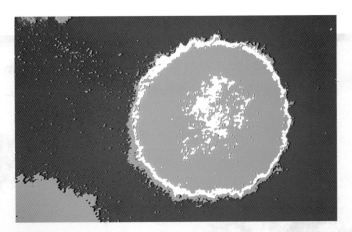

▼ **MOSQUITO**
In 1897, Ronald Ross made the discovery of malaria parasites in an *Anopheles* mosquito. This finally proved the link between these insects and the killer disease.

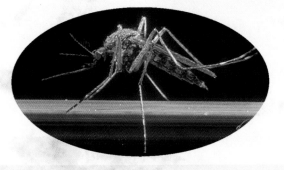

▲ **HIV VIRUS**
The discovery of the virus causing HIV in 1983 finally explained the mysterious appearance of AIDS. The HIV virus attacks and weakens the immune system. This allows the body to be attacked by other organisms and causes AIDS.

Key Dates

- 1673 Antonie van Leeuwenhoek describes the tiny life forms he has seen under a microscope.

- 1858 Rudolf Virchow states 'All cells come from cells.'

- 1878 Louis Pasteur presents his germ theory of infection to the French Academy of Medicine.

- 1882 Robert Koch isolates the tubercle bacillus that causes TB.

- 1883 Robert Koch isolates the bacterium that causes cholera.

- 1897 Ronald Ross explains how mosquitoes carry malaria.

- 1983 The HIV virus is discovered.

Immunization

▲ THE END OF SMALLPOX
One of the reasons for the success in wiping out smallpox was widespread advertizing explaining the need for vaccination. This example comes from China.

THE STORY OF VACCINATION is largely also the story of smallpox. This viral disease killed or disfigured people throughout Europe and the American colonies, where it wiped out the civilizations of the Incas and Aztecs.

In 1717, Lady Mary Wortley Montagu, wife of the British Ambassador in Constantinople, reported that the Turks had a traditional method to prevent smallpox. They took pus from infected smallpox sores and scratched it into the skin of another person. This caused a mild infection that did not produce scarring. Most importantly, it seemed to make the person immune from later infection. Lady Montagu was confident enough to try this on her own child. Soon the method was used widely across Europe.

The next development came when Edward Jenner, a British physician, heard that milkmaids who caught cowpox from their cattle did not seem to catch smallpox. Cowpox was a mild disease. In 1796, Jenner injected a local boy with the cowpox virus. Six weeks later Jenner tried to infect the boy with smallpox in an experiment that would have landed him in prison today. Fortunately the boy survived and the technique spread. Because smallpox does not infect any animals other than humans, it was possible to completely eradicate (wipe out) the disease by the 1970s. Smallpox was the first organism that we have deliberately made extinct.

Immunization works by using the body's own natural

◀ EDWARD JENNER
This statue commemorates Jenner's first experimental vaccination of James Phelps with cowpox. This protected Phelps against smallpox infection.

PROTECTING PEOPLE

Viruses such as the influenza (flu) virus and HIV mutate, or change very quickly, so the pattern of proteins on their surface also alters. This means that the body finds it difficult to produce strong immunity, because the disease is always changing. Other diseases such as polio and measles tend not to change, so vaccination provides powerful and permanent immunity.

▶ THE RABIES VACCINE
Louis Pasteur was able to produce rabies vaccines by growing the virus in rabbits' brains. Drying their brains and spinal cords for two weeks weakened the virus so much that it could be injected into people. This gave them immunity without them catching rabies.

▲ POLIO SUFFERER
In 1921, Franklin Roosevelt fell victim to polio. At the time, the disease was called 'infantile paralysis,' although it struck Roosevelt at the age of 40. The disease crippled Roosevelt's legs, but he eventually went on to become president of the USA.

▶ COWPOX
Once the value of Jenner's discovery became widely known, people rushed to be inoculated with cowpox in order to be protected from smallpox. This cartoon shows what some people feared might happen when they were injected with cowpox – cows start growing out of their bodies!

defences against an invading microbe. This works whether the microbe is a bacterium, virus or animal parasite. In a way this reflects the views of the ancient Greeks, who believed that the body could heal itself.

The immune system uses white cells in the blood, which recognize our own body cells by the pattern of proteins on their surface. When they come across invading microbes, they attack them because they do not recognize them. They produce substances called antibodies that destroy the microbes, then other white cells eat up the microbes' remains. In this way the infection is cleared up. Next time that kind of microbe gets into the body, the white cells 'remember' which antibodies they used to eliminate it last time. They produce an army of antibodies so quickly that the infection cannot become established.

Vaccination creates immunity in the same way. The vaccine contains microbes that produce only a mild version of a disease. It usually contains dead microbes or even just parts of the microbes. This is enough for the body to mount an attack and produce antibodies. These give protection later if they are exposed to more dangerous forms of the microbe, so long as these are the same type of microbe used in the vaccine.

▶ SINGLE-DOSE SYRINGE
Modern syringes are disposable, to reduce the risk of infection. They come ready-filled with vaccine.

▶ FIRING A VACCINE
For mass vaccination programmes, a gun was sometimes used. It fired the vaccine through the skin under very high pressure, without using a needle. These guns have now been replaced with single-dose disposable syringes.

▼ QUEUING FOR JABS
Vaccination is especially important in developing countries where there is little access to healthcare. Charities and governments carry out vaccination programmes against many killer diseases.

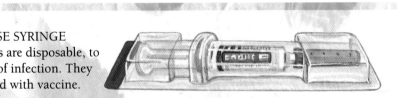

Key Dates

- 1717 Lady Wortley Montagu reports on the traditional Turkish practice of inoculation to prevent smallpox.

- 1796 Edward Jenner inoculates a boy with cowpox and demonstrates that he is then immune to smallpox.

- 1885 Pasteur tests his rabies vaccine.

- 1955 Jonas Salk's polio vaccine is introduced.

- 1974 Smallpox is eradicated (although a later single case followed a laboratory accident).

Germ Killers

Howard Florey

Ernst Chain

▲ ▼ PRIZE SCIENTISTS
Howard Florey and Ernst Chain researched penicillin together. They developed a way to mass produce this life-saving drug, and were awarded the Nobel Prize.

WHILE VACCINATION COULD PREVENT many diseases, very few infections were treatable. The first was malaria, which could be treated with quinine, extracted from the bark of the South American cinchona tree. Mercury was used to treat syphilis but proved very toxic (poisonous). A new and synthetic (manufactured) treatment called Salvarsan was introduced by Paul Ehrlich in 1910. Then in 1932 the German scientist Gerhard Domagk produced Prontosil, a red dye that attacked the streptococcus bacterium that caused many infections, such as meningitis.

A range of antibacterial drugs was developed from Prontosil. They are known as sulphonamides and prevent the multiplication of bacteria. This gives the body's immune defences time to create antibodies to destroy the bacteria. Sulphonamides were not always effective, however, and sometimes caused unpleasant side effects. Also, they were completely inactive against some types of bacteria. The search for new drugs continued.

Alexander Fleming was a researcher studying the natural antibacterial substances that are produced by the body. He was particularly interested in lysozyme, a substance that is found in tears.

▼ ALEXANDER FLEMING
Fleming's discovery of penicillin was a lucky accident, but he did not realize the importance of his discovery. It was another ten years before Florey and Chain saw the potential of penicillin and developed it further.

LIFE SAVERS
Antibiotics have been used to treat all sorts of infections. They are also given to livestock and poultry to prevent disease and to make them grow quickly. As a result of being exposed to antibiotics over long periods, some bacteria have evolved methods of avoiding their effects. Nowadays, doctors try not to prescribe antibiotics for minor infections, such as sore throats, so that bacteria cannot get used to them.

◀ WORLD WAR II
When war broke out, the UK and US governments realized that there would soon be many wounded soldiers at risk of infection. They invested lots of money in finding a way to produce enough penicillin.

◀ ANTIBIOTICS
Most antibiotics are given in the form of a powder, inside gelatine capsules, that are swallowed. However, some antibiotics are damaged by digestive juices so these have to be injected.

▼ ANTIBIOTIC ATTACK
Antibiotics work by damaging the cell wall of a bacterium.

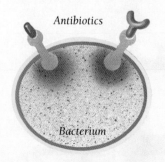

Antibiotics

Bacterium

▶ PAUL EHRLICH
In the early 1900s Ehrlich produced and tested more than 600 new arsenic compounds, in an attempt for find a cure for syphilis. One of these substances, later named Salvarsan, proved very effective. It was the first drug to have a specific antibacterial effect.

Lysozyme protects the delicate surface of the eye from bacterial attack. Fleming's discovery of penicillin was a complete accident. He had been working with staphylococci, the bacteria that cause boils. He grew colonies of these bacteria on plates of agar jelly. Returning from holiday in 1928, he noticed that a mould was growing on a discarded plate, and that the colonies of staphylococci that should have been growing around the mould had died off. Fleming identified the mould and discovered that it produced an antibiotic called penicillin. He did not realize the importance of penicillin at the time, but, ten years later, researchers in Oxford found Fleming's report. They carried out lots of tests and found penicillin to be amazingly effective.

The new drug proved so successful that there was a huge and immediate demand. After a huge effort, two scientists called Howard Florey and Ernst Chain found a way to produce large quantities of the mould. The drug was used during World War II to treat battle wounds. The only problem with it was that it did not kill every type of bacterium.

The worldwide search for natural organisms that will produce new antibiotics continues to this day, with deep-sea missions and journeys into tropical rainforests. When researchers find a natural antibiotic, they work out what the active parts of it are, so they can recreate this ingredient synthetically.

Most antibiotics work by stopping the bacteria from being able to build proper cell walls when they divide. Without complete cell walls, the bacteria die. Antibiotics do not usually damage human cells, because they do not have a rigid cell wall.

▲ SELMAN WAKSMAN
This American scientist invented the word 'antibiotic' in 1941. After the discovery of penicillin, Waksman looked for more antibiotics in soil microbes. In 1943 he found streptomycin, the first drug to treat TB. He received a Nobel Prize for his work.

▼ ANIMAL FEED AND ANTIBIOTICS
Antibiotics are often added to animal feed to make them grow bigger and stop them from catching disease. However, this practice has proved to be a medical disaster, because it encouraged the appearance of bacteria that could resist the effects of antibiotics. As a result, some antibiotics are now almost useless.

Key Dates

- 1910 Salvarsan is discovered by Paul Ehrlich.

- 1928 Alexander Fleming discovers penicillin by accident.

- 1935 Gerhard Domagk develops Prontosil.

- 1939 Howard Florey and Ernst Chain find a way to mass produce penicillin.

- 1943 Selman Waksman discovers streptomycin, the first drug to successfully treat TB.

- 1945 Fleming, Florey and Chain are jointly awarded the Nobel Prize for their discovery of penicillin.

Women Pioneers

WOMEN HAVE ALWAYS played a role in medicine, although right through history as late as the 1950s they were often dismissed by male doctors. Childbirth was an event from which men were usually excluded. Midwives looked after pregnant women and sometimes got rid of unwanted pregnancies. Midwives passed down their knowledge from mother to daughter, with the result that there is little written evidence of their work. Doctors rarely recognized the importance of midwives, although a few wrote about their techniques.

There were several famous women healers during the Middle Ages. One of these, called Trotula, practised at Salerno in the 1000s. She wrote a book called *On the sufferings of women* which was used as a medical text for the next 700 years. She gave detailed instructions on the technique of diagnosis, and also published works on the diseases of children and on skin diseases.

▲ FLORENCE NIGHTINGALE
Grateful soldiers in the Crimean War nicknamed Florence Nightingale the 'Lady with the Lamp.' In the 1850s Nightingale pioneered hygienic nursing techniques.

▶ SCUTARI HOSPITAL
Florence Nightingale and her team of nurses brought in strict nursing practices. Before their arrival the field hospital at Scutari (modern-day Usküdar, in Turkey) had a very high death rate. Nightingale used her experiences to improve nursing standards when she returned to England.

STRUGGLING TO SUCCEED

Women were not usually allowed to train as doctors. They were opposed by the Church, and by male doctors, too. It was not until 1849 that a woman called Elizabeth Blackwell became the first graduate doctor. In the early 1900s, suffragettes (women's rights activists) inspired many women. Marie Stopes in Britain and Margaret Sanger in the USA championed birth control. This freed women from having very large families and improved the health of women and children.

◀ DRESSING-UP
Mary Walker was an assistant surgeon in the American Civil War (1861–5). Her solution to men's distrust of female medics was to disguise herself as a man.

▶ MARIE CURIE
Women were excluded from all areas of science, not just medicine. An exception was Polish-born Marie Curie. With her French husband, Pierre, she discovered radium in 1898. Thanks to their investigations into radioactive materials, a revolutionary treatment for cancer was discovered.

▲ ELIZABETH BLACKWELL
Many medical schools turned down Blackwell before she finally qualified as a doctor in the USA in 1849. The idea of a woman doctor scandalized the medical profession. It was many years before Blackwell was fully accepted.

▶ MILITARY NURSES
By World War II (1939–45), the armed forces had a well-developed system for providing nursing care to the wounded. Mobile field hospitals and ambulance services were established. These were staffed mainly by women, who were thought too delicate for combat duties.

Hildegard was a German healer living at about the same time as Trotula. She combined religious and medical writing, together with natural history. In particular she gave detailed descriptions of herbal remedies and other treatments, and was greatly respected by kings and popes.

In hospitals of the Middle Ages and the Renaissance, most nursing was carried out by nuns and other women attached to religious orders. When large hospitals were built in the 1800s, nuns played a less important role. Instead, working-class women were recruited, but they were not given any training, so the standard of nursing was poor.

The first non-religious school for nurses was set up in 1842 in Germany. Students took a three-year course, followed by exams. A woman called Florence Nightingale briefly attended this school in 1851. She completed her training in Paris and then became head of the nurses at King's College Hospital.

In 1854 Florence Nightingale was sent out to nurse the troops during the Crimean War (1853–6). Conditions in the field hospital were very bad, but by improving the hygiene in the hospitals Nightingale lowered the death rate from 40 per cent to 2 per cent. After the war, she opened a school of nursing at St Thomas' Hospital, London.

It took a long time, and the hard work of many brave pioneers, to change attitudes towards women in the medical profession. One such pioneer was Dr Elizabeth Blackwell. In 1869, Blackwell returned to England from the USA where she had trained in New York, despite opposition from her fellow students. She helped to found the London School of Medicine for Women. Even so, medicine remained a male dominated profession right up to the 1950s.

▲ MARGARET SANGER
A pioneer of birth control in the USA, Margaret Sanger was a nurse working mainly in slum areas. She was sent to prison for a month after opening the USA's first birth control clinic in 1916.

▼ MARIE STOPES
In 1921 Marie Stopes opened Britain's first birth control clinic, offering free consultations and contraceptives. She recommended planned families. This meant that parents would be able to limit the number of children that they had.

Key Dates

- 1849 Elizabeth Blackwell qualifies as a doctor in the USA.

- 1854 Florence Nightingale arrives at Scutari field hospital.

- 1857 Elizabeth Blackwell opens the New York Infirmary, staffed entirely by women.

- 1898 Marie Curie discovers the radioactive element radium.

- 1911 Marie Curie receives a second Nobel Prize for her work.

- 1916 Margaret Sanger opens the first birth control clinic in the USA.

- 1921 Marie Stopes opens the first birth control clinic in Britain.

Rebuilding the Body

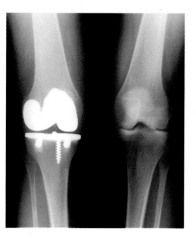

▲ ARTIFICIAL JOINTS
Many of the body's joints wear out in later life, often due to arthritis. This x-ray shows a replacement knee joint, made of metal and plastic. Many other joints can be replaced in the same way.

Prostheses are artificial body parts. False teeth are a type of prosthesis. They have been around for thousands of years, but thanks to modern plastics they are now hard to tell from the real thing.

Prostheses made huge advances during the 1900s. Artificial limbs became much lighter and looked more realistic. They can now be connected to the nervous system, so they can move like real body parts.

When limbs are broken, splints and plasters are applied

▶ HEART TRANSPLANT
Surgery to replace the heart is long and complicated. It depends of having a suitable transplant heart available. This has to be taken from a donor who has died in an accident, and must match the tissues of the recipient.

to hold them in position until the bone heals. If bones are badly shattered, metal plates are screwed onto the bone to them to give extra support. Sometimes the bone is replaced with a material such as coral. New bone cells grow into the coral, replacing it with living bone.

Heart valves damaged by disease can be replaced with mechanical ones. If the heart's natural pacemaker (that produces the heart's regular beat) is faulty, a small artificial one can be fitted. This device produces regular tiny pulses of electricity that force the heart to beat.

Transplants are another way to rebuild the body. Skin grafts are one type of transplant and blood

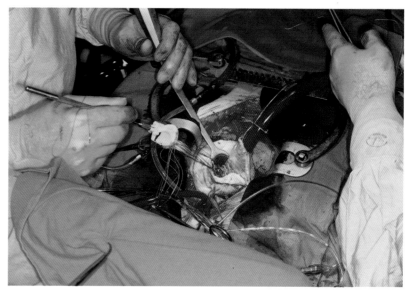

EARLY DAYS
The first example of a prosthesis was probably a tree branch. This would have been used as a simple crutch by a person with a broken leg. When surgery was developed, amputation of limbs was a common operation, though many patients died of infection. Survivors were fitted with wooden replacement limbs and hands. Sometimes simple metal hooks were used instead of hands.

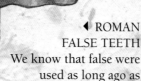

◀ ROMAN FALSE TEETH
We know that false were used as long ago as ancient Egyptian times. The Romans made complex gold bridges that held false teeth made from metal or ivory. Roman dentists also had various recipes for toothpastes that would keep the teeth healthy.

▲ NOSE GRAFT
In the 1700s Western doctors were amazed to find that Indian surgeons were carrying out complex reconstructive surgery. This severed nose was rebuilt and then skin was grafted on. Westerners soon copied these methods for themselves.

▼ WOODEN LEGS
This pirate was unlucky enough to lose a leg and an arm. With a wooden leg and a hook for a hand, he could get about for himself. However, modern artificial limbs are far more realistic and comfortable. They have working joints and are made of lightweight plastic.

transfusion is another. It was tried back in the 1600s, but only became safe with more knowledge of blood groups in the 1800s.

Transplants from another person are difficult, because the immune system immediately attacks any 'foreign' organ. Very powerful drugs are needed to prevent rejection. This is why in blood transfusion the blood group of the donor (giver) has to match the recipient's (receiver's). Another problem is finding availabile organs. Everyone has two kidneys and lungs, and so sometimes a donor will offer one of their's to help a sick person. Other organs, such as the liver and heart, must be removed from a healthy person who has died in an accident, so there is always a shortage of them. The first human heart transplant took place in 1967. Since then, thousands of people have received donor hearts. Most survive for a long time, but they need to take anti-rejection drugs for the rest of their lives.

Current research is looking at ways to grow complete new organs from a patient's own tissues, so they would not be rejected. Another controversial possibility is xenotransplantation, using organs from animals such as pigs.

▲ ARTIFICIAL HEART VALVE
Leaking heart valves can cause ill health or death, so they are often replaced with artificial substitutes. These are simple one-way valves made from metal and plastic that will not be attacked by the immune system. Sometimes specially-treated pig's heart valves are transplanted.

▶ PROSTHETIC ARM
Artificial arms can provide limited movement. Hooks or fingers are connected to the remaining arm muscles. New research is aimed at restoring more natural movement by making connections to the nerves in the arm.

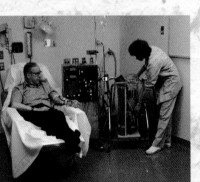

Washable, lifelike plastic sleeve covers the arm

Beneath the plastic , a moveable metal 'frame' forms the hand

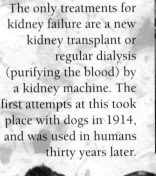

▲ BLOOD GROUPS
Karl Landsteiner identified blood groups in 1901–2. He labelled the blood types O, A, B and AB. This made it possible to give patients blood from donors who match their own group.

▶ KIDNEY MACHINE
The only treatments for kidney failure are a new kidney transplant or regular dialysis (purifying the blood) by a kidney machine. The first attempts at this took place with dogs in 1914, and was used in humans thirty years later.

Charles Best   *Frederick Banting*

◀ TREATING DIABETES
In 1921, Charles Best and Frederick Banting saved the life of a diabetic dog with insulin, taken from another animal's pancreas. This led to the modern use of artifically-produced insulin to treat diabetes.

Key Dates

- 2500BC Egyptians use false teeth.

- 1901–2 Karl Landsteiner describes blood groups, making blood transfusion a practical possibility.

- 1921 Banting and Best use insulin to treat diabetes in dogs.

- 1950s Synthetic insulin is produced.

- 1954 First successful kidney transplant.

- 1960 First pacemaker is fitted.

- 1960s Artificial hips and other joints are introduced.

- 1963 First lung transplant.

- 1964 Christiaan Barnard performs the first heart transplant.

Healing the Mind

AFTER THEY had been neglected for centuries, hospitals for the insane were eventually developed in the 1400s, mostly to keep the inmates away from the rest of society. The Bethlehem Royal Hospital in London was among the earliest of the asylums. It took in live-in patients from 1403. The inmates were kept in terrible conditions. Most were chained up, and visitors were encouraged to come and view the patients as a form of entertainment. This was common throughout Europe.

The first real advance came around 1800. Philippe Pinel, a Parisian psychiatrist (doctor for the mentally ill), abolished the practice of chaining up the patients in the Bicêtre asylum for men and Salpêtrière asylum for women. Pinel's pupil, Esquirol, came up with the idea of a community where patients lived together with their

▲ STRAIGHTJACKET
Before there were drugs to calm violent patients, straightjackets were used to restrain them.

▶ THE MADHOUSE
In its early years, the Bethlehem Hospital, known as Bedlam, was a place full of suffering. Patients were often kept chained up and even beaten.

MODERN FORMS OF THERAPY

Psychotherapy marked a departure from traditional ideas about the cause and treatment of mental illness. Psychiatrists began to look closely at the emotional problems that seem to cause mental illness and to explore these with their patients in order to give them an insight into their condition.

▶ ECT
Electroconvulsive therapy (ECT) was widely used in the 1950s and 1960s to treat severe depression. Doctors pass a powerful current through the brain, causing a convulsion and, sometimes, relief of depression. It can also cause memory loss, however, so ECT is now only used as a last resort.

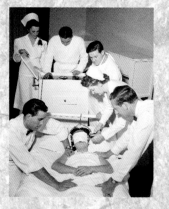

▲ ART THERAPY
Modern psychiatric clinics encourage patients to express themselves through painting. This is especially helpful to patients who bottle up their emotions because they are unable to speak freely about how they feel.

▼ PSYCHIATRIST'S CHAIR
It is very important, when a patient is being examined by a psychiatrist, that they are relaxed. This is why many psychiatrists will have comfortable chairs, like this one, or even couches, for their patients.

doctors in a group. Instead of being treated as crazed brutes, patients were seen as individuals who could be helped. This treatment sometimes improved their condition enough for them to be discharged (let out) into society.

Not all treatment became humane. Many famous psychiatrists still chained up their patients, beat them, or plunged them into cold baths in a form of shock treatment. However, living conditions in most asylums improved greatly.

In the mid-1800s Charcot, another physician at the Salpêtrière hospital, made a unique study of the patients in his care. He described their condition in great detail, and also studied hypnosis as a form of treatment. Then, at the end of the 1800s, the German doctor Emil Kraepelin began to classify the most serious mental illnesses. He was the first to accurately describe schizophrenia.

From the 1880s, Sigmund Freud developed psychoanalysis, which

▲ FREEING THE INSANE
Philippe Pinel was the first doctor to introduce humane treatment of the insane. He ordered the chains and restraints to be removed from patients in the French hospitals where he worked.

▶ SIGMUND FREUD
Freud's great innovation was to try to understand what caused mental illness. He encouraged his patients to talk about their past experiences. This is a very long, drawn-out process. It is not as practical as drugs for treating large numbers of people.

attempted to show how a patient's problems were the result of previous experiences. Carl Jung developed Freud's ideas further. Some Freudian and Jungian methods of exploring a patient's history are still used today.

The other big development during the 1900s was the use of drugs. Once it was known that there are chemical changes in the brains of the mentally ill, drugs were designed to help the brain chemistry become normal again. However, drugs brought a new set of problems, including addiction, and so the search for a perfect solution continues.

▲ WHAT MIGHT THIS BE?
The Swiss psychiatrist Hermann Rorschach came up with his inkblot test in 1918. He asked the patient what the spilt ink looked like. Their answers might give a clue as to what was worrying them.

▼ CHEMICAL TREATMENT
Prozac is one of a class of new drugs that is intended to restore the balance of brain chemicals. Scientists try to find drugs that restore normal mental health without causing serious side effects. Drugs are used to treat people suffering from depression, schizophrenia and other psychiatric problems..

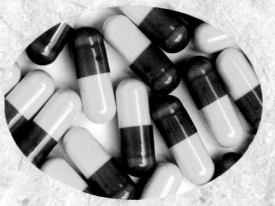

Key Dates

- 1377 Bethlehem Hospital begins to admit insane patients.

- 1793 Philippe Pinel frees the insane from their chains.

- 1856–1939 Life of Sigmund Freud, pioneer of psychoanalysis.

- 1943 The accidental discovery of LSD stimulates scientific interest in the effect of drugs on the brain. This leads the production of drugs to treat conditions such as anxiety and schizophrenia.

- 1950s–60s ECT is widely used to treat severe depression.

- 1990s Prozac and related drugs are used to treat depression.

Plants and Pills

ERBS HAVE BEEN used by people to treat disease since prehistoric times. They have been found in some of the most ancient tombs and burials. Some herbs were used because of their obvious benefits, while others were used for magical or spiritual reasons. The belief that the appearance of a plant revealed its possible use as a medicine was known as the doctrine of signatures.

It is said that 80 per cent of the world's population still depends upon herbal medicine, though only a few herbal remedies form part of conventional Western medicine. Many of those used today are the same as those mentioned in ancient records of the Egyptians.

▲ DIGITALIS
Foxglove contains the drug digitalis, which is still used for the treatment of heart failure.

▸ APOTHECARY
The medieval apothecary diagnosed illness and carried out treatments, as well as making herbal remedies and other drugs.

ADMINISTERING DRUGS
Most drugs are given by mouth in the form of tablets or medicine, but they come in many other forms. Lung diseases can be treated by breathing in a finely powdered drug, straight into the lungs. Injection is used to give large amounts of a drug very quickly, or to give a drug that would be damaged by the digestive system. Some drugs given by injection are in a form that is absorbed only very slowly into the tissues, so they have a prolonged effect.

▾ DRUG MANUFACTURING
Modern drugs companies use high-tech production lines to prepare medicines on a large scale. The process needs to be checked at every stage to ensure the quality of the drugs.

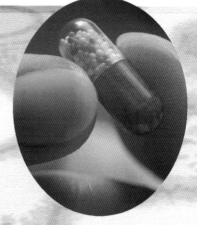

▲ SLOW-RELEASE CAPSULES
Some drugs disappear from the body very rapidly. People would have to take many doses throughout the day to keep enough of the drug in the bloodstream. Slow-release capsules let the drug out very gradually, so patients only need to take one or two capsules each day.

The herbal preparations described by Galen and other Greek doctors were preserved by Arab scribes. They continued to be used in the Middle Ages. Many monasteries and apothecaries grew herb gardens. Renaissance explorers brought back new herbs from freshly discovered lands. The herbal written by Nicholas Culpeper in 1649, titled *A Physicall Directory*, contains a wealth of detailed observation, and remains in print today.

Over the years, many of the plants listed in the old herbals fell out of fashion, but some of the most effective remedies are still used. Cinchona bark contains quinine and was introduced into Western medicine in the 1600s as a cure for malaria. Foxglove was used from 1785 to treat dropsy and doctors slowly saw that this was a valuable treatment for certain types of heart disease.

Many herbs were extremely poisonous unless they were carefully prepared. For example, colchicine, extracted from the crocus flower, can be lethal, but is a good treatment for gout. The extraction of the active part of herbal remedies soon became a science, after alchemists discovered the technique of distillation. This involved boiling up a liquid so that the water evaporated (turned into steam), leaving behind a concentrated essence.

These techniques of purification led to the founding of the modern pharmaceutical (drugs) industry. Many modern drugs are synthetic, or artificially manufactured, versions of plant extracts. There are continuing worldwide searches to identify traditional remedies and to investigate their active ingredients.

◀ THE GARDEN OF HEALTH
The Hortus Sanitatis (Garden of Health) *is a typical herbal written in Germany in the 1400s. It lists the drugs used by apothecaries and the properties the drugs were believed to have. Most of the information comes from the time of Hippocrates.*

◀ WILLOW BARK
Extracts of willow bark have traditionally been used as a painkiller, but it was not until 1852 that a version of the active drug was made synthetically. It was soon marketed as aspirin.

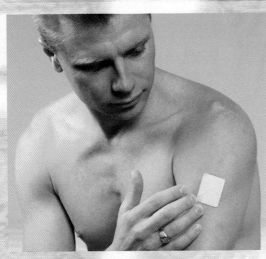

▲ NICOTINE PATCH
Some drugs can be absorbed through the skin. The nicotine patch allows small amounts of nicotine to flow into the bloodstream, helping smokers overcome their addiction to cigarettes.

▼ INHALER
Drugs for asthma are usually delivered straight into the lungs, by means of an inhaler. These drugs are sometimes in the form of a very fine powder. This puts the drug where it needs to be to work, and reduces any side effects elsewhere in the body.

Key Dates

- 1852 Aspirin is first synthesized.

- 1903 Barbiturate sedative (calming) drugs are introduced. They contain barbituric acid naturally found in the lichen *Usnea barbata*.

- 1930s Cortisone is isolated, leading to the development of modern steroid drugs.

- 1935 Sulphonamide antibacterial drugs are developed.

- 1961 The sedative thalidomide is withdrawn after causing terrible damage to unborn babies.

- 1980s AZT is developed as a treatment for AIDS sufferers.

Alternative Therapies

SOME PEOPLE TOTALLY reject modern medicine. Christian Scientists, for example, believe that prayer and faith can cure all disease. Jehovah's Witnesses reject only some aspects of conventional medicine, such as transfusions.

Not all people reject traditional treatment for religious reasons. Some people find that their condition cannot be cured by orthodox (traditional) medicine, so look for an alternative. Also, while many people still respect a doctor's advice so much that they would never dream of questioning it, others may be well-informed about their illness, and wish to take treatment into their own hands.

In the 1990s there was increased interest in alternatives to traditional medicine. There is a difference between alternative therapies, in which a person rejects conventional medicine and seeks some other form of

▲ CAMOMILE
Extracts of camomile are widely used for pain relief in homeopathic medicine. Homeopathists use tiny quantities of drugs that produce similar symptoms to those of the condition they wish to treat.

▶ MOXIBUSTION
One type of acupuncture is moxibustion, in which cones of herbs are burned on the skin at points on some of the meridians (channels) described by Chinese medicine.

MANIPULATION
The trend towards unconventional therapies is continuing in Western Europe, and is especially strong in the UK, France and Germany. People who feel excluded from their treatment are now able to choose and to take control of their healthcare, knowing they can fall back on conventional medicine in emergency. People who suffer conditions such as nagging back pain often prefer not to use strong painkilling drugs because they have inconvenient side effects, such as sleepiness. Osteopathy, chiropractic and massage provide alternatives.

◀ WORKING ON THE SPINE
Both osteopathy and chiropractic involve manipulation (massage) of the body, especially of the spine. Although the methods vary, the outcome of this manipulation can often bring relief from back pain. Family doctors often recommend these practitioners to their patients.

▼ THE CHIROPRACTOR AT WORK
Chiropractors believe that parts of the spine may press against nerves, causing pain and illness. The founder of the method, David Palmer, is even said to have cured deafness. Chiropractors often use very strong manipulation to treat a whole range of disorders including pain.

therapy, and complementary medicine, in which patients take extra steps as well as the treatment prescribed by their doctor. Most doctors accept that their patients may use complementary therapies and do not mind as long as these do not interfere with conventional treatments. In Britain, 40 percent of family doctors routinely refer patients to complementary therapists. Alternative therapies, though, can mean that a sick person delays going to their doctor and this can make their problem much more difficult to treat.

Some of these therapies are difficult to define. Herbal treatments, for example, can be a form of conventional medicine if they are known to contain medically active ingredients. Where their effectiveness is not proven, they are classed as alternative or complementary therapies.

Acupuncture is an ancient Chinese healing technique where needles are inserted into the body. Science dismissed this technique as quackery until, in recent years, it was found that acupuncture at certain points has a powerful painkilling effect. Acupuncture is especially helpful for lingering pains that do not respond to drugs.

What is common to all forms of complementary and alternative medicine is that is no scientific explanation believe that they work because of the placebo (inactive drug) effect. Placebos given to patients in medical trials often work as well as the real drugs, probably because the patient really believes that they will.

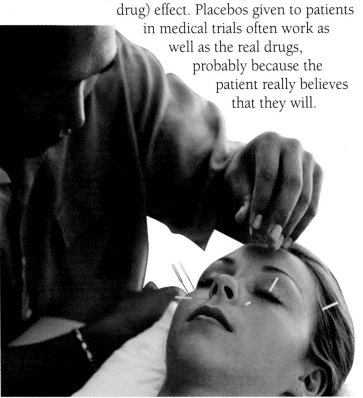

▲ ACUPUNCTURE
Scientific research has shown that acupuncture, the Chinese practice of inserting needles into the skin, really does kill pain. Serious operations have been performed in China with no other form of painkiller except acupuncture.

▶ AROMATHERAPY
Smells have a powerful effect on the body and on mood. Aromatherapy depends on massaging the body with scented oils, or on breathing in the fumes of heated oils. This helps the patient to relax and may have an effect on some illnesses.

◀ SHIATSU
This is a technique to relieve pain that evolved in Japan during the 1900s. Practitioners of shiatsu use their fingers to press hard on acupuncture points, and also use massage and meditation to treat their patients.

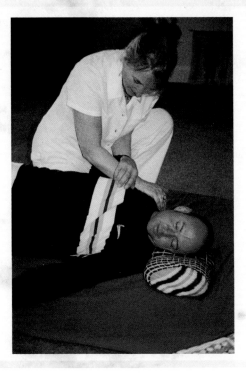

▶ FEET FIRST
Reflexology is based on the idea that different areas on the feet represent different parts of the body. Massage and stimulation of these areas can help treat illness and generally improve health.

Key Dates

- 300BC First descriptions of acupuncture in the *Nei Ching*.

- AD1601 Acupuncture discussed in detail by Yang Chi-chou.

- 1796 Samuel Hahnemann says that 'like cures like' and develops homeopathy in Germany.

- 1874 American doctor Andrew Still introduces osteopathy.

- 1895 Chiropractic is developed in the USA by David Palmer.

- 1900s Shiatsu is developed.

- 1930s Reflexology is introduced by Eunice Ingham.

Holistic Medicine

THE OLDEST FORMS of medicine are enjoying a comeback. Modern holistic medicine is an approach that treats the whole patient, not just the disease. It is a way to maintain good health rather than cure illness. The most important influences on today's holistic medicine are ancient Chinese medicine and Indian Ayurvedic medicine, both of which promoted whole body health.

Holistic medicine usually combines diet, physical exercise and meditation, together with other alternative techniques such as aromatherapy, reflexology and acupuncture. Herbal treatment is influenced by the writings of Culpeper as well as Chinese and Ayurvedic medicine. Homeopathy is one of the forms of holistic medicine which is widely practised in Europe and the USA.

Homeopathy began in Germany in the early 1800s, when Samuel Hahnemann described how very tiny doses of a drug had an effect on his patients. According to Hahnemann, the more the drug was diluted, the stronger its effects. The substance selected would produce similar effects to the disease itself if given in large doses. In the UK homeopathy is regarded as an unconventional but just about acceptable therapy.

Meditation and contemplation have an important role in holistic therapy. They were brought to Europe by Indian teachers who combined Ayurvedic medicine with Western beliefs. Transcendental meditation is one

◀ HEALTHY FOOD
There is growing awareness of what a healthy diet must contain and how this improves health. Most people know that they should cut down on junk foods, and especially sugar, salt and fats, if they want to reduce the risk of health problems later in life. Fresh fruit and vegetables are an important part of a healthy diet. They contain vitamins that supply the body with essential minerals.

DEALING WITH STRESS

Stress is an inescapable part of modern living. It can lead to illnesses such as high blood pressure and ulcers and to emotional problems such as panic attacks and depression. The conventional solution is to take drugs for these conditions. The holistic approach is to relieve stress by relaxation techniques such as yoga, t'ai chi and meditation.

◀ EASTERN ART
T'ai chi is an ancient martial art that was developed in China in the 1700s. It uses the principles of *yin* and *yang* to balance body and mind in slow-motion exercises.

▼ INDIAN EXERCISE
Yoga is an ancient Indian discipline designed to exercise the body and the mind. The body is placed in various postures, some of which require a lot of training. Yoga helps to keep the body supple and the joints healthy.

▲ YOGIC MEDITATION
This yogi is meditating in a form of the lotus position, known as the half-lotus. Yogic meditation was made popular in the West by Indian mystics such as the Maharishi Mahesh Yogi and his movement for Transcendental Meditation.

◀ KEEPING FIT
Exercise is an important part of holistic therapy. It is used to burn up excess body fat, and build up muscle. Another very important benefit is that exercise is fun! Feeling happy has been shown to have a good effect on people's health.

▼ LIFE ON THE STOCK EXCHANGE
Modern business life means constant stress and this can eventually produce changes in the body that cause illnesses such as anxiety, depression and ulcers. Many holistic techniques try to work against this stress.

of the best known of these techniques. People repeat a mantra (chant) inside their head to reach a state of deep relaxation.

The holistic movement has made many conventional doctors look at the whole patient, not just the disease. Lifestyle, emotional problems and diet are just some of the factors that can affect a person's health. Holistic therapy emphasizes good diet, exercise and fresh air, all of which contribute to health. Some clinics now offer holistic therapy along with traditional treatments, so that their patients can choose a combination of therapies that suits them. One problem with holistic therapy is that it is difficult for a people to be sure a therapist is reputable. To solve this, many countries want alternative therapists to form professional bodies.

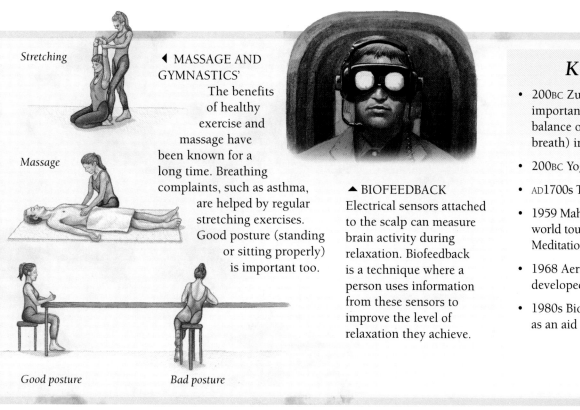

Stretching

Massage

Good posture   Bad posture

◀ MASSAGE AND GYMNASTICS'
The benefits of healthy exercise and massage have been known for a long time. Breathing complaints, such as asthma, are helped by regular stretching exercises. Good posture (standing or sitting properly) is important too.

▲ BIOFEEDBACK
Electrical sensors attached to the scalp can measure brain activity during relaxation. Biofeedback is a technique where a person uses information from these sensors to improve the level of relaxation they achieve.

Key Dates

- 200BC Zuang Zi describes the importance of maintaining balance of *ch'i* (vital energy or breath) in the body.

- 200BC Yoga develops in India.

- AD1700s T'ai chi develops in China.

- 1959 Maharishi Mahesh Yogi's first world tour brings Transcendental Meditation to the West.

- 1968 Aerobic exercise is developed by Kenneth Cooper.

- 1980s Biofeedback is developed as an aid to relaxation.

Modern Technology

Since the 1960s medical technology has advanced faster than earlier doctors could ever have dreamed. For example, the laser, which produces a thin beam of intense light, was created. It can be used as a scalpel to cut through tissue painlessly. The laser beam can be moved very precisely, which means it can be used to remove tumours and to perform delicate surgery on the eye or even inside the brain, without any damage to healthy tissues.

▲ LASER SCALPEL
The intense beam of light produced by a laser can be used for very precise surgery. As it burns through tissue it seals the wound. Lasers are often used in skin surgery to remove birthmarks and tattoos.

▶ KEYHOLE SURGERY
Some modern operations are carried out through a tiny hole made in the patient's body. A small probe is fed through the hole. This sends a picture of the inside of the patient to a large screen, so that the surgeon can see what he or she is doing.

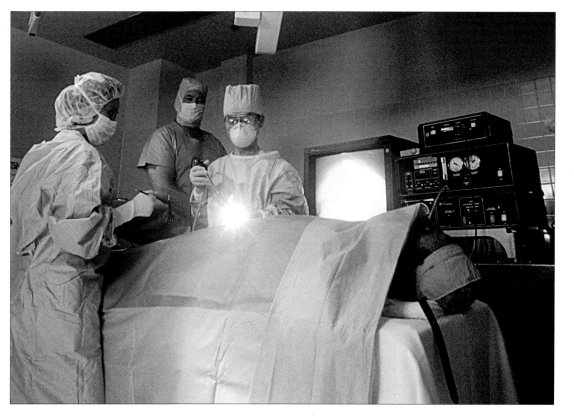

LATEST TECHNIQUES
Technological advances are constantly being made, along with more effective drugs. Sometimes simple devices can transform the life of a sick person, such as a tiny tube inserted into a blocked blood vessel to keep it open. Some technology, however, is extremely complex, such as the computerized monitoring equipment used in life support systems. Many modern techniques, such as keyhole surgery, have a quicker recovery time and this cuts down how long a patient has to spend in hospital.

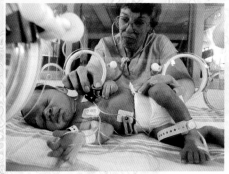

◀ THE CHANCE OF LIFE
Tiny premature babies would once have died. Today they survive in special care baby units. They breathe filtered, warm air and all their body functions are monitored. Sometimes they are given special drugs to improve their lung function.

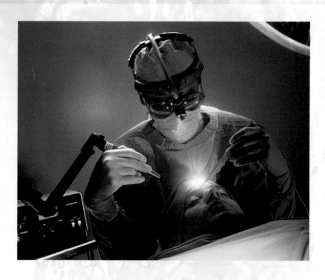

▲ HI-TECH EYE SURGERY
Lasers can be used for surgery on the eye without the need to cut open this delicate organ. The laser fires its beams through the pupil, burning a series of tiny spots that weld the retina back into place.

Pain relief is usually achieved with the use of drugs, but sometimes other technology is used to reduce the patient's dependence on these painkillers. The success of some types of acupuncture in controlling pain led to the experiment of applying tiny electrical currents to the nerves controlling pain. The experiment worked and now TENS (transcutaneous (through the skin) electrical nerve stimulation) is a common method for the relief of chronic pain.

Patients suffering extreme pain, for example in advanced cancer, need analgesic (pain-relieving) drugs continuously. This is achieved by implanting a needle in the affected area. The drug is drip-fed using a tiny battery-powered pump worn at the waist on a belt.

Premature babies (babies born early) are always at risk because their lungs are not properly formed. The earliest technology to help these tiny babies was heated incubators that kept them warm. Today even a tiny infant weighing just one kilogram can survive in a special care baby unit. Computers monitor the amount of oxygen in the baby's blood, its body temperature and breathing. In the same way, life support systems keep people alive after devastating brain injuries that would once have killed them. People in a coma can be supported for many years, although after this time they rarely recover.

Electric shocks can kill, but the defibrillator is a device that delivers a powerful shock to the heart to restart it after a heart attack. It forms an essential part of the emergency equipment in a modern hospital.

Kidney dialysis is a method that removes wastes from the blood of people whose kidneys do not work. Normally the build up of these wastes would quickly poison them, but with dialysis several times a week they can live a relatively normal life, although a kidney transplant is their only chance of complete recovery.

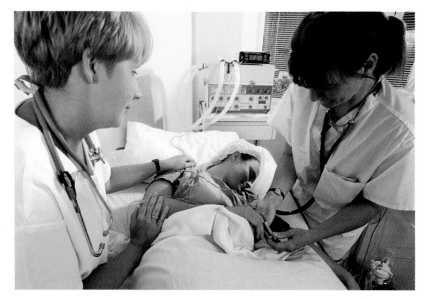

▶ LIFE SUPPORT MACHINE
A life support machine can carry out many of the vital functions of the body. People who have been severely injured in an accident can be looked after by the life support machine. This allows time for their body to heal itself. Sometimes people with severe brain damage can be kept alive for many years on a life support system.

▼ BRAIN SURGERY
The brain does not have any sensory organs on its surface, so brain surgery can be carried out on a fully conscious (awake) patient. A hole is drilled in the head under local anaesthetic. This stereotactic frame allows the surgeon to position his or her instruments very precisely.

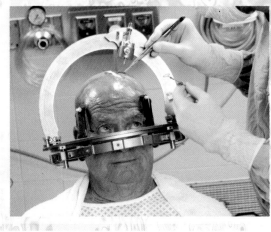

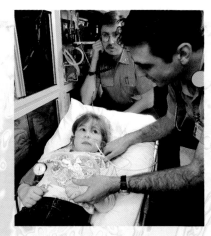

▲ TREATMENT ON THE ROAD
The original idea of an ambulance was to get a sick person to hospital as fast as possible. Today, treatment is often begun during the journey. Paramedics trained in emergency medicine save the lives of many people who may otherwise have died before reaching hospital.

Key Dates

- 1917 Albert Einstein defines the scientific principles of the laser.

- 1928 The 'iron lung' is invented to assist the breathing of people paralyzed by polio. It is widely used up to the 1950s.

- 1960 The laser scalpel is invented.

- 1978 The first 'test-tube baby' is born after research by Patrick Steptoe and RG Edwards. This is opposed by the Church, but becomes widely used.

- 1985 Keyhole surgery becomes popular. Patients recover more quickly from this form of surgery.

Imaging the Body

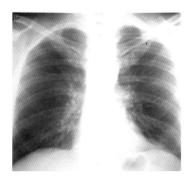

▲ CHEST X-RAY
X-rays pass more slowly through solid bone than through soft tissue. This means bones show up in an x-ray image, but flesh does not. X-rays got their name because Wilhelm Röntgen, who discovered them, did not know exactly what they were. They are now also called Röntgen rays, and as well as in medicine, they are also used for looking for defects in solid objects.

THE ONLY WAY that early doctors could know what was going on inside their patients' bodies was to open them up, or to peer in through natural openings into the body. Stethoscopes helped to reveal the working of the heart, and soon ophthalmoscopes allowed doctors to look inside the eye. Endoscopes were developed in 1805 and worked rather like a slim telescope. They were inserted down the gullet to view the stomach lining, up the anus to examine the rectum or through the vagina to explore the condition of a woman's reproductive organs. Early endoscopes were rigid and extremely unpleasant for the patient, but in the 1930s flexible ones were introduced. These worked by fibre optics, in which a bundle of tiny flexible glass fibres was used

▼ AN EARLY X-RAY
Wilhelm Röntgen, who discovered x-rays, took the first x-ray photographs. This image shows his wife's hand. Her wedding ring is clearly visible, along with an old penny and a pair of compasses, because x-rays cannot pass through metal.

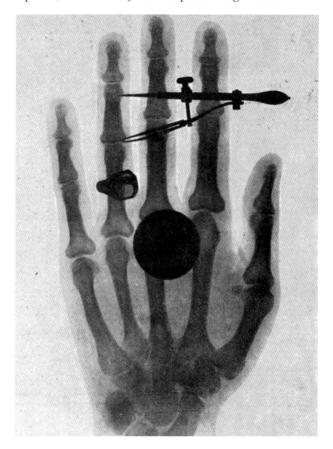

▲ ENDOSCOPE
The endoscope is a telescope-like device that is inserted into the body through a small cut. It can be moved around so that surgeon can identify a diseased area.

INSIDE VIEW
Accurate imaging of the internal parts of the body makes surgery safer and more accurate. Massive scanners are used for non-invasive investigations. The endoscope has now been refined so much that, in a procedure called a laparotomy, a tiny fibre-optic tube is inserted through a small hole in the abdomen. This allows the doctor to view the internal organs while the patient is under a local anaesthetic. Sometimes a form of keyhole surgery can be carried out with tiny instruments fitted to the same device.

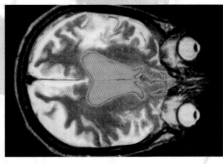

◀ SLICE OF LIFE
MRI produces a 3-D picture of the inside of the body. It uses powerful magnetic energy to photograph soft tissues that are not visible to x-rays.

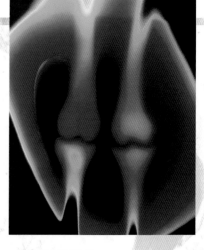

▲ HOT SPOTS
Infection or inflammation can raise the temperature of the affected part of the body. Thermal imaging cameras detect these temperature changes and produce a thermogram (heat picture), to show the doctor where the hot spots are.

to conduct an image. Modern endoscopes have been refined so that they carry their own light source and tiny instruments such as scalpels and grabs that retrieve samples of tissue. The bundle of light fibres can even take photographs inside the body.

The most important discovery to help doctors view the inside of the body was accidental. In 1895 the German scientist Wilhelm Röntgen discovered x-rays while investigating cathode rays. He received the Nobel Prize for his discovery six years later. Almost at once, people realized how useful x-rays could be for medical diagnosis. By the 1920s, x-ray clinics had become an important part of the war against tuberculosis.

A new method for imaging the inside of the body was developed in the 1950s, as a result of research during World War I. Sonar (sound navigation and ranging) used high-frequency sound waves that bounced off a submerged submarine and could be recorded at the surface. Using this technique, ultrasound could pick up echoes from soft tissues, such as tumours, that could not be readily seen on x-rays. The technique worked just as well on the foetus within the womb. Ultrasound scanning is now a routine procedure during pregnancy.

X-rays and ultrasound scans produce a simple image, but in 1967, Godfrey Hounsfield hit on the idea of producing sections through the body that could be put together by a computer to create a 3-D image. This resulted in the development of the CAT (computerized axial tomography) scanner in which patients are placed in a huge machine while the x-ray device revolves

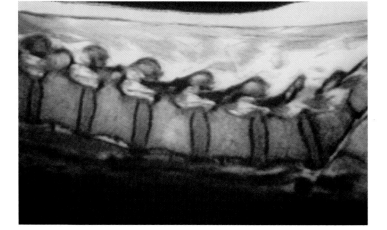

▲ CAT SCAN OF THE LOWER BACK
To produce a CAT scan, an x-ray machine is rotated about the patient's body, taking a series of pictures. Then a computer generates a scan picture that looks look a section through the complete body. CAT scans even show soft tissues that do not normally appear on x-rays.

around them, photographing slices through their bodies. A similar method is to inject the patient with a radioactive dye that shows up in the photographs taken by the scanner.

The MRI (magnetic resonance imaging) scanner is one of the most recent innovations. It is safer than other imaging techniques, because it uses magnetic energy, not harmful radiation. It can even show changes in body chemistry as they take place. For example, it can show which parts of the brain become active as we think, talk or move.

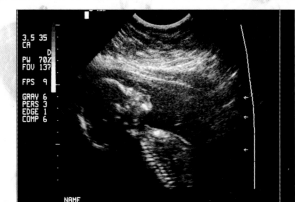

▲ UNBORN BABY
Ultrasound is used to check on the health of babies in the womb. They produce live images that even show the baby's heart beating.

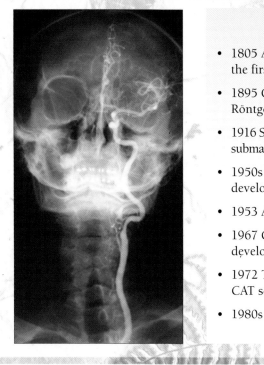

▶ ARTERIOGRAM
Damage to arterial (blood vessel) walls shows up when a dye is injected into the artery. X-rays cannot pass through this dye, and shows the shape of the artery in the x-ray.

Key Dates

- 1805 AJ Desormeaux develops the first endoscope in Paris.

- 1895 German physicist Wilhelm Röntgen discovers x-rays.

- 1916 Sonar is used to detect enemy submarines in World War I.

- 1950s Ultrasound scanning is developed by Ian Donald.

- 1953 Arteriography is perfected.

- 1967 Godfrey Hounsfield develops the CAT scanner.

- 1972 The first clinical test of CAT scanning is a success.

- 1980s MRI scans are introduced.

Looking to the Future

SCIENCE AND MEDICINE are still advancing at an ever-increasing rate. Modern innovations are usually the work of teams of people, each with their own special knowledge, rather than talented individuals.

One of the most important innovations has been techniques that allow us to read the genetic structure of the human cell. Before long every one of the millions of genes in every human cell will have been mapped, and the function of many of them will be understood. This is significant because many devastating diseases are caused by genetic abnormalities (accidental changes that occur in the genes as cells reproduce). These affect the function of the body and cause disease. It will be possible to identify people carrying these defective genes so they can make a decision about whether or not to risk having children. Research is already taking place into gene therapy, where corrected genes are inserted into an affected person's body. This is being tried in cystic fibrosis, an inherited lung disease. Modified genes are sprayed into the lungs of affected children to try and correct the condition.

Drugs are providing treatments for more and more diseases. New drugs are designed on computers that produce images of the molecular structure of a whole range of similar drugs. This can show researchers how to modify the molecule to produce

▲ CODE OF LIFE
DNA holds the code for the structure of the whole human body inside each living cell. Research into DNA is revealing the causes of many diseases.

▶ VIRTUAL SURGERY
Virtual reality (VR) allow students and surgeons to practise surgery without endangering a real patient.

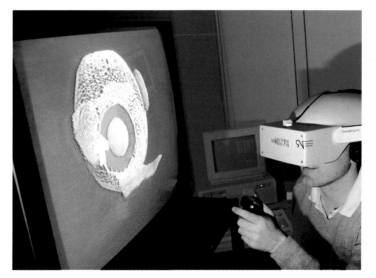

WHAT NEXT?
Medical techniques are becoming more sophisticated and, at the same time, far more expensive. Some medical innovations are so costly that there might have to be rationing if routine medical care is to continue. Already there are long waiting lists for certain operations, and the latest anti-cancer drugs are too expensive for all patients to be given these life-saving treatments.

◀ WORKING WITH THE IMMUNE SYSTEM
Immunology (studying the immune system) is a very important branch of medical science, because it makes sense to encourage the body to protect itself. At the same time, the wrong type of immune reactions can cause disease.

◀ GM FOODS
Bioengineers can already genetically modify (alter the genes of) our foods. For example, some crops now have built in resistance to insect pests. Maybe one day scientists will be able to give foods built in medicines for good health. However, some people question the safety of GM crops.

▶ BUILT TO ATTACK
Bacteriophages are forms of virus that prey on bacteria. Genetic engineering may be used to design bacteriophages that fight specific diseases.

effects, even before a drug has been synthesized.

Modern technology is already helping many family doctors. Sometimes, the doctor may need to refer a patient to a specialist for a detailed diagnosis. Modern teleconferencing means that, via his or her computer, the doctor can speak directly to a specialist who could even be in another country. The specialist could then examine the patient by video link.

Technology concentrates mostly on medicine in developed countries, but throughout the world, millions of people do not have access to medical care at all or, if they do, cannot afford the treatment. It is a challenge for doctors and governments around the worlds to improve the standards of health for everyone. Agencies such as the World Health Organisation have made huge efforts to set up global health programmes. These are aimed at diseases that could be easily controlled by vaccination or the use of inexpensive drugs.

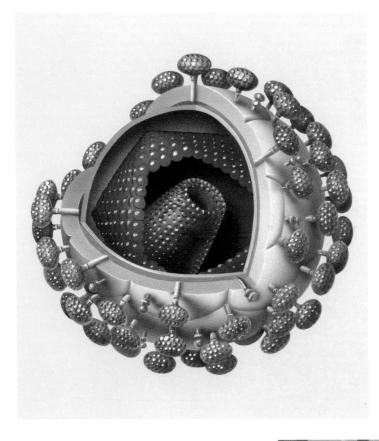

◀ HIV VIRUS
The HIV virus associated with AIDS has been studied more closely than any other virus, and its structure is well understood. What is less clear is how the virus constantly changes to avoid being attacked by the immune system. Frantic efforts are underway to find more effective treatments and vaccines to prevent the infection.

▶ SMART LOO
A diagnostic toilet has been developed in Japan. Sensors check the weight of the user and measure the fat and sugar content of their wastes. The toilet sends its results direct to the doctor.

▼ ZERO GRAVITY
Research has already taken place in orbiting spacecraft to investigate new ways to purify drugs. Zero gravity has profound effects on the body. It is possible that people weakened by muscle-wasting diseases could survive for longer under these conditions.

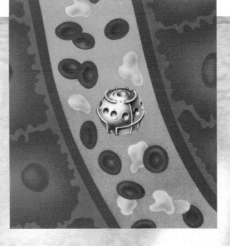

▲ NANO ROBOTS
There are plans to produce nanobots, robots small enough to travel around the body in the bloodstream. These robots could be programmed to monitor a person's health, attack tumours, or remove cholesterol (fatty build ups) from blocked arteries.

Key Dates

- 1869 DNA is discovered.

- 1943 Scientists discover that DNA passes on genetic information.

- 1953 James Watson and Francis Crick discover the double-helix structure of DNA.

- 1961 Yuri Gagarin is the first man to travel into space.

- 1970s Genetic engineering begins.

- 1980s Virtual reality is developed.

- 1990s Medical research in zero gravity begins.

- 1990 GM yeast goes on sale in the UK.

MODERN WEAPONS AND WARFARE

From hand-held rifles to stealth bombers, modern advances in technology have armed human beings with more powerful weapons than ever before. This section explores the killing machines that have been designed over the last 300 years.

BY WILL FOWLER

The Technology of Destruction

ETWEEN THE YEAR 1700 AND THE PRESENT DAY, the ways that wars are conducted have changed beyond all recognition. Flintlock muskets have been replaced by automatic machine guns, and horses have been replaced by armoured tanks and assault helicopters. Change has been most rapid in the last hundred years. World War I was fought mostly hand-to-hand, but the main battles of the Gulf War were fought by missiles and planes.

The introduction of steam power and petrol engines meant that soldiers did not have to rely on animals for transport, which could get tired or injured. The ships that relied on the wind for power were replaced by vessels that moved at greater speeds against winds and currents when powered by steam.

Armour plating, that had protected knights in the Middle Ages, found new uses protecting ships, land vehicles and even aircraft. New lighter, stronger, and even fire resistant materials were developed. These new materials were initially used to provide clothing to protect crews, but were later also used for fire fighters and the emergency services.

Before World War I people were optimistic about science. They believed that technological advances would make life safer, healthier and easier. In part this has been true, but science has also been used for war. Destruction on a huge scale has now become a reality. But though the two world wars led to the development of weapons of mass destruction (nuclear, chemical and biological weapons), they were also the spur for life-saving medical techniques.

▲ RIFLES
Ever since they were first invented in the 19th century, rifles have played a critical role in warfare.

▼ KEY DATES
The panel charts the development of modern weapons, from Leonardo da Vinci's sketches of a helicopter, to the introduction of stealth technology in modern aircraft.

▼ FORTIFICATIONS
As the technology of warfare has developed, the means of defending against ever-changing weaponry has altered dramatically.

PISTOLS AND ARTILLERY

The Gatling gun

- **1784** Invention of the Shrapnel shell
- **1807** Forsyth patents the percussion ignition
- **1835** Lefaucheux patents the pin-fire cartridge
- **1835** Colt patents his revolver design
- **1883** Maxim patents fully automatic machine gun

- **1901** British 10-pounder cannon introduced
- **1914–1918** World War I: long-range artillery in use
- **1934** First general-purpose machine gun introduced
- **1939–1945** World War II: self-loading rifle developed. Recoilless guns, rocker artillery and anti-tank guns in use
- **1947** Kalashnikov designs the AK47 assault rifle
- **1957** Italian 105mm Model 56 pack howitzer appears

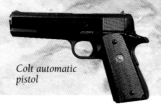

Colt automatic pistol

FIGHTING ON THE LAND

- **1850** Morse Code invented
- **1858** First aerial photography
- **1865** First antiseptics used
- **1882** Armoured steel developed
- **1914–1918** World War I: land and sea camouflage developed
- **1916** September: first tanks used in World War I
- **1925** French demonstrate the half-track vehicle
- **1939–1945** World War II: aerial photography and infra-red technology developed
- **1943** Infra-red night-vision viewer used

- **1944–1945** German missiles launched against Britain
- **1944** June 6: D-Day, the largest amphibious operation in history, takes place
- **1957** First space satellite launched
- **1991** Iraqi SCUD surface-to-surface missiles launched in the Gulf War

World War II Sherman tank

▼ AVIATION
The development of military air power has been one of the most important changes to modern warfare. Controlling the skies above any battlefield has become critical to modern tactics, and critical to military success. Aircraft are now more deadly than ever. They can fly faster and for longer, and over greater distances carrying more weaponry than ever before.

The 1940s saw the rapid development of the aircraft as the jet turbine replaced the piston engine. New planes could fly further and with more weapons than ever before.

Radio communications began at the end of the 1800s as a laboratory experiment. One hundred years later it had become an essential part of the equipment of war. The world wars showed how important communication was, and scientists developed the technology to meet the demands of soldiers.

Helicopters had existed in a basic form before World War II, but by 1945, engineers in the United States and Britain were designing new, more powerful versions of these rotary wing craft. By the end of the 1900s the helicopter had become a life saver, lifting sailors from the sea or survivors from burning buildings.

The soldiers of the developed world are no longer troops sent to fight. They have become peace-keepers, attempting to prevent brutal wars. Fast communications allow them to keep their national leaders informed about developments on the ground on an hour by hour basis.

▲ MOBILITY
The ability to move large numbers of troops and equipment quickly and easily is an essential part of any successful campaign.

▼ TECHNOLOGY
Warfare has always pushed back technological boundaries, from the first tanks to stealth bombers like this B2 bomber.

FIGHTING ON THE SEAS

- **1805** Battle of Trafalgar
- **1863** The steam-driven submersible *David* attacks Federal iron-clad ship
- **1904** *Aigret*, first diesel-powered boat
- **1906** Launch of HMS *Dreadnought*
- **1914–1918** World War I
- **1916** May 31: Battle of Jutland
- **1939–1945** German U-boats use "wolf pack" tactics against Allied shipping
- **1941** May 27: sinking of the *Bismarck*
- **1942** June 4–7: Battle of Midway

- **1944** June 6: D-Day
- **1954** *USS Nautilus*, the first nuclear-powered submarine, is commissioned
- **1961** *USS Enterprise* is first nuclear-powered carrier
- **1966** Soviet Osa-class missile-armed craft enter service
- **1990-1991** Osa-class craft see action in the Gulf War

US Knox-class frigate

REACHING FOR THE SKIES

F86 Sabre

- **1903** Wilbur and Orville Wright make the first powered flight
- **1907** September 29: first helicopter lifts a man off the ground into the air
- **1912** Machine gun fired from aircraft for first time
- **1914–1918** World War I
- **1914** October 5: first aircraft to be shot down
- **1939–1945** World War II: first strategic bombing
- **1945** August 6 and 9: atomic bombs dropped on Japan
- **1945** December 3: the first jet landing and take-off from an aircraft carrier

- **1950** First jet-versus-jet victory in the Korean War
- **1951** Canberra bomber is the first jet to fly across the North Atlantic non-stop
- **1955** B-52 enters service with the United States Air Force
- **1977** December: first flight of Lockheed Martin F-117
- **1989** July 17: first flight of Northrop Grumman B-2A Spirit stealth aircraft
- **1991** February 24: 300 helicopters used in Gulf War in the largest aerial assault in the history of aviation

Pistols and Rifles

▲ RIFLEMAN
A 19th-century French soldier carries a bolt-action rifle.

YOU CAN SEE PISTOLS every day in most countries because police officers carry them. In thrillers and westerns, the heroes and villains are usually armed with pistols. You have probably seen lots of pistols, but do you know how they work?

There are two sorts of pistols. A revolver has a cylindrical magazine with six rounds of bullets. Newer pistols are self-loading, with a detachable box magazine that fits into the handle and can hold up to 14 rounds of ammunition. Rifles are bolt-action, semi-automatic or automatic weapons, and have a magazine that holds between 5 and 30 rounds. An automatic weapon automatically places the next round in the chamber for firing, so fires repeatedly when the trigger is pulled.

▶ RIFLES
British soldiers of the late 19th century use their massed firepower to compensate for the short range and inaccuracy of their flintlock muskets.

The most famous revolvers are the "Six Guns" used in the 1800s in the United States. These were famous as they enabled the user to fire six shots in quick succession. In World War I (1914–1918) and World War II (1939–1945), British troops used the .455in Webley MarkVI revolver or the .38in Enfield Number 2 Mark1.

The Germans used the Luger pistol as it was easy to reload. It was named after Georg Luger, a designer at the Ludwig Löwe arms factory in Berlin. It weighed 850g, had an eight-shot magazine and fired a 9mm round.

The US Army carried the .45in Colt 1911 self-loading pistol throughout both world wars, the Korean War and the Vietnam War. It weighs 1.11kg and has a seven-round magazine. The Belgian 9mm Browning High Power was first manufactured in 1935. It weighs 1.01kg when loaded and has an effective range of 50–70m. Its magazine holds 13 rounds in two staggered rows – a feature copied in later designs. The British used the bolt-action .303in Short Magazine Lee Enfield (SMLE) rifle during World War I

A SOLDIER'S TOOLS

The rifle and pistol have always been the tools of the infantryman. They are light and portable, and have become more accurate and faster firing. Cavalry, artillery and support troops such as engineers also carry these weapons, primarily for self-protection rather than attack. The rifle and pistol cartridge have also allowed the weapons' mechanical feed to be improved.

▲ THE US ARMY RIFLE
In the years before the American Civil War, the US Army used a .58in rifle. Rifling made the bullet more accurate by spinning it, causing the bullet to fly straighter. The bayonet was used in close-quarter fighting.

▲ SHORT MAGAZINE LEE ENFIELD (SMLE) BOLT-ACTION RIFLE
The compact bolt-action rifle was 1.132m long, weighed 3.96kg and had a ten-round magazine. It was used by the British Army from 1907 to 1943. More than three million were made in Britain, India and Australia.

▲ BOLT ACTION
The Mauser action had five rounds. They could be loaded into the breech, the back part, by moving the bolt.

▲ THE AUTOMATIC
The US Colt 1911A1 (right) and Browning 1903 are two classic self-loading pistols. Their ammunition is in a magazine in the pistol grip.

▲ THE MI6
The MI6 is now widely used throughout the world. It was first used by the US Army in Vietnam. At that time the M16 was revolutionary because it fired a 5.56mm round, was made from plastics and alloys and weighed only 3.18kg.

and for much of World War II. The German 7.92mm Karabiner 98K was a very accurate weapon but only had a five-round magazine. The US Garand M1 rifle and M1 carbine were popular self-loading rifles during World War II as they were tough and reliable.

Two weapons have dominated armed conflicts since 1945; the US 5.56mm M16 Armalite rifle weighing 3.18kg, and the Soviet-designed 7.62mm AK47 weighing 4.30kg. Both can fire on full automatic at 700 (M16) and 600 (AK47) rounds per minute (rpm).

▲ THE ENFIELD L85A1 RIFLE
This is the current rifle issued to British troops. It weighs 3.8kg and is 785mm long. On automatic it fires 5.56mm rounds at 700 rounds per minute (rpm). The Enfield L85A1 has been used in action in the Persian Gulf, in Kosovo and in Northern Ireland.

▼ THE SNIPER'S HIDE
In World War II, snipers built camouflaged positions called hides in which they could observe and shoot at the enemy. They were often concealed for long periods in the hides, which needed to be well built and weatherproof. This hide has an angled roof covered in turf.

A turf roof conceals the hide.

The hide is deep enough to allow the sniper to stand.

▲ THE SNIPER
A soldier is camouflaged to blend into the woodland. He aims his Accuracy International L96A1 7.62mm sniper's rifle. It is fitted with an optical sight.

Key Dates

- 1807 Dr Forsyth patents the percussion ignition

- 1812 Pauly patents the first cartridge breech-loader

- 1835 Lefaucheux patents the pin-fire cartridge

- 1835 Colt patents his revolver design

- 1849 The Minié rifle replaces smooth-bore rifles

- 1886 French adopt the first small-bore smokeless-powder cartridge

- 1888 Britain adopts Lee–Metford bolt-action repeater

- 1939–1945 Self-loading rifle developed

Automatic Weapons

▲ THE GARDNER
This early water-cooled, hand-cranked machine gun is mounted on an adjustable tripod. Its ammunition is fed into the chamber from the top.

THE FIRST MACHINE GUN dates back to 1718, when Puckle's gun was developed in Britain. It was a large hand-cranked revolver on a stand that fired seven rounds per minute (rpm). The Gatling gun was also hand-cranked. It fired at a rate of 100–200rpm. It was developed in the US in 1862 and used in the American Civil War.

The first successful automatic machine gun was the 7.92mm Maxim gun designed by the American (Sir) Hiram Maxim. It used the energy of the exploding cartridges to operate the mechanism and fired at 500rpm. This rapid firing rate heated up the barrel, so it was cooled by a water-filled jacket. The British used the Maxim gun in action in 1895.

The French Hotchkiss machine gun used the gases of the exploding cartridges to operate its mechanism. It had a heavier barrel designed not to need a water jacket, but that

cooled in the air. Ammunition was fed in on a cloth belt, where other similar weapons used metal belts.

The belt-fed British Vickers .303in machine gun was designed in 1891 and was not withdrawn from service with the British Army until 1963. The World War II German MG42 was a 7.92mm general-purpose machine gun (GPMG). Stamping and spot welding speeded its manufacturing process. It had a top range of 2,000m and fired 1,550rpm. Features of its design were copied in the postwar Belgian FN MAG and in the US M60 machine guns.

The first sub-machine guns (SMGs) fired

◀ THE GATLING GUN
The hand-cranked Gatling gun, used here by British soldiers, was introduced in 1862. Designed by Dr Richard Gatling, it had between six and ten barrels. It saw action in the American Civil War and was formerly adopted by the US Army during the Spanish-American War. Later models were mounted on a light artillery carriage.

SUB-MACHINE GUNS (SMGS)

The first sub-machine gun to go into service was the Italian Villar Perosa, which was used in World War I. SMGs fire pistol-calibre ammunition such as 9mm or .45in at the same rate as a conventional machine gun. They are not accurate over long ranges, but are ideal in situations where intense close-range firepower is required.

▶ THE STEN MK II SMG
This 9mm SMG weighs 3kg empty and fires at 550rpm. Over two million were made in World War II.

◀ THE AK47
The AK47 assault rifle fires a 7.62mm round, which is halfway between a rifle round and a pistol round.

◀ THE TOMMY GUN
The Thompson M1 was the simplified World War II version of this SMG. It had a 30-round box magazine and weighed 4.74kg empty.

▶ THE UZI SMG
The Uzi is a 9mm SMG developed in Israel. It weighs 3.5kg empty and fires at a rate of 600rpm.

pistol-sized ammunition and could be carried by one person. They were developed at the end of World War I. The .45in Thompson (Tommy) gun, designed in the 1920s in the US, became notorious in the US gang wars of the 1920s. It was widely used by British and American troops in World War II.

The World War II German MP38/40 was the first sub-machine gun to have a folding metal butt. This

feature reduced its size from 833mm down to 630mm. It fired at 500rpm and had a thirty-round magazine.

Modern SMGs are compact and lightweight weapons. They are a common weapon for bodyguards as they can be carried inside jackets or briefcases.

▲ HELICOPTER MOUNTED
Machine guns were first fitted to helicopters by the French in the 1960s. They are now used by helicopters to protect the aircraft when flying into "hot" landing zones or to attack enemy infantry.

▲ VEHICLE MOUNTED
A Belgian 7.62mm MAG machine gun is mounted on a vehicle in the desert. The MAG is in service in many countries and can be mounted on a tripod for long-range fire, or on a built-in bipod for shorter ranges.

▶ THE M60
The poor reliability of the US 7.62mm M60 general-purpose machine gun in Vietnam earned it the nickname of "the Pig". It has since been modified and improved and is widely used across the world.

▼ BEATEN ZONE
A machine gun fires long bursts over long ranges, spreading its bullets in to a cone-shaped area called a "beaten zone". It is fatal or very risky for soldiers to enter this bullet-swept zone.

Machine guns are very effective defence weapons when used in pairs. Two machine guns can be positioned so that they fire from the side across the path of an aproaching enemy. This arrangement makes their fire overlap, creating two overlapping "beaten zones". This combined fire power creates a doubly dangerous area for the enemy.

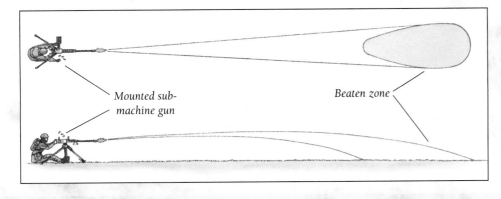

Mounted sub-machine gun

Beaten zone

Key Dates

- 1883 Maxim patents fully automatic machine gun

- 1896 United States order Browning-Colt gas-operated gun

- 1926 Czech ZB/vz26 light machine gun designed

- 1934 MG34 introduced, the first general-purpose machine gun

- 1942 MG42 creates the basis for many post-war designs

- 1947 Kalashnikov designs the AK47 assault rifle

- 1961 US Army evaluates Armalite rifle

Artillery – Cannons and Mortars

BATTLES IN EUROPE and North America between the 1500s and 1800s were thundering smoke-filled affairs as artillery soldiers manned their cannons and each side bombarded the other.

Cannons were loaded from the muzzle (front end) and fired round shot or cannon balls. The major development in artillery weapons came with the introduction of rifled barrels in 1858. A rifled barrel makes a shell spin in flight and so it is more accurate. Breech loading, loading the gun from the back, was introduced in around 1870. Recoil mechanisms to absorb the "kick" of the firing followed in 1888.

▼ RAPID-FIRE CANNON

These cannons were mounted on warships or used for close-range coastal defence. They entered service in the late 19th century. Improved recoil mechanisms meant that the gun remained stable while firing. The crew were protected by an armoured shield, but in later years they would be enclosed in a turret.

▼ DESERT FIREPOWER

A howitzer is an artillery piece designed to fire at a steep angle, usually over fortifications. US M198 155mm howitzer in action during the Gulf War of 1990–1991. It entered service with the US Army and US Marine Corps in 1979. The howitzer weighs 7,163kg and has a crew of 11. It has a maximum range of 18,150m with standard ammunition, but this increases to 30,000m with a rocket-assisted projectile (RAP).

BIG BOYS

Before aircraft that could drop large bomb loads had been developed, artillery was used to bombard fortifications or defend important locations such as ports and capital cities. The bigger the calibre (diameter of the barrel), the bigger the shell and so the greater the volume of explosives that could be enclosed in the gun. Big shells were therefore more destructive.

▶ US ARMY BREECH-LOADING HOWITZER
This siege howitzer is mounted on a turntable and has a hoist for loading.

▲ RAILGUNS
Railways have been used to carry heavy guns and mortars since the American Civil War. The world's biggest guns were the German guns used in World War II.

▼ MODERN MORTAR
A soldier loads a British 81mm mortar with a high-explosive (HE) bomb. On the left a second soldier kneels ready with another bomb to ensure a rapid rate of fire.

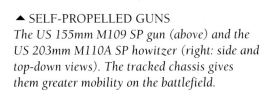

▲ SELF-PROPELLED GUNS
The US 155mm M109 SP gun (above) and the US 203mm M110A SP howitzer (right: side and top-down views). The tracked chassis gives them greater mobility on the battlefield.

Mortars were muzzle-loading weapons, which fired their shells in a high-angled trajectory (curved path). The modern mortar can be traced back to the British Stokes mortar of World War I.

Modern artillery ranges from World War II weapons such as the huge German railway siege guns – the 80cm K(E) Gustav bombarded Sevastopol and Leningrad – to the tiny Japanese 70mm battalion gun Type 92. The K(E) Gustav fired a 4,800kg shell to 47km. It had a crew of 1,500 men. The Japanese gun, with a crew of five, fired a 3.7kg shell to 1,373m.

World War II mortars included the massive German 60cm Karl, which was also used to bombard Sevastopol, as well as Warsaw. It fired a 1,576kg shell to a maximum range of 6,675m. It was mounted on a tracked chassis, but this gave it very limited mobility and it crawled along at only 10kph. Karl mortars had a crew of 18. There was also the little British 2in (51mm) mortar. It weighed 4.1kg, fired a 1.02kg bomb to a maximum range of 456m and had crew of two.

Future artillery designs may include a 155mm howitzer built with new materials that is as light as a 105mm weapon. Shells will soon be guided and capable of changing their path during flight.

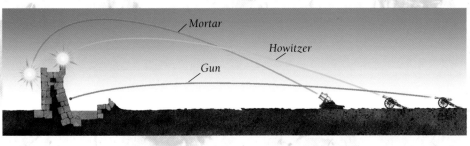

▲ TRAJECTORIES
Mortars and howitzers have a high-angled trajectory and can lob shells over obstacles. Field artillery has a flatter trajectory.

▶ INDIRECT FIRE
An artillery battery may not see its target when it fires. It can be instructed to adjust its fire by an observer who watches where the shells fall.

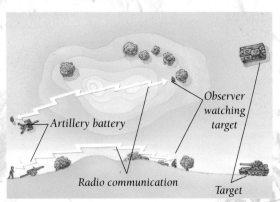

Key Dates

- 1784 Invention of the Shrapnel shell

- 1858 French adopt rifled artillery

- 1870 Breech loading widely used

- 1884 French develop smokeless gunpowder

- 1888 Konrad Hausser develops long-recoil cylinder

- 1899 Maxim "Pom Pom" automatic cannon in use

- 1914–1918 World War I: long-range artillery developed

- 1939–1945 World War II: recoilless guns, rocker artillery and anti-tank guns

Artillery – Pack Guns

▲ FIELD PIECE
Horse-drawn artillery consisted of the gun, the limber that contained the ammunition and charges, and the team of horses.

IN JULY 1999 the last Royal Tournament was held in London, England. It marked the end of the annual Royal Navy field gun race between crews from Portsmouth and Plymouth. The crews dismantled a Victorian 10-pounder mountain gun and raced across a series of obstacles before re-assembling it and firing a blank shell. It was an exciting test of strength and co-ordination. Pack howitzers like the 10-pounder were designed to be dismantled and carried by men or five mules across mountainous or rough terrain. If the pack artillery could then be assembled on a mountain ridge, their fire could dominate the roads through the valleys below.

The 10-pounder was used in India on the North-west Frontier between 1901 and 1915.

▶ ITALIAN PACK GUNS
Alpine mountain troops move their guns to new positions in World War I. Pack guns could be broken down into about four sections for ease of transport.

It fired a 4.5kg shell out to 5,500m. The gun became famous as the "screw gun" because its barrel broke down into two sections that were screwed together when it was assembled for firing.

The 10-pounder was replaced by the 3.7in (94mm) pack howitzer that soldiered on during both World Wars. The howitzer's maximum weight was 2,218.2kg and it fired a 9.08kg shell out to 5,490m.

MOVING ABOUT
Pack howitzers, or mountain artillery, and light anti-aircraft guns were designed to be dismantled so that they could be carried by troops or mules to remote mountaintop positions. Today's light guns can be carried by helicopter, which is faster and more reliable.

◀ MUSCLE POWER
Royal Navy sailors at the Royal Tournament in London, demonstrating how the British 10-pounder mountain gun can be dismantled and reassembled.

▲ ANTI-AIRCRAFT GUN
A Soviet-made, Iraqi ZPU-4 23mm anti-aircraft gun in a coastal position. It was captured in 1991 in Kuwait at the end of the Gulf War.

good that it has been effectively copied in India with a 75mm pack gun howitzer. The Model 56 can be broken down into 11 parts that can be transported by mules or even carried on soldiers' backs for short distances. It weighs 1,290kg and can fire a 19kg high-explosive shell out to 10,600m.

The use of helicopters, and the widespread need for air mobility, make the requirement for light guns and pack howitzers almost universal. They can be transported slung beneath helicopters and brought into action very quickly.

The guns of the future will be constructed from new materials, many of which are currently used in modern aircraft design. These materials are strong but much lighter than steel and alloys.

▲ CIVIL WAR CANNON
The breech-loading cannon used in the 1860s in the United States were very similar to those used during the Napoleonic Wars.

During World War II, the US 75mm M1A1 pack howitzer proved a very effective weapon for airborne forces. It was originally designed for carriage by six mules. The M1A1 fired a 6.24kg high-explosive shell out to 8,930m and weighed 588.3kg. The 105mm M3 howitzer was a bigger version of the M1A1 and weighed 1132.7kg. It could fire a 14.98kg shell out to 6,633m.

Postwar mountain artillery has been dominated by the Italian OTO Melara 105/14 Model 56 105mm howitzer. It was introduced in 1957 and since then more than 2,500 have been built. The Model 56 has been used by more than 17 countries. Its design is so

▲ PACK HOWITZER
The Italian 105mm Model 56 pack howitzer in action. The shield can be removed to save weight. The howitzer's hinged trail legs can be folded, making the gun easier to transport.

▼ ANTI-AIRCRAFT FIRE
Anti-aircraft gun crews developed the skill of aiming just in front of a moving aircraft. This meant that the shell, with its time fuse, exploded as the aircraft flew into the blast and fragments. Radar now makes the job faster and easier.

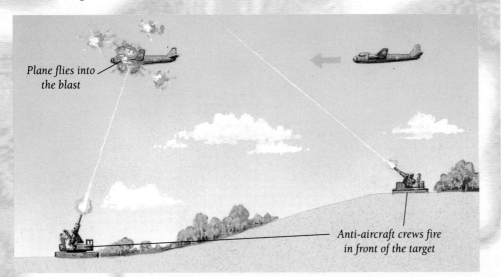

Plane flies into the blast

Anti-aircraft crews fire in front of the target

Key Dates

- 1901 British 10-pounder introduced

- 1901-1915 The 10-pounder used on Indian North-west Frontier

- 1914–1918 World War I: anti-aircraft guns used

- 1932 Swedish 40mm Bofors anti-aircraft gun appears

- 1936 German 8.8cm Flak 36 anti-aircraft gun developed

- 1939–1945 World War II: US 75mm M1A1 pack howitzer used

- 1957 Italian 105mm Model 56 pack howitzer appears

Bombs, Rockets and Torpedoes

Rockets propelled by gunpowder are a common sight across Britain on 5 November (Guy Fawkes' Night) and in the United States on 4 July (Independence Day). People watch as the rockets streak into the sky and burst into a shower of coloured stars. Rockets were originally used by the ancient Chinese as a weapon. They called them "fire arrows".

Later, in the 1800s, the British employed rockets against the French during the Napoleonic Wars. They were used in 1815 by a Royal Artillery troop at the battle of Waterloo. American and European armies experimented with them throughout the 1800s.

▶ STINGER SAM
The US low-altitude surface-to-air missile (SAM) has a maximum range of about 4,000m and a maximum speed of Mach 2.2. It has a 3kg high-explosive warhead.

The self-propelled, or "fish", torpedo developed in the late 1800s revolutionized naval warfare. In World War I rockets were fitted to British fighter planes to attack German Zeppelin airships.

The first aerial bombs were used in World War I when pilots threw hand grenades at enemy troops. By the end of the war British bombers, such as the Handley Page 0/400, were carrying 600kg bombs to attack targets in Germany.

From World War II to the present day, bombs have been either high-explosive (HE) or incendiary devices. HE bombs are designed to explode on the surface or to penetrate reinforced concrete. Incendiary bombs burn at great heat and include napalm, a jellied fuel that splashes over a wide area. Cluster bombs are small HE bombs that are scattered from a larger container over a much wider area.

World War II rockets included the huge liquid-fuel German V-2, which was designed by Werner von Braun.

FLYING BOMBS

Aircraft and artillery use rockets and bombs to deliver high-explosive or incendiary payloads to target areas. Torpedoes launched from ships and submarines or dropped from the air proved very effective against ships of all sizes in World War II. Rockets have become a more effective weapon and are now launched from helicopters as well as from ships.

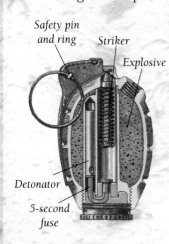

Safety pin and ring *Striker* *Explosive* *Detonator* *5-second fuse*

◀ HAND GRENADE
The British 36 grenade was introduced in 1915. It uses a mechanism with two safety features; a pin and also a handle.

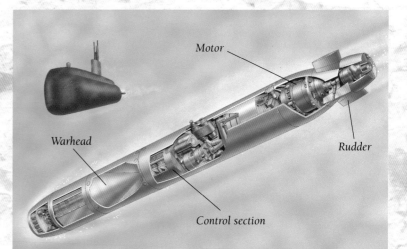

Motor *Warhead* *Rudder* *Control section*

▲ TORPEDO
A torpedo consists of a warhead, fuel supply, motor and rudder. Modern weapons also have wire guidance systems and warheads like those of an anti-tank weapon. When the warhead explodes it can penetrate deep into a ship's hull.

◀ MULTIPLE ROCKET LAUNCHER
The US Multiple Rocket Launcher System (MRLS) was used in action during the Gulf War of 1990–1991. Its tracked chassis allows it to move rapidly around the battlefield, and it can reload in a few minutes.

It weighed 13.6 tonnes and had a range of more than 300km. Another World War II rocket was the crude but effective solid-fuel 8in rocket projectile (RP) fired from Allied aircraft.

Postwar rockets include intercontinental guided missiles with nuclear warheads, air-to-air missiles for combat aircraft, and anti-tank missiles with ranges of between 3,000 and 5,000m.

Robert Whitehead and Giovanni Lupis developed the first torpedo in 1866. It took its name from a Caribbean electric-ray fish. Torpedo boats were designed to carry the new weapon, and ships designed to destroy torpedoes, known as "destroyers", were in turn developed. The torpedo

Warhead

▲ SMART BOMB
The US Paveway laser-guided bomb follows the reflected laser energy bounced back from its target. Laser- guided bombs were first used in the Vietnam War.

Computer   Fuse

made battleships vulnerable to attack by smaller vessels and submarines. In World War II torpedoes were also launched from aircraft. Modern torpedoes, with sophisticated guidance systems and warheads, are still carried by submarines. Torpedoes are also designed to seek and destroy submarines.

▶ ANTI-AIRCRAFT MISSILE
The British Rapier surface-to-air missile was first used during the Falklands War in 1982. It has a maximum speed of 650m per second and a range of 7,000m.

▶ ALFRED NOBEL
Swedish scientist Alfred Nobel (1833–1896) developed a range of high explosives. These included dynamite (1863) and nitrocellulose (1888), from which smokeless propellant was developed. Nobel's explosives changed warfare in the 20th century.

▲ CLUSTER BOMB
The cluster bomb unit (CBU) dropped from aircraft contains smaller bombs, or submunitions, that are ejected to scatter across the ground. The CBU is used against soldiers in open or unarmoured vehicles.

Key Dates

- 1860–1880 Hale rockets in use in Britain and US

- 1890 Whitehead develops torpedo

- 1903 Russian rocket engineer Konstantin Tsiolkovsky develops liquid-fuel rockets

- 1944–1945 German V-1 and V-2 cruise missiles and ballistic missiles launched against Britain

- 1981–1986 Air-launched cruise missiles enter service with US Air Force

- 1991 Iraqi SCUD surface-to-surface missiles launched in the Gulf War

Mines and Fortifications

▲ ANTI-TANK MINE
An Italian plastic-bodied anti-tank mine that could destroy a truck and cripple a tank or armoured vehicle.

SINCE THE US CIVIL WAR mines have been used as part of defensive fortifications to create obstacles and defend positions. But they are a major problem in the developing world today as they have been laid by warring parties in civil wars, causing injury to innocent civilians

The first mines were used as long ago as the American Civil War of 1861–1865, but these were crude devices. In the same war trenches were employed in field fortifications for the first time.

The design of forts had changed with the development of gunpowder. They were now no longer built upwards but outwards instead, with bombardment-proof barracks and gun batteries. From the late 17th century the French military engineer Sebastian Vauban was a major

influence. He designed huge star-shaped fortresses that allowed artillery to be used effectively. He also developed siege techniques for attacking fortresses.

Concrete was developed in the 20th century and was quickly adopted for fortifications. Barbed wire was first used extensively in the Boer War (1899–1902). In World War I the trenches of the Western Front were made of concrete, barbed wire and corrugated iron. They stretched from Switzerland to the English Channel. At the end of the war the Germans produced

Berm

Revetting

Parapet

Dugout

Firing step

▶ WORLD WAR I TRENCHES
Trenches were dug deep enough so that men could walk along them below ground level. When the soldiers needed to shoot they climbed up on to the firing step. To prevent the trenches collapsing they were reinforced with material called revetting.

PROTECTION
Trenches and bunkers were first dug in the American Civil War, although earthworks had been built in the Napoleonic Wars. The Victorians built coastal forts to protect key harbours.

By World War I improved artillery and the introduction of large numbers of machine guns forced the infantry underground. Materials such as steel girders and concrete make modern defences very strong.

▶ ANTI-TANK OBSTACLES
American soldiers stand among concrete anti-tank obstacles called "dragon's teeth". They were built by the Germans in World War II to protect the western borders of the Third Reich.

▼ TUNNELS
In the Vietnam War the Vietcong (North Vietnamese) used tunnels like this one for concealment and as protection from bombs and shellfire.

Sentry   *Concealed entrance*   *Accommodation / storage chamber*   *Escape route into water*

◀ PORTABLE DEFENCES
British soldiers deploy "concertina" wire in the desert in the Gulf War of 1990–1991. Barbed wire was first made in 1874. It is a portable, economical and rapid form of perimeter defence used by armies across the world.

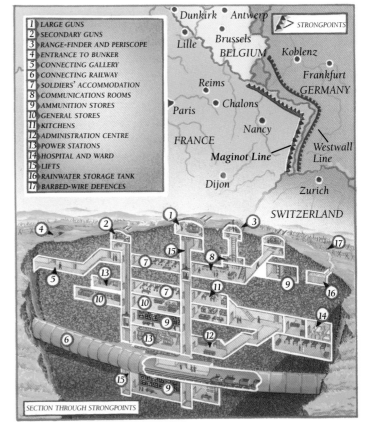

1	LARGE GUNS
2	SECONDARY GUNS
3	RANGE-FINDER AND PERISCOPE
4	ENTRANCE TO BUNKER
5	CONNECTING GALLERY
6	CONNECTING RAILWAY
7	SOLDIERS' ACCOMMODATION
8	COMMUNICATIONS ROOMS
9	AMMUNITION STORES
10	GENERAL STORES
11	KITCHENS
12	ADMINISTRATION CENTRE
13	POWER STATIONS
14	HOSPITAL AND WARD
15	LIFTS
16	RAINWATER STORAGE TANK
17	BARBED-WIRE DEFENCES

SECTION THROUGH STRONGPOINTS

▲ MAGINOT LINE
Built by the French before World War II, the Maginot Line was a series of fortifications 320km long, built to defend France's border with Germany. It took more than ten years to construct. It has been described as "a concrete battleship on land". Strongpoints in the Line had extra guns and equipment. They had underground tunnels and storage rooms, and air-conditioned barracks that protected against gas attacks. The fortifications included long-range artillery, mortars and machine guns. When the Germans attacked they outflanked the Maginot Line through neutral Belgium and Luxembourg.

the first anti-tank mines. They rigged standard artillery shells to explode when run over by a tank.

The two types of mine – anti-tank (AT) and anti-personnel (AP) – were developed in World War II. AT mines are designed to destroy trucks or to stop tanks by damaging their tracks or wheels. The German Teller AT mine contained 6kg of high explosive and has been the model for Russian and Israeli AT mines since 1945. AP mines kill or injure soldiers and civilians. Modern mines are made from plastic, which makes them almost impossible to detect. Techniques have been developed for detecting and clearing mines. Alternatively engineers may simply blast a path through a minefield.

In World War II lines of concrete fortifications were constructed, such as the coastal Atlantic Wall, built by the Germans, and the 320km long Maginot Line, built by the French. However, the use of tanks and aircraft had made this kind of static defence outdated.

▲ ATLANTIC WALL
This German 15cm naval gun was part of a coastal defence battery at Longues-sur-Mer in Normandy, France. The slots on each side of the opening give the gun a wider range of movement.

▼ AP MINE
The US M16 jumping anti-personnel mine scatters metal pieces across 3–5 metres.

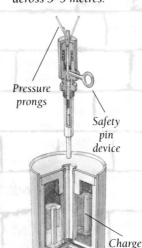

Pressure prongs

Safety pin device

Charge

Key Dates

- 1659 Vauban (1633–1707) devises new fortification systems to defeat artillery

- 1861–1865 American Civil War trench warfare near Richmond

- 1874 Barbed wire produced

- 1899–1902 Boer War: first extensive use of barbed wire

- 1904–1905 Russo-Japanese War

- 1914–1918 World War I: fight for forts at Verdun

- 1930s Construction of the Maginot Line and Westwall Line

- 1942–1944 Construction of Atlantic Wall in World War II

Guerrilla Warfare and Terrorism

▲ CHE GUEVARA
The Argentinian-born Cuban guerrilla leader was executed in Bolivia in 1967. Guevara was an icon for the young revolutionary movement during the 1960s.

EVEN DURING PEACETIME terrorism is a threat on the streets of many cities and towns. Political groups and campaigners who have decided to break the law to further their aims use terrorism. They hope to frighten governments and the public into accepting their views. Together with revolutionary and guerrilla warfare, terrorism is war waged by the weak against the strong.

One of the most famous revolutionary wars was the revolt of the American colonists against the British between 1765 and 1775. It led to the formation of the United States.

▶ COUNTER-TERRORISM
Armed with Heckler and Koch MP5 sub-machine guns, a counter-terrorist team prepares to board an airliner. They wear respirators with darkened eyepieces to protect against exploding stun grenades.

The first example of guerrilla war was during the Peninsula War of 1808–1814, when the Spanish attacked French troops in the mountains of Spain. Their operations were called *guerrilla, or* "a little war".

In 1871 in Paris, following the defeat of the French by the Prussians, the population rose in revolt against the French government. The people felt the government had betrayed them. They formed the Commune which ruled Paris from 19 March 1871 until May 1871 when it was brutally suppressed by the French Army.

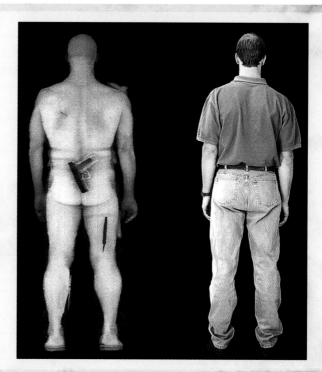

TERRORISM: THE WAR OF THE WEAK

The word "terrorism" dates back to the so-called Reign of Terror that followed the French Revolution in 1789. Between 1793 and 1794 more than 17,000 French citizens were executed, and many more perished in less formal circumstances.

Modern terrorism uses the shock value of an act, such as a random bombing, a hijack, a kidnap or a shooting, to create a widespread sense of fear and insecurity in the community. The terrorists hope this fear will eventually affect government policies. Terrorists who overthrow repressive governments can in turn sometimes fail to respect human rights.

The driving force behind a terrorist group may be politics, nationalism or religion. Terrorist tactics have also been employed by criminal organizations for blackmail, extortion or punishment.

▶ CONCEALED WEAPONS
Terrorists have devised various ways of carrying hand guns, knives and grenades in places where they will not be detected in quick body searches by police or security forces.

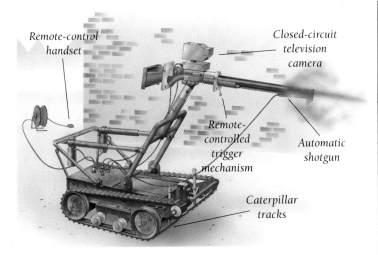

▲ ROBOT AID
Robot-tracked vehicles have been developed to approach, examine and disrupt terrorist explosive devices. TV cameras mounted on the robot allow the operator to see the device on remotely-located monitors, and shotguns or very high-pressure water blast the device apart before it can explode.

The Paris Commune no longer exists, but the name its members gave themselves – Communists – lives on.

In Russia from 1917 to 1921 the revolution against the Tsar (emperor) and his government turned into a civil war. The two opposing sides were the Bolshevik "Reds" and the pro-Western "Whites". The 20th century also saw the growth of guerrilla war as those countries defeated and occupied by Nazi Germany continued to fight secretly and "resist" their occupiers. The French Resistance, for example, was assisted with weapons and equipment sent from Britain by parachute at night.

Mao Tse Tung led the Chinese Communists against the Japanese in World War II, and against the Chinese Nationalists both before and after World War II. Together with Che Guevara who fought for Castro in Cuba, Mao Tse Tung is one of the most famous writers on the subject of guerrilla warfare.

During the Cold War, the period of tension between the former Soviet Union and the West between the years 1945 and 1989, the Soviet Union supported wars of national liberation or decolonization. In most of these campaigns guerrilla or terrorist tactics were used. Modern society is very vulnerable to such pinpoint attacks that can throw ordinary life into chaos. The targets are usually public figures, policemen or small groups of soldiers who are ambushed. Public utilities, transport and communications can be attacked with explosives. The aim of the terrorists is to make a country ungovernable so that the population force its government to strike a deal in order to achieve a peaceful life.

◀ CLIMBER
The rubber tracks on this explosive ordnance device (EOD) vehicle allow it to climb steps and enter buildings where a device may be hidden in a totally inaccessible location.

▼ THE TERRORIST CELL
The cell structure has evolved in terrorist organizations during the 20th century. By avoiding contact between large numbers it is harder for the security forces to insert their own secret agents into the organizations. By keeping the number of members in contact with each other down to two or three, it is difficult to break up an organization even if some of its members have been arrested.

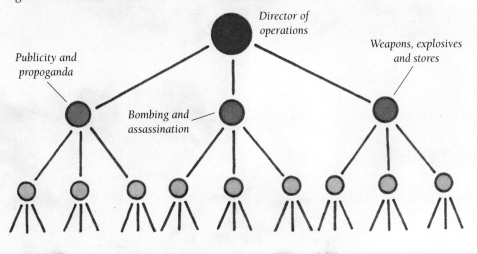

Publicity and propoganda

Director of operations

Weapons, explosives and stores

Bombing and assassination

Key Dates

- 1789 French Revolution
- 1808–1814 Peninsula War
- 1871 Paris Commune
- 1917 Russian Revolution
- 1923–1949 Chinese Revolution
- 1934– Arab-Israeli conflict
- 1939–1945 Resistance operations in Nazi-occupied Europe
- 1945–1962 War in South-east Asia
- 1949–1962 Algerian War
- 1945–1975 Indo-China War
- 1956–1960 Cuban Revolution
- 1978–1982 Islamic revolution

Tanks

▲ WORLD WAR I TANK
The Mark I tank could cross a 3m trench and had a range of 24km.

WHEN THE FIRST TANKS lumbered through the smoke and mud towards German trenches in World War I, the startled Germans thought that they had seen monsters from hell.

The first tank was the idea of Colonel Ernest Swinton in World War I. He took the tracked chassis of the petrol-driven Holt tractor and combined it with armour plate protection and field-gun or machine-gun armament. These vehicles were called "land ships", but when they were shipped from Britain to France hidden under canvas sheets they were described as "tanks". Curious soldiers were told that they were large water tanks. The name "tank" stuck. Large numbers of these

▶ TIGER TANK
The German Tiger tank weighed 57 tonnes and was armed with an 88mm gun.

armoured tracked vehicles went into action in France, at Cambrai in 1917 and at Amiens in 1918.

In the interwar years tank designs changed. New features included improved suspension and radio communications, and the main armament was mounted in a rotating turret. World War II saw the development of fighting tactics that used the protection, firepower and mobility of tanks to attack and advance quickly, outflanking or encircling a less mobile enemy. Tanks grew in weight and firepower throughout World War II, finishing with the Soviet IS-3 that weighed 45 tonnes and was armed with a 122mm gun.

In the postwar years, changes in tank design included improved engines, suspension, armour, fire control systems and armament. The American M-60 and the British-designed Centurion saw action in Asia and the Middle East. The Soviet T-54/55 was used throughout the 1950s and 1960s by many countries.

New armour developed in the 1980s includes systems that explode outwards if hit by an anti-tank missile, and plates of very hard materials that can be bolted on as extra protection. Fire control systems consist of onboard computers that automatically give the correct elevation, the angle of the gun's barrel, and

CLASSIC TANKS

Since 1916 tanks have played a major part in all significant land actions. In World War II some tanks achieved fame because of the quality of their design, for example the Russian T-34 or German Panzer. Others, such as the Sherman, were mass produced and it was their quantity that caused the greatest impact. However, tank designs since World War II have become increasingly like combat aircraft, with electronics and automation taking over many of the functions that used to be taken on by the crew.

◀ CHALLENGER II
Britain's Challenger tank of the 1980s and 1990s has four crew and weighs 62,000kg.

▶ AMERICAN 1940S SHERMAN
The Sherman weighs 30,160kg, has a 160km range and carries a crew of five.

▲ SWEDISH CV90
This tank weighs 26,000kg and has three crew and eight soldiers.

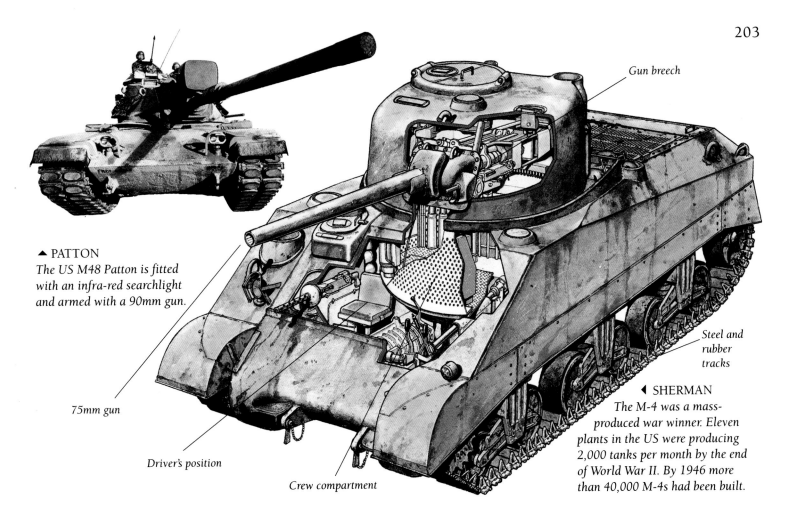

▲ PATTON
The US M48 Patton is fitted with an infra-red searchlight and armed with a 90mm gun.

75mm gun

Driver's position

Crew compartment

Gun breech

Steel and rubber tracks

◄ SHERMAN
The M-4 was a mass-produced war winner. Eleven plants in the US were producing 2,000 tanks per month by the end of World War II. By 1946 more than 40,000 M-4s had been built.

ammunition type to the gun once a target has been identified. The fire control is linked with sights that allow the crew to see the heat patterns of enemy vehicles by day and night. The new armament includes guns that fire shells or guided missiles. The new shells are made from very hard materials and are designed to punch through the armour of enemy tanks. One of the most recent major tank actions was fought as part of the Gulf War, between the Coalition Forces and the Iraqis in 1991 following the invasion of Kuwait by Iraq. The new, state-of-the-art technology of the British Challenger and American Abrams tanks gave them the advantage over the older Russian- and Chinese-built T-72 and Type 59 tanks.

▼ TANK TACTICS
Using the terrain, an experienced crew locates the enemy. They can fire at the enemy without exposing themselves. If the main armament can be depressed low enough, the tank can fire from this position. If it drives forwards, the gun can still be depressed to point at the enemy tank, but would be more exposed to attack.

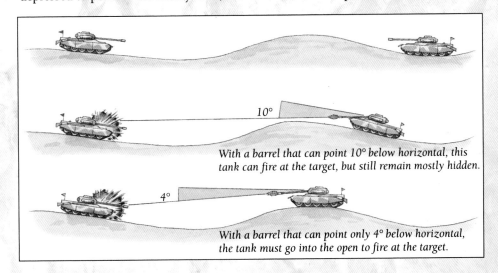

With a barrel that can point 10° below horizontal, this tank can fire at the target, but still remain mostly hidden.

With a barrel that can point only 4° below horizontal, the tank must go into the open to fire at the target.

Key Dates

- 1916 September: first tanks used in World War I

- 1943 July–September: Battle of Kursk – 2,700 German tanks against 3,300 Soviet tanks

- 1945 August: invasion of Manchuria – 5,500 Soviet tanks attack 1,000 Japanese tanks

- 1967 Middle East War – 1,000 Israeli tanks vs 2,050 Egyptian, Syrian and Jordanian tanks

- 1973 Middle East War – 2,000 Israeli tanks vs 4,800 Egyptian, Syrian, Jordanian and Iraqi tanks

- 1991 Gulf War – 2,200 Coalition tanks vs 4,000 Iraqi tanks

Anti-Tank Weapons

▲ EXPLOSION
A Swedish BILL anti-tank missile explodes above the turret of a target tank.

ANTI-TANK GUNNERS need to have the cool nerve of an old-style big-game hunter. As the enemy tank crashes towards them, perhaps firing its machine guns, the anti-tank crew must wait until their enemy is in range and then fire at its most vulnerable point.

As soon as tanks had appeared on the Western Front in World War I, all the combatants began to think of ways of stopping or destroying these machines by using anti-tank weapons.

The Imperial German Army developed a powerful bolt-action anti-tank rifle firing a .50in bullet. Most armies, however, relied on the crews of field guns to shoot it out with these early tanks. Anti-tank rifles were used by the British and Soviet armies in the opening years of World War II, but thicker armour and new weapons soon made them obsolete.

The true anti-tank gun, which was developed in the 1920s and 1930s, fired a very hard shell at high velocity. Early guns were between 37mm and 57mm in calibre. As World War II progressed the guns grew bigger, and the Germans used the 88mm anti-aircraft gun as a very effective anti-tank gun. The Russians used a huge 100mm gun.

The major change in anti-tank weapons came with the development of the shaped charge and short-range rockets. The shaped charge penetrated all conventional armour, while there was no recoil with a rocket projectile. The weapon that combined rocket and shaped charge was the American 2.36in rocket launcher M1. It was nicknamed the "Bazooka" after the musical instrument played by the US comedian, Bob Burns.

▲ INFANTRY ANTI-TANK
Anti-tank weapons may have a crew, for example the M40 106mm recoilless rifle or the TOW or Milan missiles, or they may be single-shot one-man weapons such as the M72 or the RPG-7.

PENETRATION

Most infantry anti-tank weapons have a shaped charge warhead. This consists of explosives shaped around the outside of a copper cone. When the warhead explodes the energy of the explosion is pushed inwards and forwards, creating a jet of molten metal and gas. A slug of metal at the front then melts its way through the armour of the tank.

◀ CARL GUSTAV
Canadian soldiers use the Swedish 84mm recoilless anti-tank weapon called the Carl Gustav. It can fire a wide range of ammunition.

▲ BILL
The launcher of the revolutionary Swedish BILL missile is fitted with a thermal imaging (TI) sight. It can detect the heat generated by the engine of a tank or fighting vehicle and use it as a target. This technology can also be used just as a night-vision device by troops on reconnaissance missions during darkness.

▶ FAIRCHILD A-10

The Fairchild A-10A has the official title Thunderbolt II, but is known as "the Warthog" by its crews. It has a powerful multi-barrel 30mm GAU-8 cannon in the nose and can also carry anti-tank missiles and bombs.

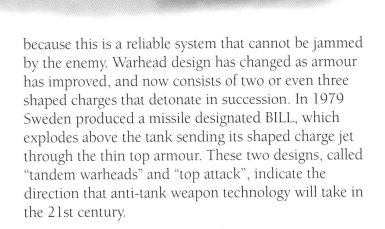

At the close of the war the Germans had looked at the concept of an anti-tank guided weapon (ATGW), which they designated the X-7. It had a range of 1,000m, weighed 10kg and would be guided to its target by signals passed along a light wire that was on a spool on the launching mount. The X-7 was reported to be capable of penetrating 200mm of armour.

Most modern ATGWs are wire guided because this is a reliable system that cannot be jammed by the enemy. Warhead design has changed as armour has improved, and now consists of two or even three shaped charges that detonate in succession. In 1979 Sweden produced a missile designated BILL, which explodes above the tank sending its shaped charge jet through the thin top armour. These two designs, called "tandem warheads" and "top attack", indicate the direction that anti-tank weapon technology will take in the 21st century.

◀ TANK DESTROYER

A British Alvis Striker firing a wire-guided Swingfire anti-tank missile. The Swingfire has a maximum range of 4,000m.

▼ LAW

The M72 LAW is a telescopic rocket launcher that weighs 3.45kg. It has an effective range of 220m. It was first used in action in the Vietnam War, and later by the British in the Falklands in 1982.

▼ DESTRUCTION

An Iraqi tank destroyed by American A-10s during the Gulf War. The tank has almost blown apart because the ammunition and fuel inside have exploded. Internal explosions are a constant worry for all armoured vehicle crews.

Key Dates

- 1918 German 12mm anti-tank rifles in use

- 1927 First dedicated anti-tank guns developed

- 1942 "Bazooka" rocket launcher developed in US

- 1943 German PaK 43/41 anti-tank gun enters service

- 1956 French introduce Nord SS10 wire-guided missile

- 1972 Euromissile Milan produced

- 1973 Egyptians use Sagger guided missiles in Sinai

- 1979 Swedish BILL developed

Transport

▲ AIRBORNE
A rocket-armed Blackhawk helicopter carries a two-man reconnaissance vehicle as an underslung load.

WHEN ARMIES GO to war they use similar forms of transport to ordinary people – car, train, ship and aircraft. For centuries they relied on human or animal power for transport. Oxen, horses and mules pulled wagons and guns; and troops carried heavy loads in packs.

Ships were vital for island nations such as Britain because they could transport troops overseas and, if necessary, evacuate them. In World War II amphibious operations became highly specialized, with landing craft designed to put troops and vehicles ashore on open beaches.

The steam locomotive made troop transportation faster and allowed large numbers of troops and equipment to be moved around. The American Civil War (1861-1865) demonstrated the importance

of a reliable railway system. Railway lines and particularly bridges became a key target for raids by troops and, later on, by aircraft.

At the beginning of World War I vehicles such as taxis and buses were used to move troops quickly. Later, trucks became more readily available. Huge numbers of trucks were used in World War II, increasing the need for fuel supplies. After D-Day in June 1944 a fuel pipeline was laid from Britain to northern France across the Channel. It was codenamed PLUTO, which stands for Pipe Line Under The Ocean.

Among the wheeled vehicles produced in World War II the ¼-tonne Jeep remains the

◀ MOTORBIKE
A German Afrika Korps BMW R75 motorcycle combination, armed with an MG34 machine gun, roars through the Libyan desert in 1942.

AMPHIBIOUS OPERATIONS

World War II saw the development of specialized landing craft to carry vehicles, troops, and stores for amphibious operations. Before 1942 soldiers went ashore from small boats, ships or modified freighters. In the Pacific, the US Marine Corps used tracked amphibious APCs to carry marines ashore.

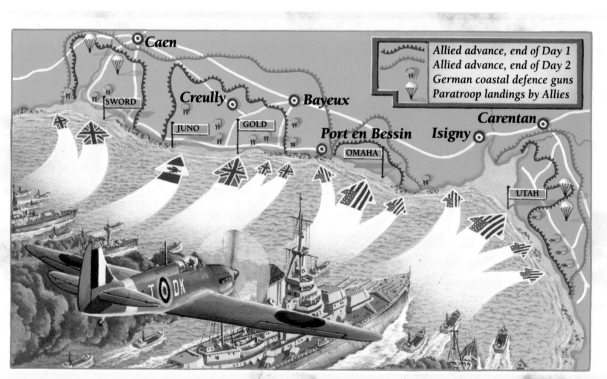

Allied advance, end of Day 1
Allied advance, end of Day 2
German coastal defence guns
Paratroop landings by Allies

Caen
SWORD
Creully
JUNO
GOLD
Bayeux
Port en Bessin
OMAHA
Carentan
Isigny
UTAH

◀ *EXTRA ARMOUR*
An Israeli M113 APC, in desert camouflage, is fitted with extra armour and carries a .50in Browning machine gun. APCs have enough internal space to make them ideal weapons carriers for missiles, AA guns or spare ammunition. They are also used as ambulances and for radio communications.

▼ *HUMVEE FIREPOWER*
A TOW anti-tank missile streaks away from its launcher, which is mounted on an HMMWV, a wheeled utility vehicle known to US soldiers as a "HumVee". The rugged, stable and reliable HumVee is popular with US service personnel because it is easy to drive.

most enduring symbol. The US produced 639,245 Jeeps before the war ended, and the Jeep continued to serve in many armies into the 1960s. In World War II the US-designed DUKW, a six-wheeled amphibious truck, was used during amphibious operations to ferry stores from ships to the shore. Despite their age, DUKWs were still being used by the British Royal Marines in the late 1990s.

Most armies now use 4-tonne trucks and light $^3/_4$-tonne vehicles. However, some specialized Alpine regiments still use mules to carry heavy equipment such as mortars, pack howitzers and ammunition up narrow mountain tracks.

◀ D-DAY LANDINGS
Landings at beaches in Normandy, codenamed Utah, Omaha, Gold, Juno and Sword, began at 06.30 on 6 June 1944. By midnight 57,000 US and 75,000 British and Canadian troops and their equipment were ashore.

▲ LANDING CRAFT
US soldiers approach Omaha Beach in Normandy in June 1944. They are in a Higgins boat, a landing craft designed to carry soldiers.

◀ DUCK
The DUKW, a wartime amphibious truck, was nicknamed the "DUCK". It is still in service with the Royal Marines in Britain.

Key Dates

- 1885 Four-wheel motor carriage developed

- 1914 French use 600 taxis to transport troops at the Marne

- 1925 French demonstrate the half-track vehicle

- 1927 British Army tests mechanized warfare tactics

- 1940 Germans conduct trials for an amphibious invasion of Great Britain

- 1943 US DUKW used in combat

- 1944 D-Day, the largest amphibious operation in history, takes place in northern France

Reconnaissance

IMAGINE PLAYING CHESS or another tactical board game, but you only see the board occasionally or are told about its layout by someone else. You would be "in the dark". A chess player wants to see how the game is developing, perhaps look at the opponent's expression and make moves based on this information.

In war, reconnaissance is rather like watching the board and the player. It is the tactical method of learning about enemy positions, movements or plans and finding out about the terrain or weather in which combat may take place.

For many centuries the job of reconnaissance was done by small patrols of light cavalry riding ahead of the main body of troops. The only special equipment available was a telescope or a pair of binoculars. If they

▲ SAS JEEP
A US-made Jeep fitted with Vickers K machine guns in service with the SAS in North Africa.

saw the enemy they would then ride as fast as possible to pass the information back.

The pedal bicycle was popular at the turn of the 19th century because cyclist troops were fast, silent and very mobile. However, reconnaisance changed dramatically with the development of the internal combustion engine and of small reliable radios.

Armoured cars and motorcycles had been developed in World War I. Between 1939 and 1943 German soldiers used them most effectively and set the style for armoured reconnaissance. Pushing ahead, they would find undefended bridges, gaps in minefields and weak

▼ FRENCH VBL
This armoured amphibious vehicle is fitted with both machine gun and Milan missile.

MODERN VISION
Reconnaissance by land, sea and air uses a huge range of sensors to gather information about the enemy and its plans and forces. Once this information has been collected, the most important step is to put it all together and assess its value. This assessment must then be passed as quickly as possible to the commanders and units so that they can make best use of it.

▶ PHOTOGRAPHY
Photographs are useful because they can be processed quickly and are easy to handle. Extra information can be overprinted on them, combining the accuracy of a photo with the information found on a map.

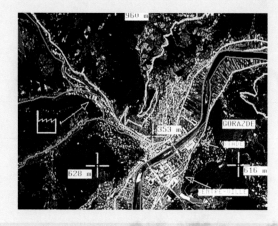

▲ DRONE LAUNCH
A remotely piloted vehicle (RPV) is also known as a drone. It is a small aircraft fitted with cameras and sensors. Drones are designed to be flown by remote control over enemy territory.

◄ AERIAL RECONNAISSANCE
Aerial reconnaissance began as long ago as the Franco-Prussian War when a photograph was taken from a hot air balloon. Even today manned flights are still used to gather photographic intelligence.

▼ SATELLITES
Modern cameras aboard satellites can produce remarkably clear images. They have made every part of the world accessible.

points in defended positions. This valuable information would be quickly radioed back and the main forces would follow up.

Reconnaissance could also be undertaken by foot patrols working away from their vehicles, and even by scuba divers and midget submarines. In the months before D-Day in 1944 the beaches of northern France were visited by small groups of divers. They swam ashore to check the gradient of each beach and its defences, and to discover whether it was sand, shingle or mud, as this was important for the landing troops.

In the war in the Falklands in 1982, men of the Special Boat Service (SBS) and the Special Air Service (SAS) landed on the islands to observe Argentinian positions. They helped the planners to build up a picture of the strength and quality of the garrison. In the 1990-1991 Gulf War, the British SAS entered Iraq to report on the terrain. It was what they hoped for, a gravel desert that was better for the tanks and armoured vehicles.

Reconnaissance intelligence is also gathered from aerial photographs and radar images taken by special reconnaissance aircraft. The most recent technique for gathering reconnaissance intelligence is by remotely piloted vehicles (RPVs). They are usually small aircraft fitted with cameras that transmit TV images of the terrain to the base from which the RPV is being operated. They give information about enemy movements and positions.

▼ DRONE FLIGHT
Modern drones send back "real-time" TV and sensor information as they fly a search pattern over a designated area. If the operator "sees" something of interest, the drone can fly lower or use more powerful sensors.

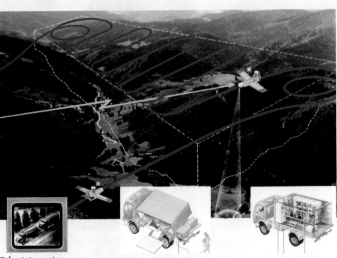

Drone flies a set route over the target area in order to ensure the best possible coverage

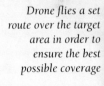

Communications mast

Television picture display

Launch vehicle

Control centre

Key Dates

- 1858 First aerial photography
- 1866 Typewriter invented
- 1888 First portable roll-film camera
- 1923 Cathode ray tube, used in televisions, invented
- 1943 Infra-red night-vision viewer used
- 1957 First space satellite launched
- 1960 U-2 reconnaissance aircraft flown by Gary Powers shot down over the former Soviet Union
- 1982 SAS and SBS forces used for reconnaissance in the Falklands

Communications

▲ CARRIER PIGEON
A homing pigeon carries simple messages in a capsule attached to its leg.

I N A FAST-MOVING GAME such as a football match, information can mean the difference between victory or defeat, communicating tactics and positions. In wartime, this sort of communication is even more critical – the lives of thousands of soldiers are at risk. Ships, aircraft and many other military units report their positions, which allows a commander to build up a picture of the battle.

For centuries messages were sent either verbally or as a written despatch and carried by foot or horseback. Beacons positioned on high hills were lit if there was a threat of enemy invasion or attack. Signal flags used at sea were a key to the British victory at Trafalgar on 21 October 1805. In 19th-century India and South Africa, where the air was clear and the sunshine constant, devices called heliographs used reflective mirrors to flash Morse code signals.

The Morse code could also be used with signal lamps; this method of communication was particularly effective at sea. The telegraph, which allowed Morse messages to be sent over long distances, was first used in the American Civil War (1861–1865).

▲ FIELD RADIO
A modern field radio is light and reliable. It may even have a built-in security system that makes it impossible to decode a message without the correct equipment.

CODES AND SIGNALS

Signalling systems were initially visual ones, using flags, light or even smoke. They allowed people to communicate beyond the range of the human voice. Telegraph, telephone and radio increased the range. However, the danger of interception by the enemy made it essential that signals should be in code.

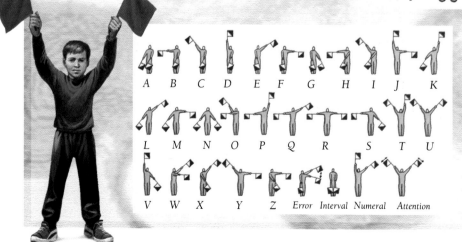

◀ SEMAPHORE
The British Army and the Royal Navy used this signalling system before radio was developed. The advantage of semaphore is that flags don't operate from an electronic system that can break down.

▲ MORSE CODE
Invented by Samuel Morse in 1850, this "dot and dash" code was the key to the telegraph system. It was first used operationally during the Crimean war.

◀ WARTIME RADIO
French troops with American uniforms and equipment operate a radio during fighting in Germany in 1945.

▶ CONCEALED
Men of the US Army's 82nd Airborne Division during the invasion of Grenada in 1983. The soldier carries the radio in a medium pack to conceal it.

The telephone was in widespread use by 1880 and was used in the Boer War (1899–1902) and the Russo-Japanese War (1904–1905). In World War I, field telephones were developed and telephone cables were laid quickly to connect headquarters with the artillery batteries.

The first radios were cumbersome and required a wagon and team of horses to transport them. In 1915, an observer used a radio in a hot air balloon over the Dardanelles in Turkey. During the interwar years radios became small enough to fit in a backpack.

Most military radios operate in the very high frequency (VHF) range between 30 and 200megahertz (MHz) and in the high frequency (HF) range between 1 and 30MHz. Anyone with a radio receiver tuned to the right frequency could listen to a radio conversation, and so codes were introduced. However, even if a message

was encoded the station could be jammed by a powerful signal. One technique for ensuring security and avoiding jamming was "burst transmission". A message would be prepared and then sent in a few seconds to another station that would display it on a screen. In the 1980s radios were designed that could change frequencies at random intervals. If the receiving station was correctly tuned it would follow the "hops" and so a conversation could take place without interruption.

The latest development in radio communications are satellites. They receive radio signals and re-broadcast them, allowing messages from remote locations to be transmitted reliably over huge distances.

▲ SUNLIGHT
A British soldier uses a signalling mirror to contact a circling helicopter. It is a silent but effective communications tool.

▶ THE ENIGMA CODE
During World War II the Germans used a variety of codes. Most of them used a machine to jumble up the letters of the message. The British, assisted by the French, Poles and Americans, were able to break the German codes. This literally saved Britain from starvation because some of these codes were for the U-boats, which were sinking ships carrying food and fuel to Britain. The code machines were like very complex typewriters.

Key Dates

- 1850 Morse Code invented
- 1858 Heliograph invented
- 1876 Telephone invented
- 1892 First detected radio signal
- 1901 Transatlantic radio link established
- 1921 Teleprinter developed
- 1925 Short-wave, crystal-controlled radio invented
- 1926 Enigma coding machine developed
- 1949 Transistor invented
- 1960 Microchip first used

Protecting the Soldier

▲ THE HELMET
The helmet, such as this M1 steel helmet, is the oldest and most effective protection for a soldier.

ARMOUR HAD PROTECTED soldiers when firearms were awkward and heavy and the sword was still used in warfare. However, armour was no longer worn once firearms improved and freedom of movement had become more important.

Like the "hard hats" worn by construction workers on building sites, the steel helmets introduced in World War I were intended to protect soldiers from objects falling on their heads. Such objects are normally shrapnel, the tiny fragments that fall from the sky when a shell explodes. During World War I armoured protection was introduced for snipers – soldiers who use powerful rifles with telescopic sights to shoot at an unwary enemy or important targets such as officers. This protection was very unwieldy and heavy, and resembled the breastplates of medieval soldiers.

Following the use of poison gas by the Germans on the Western Front in World War I, gas masks or respirators were produced. The first masks were simply cotton pads worn with goggles, but by the end of the war respirators were not only more effective but also more comfortable to wear. Modern masks use charcoal filters. Charcoal is a very useful filter against impurities, hence its use in domestic water filters. It is also used in soldiers' protective jackets and trousers.

▲ REACTIVE ARMOUR
Explosive reactive armour (ERA) comes in bolt-on slabs. It explodes outwards when hit, counteracting the penetration of charges.

PROTECT AND SURVIVE

As weapons became more effective and more lethal, soldiers looked for ways of improving their protection. Soldiers who were fighting a defensive battle dug themselves in, built log or sandbag defences or, even better, reinforced concrete ones. The difficulties came when they were in the open. Thick steel plates gave protection, but their weight meant that soldiers could move only short distances at low speed.

In the 1980s and 1990s new materials have allowed soldiers to move freely with protection from shell fragments and bullets. Fireproof materials, used in tank and aircraft crew overalls, protect the wearer against flash burns from exploding fuel tanks. In bad weather troops now have the comfort of breathable waterproofs.

British helmet, World War I

British paratrooper's helmet, 1944

British helmet no. 4, 1944

US M1 steel helmet, World War II

Current British no. 6 helmet

Current US PASGT Kevlar helmet

◀ EVACUATION OF CASUALTIES
US soldiers carry a casualty on a litter to a Blackhawk helicopter. Helicopters were first used for flying wounded from the battlefield during the Korean War and have become a vital link in the casualty evacuation chain. Nicknamed "Dust Off" in the Vietnam War, helicopters could literally take an injured man from deep in the jungle and fly him to a modern hospital. He could be admitted to a fully equipped operating theatre in less than an hour. Many troops who would have died in earlier times because of a lack of prompt and thorough medical support now survive terrible battlefield injuries.

In World War II protective jackets with overlapping steel plates were produced to protect American bomber crews from the shrapnel from German anti-aircraft (flak) guns. The jackets were called "flak jackets".

Today's body armour is made from materials such as Kevlar, which is light and strong. Its woven form is used for jackets and even boots; it can also be bonded into a plastic for used in helmets. These new materials can protect a soldier, even at close range, from shots from hand guns and even rifles.

In the confined spaces of aircraft, warships and armoured vehicles, fire has always been a major threat. In World War II, leather jackets and gloves, as well as goggles, provided some protection. The crews on warships wore steel helmets and anti-flash hoods made from an asbestos-based fabric.

The development of artificial fire-resistant fabrics such as Nomex has allowed gloves, flying overalls, jackets and trousers to be made from a material with a high level of protection. Tanks and aircraft now have fire detection systems that operate instantly, swamping potential fires with a gas that cuts off the oxygen.

▶ ANGLE OF ARMOUR
If the armour on an armoured fighting vehicle is sloped, this increases the distance through which a projectile has to pass before it breaks through to the interior. If a projectile strikes the armour at an oblique angle it may even ricochet and fall away harmlessly.

Armour that is 8mm thick when vertical, is 11mm thick when tilted

8

8

11

Key Dates

- 1856 Bessemer steel produced

- 1865 First antiseptics used

- 1882 Armoured steel developed

- 1914–1918 World War I: steel helmets introduced to protect soldiers from shrapnel

- 1920s Gas masks and respirators introduced after the use of poison gas in World War I

- 1939–1945 World War II: penicillin, plastic surgery and blood transfusions introduced

- 1970s Explosive reactive armour, ceramic armour, Kevlar and Nomex developed

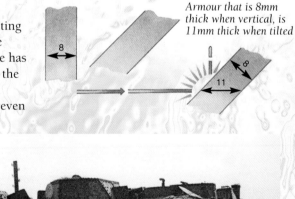

▲ ARMOURED TRAIN
A Soviet armoured train captured by the Germans in World War II. Armour protected the crew, but the train was vulnerable if the tracks were destroyed or damaged.

Armoured Vehicles

▲ ARMOURED CAR
The first armoured car, the Charron Girardot et Voigt, was built in France in 1904.

As far back as 1482 the idea of an armoured fighting vehicle (AFV) appeared in sketches drawn by Leonardo da Vinci. It was propelled by muscle power, with the crew operating geared hand cranks and firing muskets through slits. However, it was the British War Office that saw the first true AFV in 1902 when the Simms "War Car" was demonstrated. It used a petrol engine to drive a wheeled vehicle at a maximum speed of 18kph. It was protected by 6mm of armour and armed with two machine guns and a one-pounder gun.

The Belgians and British Royal Navy used armoured cars with machine guns in 1914. However, the mud of the Western Front was unsuitable for wheeled vehicles. Armoured cars were used in the Middle East by the British when fighting against the Turks.

The interwar period saw the development of six- and even eight-wheeled armoured cars and the half-track. This vehicle had tracks at the rear of its chassis and wheels at the front. It had the cross-country performance of a tank but could be driven like a truck. The German Sdkfz 251 and American M3 half-track were widely used in World War II.

◀ ARMOURED PERSONNEL CARRIER (APC)
This M113 APC is fitted with TOW anti-tank missile launchers. APCs are used in both wartime conflicts and civil disturbances.

PROTECTION AND MOBILITY

Armour protection is used for combat vehicles and also to protect VIP (Very Important Person) cars and vehicles used by the media in hostile locations. Protection may be quite basic, consisting of plates and panels, or it may be a system that is both bulletproof and mineproof.

◀ ARMOURED INFERNO
A Swedish APC burns after being hit by an anti-tank weapon in a demonstration on an army range. APCs contain fuel, hydraulic fluid under pressure and ammunition, so internal fire can be catastrophic. This vehicle had its rear doors closed, but the explosion has blasted one open. Fire suppression systems need to operate quickly for soldiers to survive a fire. Recently, if not under fire, troops have sat on the roof of their moving APC in case it hits an anti-tank mine, catches fire and explodes.

▲ BRITISH SAXON APC
The 4 x 4 Saxon is effectively an armoured truck. It weighs 9,940kg, can carry 10 soldiers and has a top speed on roads of 96kph. It has been used in Northern Ireland and Bosnia to transport troops under armour.

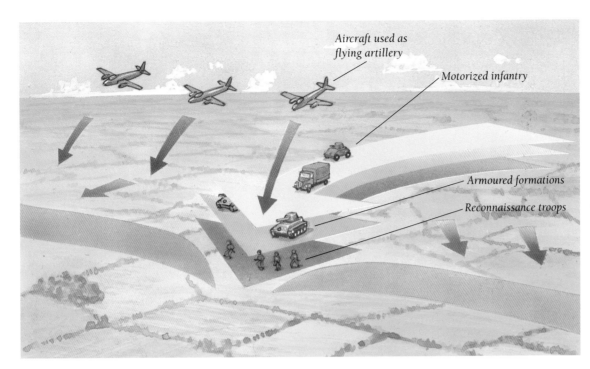

Aircraft used as flying artillery

Motorized infantry

Armoured formations

Reconnaissance troops

◀ ARMOURED ATTACK
The armoured tactics pioneered by the Germans in 1939–1942 used aircraft as flying artillery. At the front were reconnaissance troops, followed by armoured formations and backed by motorized infantry in trucks. The tanks were massed to punch through enemy defences. The infantry secured the flanks as the armoured troops plunged deeper into enemy territory.

After the war the M3 was used by the Israeli Army up to 1967. The half-track also allowed infantry to keep pace with fast-moving tanks. Artillery mounted on tracked chassis could bombard enemy positions before the infantry and tanks attacked.

Before D-Day on 6 June 1944, the British developed several special tanks, nicknamed "Funnies". They included tanks that could clear paths through minefields, lay special matting roads across shingle beaches or lay bridges over ditches. Another of these special tanks was the Armoured Vehicle Royal Engineers (AVRE) that could fire an 18kg demolition bomb 210 metres against German fortifications. The armoured engineer vehicle that can lay bridges or bulldoze rubble is now a standard vehicle in most major armies.

Since the end of World War II AFVs have been developed as armoured ambulances, recovery vehicles, mobile workshops, headquarters, nuclear biological and chemical (NBC) detection vehicles and troop carriers. They are wheeled like the French VAB or fully tracked like the American M113. The wheeled APCs are widely used in United Nation peace-keeping operations because they give protection against rifle and machine gun fire as well as shell fragments.

▲ FRENCH PANHARD ERC
Armed with a 90mm gun, the French ERC Sagaie armoured car has a top speed of 95kph on roads. Its six wheels give it a better cross-country performance than a normal four-wheeled vehicle. The ERC saw action during the Gulf War of 1990–1991 against Iraq.

Key Dates

- 1904 First armoured car

- 1914 Armoured car shoots down German Taube aircraft

- 1919–1922 Armoured cars used in Ireland against the IRA

- 1920 Rolls Royce armoured car introduced; it serves until 1941

- 1931 First cast turrets introduced by France for the D1

- 1932 Japanese field the first diesel-powered armoured vehicle

- 1936 Torsion bar suspension introduced by the Germans

- 1944 Tetrach light tanks land by glider in Normandy, France

Camouflage

EXAMPLES OF CAMOUFLAGE exist all around us in nature. Birds, fish and other animals have self-protection in the form of colours that help them blend into the background of vegetation, sky, water or sand.

The earliest military camouflage consisted of the dark-green tunics and black buttons adopted by the British rifle regiments during the Peninsula War of 1808–1814. The British had learned camouflage and field craft from the experience of fighting the American colonists and Native Americans in North America in the late 18th century. The red coats of the British stood out clearly in battle, making them easy targets.

In 19th-century India, British troops dyed their white tropical uniforms with tea to produce a shade of brown that Indians called *khak*, or dust coloured. These "khaki" uniforms helped the troops to blend into the dry terrain as they fought against tribes on the North-west Frontier.

In World War I camouflage, a word taken from the French *camouflet* meaning "smoke puff", became a serious technique. The French Army used conscripted artists to devise colour schemes to conceal artillery and vehicles. Some were in fantastic shapes and colours, and also included nets with strips of coloured cloth that were draped over buildings, guns and vehicles.

▲ GREEN AND BROWN
A British soldier in the black, green, brown and buff camouflage that was introduced in the early 1970s. It is designed to mimic the shadows and highlights of natural vegetation. It is effective in tropical and temperate terrain, and has been adopted by the Dutch and Indonesian armies.

▲ DESERT
A soldier in the desert with his helmet garnished with nylon "scrim" to break up its outline. His equipment and clothing have softened with use and do not present hard unnatural lines and shapes.

MEN AND MACHINES

Camouflage conceals soldiers, vehicles and buildings. It may consist of paint patterns, netting, painted screens, planted vegetation or even fake buildings and vehicles. Good camouflage fools the naked eye, but special photographic film and night-vision equipment will penetrate ordinary camouflage. Special nets and paints have in turn been developed to counter this technology.

▶ FACE PAINT
A soldier with some of the elaborate patterns that can be painted to break up the shape and colour of the human face. Grass has been added to his helmet.

▲ HELMET COVERS
US military helmets with cotton drill desert camouflage covers. This spotted pattern is known to US service personnel as "chocolate chip cookie" camouflage. The elastic band around the helmet is used to secure vegetation for camouflage.

US soldiers armed with M16 rifles and carrying rucksacks slog through the dust. They are wearing camouflaged uniforms. Their Kevlar helmets have cloth covers made from the same material.

▲ SNOW
In the course of an exercise in the 1980s in northern Canada, Canadian Army Special Forces slog through the snow in white camouflaged uniforms and backpack covers. They have fixed white tape to their weapons to break up the outline.

The development of aircraft and aerial photography during the two World Wars made camouflage essential. Elaborate deception schemes included building fake vehicles and constructing huts with lighting that operated by itself at night.

By the end of the 20th century new methods of detection took camouflage out of the simple visual detection range. These methods included night-vision equipment and thermal imaging, enabling the viewer to see the heat generated by humans or equipment. Modern camouflage can conceal the shape, colour, heat and radar picture of aircraft, ships and tanks.

◀ FOOLING THE EYE
A USAF Rockwell B-1A bomber in "viscam", the visual camouflage designed to make the bomber blend into the background over which it is flying. Although electronic aids such as radar and thermal imaging can be very accurate, pilots and soldiers also rely on their eyes to double check.

▼ JETS OVER THE DESERT
Two F-15 Eagles are in flight with a chase plane over the desert. The Eagles are painted in pale "air superiority" camouflage that is designed to blend into the sky.

Key Dates

- 1775–1783 American War of Independence: use of field craft by colonists

- 1808–1814 Peninsular War: the British riflemen wear dark-green camouflaged tunics

- 1857–1858 Indian Mutiny: white uniforms dyed "khaki"

- 1914–1918 World War I: land, sea and air camouflage developed

- 1939–1945 World War II: aerial photography and infra-red technology developed

- 1970s Black, green, brown and buff camouflage introduced

Battleships

▲ NELSON
Nelson was one of the greatest naval commanders. One of the secrets of his victories was an efficient flag signalling system.

A CAPITAL SHIP IS A major naval warship. Today's capital ship is probably a submerged submarine with nuclear missiles aboard, or an aircraft carrier. Yet for centuries the capital ship was a battleship such as HMS *Victory,* which was powered by sail and armed with cannons along its hull.

Sea war in the 18th and 19th centuries was a test of sailing skills, stamina and courage. The gunners learned to load and "run out" the cannons and fire them as quickly as possible to ensure that there was a steady barrage against enemy warships. The wooden-hulled ships were very strong, and when soaked with salty seawater they did not burn easily.

The change came in the mid-19th century with the development of steam propulsion, armour plating and breech-loading guns. In 1859 the French launched the first steam-powered iron-clad battleship, *La Gloire*. It was armed with 36 163mm guns. Within two years the British had launched the *Warrior,* an iron-clad ship with superior protection and armaments.

During the American Civil War the indecisive battle between the iron-clad battleships *Merrimack* and *Monitor* in 1862 gave some clue about the outcome of future naval battles.

The battle of Tsu Shima (Toshima) on 27and 28 May 1905 pitted Russian battleships against Japanese ones. The battle ended with a decisive victory for the Japanese naval forces. The Russian defeat at Tsu Shima led ultimately to defeat for the Russian forces in the Russo-Japanese War.

◀ ABOARD THE *MONITOR*
The battle of Hampton Roads, Virginia, on 8-9 March 1862, saw the Confederate armoured steam frigate *Merrimack* fight an inconclusive battle with the USS *Monitor*. The *Monitor* had 11in guns in a revolving turret.

FROM WOOD TO IRON
Steam power and armour plate made the new iron-clad warships "wolves among a flock of sheep" when they first appeared in a world dominated by wooden sailing ships. An "arms race" developed with new and more sophisticated iron-clad ships being built throughout Europe in the 19th century.

Muzzle —

▶ US CANNON
This 19th-century muzzle-loading ship's cannon has simple gearing on its wooden carriage, which allows the muzzle to be lowered or raised.

— *Muzzle*

◀ A US 8IN GUN
This gun could be used aboard capital ships or for coastal defence. It is breech loading and is mounted on a turntable trackway to allow it to rotate fully through 360 degrees.

Breech loading

▼ BATTLE OF TRAFALGAR
The Battle of Trafalgar was fought on 21 October 1805 off the Spanish coast. It involved 27 British and 33 French and Spanish ships. The battle was a victory for the British under Nelson.

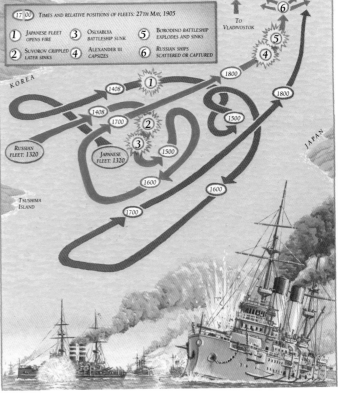

▲ BATTLE OF TSU SHIMA
This battle between the Imperial Russian Baltic fleet and the Imperial Japanese fleet took place off Korea between 27 and 28 May 1905.

At the beginning of the 20th century the launch of HMS *Dreadnought* in 1906 marked a further change in the design of capital ships. It was armed with 10 12in guns and 27 12-pounder guns. By this time battleships had a speed of 18 knots and weighed 15,000 tonnes.

▲ SEA BATTLE
In a sea battle in 1862, during the American Civil War, the *Merrimack (right)* fights it out with the USS *Monitor*. This battle saw the first operational use of armoured steam-powered craft in war.

Key Dates

- 1805 October 21: Battle of Trafalgar

- 1859: French launch the first steam-powered, iron-clad battleship, La Gloire

- 1862 March 8–9: Battle of Hampton Roads

- 1864 August 5: Battle of Mobile Bay

- 1866 July 20: Battle of Lissa

- 1898 May 1: Battle of Manila Bay

- 1905 May 27–28: Battle of Tsu Shima

- 1906: Launch of HMS Dreadnought

20th-Century Battleships

▲ NIGHT SALVO
A US battleship fires a battery salvo at night.

THE BATTLE OF JUTLAND in 1916 during World War I was fought between the capital ships of the Royal Navy and the Imperial German Navy. The outcome was indecisive.

In the interwar years several countries attempted to reduce the weight of capital ships and the size of their fleets. However, both the Japanese and the Germans were building warships in secret, and they entered World War II with powerful modern ships. The Germans saw their ships as a powerful weapon to attack Allied merchant shipping. As a result, German warships, such as the 50,153-tonne battleship *Bismarck*, became a priority target for the Royal Navy. The *Bismarck* was sunk on 27 May 1941 after being pounded by the guns of the battleships HMS *King George V* and HMS *Rodney*.

The development of aircraft carriers and submarines made capital ships very vulnerable. The Japanese battleships *Yamato* and *Mushashi*, the largest and most heavily protected ships of their class in the world, displaced 64,170 tons each. They were armed with nine 18in guns and twelve 6in guns. They had crews of 2,500 men and carried six spotter aircraft. The *Yamato* and the *Mushashi* were sunk by torpedo and dive-bomber aircraft from US carriers on 7 April 1945 and 24 October 1945 respectively. Earlier, HMS *Prince of Wales*, which had fought against the *Bismarck*, was sunk by Japanese aircraft on 10 December 1941.

Battleships fired huge shells, which were very effective in the bombardment of coastal defences before an amphibious landing. During World War II battleships were used on D-Day and to support the US Marine Corps landings throughout the Pacific.

Today the title of capital ships has passed to aircraft carriers and nuclear submarines armed with ballistic

▶ CLOSE IN SUPPORT
This US Navy 20mm Phalanx system is radar controlled. The gun fires at 1,000–3,000rpm. Its very hard depleted-uranium rounds are designed to destroy surface-skimming anti-ship missiles such as the Exocet. The Phalanx has a maximum range of 6,000m. It can rotate through 100 degrees in one second, and elevate up to 68 degrees in one second. The gun has a 989-round ammunition drum that can be reloaded in 10–30 minutes.

CAPITAL SHIPS

Capital ships, the big warships around which naval fleets are formed, were originally big-gun battleships. Today's surface fleets and task forces are based around the aircraft carrier. Carriers and submarines are nuclear powered, which gives them the ability to stay at sea almost indefinitely and to travel huge distances.

▶ PRESTIGE
Capital ships were the centrepiece of the great navies of the 20th century. In peacetime these great ships would travel the world "showing the flag", visiting the ports of other nations whom their government wished to impress. In wartime capital ships were the flagships for the admirals in command of battle fleets.

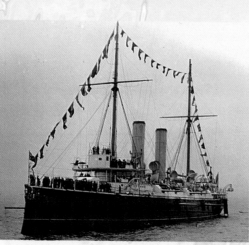

▲ DRESSED OVERALL ▼
These armoured, steam-powered warships are "dressed overall" with signal flags displayed as decoration. Modern warships have a more streamlined appearance.

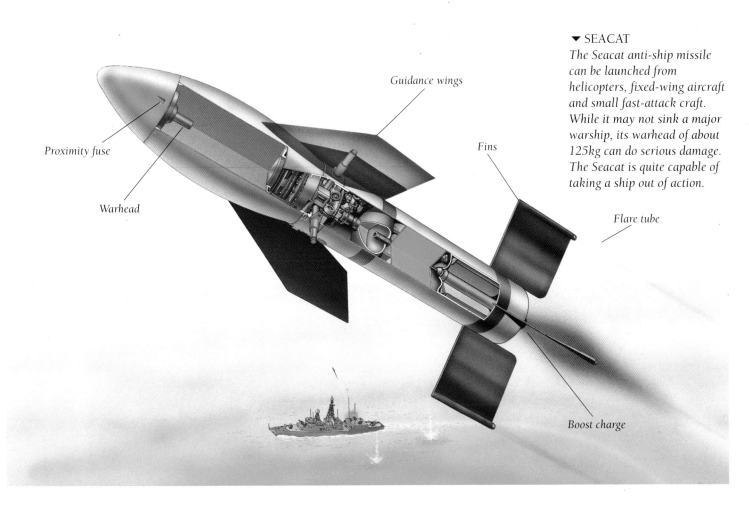

The Seacat anti-ship missile can be launched from helicopters, fixed-wing aircraft and small fast-attack craft. While it may not sink a major warship, its warhead of about 125kg can do serious damage. The Seacat is quite capable of taking a ship out of action.

Proximity fuse

Warhead

Guidance wings

Fins

Flare tube

Boost charge

missiles (SSBNs). The United States Navy has the largest number of SSBNs in the world.

In March 1992 the US Navy decommissioned the last operational battleship in the world, the USS *Missouri*. The 45,000 ton *Missouri* was launched in 1944 and served in the Pacific during World War II and later in the Korean War. The *Missouri* was armed with nine 16in guns. These were last used in action as recently as 1991 when the battleship bombarded Iraqi positions in Kuwait during the Gulf War.

▼ BROADSIDE
A Missouri-class battleship lets rip a broadside with her 16in guns. The guns have a maximum range of 41,600m and fire an 850kg shell. The US Navy was the last force to use battleships in action.

Key Dates

- 1914–1918 World War I
- 1914 November 1: Battle of the Coronel
- 1914 December 8: Battle of the Falklands
- 1916 May 31: Battle of Jutland
- 1939 December 13: Battle of the River Plate
- 1941 May 27: Sinking of the *Bismarck*
- 1944 June 6: D-Day
- 1945 April 7: Sinking of the battleship *Yamato*

Smaller Fighting Ships

THERE WAS SHOCK and surprise among senior naval officers in both Europe and North America when the first torpedo boat was launched in 1878. It was the 19 knot British-built *Lightning,* with a torpedo tube in its bow. This compact torpedo boat had the speed and fire power to race after larger ships and to sink or damage them.

Japanese torpedo boats proved very effective against the Russians in the Russo-Japanese war during night-time action at Wei-Hai-Wei in 1895 and again at Port Arthur on 8 February 1904.

In World War I the Royal Navy deployed coastal motor boats (CMBs) and motor launches (MLs) in the narrows of the English Channel.

During World War II the German motor torpedo boats were designated *S-Boot,* or *Schnellboot* meaning "fast boat". They were known by their crews as *Eilboot (E-Boot)* meaning "boat in a hurry". Several classes of *S-Boot* were built. Most were powered by three-shaft Daimler–Benz or MAN diesel engines and had a maximum speed of 39–42 knots with a range of 350km.

World War II armament was varied, but for most of the war it consisted of two 2cm anti-aircraft (AA) guns and two 21in torpedo tubes. From 1944, defensive armament was upgraded and became one 4cm and three 2cm AA guns, or one 3.7cm and five 2cm AA guns. Larger types of ship could also carry six or eight mines in place of reloading torpedoes.

During World War II John F. Kennedy, the future President of the United States, commanded a US Navy patrol torpedo

▲ PATROL
A warship fires one of its Harpoon missiles

▶ PATROL
US warships patrol, their masts cluttered with radar and radio antennae.

INDIVIDUAL SHIPS

The anti-ship missile and torpedo have given smaller craft a powerful punch, making them a dangerous enemy for larger, slow-moving naval vessels. Modern materials and improved engine design give these craft a performance similar to racing speedboats. They are able to dart towards larger, slower ships, launch their missiles and retreat very quickly.

▼ SAETTIA
An Italian Saettia-class small-missile craft has a crew of 33, a maximum speed of 40 knots and weighs 400 tons fully loaded.

▼ PATRA
A French Patra-class craft has a crew of 18, a maximum speed of 26 knots and weighs 147.5 tons fully loaded.

▼ SPICA
A Swedish Spica II-class torpedo attack craft has a crew of 27, a maximum speed of 40.5 knots and weighs 230 tons fully loaded.

◀ PATROL BOAT
Small nations with coastlines to protect make extensive use of patrol craft such as this one. These boats are used to police maritime borders and for anti-piracy and anti-smuggling operations.

(PT) boat in the Pacific. The boat was powered by three petrol engines which gave it a maximum speed of 40 knots.

The surface-to-surface missile was developed after World War II and gave small craft new hitting power. The postwar Soviet Osa ships were capable of speeds up to 38 knots and were armed with four SS-N-2A "Styx" missiles. Nearly 300 Osas were built and were used to equip 20 navies throughout the world. Osas saw action in the Middle East in the 1973 Yom Kippur War between Israel and her Arab neighbours, and also in the Gulf War in 1990–1991.

Patrol boats are ideal for landing small groups of special forces. These sorts of attacks are usually undercover, amphibious attacks. Patrol boats are also widely used in peacetime for search and rescue missions, fishery patrols and anti-piracy operations.

◀ KNOX
A US Knox-class frigate has a crew of 300, a maximum speed of 27 knots and weighs 4,260 tons fully loaded. It is armed with guns, torpedoes and missiles. Knox class frigates are no longer in service with the US navy, but are still used by smaller nations.

▼ TESTS
Verifier, a British Aerospace trials craft, launches a Sea Skua anti-ship missile during evaluation trials. Missiles such as the 145kg Sea Skua with its 9kg warhead, although originally designed as an airborne anti-ship missile, give even the smallest craft a considerable punch.

Key Dates

- 1878 *Lightning* 19 knot torpedo boat launched

- 1914–1918 World War I: Royal Navy coastal motor boats and motor launches reach 35 knots

- 1939–1945 World War II: German E-boats reach 42 knots

- 1958 Soviet Komar class missile-armed craft enter service

- 1966 Soviet Osa class missile-armed craft enter service

- 1973 Soviet Osa class craft see action in the Middle East

- 1990–1991 Osa class see action in the Gulf War

Submarines

▲ THE *TURTLE*
This hand-propelled craft was devised by the American David Bushnell in the early 19th century.

THE FIRST SUBMARINE attack was carried out by the semi-submersible steam-propelled craft called *David* during the American Civil War. It damaged a Federal iron-clad ship with a spar torpedo. No one would have guessed that this crude underwater craft would be the forerunner of the most sophisticated and powerful weapons that the world has ever known.

Electric and oil fuel motors made fully submersible boats practical. In 1886 Lt Isaac Peral of Spain built an electrically powered boat. The following year the Russians built a boat armed with four torpedoes. In 1895 the streamlined *Plunger* was built in the United States by John Holland. On the surface it used a steam engine to charge the batteries which powered it when moving underwater.

The German U-boats in World War I showed how submarine warfare could be a strategic weapon in attacking commercial shipping as well as launching tactical attacks on enemy warships.

On 8 August 1914, the U-15 fired a torpedo at the battleship HMS *Monarch*. Although the torpedo missed, it was the first time that an automotive torpedo had been fired against an enemy from a submarine.

In World War II the Germans capitalized on this experience by concentrating U-boats into "wolf packs" to attack British convoys in the North Atlantic. The Allies were able to defeat the U-boats by breaking the coded signals transmitted to them and by using improved detection systems and weapons. In the Pacific, the US Navy waged a highly effective submarine campaign against Japanese commercial and naval ships.

In the postwar years nuclear power changed submarines forever. Now they could, in theory, stay submerged for indefinite periods of time. The first

Navigation instrument panel

Forward battery

Speed control

◀ TWO-MAN SUBMARINE
Pioneered by the Italians in World War II, these vessels could be steered by two divers. They would position the detachable warhead beneath an enemy warship.

Control box

Control stick

Breathing mouthpiece

Aft battery

Explosive charges (110 TNT each)

Propulsion motor

HUNTER KILLER

Modern submarines are divided into two classes: the nuclear-powered submarines armed with nuclear missiles (SSBNs) and the hunter killers (SSNs). The latter may attack enemy surface ships, but they are also very effective at hunting SSBNs. In World War II Allied submarines made torpedo attacks on surfaced enemy U-boats. However, modern SSNs can hunt and kill underwater, using sonar to locate the enemy and firing sophisticated guided torpedoes.

▼ DIESEL POWER
A diesel-powered hunter-killer submarine. Diesel power is a very quiet form of propulsion.

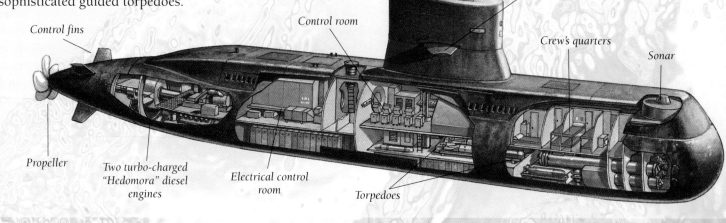

Periscope

Hydroplanes

Control room

Crew's quarters

Sonar

Control fins

Propeller

Two turbo-charged "Hedomora" diesel engines

Electrical control room

Torpedoes

nuclear submarine was the USS *Nautilus*. It was commissioned in 1954 and could dive to more than 200m. In 1959 the launch of the USS *George Washington* marked the arrival of the world's most formidable weapon. This nuclear-powered submarine was armed with Polaris nuclear missiles that could be launched while the boat was submerged.

On 2 May 1982, off the Falklands, the submarine HMS *Conquerer* torpedoed and sank the Argentinian heavy cruiser *General Belgrano*. Despite the use of very efficient anti-submarine tracking systems and weapons, submarines remain a powerful weapon because of the secret nature of their operations.

▶ BOMBER
An SSBN is known in the Royal Navy as a "bomber". Its missiles are housed in launch tubes astern of the fin, or conning tower.

Type A3 Polaris missile

Periscopes and radar mast

Bridge (for surface use)

Machine control room containing nuclear reactor control panels

Communications room

Electrical generating plant

Nuclear reactor (top secret)

Missile compartment

Navigation centre

Torpedo tubes

▲ ATOMIC SUBMARINE
First developed by the US, the nuclear-powered submarine is the most powerful warship in history. It is armed with intercontinental nuclear missiles which can be fired from underwater.

▼ NEGATIVE BUOYANCY
A submarine dives by letting water into its buoyancy tanks and this makes it heavy enough to sink. To surface it "blows" its tanks, pushing air into them so that the water is forced out.

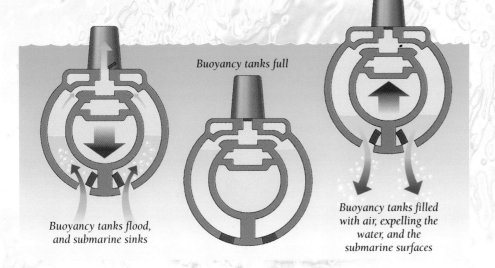

Buoyancy tanks full

Buoyancy tanks flood, and submarine sinks

Buoyancy tanks filled with air, expelling the water, and the submarine surfaces

Key Dates

- 1863 October 5: steam-driven submersible *David* attacks Federal iron-clad ship

- 1895 USS *Plunger*, the first battery-powered boat

- 1904 *Aigret*, first diesel-powered boat

- 1914–1918 World War I German U-boats wage war against Allied commercial shipping

- 1939–1945 World War II German U-boats use "wolf pack" tactics against Allied shipping

- 1954 USS *Nautilus*, the first nuclear-powered submarine, is commissioned

Aircraft Carriers

▲ VERTICAL
A Royal Navy Harrier takes off in the Falklands in 1982.

EARLY AIRCRAFT WERE FRAGILE and underpowered. They were still a dangerous and risky form of transport when US airman Eugene Ely made the first successful flight from a platform rigged on the deck of a US Navy cruiser in 1911. Two months later the intrepid Ely also made a landing onboard a ship. He had effectively become the first carrier pilot, although at that time aircraft carriers had not been conceived.

In 1913 HMS *Hermes* pioneered aircraft carrier design with its short flying-off deck and three aircraft. A U-boat sank her in 1914, but her successor, completed in 1919, was a true aircraft carrier. During World War I the British used seaplane carriers from which aircraft were lowered into the sea.

The interwar years saw a rapid development in carrier design and capability. HMS *Ark Royal*, which was commissioned in 1938, incorporated all the latest features: arrester wire to halt incoming aircraft, net crash barrier, batsmen to guide pilots and catapults to launch aircraft. In 1939 Britain had ten carriers. In 1941 Japan had eleven and the US had three. By the end of the war the US Navy had over 100 in action.

At Taranto in 1940, 21 Swordfish aircraft from the Royal Navy carrier HMS *Illustrious* attacked ships of the Italian Navy, severely damaging three battleships. The Japanese are believed to have modelled their attack at Pearl Harbor on 7 December 1941 on Taranto. They committed 360 aircraft armed with torpedoes and bombs, and sank or immobilized eight battleships, three cruisers and other craft. The US Navy carrier fleet, which was at sea at the time of the attack, formed the nucleus of a new Pacific fleet.

In May 1942, the US Navy fought the Battle of the Coral Sea against the Japanese. It was the first sea battle fought entirely by aircraft attacking ships. In June 1942,

▲ TAKE-OFF
A RNAS Sopwith Pup fighter aircraft takes off during trials in World War I.

LARGE AND SMALL

In the 20th century aircraft carriers have grown from simple "flat tops" to virtual cities at sea. The USS *Nimitz*, for example, has a crew of more than 6,000 with 50 aircraft as well as helicopters. In World War I HMS *Hermes* was the first aircraft carrier and had only three aircraft. *Hermes* was sunk by a U-boat; even today aircraft carriers are vulnerable to submarine attack.

▲ LAUNCHING
This McDonnell Douglas Hornet is preparing to take off.

◀ SIZE
A huge US carrier is manoeuvred into harbour by small tugboats.

▲ ARRESTING
A McDonnell Douglas Hornet hits an arrester net.

▲ FIGHTER POWER
McDonnell Hornet fighters aboard a US carrier. The Hornet's six Phalanx missiles can be used against six targets simultaneously.

the Battle of Midway was another complex air and sea action. These two battles cost the Japanese six of their ten carriers, and the US Navy four of the original eight.

After 1945, further enhancements were incorporated into carrier design. The addition of helicopters allowed carriers to launch operations against enemy submarines and also to land marines to secure coastal positions. The angled flight deck allowed aircraft to take off while others were landing. In 1961 the USS *Enterprise* was completed – at 75,700 tons it was the largest aircraft carrier ever built. It could carry 100 aircraft and, being nuclear powered, had a cruising range the equivalent of 20 times around the world.

In 1967 the British decided that they would phase out fixed-wing aircraft in favour of the Vertical Short Take-Off and Landing (VSTOL) BAe Sea Harrier. The upward-angled ski-slope deck made take-offs easier for Harriers, and subsequently both Italy and Spain have adopted this less expensive option of a carrier equipped with Harriers. In the mid-1970s the Soviet Union began building carriers equipped with VSTOL Yakovlev Yak-36MP "Forger" aircraft and helicopters.

Carriers were involved in the Korean War, at Suez in 1956, in Vietnam, in the Falklands and in the Gulf War of 1990–1991.

▼ CARRIER POWER
This US Navy Kitty Hawk class conventionally powered carrier has a crew of nearly 6,000. It can carry up to 50 aircraft including F-14 Tomcats and F-18 Hornets as well as helicopters.

▼ BATTLE GROUP
A modern naval battle group is built up around a carrier, with supporting vessels to provide cover against enemy aircraft, surface vessels and submarines. The carrier's combat aircraft can attack ships and installations at a safe range from the group.

Key Dates

- 1911 Eugene Ely flies off a ship

- 1913 HMS *Hermes* is commissioned

- 1940 November 11: Fleet Air Arm air attack on Italian fleet at Taranto

- 1941 December 7: Japanese carrier aircraft attack US Navy in Pearl Harbor

- 1942 May: Major carrier action in Battle of the Coral Sea

- 1942 June 4–7: Battle of Midway

- 1961 USS *Enterprise* is first nuclear-powered carrier

Early Fighter Planes

▲ RED BARON
The German fighter ace Baron Manfred von Richthofen was killed in 1918. He commanded a squadron called the "flying circus".

THE EARLY PILOTS were often wealthy and enterprising sportsmen, so the idea of shooting at each other in war was considered to be ungentlemanly. However, it was not long before pilots carried rifles and pistols when flying, and took pot shots at each other. The first true fighter action took place during World War I on 5 October 1914, when a French Voisin V89 brought down a German Aviatik aircraft with its machine-gun fire.

The interrupter gear invented by the Dutchman Anthony Fokker allowed German aircraft to fire forwards through the arc of their propeller. This meant that fighter pilots could aim their aircraft at enemy planes.

▶ FOKKER TRIPLANE
The German World War I Fokker Dr-I fighter had a maximum speed of 200kph and was armed with two 7.92mm Spandau machine guns.

Between 1914 and 1918 aircraft speeds increased from 170kph to 270kph. The first fighter flew at a height of 4,000m, but by the end of the war they were up to 6,000m.

One of the most successful British fighters was the SE-5a. It had a maximum speed of 66kph and was armed with a single synchronized Vickers or Lewis machine gun. The German D1 Albatross had a maximum speed of 55kph and was armed with twin 7.92mm Spandau machine guns.

The interwar period saw the development of the all-metal aircraft with wing-mounted machine guns and also cannon that fired explosive rounds. By 1939 the Messerschmitt Bf-109E had a top speed of 572kph, and by 1945 the 109G with a 1,900hp inline engine had a top speed of 689kph. Armament was a 30mm cannon and two 7.92mm machine guns.

The World War II Allied fighters, the Supermarine Spitfire, and the North American P-51 Mustang were classic types. The Mustang, fitted with extra fuel tanks, had a top speed of 703kph

FIGHTERS OF THE WORLD WARS
Early fighters were slow scout aircraft with simple armament. By the beginning of World War II they were all-metal monoplanes with cannon as well as machine guns. By the close of the war the first jet fighters were in action and many aircraft were equipped with radar.

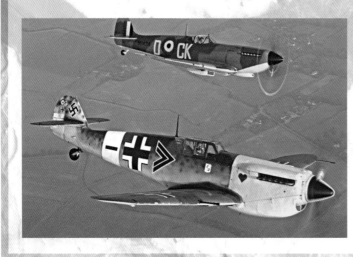

◀ BATTLE OF BRITAIN
A Spitfire with a postwar Merlin-engined Messerschmitt Me-109 photographed during the film *The Battle of Britain*. Spain used the Messerschmitt 109 after the war but put in new engines to improve its performance.

▲ P-38 LIGHTNING
With a top speed of 666kph the Lockheed Lightning, introduced in 1941, was armed with four machine guns and a 20mm cannon. It could carry 1,800kg of bombs.

Aerial

Armour plate

Radio

Battery

Reserve petrol tank (armoured)

Petrol tank

Cine camera

Merlin II engine

Ammunition boxes

Four Browning 0.303in machine guns

Landing light

◀ HAWKER HURRICANE
Armed with eight .303in machine guns, the Hurricane was older and slower than the Spitfire. However, it shot down more German aircraft during the Battle of Britain than the Spitfire did. Hurricane pilots concentrated on attacking the slower, more vulnerable bombers, while Spitfires fought with the escorting Messerschmitt 109 fighters.

▼ "THE FEW"
RAF Spitfire pilots wait on an airstrip in the long summer air battle of 1940 that was called the Battle of Britain. The small number of pilots were nicknamed "The Few" following a speech by Winston Churchill.

and sufficient range to allow pilots to escort bombers to Berlin and back. The Spitfire went through 21 different marks between 1936 and 1945, becoming a more powerful and more heavily armed fighter with each version. The Spitfire MIX, powered by a Rolls-Royce 1,660hp Merlin engine, had a top speed of 657kph and was armed with .303in machine guns and 20mm cannon.

Some of the fighters continued in service into the 1950s and 1960s as ground-attack aircraft. Those fighter aircraft that are still flying today are in the hands of aviation enthusiasts.

Single 7.9mm MG 15 machine gun

Ammunition tanks

Twin 20mm MG FF cannon

▲ THE MESSERSCHMITT ME-110
The German Me-10 "destroyer" fighter was an advanced design when it first flew. However, in the Battle of Britain in 1940 it was too slow for British fighters.

Key Dates

- 1910 Rifle fired from an aircraft for first time

- 1912 Machine gun fired from aircraft for first time

- 1913 37mm cannon fired from an aircraft

- 1914–1918 World War I

- 1914 October 5: first aircraft to be shot down

- 1939–1945 World War II

- 1944–1945 Me-262, the world's first jet fighter

Jet Fighters

▲ FLYING HIGH
*An F-15 Eagle pilot
in the cockpit*

URING THE 1930s aircraft powered by jet propulsion featured in science fiction comics, together with men from Mars and moon rockets. However, both the British and the Germans were conducting research in this field before World War II. The first jet to fly was the German He-178 in 1939, followed by the British Gloster Meteor which flew fitted with jet engines in 1941. The two aircraft never met in combat, but science fiction became reality in 1944 when RAF Meteors took to the air to chase and shoot down German V-1 flying bombs.

Deliveries of the world's first operational jet-powered fighter, the German Messerschmitt Me-262 *Schwalbe* (Swallow), began in May 1944. However, these aircraft were initially configured as bombers and the fighter did not enter service until later that year. It had a maximum speed of 869kph and was armed with four 30mm cannon and 24 5cm R4M rockets. Me-262s took a heavy toll of US Army Air Forces (USAAF) bombers during 1945. On the Allied side, the Gloster Meteor had a maximum speed of 660kph and was armed with four 20mm cannon.

The Korean War saw the first jet versus jet action when US Air Force F-86 Sabres, F-80 Shooting Stars and US Marine Corps F9F Panthers fought with Chinese MiG-15s. The first victory went to a US Air Force (USAF) F-80 Shooting Star on 8 November 1950 against a Chinese MiG-15 over the Yalu river.

Jet fighters have been in action, either in air combat or attacking ground targets, in most parts of the world since the 1950s. Over North Vietnam, in the conflicts between India and Pakistan, the Arab–Israeli wars, the Gulf Wars between Iran and Iraq and between the Coalition Forces and Iraq, US-designed aircraft have fought with Soviet aircraft. In the Falklands in 1982 British Harriers were pitted against US and French-designed aircraft. Soviet jet aircraft were used in ground attack operations during the Afghan war.

Among the most versatile jet fighter aircraft are the Russian MiG-21 and the American McDonnell Douglas F-4 Phantom, which

◀ FIGHTING FALCON
The American F-16 Fighting Falcon multi-role fighter is made by General Dynamics, and is in service in more than 14 countries worldwide. Painted in striking livery, it is flown by the USAF Thunderbirds display team.

A NEW BREED OF WAR PLANE

Immediately after World War II there was a move to design and build jet fighters. US and Chinese jets clashed in the Korean War in 1950–1953. Although missiles such as the Sidewinder have been widely used in combat, the 30mm cannon is still a very effective weapon and can be used against ground targets.

◀ MIRAGE 5
The French Dassault fighter has a top speed of 1,912kph. Operating in a ground-attack role the Mirage can carry bombs, rockets or missiles.

▲ F86 SABRE
The first woman to fly faster than sound, Jacqueline Cochran, achieved the record in a Sabre on 18 May 1953.

▼ PHANTOM
The F-4 Phantom has been built in larger numbers than any Western combat aircraft since World War II.

▲ HAWK
The British BAe Hawk is a versatile combat aircraft that can also be used as a trainer.

Weapons system
ranging radar

IFF aerials
(identification
friend or foe)

Koliesov lift
engines

GSh-23L
cannon pack

▼ FORGER
*The Russian Yak-38, or "Forger", was a vertical
take-off combat aircraft that first flew in 1971.*

▼ HARRIER
*The BAe Harrier has proved an effective
fighter and ground-attack aircraft in the
Falklands and in the Gulf War.*

have fought in Vietnam and the Middle East.

In many of these combats the AIM-9 Sidewinder
heat-seeking air-to-air missile has been the key
weapon. The AIM-9 heat-seeking missile takes its
inspiration from nature. The sidewinder snake locates
its prey by detecting their body heat with special
sensors in its head. The AIM-9 Sidewinder missile
detects the heat from the engine exhausts of its target.

▲ EAGLE
*A missile-armed USAF McDonnell Douglas F-15 Eagle multi-role
fighter manoeuvres into position during in-flight refuelling.*

▼ EUROFIGHTER
Built by a consortium of Spain, Germany, Italy and the UK, the Eurofighter Typhoon
first flew on 29 March 1994. The project has been hampered by political problems
because Germany has reduced its requirement and has argued for a less expensive
aircraft now that the Cold War has ended.

Key Dates

- 1939 German Heinkel He-178
  jet fighter flies

- 1944 German Me-262 enters
  service

- 1944 British Gloster Meteor in
  action against V-1 flying bombs

- 1944 Lockheed Shooting Star
  enters service with USAAF/USAF

- 1945 December 3: de Havilland
  Vampire makes first jet landing
  and take-off from a carrier

- 1950 First jet versus jet victory
  in Korean War

- 1966 August 31: Hawker Harrier
  makes first hovering flight

Early Bombers

▲ LANCASTER
The British bomber was used in the "Dam Buster" raids against Germany.

THE POTENTIAL FOR AIRCRAFT to operate as a platform for delivering bombs to enemy targets was realized as early as 1911. In that year the first bombs were dropped from an aircraft during the Italo-Turkish war.

In World War I bombers started as scout planes in which the crew had taken a few grenades to lob at the enemy lines. Bombers grew from these small single-engined two-seater aircraft to types such as the British Handley Page 0/400. Around 550 of these twin-engined bombers were built. When they attacked German military and industrial targets, they flew in formations of 30–40 aircraft.

The German Gotha GIV and GV bombers attacked targets in London and southern England in World War I. They carried between 300 and 500kg of bombs, had a crew of three and were capable of 175kph with a range of 600km.

In the interwar period there was considerable fear that bombers carrying bombs loaded with poison gas would attack large cities, causing huge casualties. The German Air Force was re-formed secretly after World War I, and the sleek Heinkel He-111 and Dornier Do 17, both described as airliners, were re-engineered as bombers for World War II. The He-111 carried 2,500kg of bombs and the Do 17 1,000kg. The Junkers Ju 87 became notorious as the Stuka dive bomber and the Ju 88 made the transition from bomber to heavily armed fighter.

◀ HANDLEY PAGE 0/400
With a crew of three the RAF Handley Page 0/400 could carry up to 900kg of bombs. It was armed with up to five .303in Lewis machine guns.

BOMBERS OF THE WORLD WARS

In the two World Wars the payload and range of bombers increased dramatically. At the beginning of World War II the German He-111 was carrying 2,500kg of bombs at 420kph. By the close of World War II the four-engined Avro Lancaster was carrying 6,350kg of bombs at 462kph for 2,575km.

◀ B-25 MITCHELL
A US Mitchell medium bomber escorted by a Vought F-4U Corsair carrier-based fighter. The Mitchell could carry 1,400kg of bombs. Several examples of Mitchells have been restored in the US.

▲ LANCASTER
The RAF Avro Lancaster entered service in March 1942 and became the mainstay of the bombing campaign against Germany. By 1944 there were 40 Lancaster squadrons in action.

▶ B-17 FLYING FORTRESS
The B-17 could carry 2,700kg of bombs at
503kph. By the end of the war over 4,700
were in front line service with the USAAF.

On the Allied side bombers grew in size, range and bomb load. In 1939, the Vickers Wellington could carry 3,000kg of bombs. By 1945 the Avro Lancaster could carry 6,350kg of bombs to 2,670km. The USAAF Boeing B-17 had a maximum bomb load of 5,800kg and a range of 5,310km. The Consolidated B-24 Liberator carried up to 3,600kg of bombs at 483kph.

Supporters of strategic bombing say that it made a major contribution to the Allied victory in World War II. However, despite the importance of bombing, history has shown that victory is only guaranteed when ground forces enter enemy territory and occupy it.

▼ DRESDEN 1945
German authorities sort through bodies in the ghastly aftermath of the attack on Dresden. Attacked by 773 RAF bombers by night and by the USAAF during the day, some 20sq km were destroyed by fire. In the overcrowded city more than 100,000 died in the firestorm.

Key Dates

- 1911 Bombs first dropped in the Italo-Turkish war

- 1914–1918 World War I: tactical and rudimentary strategic bombing established

- 1936–1939 Spanish Civil War: tactical bombing perfected

- 1939–1945 World War II: first strategic bombing

- 1942 Pressurized B-29 Superfortress flies

- 1944–1945 German Arado 234 jet bomber in action

- 1945 Atomic bombs dropped on Japan by B-29s

Modern Jets and Stealth

THE CLOAK OF INVISIBILITY is a feature of many ancient myths. Although it may not be a reality, new techniques in aircraft design have made them very hard to detect by systems such as radar. These features are known as "stealth", and all modern combat aircraft now have some stealth features. Stealth in aircraft design is the attempt to minimize the ways in which aircraft can be detected by ground or airborne air defence systems.

In its earliest form, camouflage paint was a stealth feature, but the echo from radar would show the location of the most ingeniously camouflaged aircraft. One technique for defeating early radars was to fly very low and so hide the aircraft among the clutter of radar echoes. Modern radars can now discriminate between clutter and moving targets, so the next move was to design an aircraft that gave very little or no radar return. This was achieved by giving the aircraft as few surfaces as possible

▶ STEALTH
The Lockheed/Boeing F-22A Rapier, the new fighter for the USAF, has "stealth" features within its design.

from which a radar beam could bounce off and so give an echo. In addition to the design of the aircraft's profile, it was coated with a radar-absorbent material that would further reduce or limit the echo.

If there is no discernible radar echo, the heat from

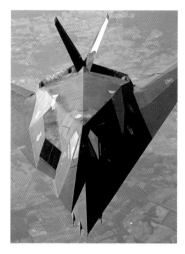

▲ NIGHTHAWK
The Lockheed F-117A Nighthawk first saw action in 1989 in Panama and later in 1991 in the Gulf. An F-117 was shot down over the former Yugoslavia in 1999.

MODERN DEVELOPMENTS

Radar and thermal detection systems have made combat aircraft vulnerable, even if they are flying low and at night. Since radar reflects off flat hard surfaces, any aircraft with a less angular shape and a "radar-absorbent" coating is less likely to be detected. The engines produce hot gases that can be picked up by radar. However, these gases can be cooled or screened before they pass into the air.

F-107 WR-400 turbofan jet engine

Folding wings

Nuclear warhead

Tercom guidance system

▲ CRUISE MISSILE
The German V-1, the earliest cruise missile, was slow and fairly inaccurate. In the late 1970s the United States produced a cruise missile that could be launched from land, sea or air. It has a guidance system that is very accurate and can fly a circuitous route to its target. Cruise missiles have been used in the Middle East and Serbia.

▶ SCALE MODEL
A wind-tunnel model of an American experimental combat aircraft. Computer modelling is used to evaluate new designs.

▼ FIGHTER
The Boeing Joint Strike Fighter will replace several types of combat aircraft from 2004.

▶ BOEING B-52
The veteran USAF B-52 strategic bomber has been used since 1955. It can carry up to 22,680kg of air - launched cruise missiles or 51 454kg conventional bombs.

▶ SPIRIT
The Northrop Grumman B-2A looks back to the German Gotha flying design which was developed at the close of World War II. The B-2A can carry 22,680kg of ordnance at 764kph and has a range of 18,520km with one refuelling.

the engines of a modern aircraft can still be detected. The solution to this problem is to position the engines so that the hot gases from them flow over the top of the wings. The gases are cooled as they pass over special ceramic plates.

The classic stealth aircraft are the US Lockheed F-117 fighter, which was used in action in 1989 as a bomber in the invasion of Panama and later in attacks on Iraq in 1991. An F-117 was shot down during the air attacks on Serbia in 1999.

The Northrop B-2 Advanced Technology Bomber is a dedicated stealth bomber. It is capable of carrying 16,920kg of ordnance over a maximum range of 9,815km.

The USAF Advanced Tactical Fighter programme took place in the 1990s. It was a competition between the Lockheed/General Dynamics YF-22 and the McDonnell Douglas YF-23, two fighters with stealth features. The Lockheed aircraft, now designated the F-22 Rapier, has been accepted and will enter service by 2011.

▼ STEALTH TECHNOLOGY
Although stealth is associated with aircraft, it has also been employed in the design of modern combat ships and even in tanks. Ships and tanks can be detected on radar and thermal imaging, so their exhausts need to be screened and any radar reflective surfaces have to be softened.

Engines are either side of the cockpit. The exhaust flows are set well forward. This allows the exhaust to cool as much as possible as it passes over the wings, minimising the heat trail.

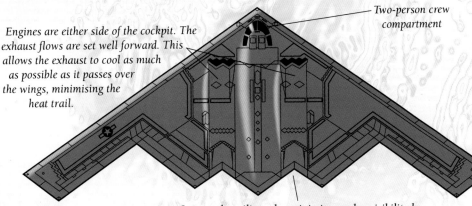

Two-person crew compartment

Saw-tooth trailing edge minimizes radar visibility by breaking up the normal straight edge of a wing

Key Dates

- 1951 Canberra bomber is the first jet to fly across the North Atlantic non-stop

- 1955 B-52 enters service with the USAF

- 1977 December: first flight of Lockheed Martin F-117

- 1983–1984 US stealth research ship *Sea Shadow* built

- 1989 July 17: first flight of Northrop Grumman B-2A Spirit

- 1991 March 14: Smyge Swedish stealth patrol craft launched

- 1991 April: F-22 Rapier selected by USAF

Airborne Troops

▲ PARACHUTE
The light fabric of a parachute traps air, slowing down the descent of the soldier or paratrooper.

I T IS HARD FOR US to realize how unusual paratroops seemed when they first appeared in World War II. Most soldiers had never travelled in an airliner, so men who arrived by parachute from aircraft seemed almost as fantastic as spacemen. The Soviet Union pioneered airborne forces in the interwar years. However, it was Nazi Germany that made first use of them in World War II.

Airborne troops could be delivered to the battlefield either by parachute or in gliders. Troop-carrying gliders carried between 10 and 29 troops and could also be used to transport vehicles and light artillery. They were particularly effective when an operation called for a formed group of men to attack a target such as a bridge or coastal artillery battery. The problem with paratroops was that they could be scattered over a large area if they jumped too high.

The German attack on the island of Crete in May 1941 involved 22,500 paratroops and 80 gliders. The airborne forces suffered very heavy losses: 4,000 were killed, 2,000 wounded and 220 aircraft were destroyed. Hitler declared that "the day of the paratrooper is over".

The British and Americans were quick to learn from the Germans mistakes, and airborne forces were used on D-Day in Normandy in June 1944. Airborne forces were also in Sicily in 1943, in Normandy in 1944, and at the Rhine crossings in 1945. In Burma in 1943, British and Commonwealth troops known as Chindits were landed by glider deep inside Japanese lines. They drew Japanese forces away from the front lines in India.

After World War II, the French made extensive use of paratroops in Indochina (Vietnam) between 1948 and 1954. However, in May 1954 at Dien Bien Phu they were defeated

▶ PARATROOPER
A British paratrooper in World War II. The buckle in the middle of his chest operates as a quick release for the parachute harness.

AIRBORNE OPERATIONS

Attacks by paratroops and glider-borne soldiers in World War II were sometimes a gamble because these lightly equipped soldiers could be defeated by ground troops with tanks and artillery. If friendly ground forces could link up with them, airborne troops could sieze and hold key positions such as bridges, fortifications and causeways. They could help to keep up the momentum of an attack.

▲ JUMPING FOR FUN
A sports parachutist exits from an aircraft in the "spread stable position". Before he pulls the release on his parachute he will enjoy a period of "free fall".

▶ TRANSPORT
Transport aircraft can carry trucks and vehicles that can be unloaded if a suitable airfield has been captured and secured.

▲ DROP ZONE
Parachutes float down and collapse in a mass military drop. The flat area allocated for such an operation is called a drop zone, or DZ. Helicopters put down soldiers on a landing zone, or LZ.

when they set up an airborne base deep inside Viet Minh lines. They lost 11 complete parachute battalions in the fighting.

On 5 November 1956 French and British paratroops landed at Port Said to recapture the Suez Canal, which had been nationalized by the Egyptians.

Today, helicopters mean troops no longer need to parachute from aircraft. However, airborne forces are still considered an elite group within all national armies.

▲ SEALS
These Seals, US Navy Special Forces troops, are wearing harnesses that clip on to a ladder. They are being lifted by a Chinook helicopter.

▶ HOW A PARACHUTE WORKS
The umbrella shape of the parachute, called a canopy, is made from silk and, later, nylon. It traps air and so slows the descent of the parachutist or cargo. A small hole in the centre canopy allows air to escape and prevents the parachute from swinging from side to side.

Modern square parachutes are called "ram air". They can be steered allowing the parachutist to land with very great accuracy. The latest development is a remotely controlled steerable canopy that can be used by special forces in remote locations to take delivery of cargo. The load is dropped at a great height.

Key Dates

- 1797 Parachute invented

- 1927 Italians are first to drop a "stick" of paratroops

- 1930s Soviet forces develop paratroops

- 1939–1945 Airborne operations in Europe and Far East

- 1941 German airborne attack on island of Crete

- 1944 British and Polish landings at Arnhem

- 1953–1954 Battle of Dien Bien Phu in Vietnam

- 1956 French and British paratroops capture Suez Canal

Helicopters

▲ SEA KNIGHT
A US Marine Corps Sea Knight with an underslung load lifts off.

As THEY CLATTER IN AND OUT of heliports, helicopters are an everyday sight. Most people think that they are a postwar invention. However, the first free flight by a tandem-rotor device was by Paul Cornu on 13 November 1907. Igor Sikorsky built two helicopters in Russia in 1909–1910.

Helicopters were used at the close of World War II, and in Korea and Indo-China the Americans and French used them to evacuate wounded soldiers from the battlefield. The most widely used helicopters in this period were the Sikorsky H-19 and the Bell H-13 Sioux. On 5 November 1956 at the Suez Canal British Royal Marines were landed by helicopter in the first airborne assault. In the Algerian war of 1954–1962 the French used helicopters to carry troops. The helicopters were fitted with anti-tank missiles and machine guns.

The American involvement in Vietnam, from 1962 to 1975, saw the use of helicopters in assault, casualty evacuation and transport and liaison missions. In airborne assaults 16 troop-carrying helicopters nicknamed "Slicks" were supported by 9 attack

▲ APACHE
The US Army's Apache attack helicopter has a crew of two and a maximum speed of 365kph.

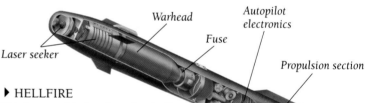

Laser seeker   Warhead   Fuse   Autopilot electronics   Propulsion section

▶ HELLFIRE
This laser-guided anti-tank missile was used in action in the Gulf by US Army Apache helicopters.

VERTICAL FLIGHT

Helicopters are used in wartime to transport troops, casualties and stores. They can rescue shot-down pilots and attack ships, submarines and ground targets. Some are even equipped for air-to-air combat.

▲ TRANSPORT
The Boeing Vertol CH-47 Chinook has a crew of two and can carry up to 44 troops.

▼ OSPREY
The American Bell Boeing Osprey tilt-rotor aircraft can carry up to 24 combat-equipped troops or 9,070kg of cargo. The US Marine Corps were enthusiastic advocates of the Osprey, which can transport troops quickly from offshore to secure beach heads.

▲ RESCUE
A Royal Navy GKN Westland Sea King has airborne early warning radar to warn surface ships about enemy missiles or warships. The Sea King can also winch people from the sea.

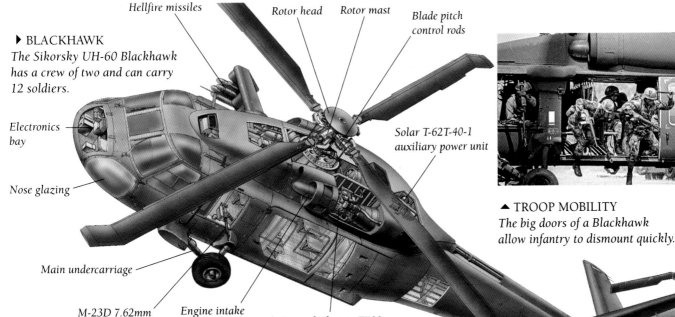

▶ BLACKHAWK
The Sikorsky UH-60 Blackhawk has a crew of two and can carry 12 soldiers.

Hellfire missiles

Rotor head   Rotor mast   Blade pitch control rods

Electronics bay

Solar T-62T-40-1 auxiliary power unit

Nose glazing

▲ TROOP MOBILITY
The big doors of a Blackhawk allow infantry to dismount quickly.

Main undercarriage

M-23D 7.62mm machine gun   Engine intake

General Electric T700-GE-700 turboshaft engine

Gear box

Titanium and glass-fibre rotor blades

helicopters nicknamed "gunships". The gunships were armed with 48 rockets and machine guns. The Bell H-1 Iroquois, which is universally known as the Huey, became the helicopter of the Vietnam War. Since 1958, some 9,440 Hueys have been built. The Bell AH-1 Cobra was the first dedicated attack helicopter and became the first helicopter to destroy tanks with anti-tank missiles from the air. The Boeing Vertol CH-47 Chinook twin-rotor helicopter was widely used to carry between 22 and 50 troops. By the end of the Vietnam War, the United States had lost nearly 5,000 helicopters.

The Soviet Union looked to the Cobra and developed the Mi-24 attack helicopter, which is known by NATO as the Hind. It saw action in Afghanistan between 1979

and 1989. Among the helicopters produced by the Soviet Union was the Mi-26 "Halo". It could carry 20 tonnes and was used to dump lead and concrete on the nuclear reactor at Chernobyl following its dramatic explosion in 1986.

The American Sikorsky H-60 Blackhawk troop-carrying helicopter and the McDonnell-Douglas H-64 Apache attack helicopter were used by the US Army in the Gulf War in 1991.

▶ HOW IT WORKS
A helicopter is sometimes known as a "rotary wing aircraft" because its main rotor can be tilted. This creates the current of air that flows over the wings to lift the aircraft into the sky. The angle of tilt of the rotor blades is called pitch, and "coarse pitch" is the sharp angle needed to lift the helicopter off the ground. The smaller tail rotor pushes against the rotation of the main rotor and so keeps the helicopter flying straight and level.

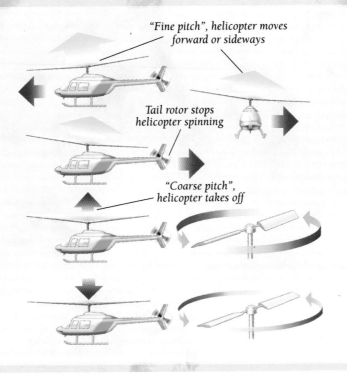

"Fine pitch", helicopter moves forward or sideways

Tail rotor stops helicopter spinning

"Coarse pitch", helicopter takes off

Key Dates

- 1500 Leonardo da Vinci sketches helicopter idea

- 1907 September 29: first helicopter lifts a man off the ground into the air

- 1914–1918 Austrians fly helicopters in World War I

- 1942 American Sikorsky R-4 becomes first military helicopter

- 1963 First true attack helicopter, the American Model 207 Sioux Scout

- 1991 February 24: 300 helicopters used in Gulf War in the largest assault in the history of aviation

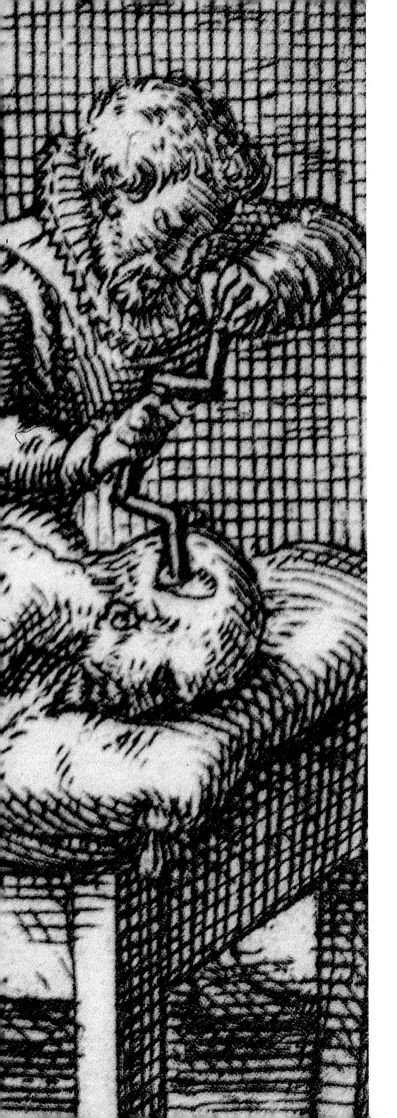

Gazetteer of

People
and
Places

Glossary

People and Places

Abbasids, dynasty of Muslim caliphs (rulers), who ruled the Arab world from AD749 until 1258.

Abu Bekr, the first caliph (ruler) of the Muslim empire, who succeeded Muhammad in AD632.

Ahura Mazda, the supreme god in the Zoroastrian religion.

Amritsar, Sikh holy city in northwest India founded by Guru Ram Das, where the sacred Golden Temple was built between AD1574 and 1581.

Appian Way, the first of the major Roman roads, constructed in 312BC.

Archimedes, Greek citizen of Syracuse (c.287–212BC) and the world's first true scientist, who used mathematical theories and practical experiments to prove his string of discoveries.

Asgard, the realm of the gods in Norse mythology.

Auenbrugger, Leopold, Austrian doctor who, in 1761, proved that listening to the chest reveals information about the state of the lungs.

Baekeland, Leo, inventor, in 1909, of Bakelite, the world's first entirely synthetic plastic.

Baird, John Logie, Scottish pioneer who demonstrated practical television in 1926.

Becquerel, Antoine, French scientist who discovered radioactivity in 1897.

Benz, Karl, German engineer who offered the first petrol-engined car for sale in 1888.

Boyle, Robert, Irish scientist (1627–1691) who said that everything in the material world is made of elements and compounds.

Brahman, the supreme Hindu god.

Canaan, the land promised to the Jews by God.

Catholic, at first, the universal Christian Church which, in AD1054, split into Western (Roman) and Eastern (Orthodox) branches. Today, the term usually refers to the Church headed by the Pope in Rome.

Celts, people who lived in central and western Europe during the Iron Age, just before these areas were occupied by the Romans.

Confucius, Chinese philosopher who lived from 551 to 479BC and whose peaceful teachings founded Confucianism.

Constantine the Great, Roman emperor who, in AD312, granted toleration of Christianity, which soon became the official religion of the Roman empire.

Copernicus, astronomer who showed that the Earth revolves around the Sun and not the Sun round the Earth.

Coral Sea, region off northern Australia where an American aircraft-carrier force inflicted the first naval blow to the Japanese in World War II.

Crete, Greek island that was invaded by the Germans in World War II after a major airborne assault in May 1941.

Crick, Francis, British scientist who, along with James Watson, discovered the double-helix structure of DNA in 1953 and helped to pave the way for modern genetics.

Culpeper, Nicholas, English herbalist who wrote the first modern herbal in 1649

Dardanelles, strait in northwest Turkey that links the Mediterranean and Black Seas, and where Allied Forces suffered a grim defeat in 1915.

Darwin, Charles, English naturalist who published his controversial theory of evolution, The Origin of the Species, in 1859.

Demeter, the Greek goddess of farming and harvests.

Dien Bien Phu, village in Indochina (Vietnam) gained by communist forces in 1954, thus signalling the end of French colonial rule.

Dionysus, the Greek god of wine.

Domagk, Gerhard, German scientist who developed Prontosil, one of the first antibacterial drugs, in 1932.

Duat, the underworld in ancient Egyptian religion.

Einstein, Albert, revolutionary physicist, who published his theories of special relativity and general relativity in 1905 and 1915 respectively.

Ely, Eugene, American aviator who made the world's first successful take off from and landing on a ship in 1911.

Empedocles, Greek philosopher who described the four humours (elements) that make up the body, in the 400s BC.

Euclid, Greek mathematician who taught at Alexandria and wrote his Elements of Geometry in about 300BC.

Falkland Islands, British colony in the south Atlantic Ocean and the scene of a short war in 1982, when British forces expelled the Argentine forces that had occupied the islands.

Faraday, Michael, English chemist and physicist (1791–1867) who made pioneering discoveries in the field of electricity.

Fleming, Alexander, Scottish bacteriologist who discovered penicillin in 1928, paving the way for treatment of infectious diseases.

Galilei, Galileo, Italian scientist (1564–1642) who was the first to use a telescope to examine the night sky and whose astronomical achievements included the discovery of four of Jupiter's moons.

Gautama, Siddhartha, generally known as the Buddha (enlightened one), the founder of the Buddhist system of belief around 500BC.

Guru Nanak, the Indian founder of the Sikh religion, who lived from 1469 until 1539.

Halstaat, the first stage of the Iron Age in Europe, from the 600s to the 500s BC, named after an Iron Age archaeological site in Austria

Harvey, William, English physician who described how the heart pumps blood around the body in 1628.

Hausser, Konrad, the designer of the first effective long-recoil mechanism for artillery in 1888.

Henry the Navigator, prince of Portugal and founder of a school of scientific navigation, who financed voyages of discovery along the coast of West Africa during the 1400s.

Hipparchus, Greek who compiled a catalogue of the stars and became the first truly great astronomer. However, much of his work was based on records left behind by the ancient Babylonians.

Hippocrates, Greek citizen of Kos, who lived from 460 to 377BC and who is known as the 'father of medicine' for his works and writings on the accurate diagnosis and treatment of disease.

Hiroshima, Japanese city on which the first atomic bomb was dropped in August 1945.

Holland, John, American engineer who developed the world's first practical submarines in the 1890s.

Homer, supposed writer of the Iliad and Odyssey, Greek epic poems about the Trojan War and its aftermath.

Hubble, Edwin, American astronomer whose discoveries of the 1920s led to the 'big bang' theory of the universe.

Hunter, John, Scottish surgeon of the 1700s, who transformed surgery into a science.

Jenner, Edward, English physician who revolutionized the prevention of disease in 1796 when he successfully inoculated a boy against smallpox.

Jerusalem, holy city for Jews, Christians and Muslims and the site of the Jewish Great Temple built by King Solomon.

Jesus of Nazareth, a Jew born around 7 or 6BC, whom Christians believe was the son of God. His life, death and teachings are the foundations of the Christian Church.

Jutland, name given to the greatest naval battle of World War I, fought in May 1916 off the west coast of Jutland, Denmark

Korea, country in Asia (now split into North and South Korea) and site of a major war between 1950 and 1953, in which jet-powered fighter planes were first used against each other.

Lao-tzu, the Chinese founder of Taoism, a philosophy based on following a natural path through life.

Lavoisier, Antoine, French chemist who helped to prove that all materials are made up of basic elements.

Leeuwenhoek, Anton van, Dutch scientist who made the first practical microscope in 1671, through which he identified microbes which he called 'animalcules'.

Luger, Georg, Austrian who, in 1899, designed the small automatic weapon called the Luger pistol, used by the Germans in World Wars I and II.

Luther, Martin, German religious reformer whose condemnation of the Roman Catholic Church in 1517 led to the Reformation and the establishment of Protestantism.

Mahavira, Indian founder of the Jain religion in the 500s BC.

Malpighi, Marcello, Italian physician of the 1600s who contributed to the understanding of the circulation of the blood by his discovery of the capillaries that link arteries and veins.

Marconi, Guglielmo, Italian-born scientist who sent the world's first radio message in 1895.

Maxim, Hiram, American-born British magnate who invented the first fully automatic machine gun in 1883.

Mercator, Gerhardus, Dutch mapmaker who, in 1552, created a new map projection of the world that accurately represented the surface of a sphere (the Earth) on a flat surface (map).

Mesopotamia, the fertile area of land between the Tigris and Euphrates rivers in the Middle East, where the world's first urban civilization emerged.

Midgard, the middle world in Norse mythology, where humans live.

Midway, Pacific islands off which American aircraft carriers inflicted a decisive defeat on the Japanese navy in June 1942 during World War II.

Moses (known as Musa in Islam), prophet who brought the Jews out of Egyptian captivity in about 1466BC and to whom God revealed the Ten Commandments.

Muhammad, prophet born in Makkah (Mecca) in AD570 and founder of Islam, which holds that Allah is the one true god.

Nagasaki, Japanese city on which the second atomic bomb was dropped in August 1945.

Nelson, Horatio, British naval hero and commander who defeated the French and Spanish navies at the Battle of Trafalgar in October 1805, but died during the battle.

Newton, Isaac, English scientist and mathematician who came up with his famous theory about gravity in 1666. He also made important scientific discoveries about motion and the nature of light.

Nightingale, Florence, British nurse who pioneered modern nursing methods during the Crimean War (1853–1856).

Normandy, part of northern France and site of the D-Day campaign which began in June 1944 when Allied troops landed on the Normandy coast, marking the start of the liberation of German-occupied territory.

Odin, also known as Wotan, the primary god of Norse mythology.

Oppenheimer, Robert, American nuclear physicist who led the development of the atomic bomb during World War II.

Pasteur, Louis, French scientist who, in the 1860s, established how bacteria cause infection and developed pasteurization, a technique for destroying microbes with heat.

Pilate, Pontius, Roman governor of Judea who condemned Jesus of Nazareth to crucifixion in about AD30.

Planck, Max, German physicist who published his quantum theory in 1900, revolutionizing scientific understanding of atomic processes.

Plate, River, also known as the Río de la Plata, South American river in whose estuary the German pocket battleship Graf Spee was trapped by British forces and scuttled (deliberately sunk) by her captain in December 1939.

Priestley, Joseph, English chemist who identified oxygen in the 1700s.

Ptolemy, Astronomer who lived in Alexandria from AD90 to 170 and whose idea that the Earth was at the centre of the universe went unchallenged until the 1500s.

Pythagoras, Greek philosopher and mathematician, born in Samos in 560BC.

Ra, the ancient Egyptian sun god.

Richthofen, Manfred von, German fighter pilot who scored 80 victories during World War I.

Röntgen, Wilhelm, German physicist who discovered X-rays in 1895.

Shiva, one of the three main Hindu gods, responsible both for preserving and for destroying life.

Snow, John, British doctor who traced the cause of the London cholera outbreak of 1854 to contaminated water supplies.

Solomon, Jewish king known for his wisdom, who completed the construction of the Great Temple in about 960BC, which had been begun by his father, King David.

Sumer, Lower Mesopotamia, where the first civilization sprang up, and the birthplace of writing and the first real mathematics.

Swinton, Ernest, British colonel who came up with the idea of the tank in 1914, during World War I.

Tsiolkovsky, Konstantin, Russian scientist who developed the liquid-fuel rocket motor in 1903 and who pioneered the idea of multi-stage rocket technology in 1929.

Tsu Shima, island between Japan and Korea, near which the Japanese scored a decisive naval victory over the Russians in May 1905.

Valhalla, the heaven of the brave in Norse mythology.

Vinci, Leonardo da, Italian engineer, inventor, architect and artist, who was a true Renaissance polymath (master of many fields).

Vishnu, one of the three main Hindu gods, responsible for preserving the universe.

Watson, James, American scientist who, along with Francis Crick, discovered the double-helix structure of DNA in 1953 and helped to pave the way for modern genetics.

Wegener, Alfred, German scientist who, in 1923, first put forward the theory of continental drift, that the continents move over the surface of the Earth, and who also suggested that there was once one giant supercontinent.

Whitehead, Robert, British engineer based in Italy who developed the first effective locomotive torpedoes from the 1860s.

Wright, Wilbur and Orville, American brothers and aviation pioneers who achieved the world's first powered and sustained flight in a controllable heavier-than-air craft during December 1903 at Kitty Hawk, North Carolina.

Yahweh, or YHWH, the Hebrew name of the single god of the Jewish religion.

Zeus, the supreme god in Greek religion.

Zoroaster, Persian priest who lived around 1200BC and whose teachings form the basis of the Zoroastrian religion.

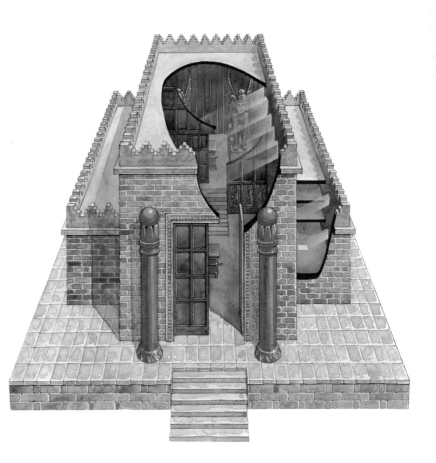

Glossary

Amphitheatre

A circular or oval open-air theatre, with seats arranged around a central area.

Anatomy

The study of the structure of the body—where everything is and how it fits together.

Antibiotic

A drug typically based on a natural substance that attacks germs.

Antiseptic

Any substance that kills or inhibits germs.

Aqueduct

A bridge that supports a canal for transporting water.

Artillery

Large weapons that need transport to move them around the battlefield and a crew to operate them.

Astrolabe

Navigational instrument used by sailors to measure the height of the Sun at noon, thus giving the ship's latitude.

Ayurveda

A series of Indian religious texts dating back to about 2000BC.

Barometer

A device for measuring air pressure.

Bible, The

The Christian holy book, divided into the Old and New Testaments, each containing many different individual books.

Capillary

Tiny blood vessel in the body, linking veins to arteries.

Cathode-ray tube

A special glass tube containing a vacuum. Inside, streams of electrons flow from a negative electrical terminal, or cathode.

Chain reaction

A nuclear fission reaction which gathers pace by itself. Neutrons split from each atom go on to split other atoms, and so split off more neutrons.

Chimera

A creature genetically engineered to include tissues from another creature.

Chronometer

Highly accurate clock used at sea to establish longitude.

Clone

A perfect genetic replica of a living thing, made from exactly the same genetic material.

Combustion

The process of burning.

Compound

A substance made by chemically combining two or more elements.

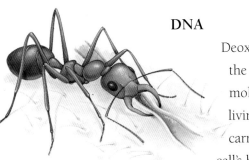

DNA

Deoxyribonucleic acid, the basic chemical molecule inside every living cell which carries the genes—the cell's basic instructions for life and the instructions to make a new organism.

Dynamo

A device for generating electricity by rotating magnets past an electric coil.

Electromagnetism

The combined effects of electricity and magnetism.

Element

One of the 100 or so basic chemicals from which all others are built. None can be split into any other substance.

Equinox

One of the two days each year when night and day are equally long (12 hours) all over the world. One is on March 21, the other is on September 23.

Evolution

The gradual change of living species over time.

Immortal

Describes someone who will live forever.

Initiation

A ceremony by which a person is introduced into a religion.

Irrigation

Using canals or watercourses to bring water to dry land so that crops can grow.

Meditation

The act of sitting and thinking about something deeply.

Messiah

The person sent by God to save his people. The Jews believe God will send a messiah to save them. Christians believe that Jesus was that messiah.

Missionary

A person who travels abroad to convert the local people to his or her own religion.

Monastery

A religious building where monks live.

Monk

A man who lives in a religious community. Monks vow to live a life of poverty and obey God.

Nirvana

Name of the state of existence that Buddhists seek to reach.

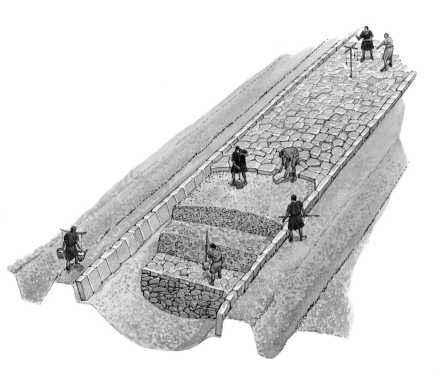

Orthodox

Traditional. There are orthodox branches of both Judaism and Christianity.

Persecute

To punish or harm someone for their beliefs.

Philosophy

A set of beliefs and values held by a person or group of people.

Pilgrimage

A journey to a holy place by a religious follower.

Pope

Head of the Roman Catholic Church, based in Rome.

Prophet

Someone through whom God speaks.

Quantum theory

The idea that, on a subatomic level, energy is always broken into tiny chunks, or quanta.

Qur'an

The holy book of Islam as spoken by Muhammad.

Radiation

The spread of energy as particles or waves, e.g. X-rays, light, or gamma rays.

Radioactivity

The gradual disintegration of large atoms, along with the emission of radiation.

Rastafarianism

Religion of the West Indies ordaining a belief in the Old Testament but worshipping Haile Selassie, emperor of Ethiopia from 1930–1974.

Saint

A Christian who lived a good life, showed great faith in God and performed miracles.

Sect

A small religious group that has split from the main religion.

Sharía

The holy laws derived from the Qur'an and Sunnah for the ordering of a Muslim's life.

Shíah and Sunni

The two primary branches of the Islamic religion, which developed from AD680.

Shinto

Major religion established in Japan during the 6th century AD.

Shrine

A sacred place or container where religious objects or images may be kept.

Submersible

Any vehicle capable of travelling under water, primarily submarines.

Sunnah

Secondary holy book of the Islamic religion, containing accounts of Muhammad and his immediate followers.

Tectonic plate

One of the 20 or so giant slabs from which the Earth's surface is made.

Torah

Hebrew name for the first five books of the Bible.

Transistor

Tiny electronic switch which works automatically.

Tribe

A group of people who are often related and share the same language and culture.

TNT

Trinitrotoluene, a powerful explosive.

U-Boat

German submarine in World Wars I and II.

Underworld

The mythical region beneath the world's surface where dead people are said to live.

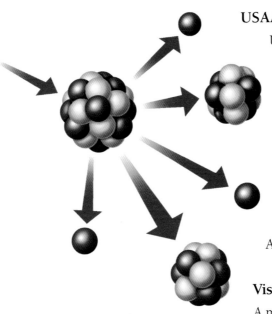

USAAF

United States Army Air Force, American air force in World War II.

USMC

United States Marine Corps.

USS

United States Ship, the title of American warships.

Vision

A mystical or religious experience when a person sees God or something supernatural.

World Wide Web

Computer system for linking computers together via the Internet.

WP

White phosphorus, a material that produces thick white smoke and causes severe burning. Used in shells and grenades.

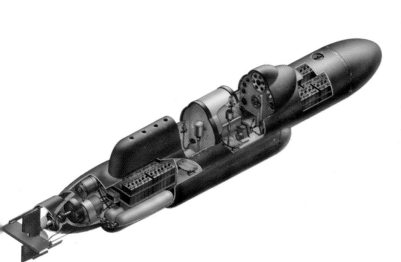

Index

A

aborigines 20-1

Abraham 50, 52-3

acupuncture 137, 175

aeroplanes 100-1

Africa 20-1, 132-3

agnostics 13

air travel 100-1

air warfare 186-7, 228-9, 230-1, 232-3, 234-5, 236-7, 238-9

aircraft carriers 226-7

alchemy 88-9, 142-3

alternative therapies 174-5

amphibious craft 206-7

anaesthetics 9, 153, 154-5

anatomists 82-3

anti-tank weapons 204-5

antibiotics 108-9, 164-5

antisepsis 9, 154-5

aqueducts 79

Archimedes 76-7

arithmetic 72-3

armour 212-13

armoured vehicles 214-15

artificial materials 122-3

artillery 186, 192-3, 194-5

astronomy 74-5, 84-5

atheists 13

atoms 88-9

automatic weapons 9, 190-1

Ayurvedic medicine 134-5

Aztecs 20

B

Babbage, Charles 114

Babylonians 70, 72-3, 74, 130-1

bacteria 160-1, 162-3, 164-5

Baird, John Logie 102-3

battleships 218-19, 220-1, 222-3

Bell, Alexander 93

Bible, New Testament 55, 56-7, 58-9

Bible, Old Testament 49, 50-1, 52-3

Big Bang 106-7

Black Death 148-9

Blackwell, Elizabeth 166-7

blood groups 169

bloodletting 138-9, 140, 152

bomber aircraft 232-3

bombs 196-7

Buddhism 32-3, 34-5, 36-7

C

camouflage 216-17

canals 90

cannons 192-3

cars 70, 98-9

Catholicism 54, 55

cauterization 128, 145, 147

celebrations 22, 28-9, 37, 40-1, 47, 52-3, 58-9, 65

Celts 18-19, 20

charlatans 156-7

chemical weapons 240-1

chemistry 66-9, 112-13

China 42-3, 44-5, 71, 73, 136-7

Christian Scientists 66

Christianity 54-5, 56-7, 58-9

clones 124

Columbus 71, 81

communications 118-19, 210-11

computers 114-15

Confucianism 42-3

constellations 74-5

continental drift 120-1

Copernicus 71, 84-5

cults 66-7

Curie, Marie and Pierre 103, 166

D

Da Vinci, Leonardo 82, 147

Dalai Lama 30

Darwin, Charles 96-7

diabetes 169

diagnosis 150-1

dinosaurs 96-7, 120

diseases 108-9, 128-9, 148-9, 160-1

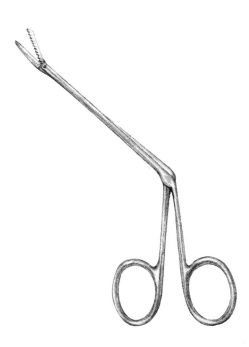

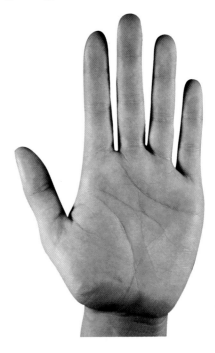

This edition is published by Southwater

Southwater is an imprint of
Anness Publishing Limited
Hermes House
88–89 Blackfriars Road
London SE1 8HA
tel. 020 7401 2077
fax 020 7633 9499

Distributed in the UK by
The Manning Partnership
251–253 London Road East
Batheaston
Bath BA1 7RL
tel. 01225 852 727
fax 01225 852 852

Distributed in the USA by
Anness Publishing Inc.
27 West 20th Street
Suite 504
New York
NY 10011
tel. 212 807 6739
fax 212 807 6813

Distributed in Australia by
Sandstone Publishing
Unit 1, 360 Norton Street
Leichhardt
New South Wales 2040
tel. 02 9560 7888
fax 02 9560 7488

10 9 8 7 6 5 4 3 2 1

For Lorenz Books:
Publisher: Joanna Lorenz
Managing Editor, Children's Books: Gilly
Cameron Cooper
Project Editor: Nicole Pearson
Designer: Joyce Mason; Axis Design

Previously published as four separate
volumes:
World Religions; Science and Technology;
The Story of Medicine; Modern Weapons and
Warfare

PHOTOGRAPHIC ACKNOWLEDGEMENTS

Page 19 (BC) Judy McCaskey; 22 (BC) Kaveh
Kazemi/ Panos Pictures; 27 (TR) Victoria and
Albert Museum/ The Bridgeman Art Library;
29 (TL) Lindsay Hebberd/ CORBIS; 30 (BR)
The National Museum of India/ The
Bridgeman Art Library; 33 (TR) The
Bridgeman Art Library; 35 (BL) Alain le
Garsmeur/ Panos Pictures; 39 (TR) Bennett
Dean: Eye Ubiquitous/ CORBIS; 40 (CR)
Dinodia Picture Agency, Bombay/ The
Bridgeman Art Library, (BC) Charles &
Josette Lenars/ CORBIS; Earl &
Nazima Kowall/ CORBIS; 46 (C)
Clare Oliver; 47 (TR, BC) Clare
Oliver; 48 (BR) Daniel
Lainé/ CORBIS; 52 (BR)
David H. Wells/
CORBIS; 53 (CR)
Dave Bartruff/

CORBIS; 57
(BC) Kevin Fleming/ CORBIS; 59 (BC) The
Bridgeman Art Library; 60 (BR) Piers Benatar/
Panos Pictures; 61 (BC) Sonia Halliday
Photographs; 62 (TR) Bettmann/ CORBIS; 63
(TR) Sonia Halliday Photographs; 64 (BL)
Robert Leslie; 65 (TL) CORBIS; 66 (TL)
Bettmann/CORBIS; (CR) Lake County
Museum/ CORBIS; 67 (TL) Bettmann/
CORBIS, (BR) Denis O'Regan/ CORBIS;
74 (C/R) Ann Ronan Picture Library; 75
(B/L) Image Select; 81 (C/R) Corbis; 82
(C) Corbis; 83 (T/R, B/L) Ann Ronan
Picture Library; 84 (T/R) Mary Evans
Picture Library; 85 (C/R) Image Select;
85 (B/L) NASA; 87 (C/L) NASA; 88
(T/R) Ann Ronan Picture Library; 88
(B/R) Corbis; 89 (B/L) Corbis; 90 (B/L,
B/R) Ann Ronan Picture Library; 92
(T/R) American Institute of Physics; 93
(B/L) Mary Evans Picture Library; 94
(B/R, B/C) Ann Ronan Picture Library;
97 (T/R) Mary Evans Picture Library; 99
(C/R) Ford Motor Company; 100 (B/R)
Virgin Atlantic Airways Limited; 101
(C) Corbis; 102 (T/R) Science Photo
Library; 103 (T/R) Corbis; 104 (T/R,
B/L) Corbis; 104 (T/L, R) Corbis; 105
(T/R) Richard Morrell/ Science Photo
Library; 108 (C/R) Corbis; 109 (T/R)
Mary Evans Picture Library; 109 (B/L)
Geoff Tompkinson/Science Photo
Library; 110 (B/C) Corbis; 113 (B/L)
Tek Image/Science Photo Library; 114
(C/R) Firefly Productions/Science Photo
Library; 115 (B/L) American Institute of
Physics; 115 (C/R) Sony Computer

Entertainment (U.K.); 115 (C) Reproduced by
kind permission of Apple Computer U.K.
Limited; 117 (B/L) NASA; 120 (T/R) Naoto
Hosaka/ Frank Spooner Pictures; 120 (B/R)
Adam G. Sylvester/Science Photo Library; 121
(B/C) Frank Spooner Pictures; 123 (T/C)
Allsport at Image Select; 123 (B/L) Science
Photo Library; 124 (B/C) R.
Benali/S.Ferry/Frank Spooner Pictures; 125
(B/L) Corbis; 131 (TL) Mary Evans Picture
Library; 132 (BR) Mary Evans Picture Library;
133 (BC) Buddy Mays/ CORBIS; 144 (BC)
Mary Evans Picture Library; 145 (TL) Mary
Evans Picture Library; 146 (CR) Ann Ronan
Picture Library; 147 (TR) Bettmann/ CORBIS;
149 (TR) The Bridgeman Art Library, (CL)
Bettmann/ CORBIS ; 152 (CR) Bettmann/
Corbis; 153 (BL) CORBIS; 156 (BL) Mary
Evans Picture Library; 158 (TL) Mary Evans
Picture Library; 159 (BL) Hulton-Deutsch
Collection/ CORBIS; 160 (C) Bettmann/
CORBIS; 162 (TL) CORBIS, (BL) Hulton-
Deutsch Collection/ CORBIS; 163(TR)
CORBIS; 164 (CR) Bettmann/ CORBIS; 165
(TR) Bettmann/ CORBIS; 167 (BL) CORBIS,
(BC) Bettmann/ CORBIS; 168 (BC) Ann Ronan
Picture Library; 169 (TL) Nathan Benn/
CORBIS; 170 (BL) Bettmann/ CORBIS; 171
(TR) Bettmann/ Corbis; 173 (TR) Mary Evans
Picture Library; 175 (CR) Lisa M McGeady/
CORBIS, (C) Linda Richardson, (BL) photo
courtesy of the British School of Shiatsu-Do
(London); 177 (CR) AFP/ CORBIS; 179 (BL)
Roger Ressmeyer/ CORBIS; 180 (TR) Ann
Ronan Picture Library, (BL) CORBIS; 182 (C)
Hank Morgan/ Science Photo Library.

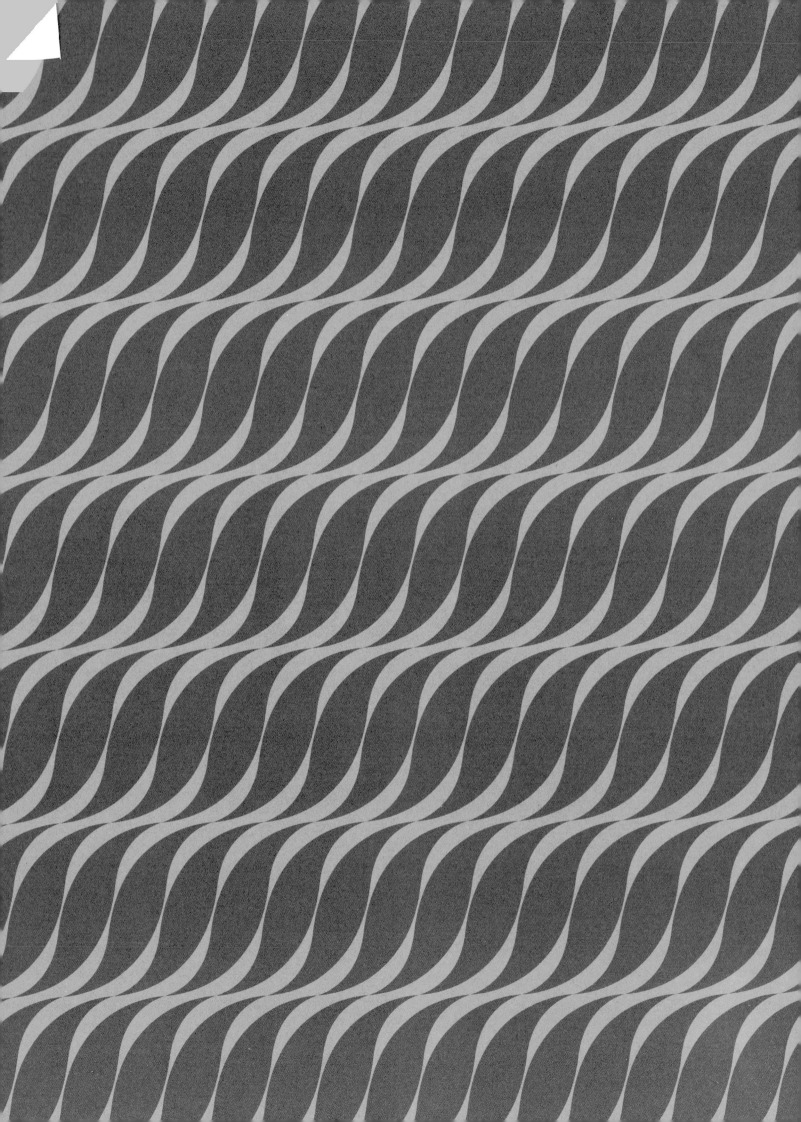